I0120600

Occupied Refuge

GLOBAL INSECURITIES

A series edited by Catherine Besteman and Darryl Li

Occupied Refuge

*Humanitarian Colonization
and the Camp in Kenya*

HANNO BRANKAMP

Duke University Press   *Durham and London*   2026

© 2026 DUKE UNIVERSITY PRESS. All rights reserved
Project Editor: Ihsan Taylor
Designed by A. Mattson Gallagher
Typeset in Garamond Premier Pro by Westchester Publishing Services

Library of Congress Cataloging-in-Publication Data
Names: Brankamp, Hanno, [date] author.
Title: Occupied refuge : humanitarian colonization and the camp in
Kenya / Hanno Brankamp.
Other titles: Global insecurities.
Description: Durham : Duke University Press, 2026. | Series: Global
insecurities | Includes bibliographical references and index.
Identifiers: LCCN 2025021994 (print)
LCCN 2025021995 (ebook)
ISBN 9781478033134 (paperback)
ISBN 9781478029670 (hardcover)
ISBN 9781478061885 (ebook)
Subjects: LCSH: Kakuma Refugee Camp. | Refugee camps—Kenya. |
Humanitarian assistance—Kenya. | Refugees—Government policy—
Kenya. | Militarism—Kenya.
Classification: LCC HV640.4.K4 B73 2026 (print) | LCC HV640.4.K4
(ebook)
LC record available at https://lccn.loc.gov/2025021994
LC ebook record available at https://lccn.loc.gov/2025021995

Cover art: Photograph by the author.

For Nelson and Kirsty
Sisi ni kitu kimoja!

Contents

Acknowledgments
ix

INTRODUCTION
1

{1}
REFUGE
37

{2}
OCCUPATION
69

{3}
DIS/ORDER
101

{4}
COMMUNITY
129

{5}
EXTRACTION
159

CONCLUSION
183

Notes
197

Bibliography
221

Index
253

Acknowledgments

Research is always necessarily one step behind the struggles of people. And it is the people we encounter in our work who inspire and remind us, through their strength, wisdom, and freedom dreams, why we do what we do. With our academic work trailing behind their courageous lead, we can only ever hope to do their stories and experiences justice while contributing, in some way, to realizing collective aspirations of liberation near and far. Given this imbalance, it comes as no surprise that I find myself deeply indebted to family, friends, comrades, colleagues, and fellow travelers who have been immensely kind and supportive over the years. Only their love has made the frequent solitude of academic writing worthwhile. However, it is especially regrettable that precisely those who have contributed the most to this book with their stories, knowledge, and precious time cannot be named due to concerns for their own safety. They welcomed me into their lives in Kakuma camp, introduced me to their families, entrusted me with secrets, showed me friendship, and shared their innermost hopes for the future—along with tea and plates of *kisra*, *ugali*, *injera*, *baasto*, and fried camel meat. I cannot repay the hospitality they have shown me in a place that most of them do not strictly call "home." Although they feature in this book not under their real names, they are its protagonists whose tenacity and resolve to seek a new life is beyond compare.

At Oxford, I was immensely fortunate to learn from my then supervisor, Patricia Daley, a trailblazer, tireless champion of students, and powerhouse without whom the university, and geography as a discipline, would be infinitely poorer. I also thank my second supervisor, Olly Owen, for being the anthropologist voice in my ear when my conceptual musings took me too far away from people's actual lives. I had two stints at the University of Oxford—first, as a doctoral student in the School of Geography and the Environment, and later as a departmental lecturer in the Refugee Studies Centre at the Oxford Department of International Development (ODID). During those years, I received support, friendship, feedback, and encouragement from many people, including Oliver Bakewell, Catherine Briddick, Neil Carrier, Jeff Crisp, Dilar Dirik, Andrew Dwyer, Matt Gibney, Ian Klinke, Sneha Krishnan, Peter Martin, Fiona McConnell, Naohiko Omata, Scott Orr, Helge Peters, David Pratten, Cory Rodgers, Diego Sánchez-Ancochea, Ruth Saxton, Tom Scott-Smith, Uttara Shahani, Andrea Smith, Jonny Steinberg, Nikita Sud, and Alex Vasudevan. I owe Loren Landau and Caroline Wanjiku Kihato much gratitude for delicious meals and red wine whenever they invited me into their home. Unforgettable also was the time when, out of nowhere, the late Barbara Harrell-Bond called me to her house when I was a still fresh doctoral student and told me, with a smile, that "Kakuma has already been done!" I sincerely hope that the present study proves the usefulness of my inquiry. Negar Behzadi and Andonis Marden deserve special acknowledgment for their friendship and for always offering me a place to stay when I needed it.

At King's College London, I was fortunate to be part of a warmhearted community of dear colleagues who received me with open arms, including Majed Akhter, Ruth Craggs, Luke Dickens, Alex Loftus, James Millington, Naho Mirumachi, Richard Schofield, Daniel Schillereff, and Kate Schreckenberg, and last (but certainly not least) the wonderful office 5.14 "alumni": Christine Barnes, Maud Borie, Margaret Kadiri, Kevin Lougheed, James Porter, and Faith Taylor. At Durham, Jonny Darling has been an incredibly kind, reassuring, and supportive mentor and remains an incessant source of guidance to this day. Other colleagues have also made me feel at home in the Northeast, including Sarah Hughes, Léonie Newhouse, Joe Painter, and Helen Wilson.

I further continue to learn from the inspiring work of stellar scholars too numerous to list here exhaustively. But they include colleagues whose writings have been formative for my thinking and whose thoughtful engagement with my work throughout the years has been nothing but humbling. I thank Sanaa Alimia, Gargi Bhattacharyya, Clayton Boeyink, Georgia Cole, Neil Wilson Crawford, Nicholas de Genova, Sara de Jong, Kelly Devenney, Elena Fiddian-Qasmiyeh, Joël Glasman, Bram Jansen, Ulrike Krause, Sophie Mackinder, Diana Martin, Claudio Minca, Daniel Morales, Ali Nobil, Polly Pallister-Wilkins, Yousif M. Qasmiyeh, Lisa Ann Richey, Martina Tazzioli, and Simon Turner. Nandita Sharma's radical vision for a global commons continues to inspire me deeply, and her advice and support have been nothing but generous. Yolanda Weima has been not only a comrade and friend but also a frequent academic coconspirator these past years. A very special thanks also goes to Catherine Besteman for believing in this book project early on.

In Kenya, my life was enriched by the most amazing people I could have hoped to meet, many of whom I share friendships with to this day. I want to highlight Berna Ataitom for being an exceptional friend in the belly of the "beast" that is the United Nations High Commissioner for Refugees (UNHCR). Siraaj was the kindest and most patient Somali teacher I could have hoped for in Eastleigh. Many others were always there for me with friendship and advice, including Qaabata Boru, Björn Euler, Joost Fontein, Vivian Gitari, Mohamed Hassan, Fred Ikanda, Eunice Jerop, Natalia Herberg Jiménez, John Kanyingi, Gabriel Lubale, Andrew Maina, Clève Massamba, Njoki wa Maina, Allan Mukuki, Syokau Mutonga, Veronica Mwangi, Kodi Arnu Ngutulu, Lucy Nimmo Nduati, Samuel Gathanga Ndung'u, Teresia Ngandi, Janet Njoroge, Ruth Nyabuto, Victor Nyamori, Boni Ongaya, Fabian Ongaya, Loice Ongere, Lilian Obiye, Fabian Oriri, Michael Owiso, Fardosa Salah, Mazen Shaweesh, Sarah Maranga, and Shane. I will also never forget Chegem and our *miraa*-fueled drive to the South Sudanese border. Celestine Adipo, Simon Wang'oe, and Zam Shidane have tirelessly helped with many transcriptions. Christine Kamau deserves a special mention for introducing me to her Nairobi "muddle-class." Finally, Faith Kasina continues to be a fearless comrade, a source of inspiration, and a good friend.

I am also grateful for the support I have received from the Lutheran World Federation (LWF), which generously provided me with long-term accommodation in their Kakuma compound; to UNHCR members of staff for tolerating my critical and (in their minds) undoubtedly annoying questions; for the openness and unexpected trust of many government officials in Kakuma, despite our ambiguous and often rocky relationship; to Kenya's Independent Policing Oversight Authority (IPOA); to the refugees and Kenyans working for the Community Peace and Protection Teams (CPPTs); and, not least, to all residents of Kakuma, both in and outside the camp. The CPPTs, in particular, helped me to navigate the camp and to experience it through their eyes. I thank them for that unique opportunity and their generosity with all my heart.

This research was made possible by funding from the United Kingdom's Economic and Social Research Council (ESRC), in conjunction with the German National Academic Foundation (Studienstiftung des Deutschen Volkes). A British Academy Postdoctoral Fellowship subsequently enabled me to return to Kenya for follow-up research trips as part of a newer project, which has generated materials that also made it into this book. At Duke University Press (DUP), it was an absolute pleasure to work with Gisela Fosado, Alejandra Mejía, and later Ihsan Taylor, who carefully shepherded this project through the publication process, from first proposal to the completed manuscript. Two anonymous reviewers have provided encouragement and thoughtful feedback that has sharpened this book's argument and analysis, though all remaining errors are mine alone. Gabriel Moss created the two beautiful maps. I also appreciate the tedious labor that goes into the making of a book at the editorial, production, and marketing stages. My full solidarity to the DUP Workers Union for this.

Of course, underpinning everything I have done and achieved are the friends and comrades who make my life worth living and a better world imaginable. I thank Aelya Salman for always staying in touch, for her love, and for meeting me in a new place and the same place every time; Mirna Abdo and Tala Fasheh, for our continued friendship, and for introducing me to Palestinian cross-stitch (*tatreez*); Shaquilla Harrigan, for choosing me as her PD; Nyacomba Githu, for our evenings listening to Daudi Kabaka; Anna Adima, Sam Awooha, Caít and Jamie, Henry and Ashley Dee, Zoltán Glück and Manissa Maharawal, Wangui Kimari, Kris Lee, Francesca Meloni and Lusungu Chikamata, Henrik Mulder and Marieke Kelm, Daudi and Simon Kisusi, Chimwemwe Phiri, Hannah Solomon-Strauss, Farida Stanley, Liah Tecle, Claire Walker and Bilal Hakeem, Jack and Rebecca WalkerWoo, and Robin White, as well as Yoav Zeevi and Vivek Nityananda. Finally, Stella Wangari has long been a superb friend whose rants about Kenyan politics and the state of the world are always invigorating.

My family has contributed immensely to all my endeavors. My parents, Doris Calovini-Brankamp and Heiko Brankamp, have afforded me the great privilege of never-ending belief in whatever path I chose to tread, and it is their immeasurable love and trust in me that has given me confidence and strength throughout my life. Our family in Mwanza, especially Sundi Sonda ("Mama Nelly"), Bujiku, Shiggi, Nkamba, Kabula, Bibi Loyce, and Mzee Sonda, deserve thanks for all they do and have done. Thanks also to our family in Canada, Ian Graham, Joe Graham and Claire Mitchell, and Carys Owen. I am also thankful to my sister-in-law, Julia Szilat, and my brother, Hauke Brankamp, who has always been an inspiration. Our little cosmonauts Laika and Sputnik are also unforgotten.

Finally, I reserve the most heartfelt gratitude for my partner, Kirsty Graham, and our son, Nelson. Kirsty sees me like nobody else does, and I am at once humbled by their love and in awe of their courage, rebelliousness, and optimism for the future. It is through them that I keep discovering the natural world in all its beauty and remember to take days off work. Nelson has brought me the greatest joy I have ever known. His care, thoughtfulness, and critical curiosity about the world are truly wonderful to witness. During an early morning school run in Mwanza many years back, he told me that he would put up a fight should the colonizers ever wish to return. I know he would. This book is for him and Kirsty.

MAP 1. Refugee camps and cities in Kenya. Created by Gabriel Moss.

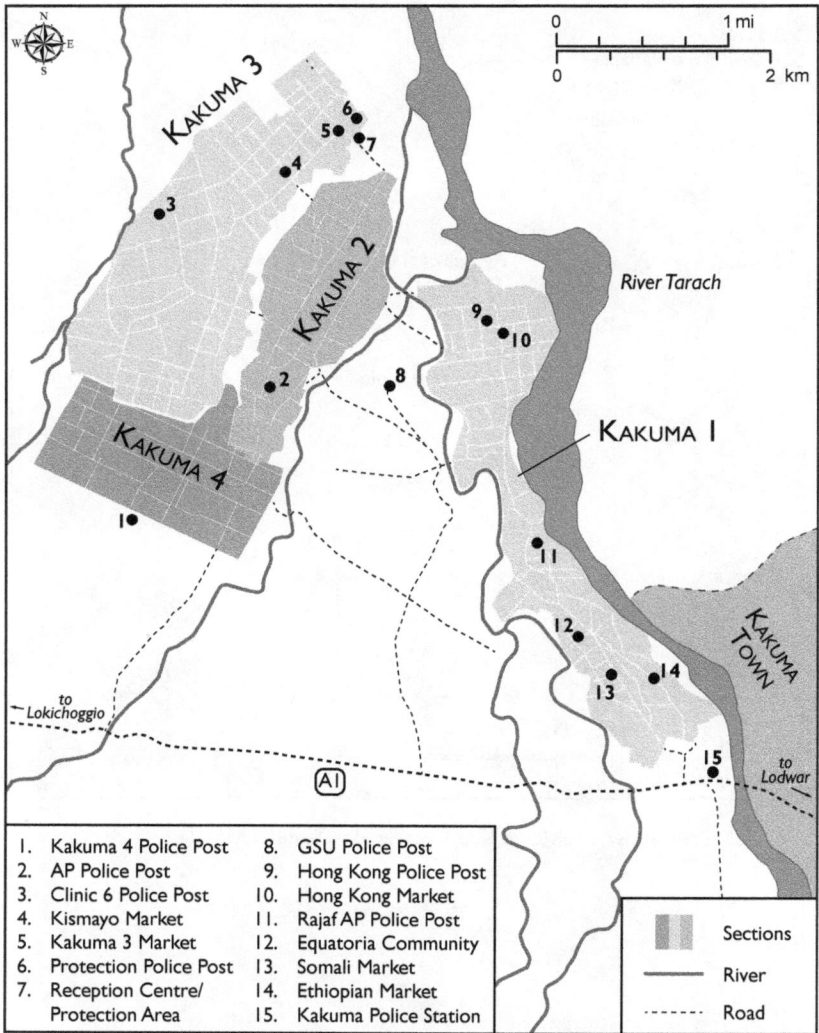

MAP 2. Key locations inside Kakuma refugee camp. Created by Gabriel Moss.

KAKUMA 3

KAKUMA 2

KAKUMA 4

KAKUMA 1

River Tarach

KAKUMA TOWN

to Lokichoggio

to Lodwar

A1

0   1 mi
0   2 km

1. Kakuma 4 Police Post
2. AP Police Post
3. Clinic 6 Police Post
4. Kismayo Market
5. Kakuma 3 Market
6. Protection Police Post
7. Reception Centre/ Protection Area
8. GSU Police Post
9. Hong Kong Police Post
10. Hong Kong Market
11. Rajaf AP Police Post
12. Equatoria Community
13. Somali Market
14. Ethiopian Market
15. Kakuma Police Station

Sections
River
Road

Your mother is UNHCR, your father is the Government of the Republic of Kenya. You must respect your parents!

—KAKUMA CAMP MANAGER (2017)

The government had come, not to help us, but to instill fear into us, and, out of fear, obedience.

—JARAMOGI OGINGA ODINGA (1967)

Introduction

It was the late evening of December 25, 2016, in Kakuma refugee camp, north-western Kenya. Abby's, one of the popular bars and clubs in this densely settled neighborhood of the camp, was once again packed with boisterous customers celebrating Christmas over beer, *nyama choma* (barbecued meat), dance, and blaring reggae music. Just as the speakers were turned up, and the party was coming into full swing, a file of olive-green Land Cruisers sped up to the entrance of the bar, and a squad of Kenyan police officers jumped out. With loaded rifles slung over their shoulders, the uniformed men surrounded the premises while partygoers, expecting the worst, desperately tried to escape by scaling the corrugated iron walls or sneaking through the latrines at the back. Two weeks earlier, the Kakuma office of the United Nations High Commissioner for Refugees (UNHCR) had sent an official request to the town's head of police, the Officer Commanding Station (OCS), asking him to enforce stricter curfews and closing times for bars, *hoteli* (restaurants), and coffeehouses during the festive season, citing an anticipated uptick in disturbances and security threats. It was no secret that aid organizations and the Kenyan authorities were suspicious of unauthorized gatherings in the camp and routinely criminalized those who took part in them. The directive to preserve "public order" was not unprecedented but illustrated how statecraft and aidcraft were joined at the hip. Emboldened by official backing of the UN, Kenyan officers dragged bewildered customers out of the bar and loaded them onto vehicles that were waiting outside, hurrying them along with yells, insults, and heavy truncheon blows.

The officers drove back and forth between Abby's, Kakuma's central police station, and smaller police outposts that littered the camp, struggling to find enough jail space for the masses of arrested refugees. Joseph, a Burundian *boda boda* (motorbike taxi) driver who witnessed the operation, remembered that "officers began to randomly arrest people at 8:00 p.m., and the police vehicles made five additional trips, picking more people up each time they returned. They must have finished at around 9:00 p.m. By that time everyone was distraught." Holding cells across Kakuma filled up quickly with more than one hundred detainees, most of them adolescents and young adults. The OCS barked instructions at subordinates, reminding them that each detainee should "defend" their own individual case, which was code for the bribes that this inevitably entailed. Late into the night, agitated family members, neighbors, and friends streamed into the police station from every corner of the camp to secure the release of daughters, sons, husbands, wives, and lovers, usually for a standard "fee" of 1,000 Kenyan shillings ($10) or 2,000 Kenyan shillings ($20). But prices also varied depending on a person's social standing, ethnicity, and personal networks. Somalis and Ethiopians, who were often stereotyped as affluent businesspeople or traders, were particularly desirable targets for extortion. Each community began collecting funds to free as many of their kin as possible. Hiywot, the young Ethiopian owner of Abby's bar, pleaded with the OCS to no avail: The price for her freedom was a hefty 10,000 Kenyan shillings ($100), which was doubled as soon as the police realized that she was in a relationship with one of Kakuma's wealthiest businessmen. After finally exiting the airless and foul-smelling cells in the early hours of the following day, Hiywot speculated whether it might have been a competitor who had paid off the police officers to disrupt her thriving business. Recounting his story of the raid, Joseph concluded cynically, "At least the police ate well that night. The New Year found them well. Everybody else suffered."

These scenes encapsulate the deep contradictions that shroud refugee camps today. Camps enjoy a default legitimacy as imagined emergency "safe havens" that offer much needed shelter, food, health services, education, and humanitarian protection for scores of people fleeing conflict, social adversity, natural disasters, and ecological collapse. By providing the minimum conditions for life and technically managing disasters, camps are the spatial bedrock of a global regime of refugee protection. Estimates suggest there may currently be more than one thousand such institutionalized spaces of refuge dotting the globe, most of which are found in countries of the so-called global South.[1] Yet they are hardly known to be particularly livable places. Camps are popularly associated with rampant insecurity and crime, gender-based and other violence, poor public health, economic dependency, and terrorist threats.[2] Echoing colonial tropes, it is sometimes implied by aid and state actors alike that camp dwellers have their own fair share in prolonging this condition due to unresolved psychological trauma, harmful cultural practices, religious extremism, and the displacement-induced erosion of social bonds. As imperfect as sanctuaries such as Kakuma may therefore always be for refugees, in the institutional imagination they create a stable, if temporary, "environment that supports their fundamental human rights to life, liberty and security of person."[3] Of course, aid agencies such as the UNHCR and its implementing partner organizations on the ground have the betterment of refugee lives at heart. Humanitarian workers, most would agree, are morally invested in their profession and do not intentionally seek to put anyone's life at risk—on the contrary. Their self-identities speak of sacrifice, compassion, and action for both an abstract ideal and the concrete sufferers they help. But the concerted efforts of the UNHCR and the Kenyan state to limit and actively suppress autonomous sociality, mobility, collective joy, and safety among Kakuma's residents—by means of crackdowns, imprisonment, curfews, physical abuse, ethnoracial profiling, and forced micro-extractions of wealth—tell a different story. They raise critical questions about what lies beneath the official mandate of "protection."

On a planetary scale, aid programs are—as of late—now increasingly being mobilized as "soft" instruments of migration control to complement "hard" containment infrastructures of walls, detention centers, barbed wire, surveillance technologies, and border guards. By funding refugee camps in formerly colonized—and still geopolitically marginalized—regions of the world, wealthy countries seem to have found a more ethically justifiable way to insulate themselves from people displaced by war, capitalist crisis, militarization, and the direct effects of climate change, without relying exclusively on politically more uncomfortable "spectacles" of border violence on their own doorstep.[4] After all, disciplinary measures to regulate the global circulation of migrants, life seekers, laborers, asylees, the dispossessed, and the racially oppressed are the hallmarks of an abiding geography of coloniality that is disguised by liberal dispensations of aid.[5] Viewed from Western corridors of power, maintaining refugee camps along the global peripheries is a useful investment to at once defuse gaping inequalities, govern human suffering, exhibit generosity, and, ultimately, curb the free migration of millions, rendering aid in the process a more discreet and, arguably, more sustainable method of "bordering beyond coercion."[6] What emerges here, then, is a camp geopolitics in which spaces of containment are becoming locations of strategic interest for state and aid actors. Even as the "dirty work" of border control is now explicitly being externalized by northern countries that prop of the military, police, and border agencies of their allied states in the global South, the popular imagination of humanitarianism as a morally progressive project of civilian protection remains largely intact.[7] Aid, many like to think, continues to embody a fallback solution to resolve global inequalities by peaceful means.

In this book I am wary of this myopic and, arguably, Eurocentric conclusion. *Occupied Refuge* challenges the idea that humanitarian refugee aid in the South represents a "nonviolent" form of surrogate borderwork, while it equally criticizes the portrayal of violence as simply a given feature of refugee camp life. Indeed, what may from afar appear as a deeply flawed yet ultimately benign international intervention to ease the plight of refugees in "far-away" regions resembles, on closer inspection, the mounting of a full-fledged militarized occupation that is primarily (and often exclusively) imposed on negatively racialized aid recipients who reside in formerly colonized societies and are deemed otherwise unmanageable. With this, aid programs follow age-old scripts of liberal empire in which some are fully recognized as subjects endowed with unalienable rights, individual freedoms, a capacity for rational conduct, and inviolable bodies, while "others" are thought to be dangerously unruly and therefore to require mobility control, moral paternalism, and physical discipline.[8] One rule was always reserved for the metropole and (usually) propertied white citizens, while yet another was applied to the racially subjugated "native" populations confined to the colonial margins. In the postcolonial world, a similar socio-spatial hierarchization was largely upheld yet encoded with the language of liberal democracy, national sovereignty, partnership, development, and aid.

Nowhere is this more apparent than in the geographically dispersed operations of liberal humanitarian and migration regimes. The further their subjects—migrants, refugees, and people on the move—are removed from centers of political power in the North, the more their struggles against institutionalized violence move out of sight and are trivialized or refuted. Although life seekers from Africa and other southern places of origin now regularly make their own way to Europe, North America, and Australia—shrinking the geographical divide between metropoles and former colonies in the process—the Eurocentric myopia that recognizes violence as such only at close quarters, while minimizing it in the distance, persists. In other words, the humanitarian governance of refugees at the global margins brings to the fore "the issue of contingent human violence."[9] The lived insecurities of contemporary refugee camp dwellers and their enduring "vulnerability to premature death," to use Ruth Wilson Gilmore's phrase, are therefore not just the result of "invisible" structural forces that gradually exhaust or weaken their bodies through many years of debilitating encampment, ill health, inadequate food rations, forced waiting, and declining life chances.[10] Rather, they are created in large part by the concrete, visible, and attributable violence of police and penal power that underpins institutionalized refugee humanitarianism today.

Drawing on ethnographic research in Kenya, this book shows that occurrences such as the Christmas raid on Abby's in Kakuma are neither exceptional events nor merely evidence of refugee aid "gone awry." Rather, delivery of humanitarian assistance is, in practice, underwritten by extraordinary levels of policing and militarization, routinely exposing refugees to the sharp end of state power. It traces the workings of this power through the eyes of those involved in the everyday management of camp affairs: police officers, government officials, aid workers, community police, and ordinary refugees. Ironically, it is against the backdrop of "pacification" through batons, guns, prison cells, and collective punishment that humanitarian workers are able to stage their purportedly benevolent missions of protection. However, I argue that rather than simply *masking* imperialist, anti-migration, security-centered, and racist policies concocted in the global seats of power, as is often readily implied, this heavy-handed administration of refugee operations itself represents a material, social, and political project of *humanitarian colonization* that has long been unfolding—seemingly out of sight—in the global South.

I use the frame of colonization not as a contained historical event limited to the structure of European imperialism but to shed light on a more persistent set of geographies and relations of rule in the present. With the advent of sovereign statehood, former colonies like Kenya made significant efforts to fully control their own territories and populations in a drive to create a new "national space." This national expansionism entailed seizing, occupying, settling, and policing the country's frayed rural margins and subjecting them to administrative control by the central state. Instead of offering a fresh start after European colonizers had departed, the new state itself continued to be a "colonizing institution," more interested in attacking than in protecting society.[11] In doing so, Kenya turned the technology of the camp—once used to defend the imperial order against disobedient Africans—into a means of violently limiting the rights and mobilities of both precaritized minority citizens and "nonnative" migrants thought to jeopardize its new national order, identity, and peace. While this nationalist project of muscular integration effectively stalled within the first decade of independence (*uhuru*), the arrival of refugees during the 1990s breathed new life into it through fresh donor funding, aid infrastructures, and diplomatic encouragement to pursue encampment. Before this humanitarian encroachment began in the late 1980s, and took off in earnest in 1991, Kenya therefore had already engaged in colonizing its own interior. This means that it is not only hypervisibly racialized encounters between the border guards of white-majority countries and nonwhite migrants along the physical threshold of the global North, but also the internal disparities, unequal mobilities, and hierarchies of belonging within postcolonial nation-states that reproduce processes of colonization.[12] This impresses on us the conclusion that "time in the colony and its afterlife is not linear but rather constructed of crossings, reversals, and re-inventions," of which recurrent forms of carceral power and nested relations of ethnoracial domination are pertinent examples.[13] The camp, I argue, is key to understanding how colonial relations are continuously reworked, reinvented, and respatialized across what often appear to be rather disparate histories and geographies today. It blurs the lines between reproducing colonial control, asserting postcolonial sovereignty, and spatially anchoring what some have referred to as "global apartheid" on a local scale.[14]

Kenya is a "high-profile" country of asylum that has attracted significant attention from international media in recent years for hosting one of Africa's largest refugee populations and serving as a hub for humanitarian interventions across the Horn of Africa. It has also long been a key ally for European and US geopolitical interests, giving diplomatic, economic, and military cover for their African designs, and it is the only country on the continent to host headquarters of two major UN organizations: the United Nations Human Settlements Program (UN-Habitat) and the United Nations Environmental Program (UNEP). Most recently, Kenya volunteered to head a multinational security support mission in Haiti to also demonstrate its dependability as a proxy for Western imperial projects abroad. Yet Kenya often slips through the cracks of even critical migration debates and receives less scrutiny than European-funded "frontline" regimes such as Libya or Tunisia that are more squarely involved in deterring migrants on their way to the Mediterranean. Far removed from European shores, "host countries" such as Kenya are nonetheless complicit as regional buffers in a segmented racialized system of global apartheid that enforces hierarchies of citizenship, differential mobilities, and labor exploitation. But it does so not just by prioritizing the wishes of its global North benefactors but also by leveraging their substantial resources to reinvigorate nation building by force along its internal frontiers.

To tell the story of humanitarian colonization, we need to look back to Kenya's colonial past and into the postcolonial era, when it started increasingly to discriminate against its minoritized citizens and noncitizens. Selected historical retellings in parts of the book lay the groundwork to better understand the parallel workings of colonial repression and newer logics of national belonging after independence. The new state, although based on Black majority rule and self-governing authority (*madaraka*), continued to rely on exclusionary land and property rights, ethnic territoriality, unequal center-periphery relations, insatiable capitalist accumulation, and permanent counterinsurgency as its guiding logics. Much like its colonial predecessor, post-*uhuru* Kenya sought to impose sovereign control over all regions and peoples within its borders. But while the colony had been worried about the *Indigenous* population's ability to subvert imperial order, the Kenyan nation-state saw the greatest peril in populations who were supposedly *alien* to its territory and began to administratively separate its national "natives" from migrant "non-natives."[15] Citizens (*wananchi*) were defined not by their shared history of colonial oppression but, first and foremost, by their nativeness to the land (lit., *Kiswahili* [children of the land]). This was not limited to legal noncitizens; it also included Kenya's minorities, who, with national independence, were made into mere "guests" on the majority's home turf.[16] The burning question of who was autochthonous ("native to the soil") to Kenya, and could plausibly belong, was thus rigidified at the same time as the central state expanded its reach across border territories containing large numbers of question-mark citizens whose loyalty to "the nation" it doubted.

The road from colonial to postcolonial rule hence was marred not only by exclusionary ideas of citizenship but, importantly, also by the state's aim to "colonize" its own peripheries afresh by bringing national unity, development, and aid. Today's refugee aid regime in Kenya, and the formerly colonized world more broadly, thus constitutes a microcosm of our liberal postcolonial order in which universal promises of freedom, development, human rights, and protection are made alongside intensifying processes of state-organized repression, border controls, dehumanization, labor exploitation, and territorial exclusion. This book reveals that, when we scratch the surface of humanitarian spaces such as Kakuma refugee camp, we inevitably stare into their colonial underbelly: a two-faced system of "compassion" based on the militarized policing of mobility, ethnoracial subjugation, indirect rule, and extraction. But rather than mere hangovers from the historical colonial era, refugee camps show how the logics of colonization and carceral containment have often been adapted by African nation builders, repurposed, and put in the service of global mobility apartheid and national development after the end of empire.

Recentering Refugee Aid in the Global Margins

Kakuma, one could argue, may be a small and insignificant outpost of the global humanitarian regime. Located in the arid lunar landscape of northwestern Kenya, where the borders of South Sudan, Uganda, Ethiopia, and Kenya meet, the camp embodies, like few other places, a position at the margins—of Kenya and the world. Yet "small or remote places are not inconsequential," the political geographer Alison Mountz reminds us. "They are key to understanding power relations that shape entry and exclusion."[17] Margins, indeed, have long been recognized as sites of special import for understanding the state, society, and even the whims of global politics.[18] They are empirically and theoretically productive because they trouble our received categories, question the limits of legibility, and expose what is sometimes hidden under the cloak of geographical distance. In fact, a significant body of work now suggests that it is precisely *not* northern metropoles but marginalized spaces in the global South that can grant us "privileged insight into the workings of the world at large."[19]

Yet over the past two decades, much of the literature on humanitarianism and forced migration has slowly reverted to privileging refugee "crises" nearer the centers of Europe, North America, and Australia.[20] The term *margins*, in this context, frequently has been used to denote the proximate borderlands of the North rather than places farther afield in Africa, Asia, Latin America, or Oceania. While this is understandable, given the deadliness of fortified northern borders to this day, it also reflects an analytical schism in policy and scholarship.[21] Refugees and other forced migrants often come into focus only *if and when* they travel to the North in search of better lives, less so when they remain in their southern "regions of origin." Europe-specific studies are also unsatisfactory substitutes for understanding humanitarian landscapes in other parts of the world, where 84 percent of refugees and displaced people reside. Unlike in the North, aid programs in the South rely more exclusively on foreign funding, exist on average for much longer periods of time, are generally larger in scale, and are staffed (for the most part) by citizens of former colonies, even if the institutional power of agencies such as the UNHCR typically rests firmly "in white hands."[22] But just as in the North, theaters of aid, migration, and asylum in the South are thoroughly steeped in forms of coloniality past and present.[23] By focusing on refugee encampment in northwestern Kenya, a marginal site even *within* these margins, this book contributes to a body of work that continues to decenter Europe-bound migrations and reexamines refugee mobilities and humanitarianism located squarely within "the South."[24] Once the default settings of displacement, in which logics of aid, development, and postcolonial geopolitics became inseparably enmeshed, southern contexts have since turned into secondary sites of inquiry in critical humanitarian and (forced) migration studies, making them appear like distant outliers rather than windows into *global* humanitarian power.[25]

In fact, not all humanitarian "crises" are the same in the dominant imagination: From the colonial era onward, emergencies, wars, and disasters closer to "home" in the North usually have been seen as momentary ruptures of a "normal" state of affairs that require temporary interventions, while crises in "remote" locations of the South have been imagined as more permanent conditions of life—or, as Sue Estroff notes, they symbolized "the temporal persistence of . . . dysfunction."[26] If the periodic arrival of migrants at European shores required a short-term "fix" in the form of pop-up humanitarian infrastructure, hotspots, and citizen-led aid activities in cities, border areas, and islands, then the humanitarian geographies in the South were imagined to be durative and unresolvable, augmenting Africa's long association with "protracted refugee situations."[27] These are situations of displacement in which large numbers of conationals live in extended exile for at least five consecutive years and are "unable to return home and without the prospect either of a solution in the country where they have sought asylum or of resettlement abroad."[28] In 2021, the UNHCR estimated that as many as 15.9 million refugees fell into this category alone.[29] Further, the division between ostensibly temporary assistance in the North and more entrenched missions in the South loosely maps onto two principal motivations for humanitarian action: first, a short-term or "minimalist" effort to deliver concrete relief and physical protection during acute crises, emergencies, or on battlefields; and second, reflecting humanitarianism's origins in European colonization and Enlightenment thought, a more long-term "developmentalist" approach that seeks to effect the economic, moral, and social uplift of the domestic poor and, subsequently, negatively racialized "others" in colonies or faraway lands.[30] Although this categorization risks creating too neat a binary, refugee assistance in Europe is usually understood to be more limited, contained, or short-lived while equivalent interventions in the Southern Hemisphere are depicted as an unavoidably protracted quagmire.

This makes humanitarian crisis a "glitch" in the normal ordering of liberal modern life in Euro-America, whereas it becomes "normal" and hardly worthy of comment when occurring outside it. As far back as in the aftermath of World War II, relief for displaced people was reserved exclusively for Europeans until the Cold War and the era of decolonization, when UNHCR-fronted refugee operations were extended from postwar Europe to its former colonies.[31] To this day, these "slow emergencies" of forced displacement are differentially racialized. "The (white) liberal subject that anticipates a future of growth, change, development and becoming" is thought of in stark opposition to Black, Brown, Indigenous, or migrant subjects, who are seen to be "suspended in a durative temporality of decline, stagnation, [and] decay."[32] Aid programs in postcolonies have long been framed as acts of managing the outfall of irreversible ruin inflicted by a combination of ethnic conflicts, kleptocratic rule, state failure, and social breakdown that reflect colonial imaginings of southern life-worlds as "uninhabitable geographies."[33] Racially oppressed southern populations were in this way permanently excluded from the possibility of recovery and relegated to a normalized life in unchangeable conditions of crisis.

During the 1960s and 1970s, aid organizations began to flourish globally in response to the new aid emergencies that then predominantly arose in the South.[34] Africa in particular became a key theater of such humanitarian interventions. During the Cold War, the continent was portrayed by Western observers in paternalistic colonial terms as an anarchic place without future, agency, or political reason and, therefore, exclusively as an "object of humanitarian concern."[35] The Algerian war of independence (1954–63), the Congo Crisis (1960–65), the Biafra War (1967–70), Ethiopia's great famine (1983–85), military-enforced aid in Somalia (1992–93), the Rwandan genocide (1994), and successive conflicts in the Great Lakes region (1996–2003), among others, gave credence to the idea that Africa had, indeed, become the modern-day "cradle of humanitarianism."[36] By 2000, the continent hosted no less than a third of the world's refugees, and the European Union (EU) was increasingly concerned about responsibility sharing between rich donors and host countries in so-called regions of origin.[37] In 2010, nearly half of all humanitarian funds were channeled to African field operations.[38] More recently, the EU's Valetta Summit on Migration in 2015 reinforced this commitment to focus resources on providing aid in African countries to stem onward migration. Initiatives like the Emergency Trust Fund (EUTF) for Africa echoed this aim and were set up to tackle regional instability, irregular migration, and the challenges of displacement. Today, the UNHCR has allocated 30 percent of its annual budget to refugee assistance in Africa—more than to any other world region—while some of the fastest-growing forced displacements are occurring, at the time of writing, in Sudan, South Sudan, Democratic Republic of the Congo, Central African Republic, and Burkina Faso.[39]

Recentering refugee aid in these global margins, especially Africa, not only contributes to "provincializing" the landscapes of humanitarian action in the North but, crucially, highlights the ways in which "distance" mediates notions of crisis, care, and violence.[40] Because so-called humanitarian crises seem more "out of place" in the North, spectacular border violence is also more likely to be made "visible" (and condemned) as a transgression. In turn, the seeming ordinariness and geographical remoteness of displacement in the South makes those refugees less threatening to the white social order of Europe and North America and more "worthy" of assistance, but ultimately also less likely to become a public concern.[41] By virtue of not reaching Europe's territorial borders, refugees who are unable to leave Africa are thought to be spared the brutal treatment and premature death experienced by those who travel to the North. This imagined difference marks humanitarian geographies of the South as far more developmentalist in nature while framing the containment of refugees as an act not of *aggression* but of *compassion*—at once "saving" people from a violent European border regime and ostensibly safeguarding their social "progress" on the continent.[42] Displaced Africans who "stay put" in refugee camps such as Kakuma therefore are not only unable to choose their migratory futures but are enveloped in reworked colonial narratives of protectionism that also conceal the violence of refuge within neighboring nation-states of the South.

Violent Humanitarianism: Beyond Malfunction

Being arrested by the Kenyan police was not a shock for Hiywot and other refugees in Kakuma, even though it heightened their fear of physical abuse and financial ruin. What might seem like a spectacular infringement on refugee rights was, for partygoers in the camp, an accepted reality. For many, aid was virtually unthinkable without accompanying threats of extortion and imprisonment. There even was a sense that recurring roundups were preferable to the far more existential danger of expulsion from Kenya that has loomed for several years. This book takes up the question of violence inflicted by, or under the eyes of, those who are officially tasked with offering asylum, relief, and protection. It demonstrates that raids, arrests, and militarized policing are by no means signs of humanitarian malfunction but precisely constitute the ways in which aid is being materialized as an everyday spatial practice.

Against popular perceptions of humanitarianism as a morally pure quest that embodies "what is good about the world" and that connotes all manner of "doing good," it is closely entangled with the waging of violence.[43] At their core, humanitarian acts are palliative: They are responses to harm experienced by people in the wake of conflicts, wars, and disasters. As such, they mobilize a moral politics to be able to give assistance to, and ease the suffering of, the destitute, dispossessed, and displaced in the name of a "common humanity."[44] Didier Fassin traces this sensibility and compassionate mode of governing precarious lives to Enlightenment ideas about what binds human beings together, calling this moral sentiment of care for one another, quite aptly, "humanitarian reason."[45] Moral obligations to help in the uplift of orphans, the disabled, the injured, the poor, and the homeless developed into an integral part of the political and moral fabric of Western modernity and imprinted how Europeans came to see themselves on the world stage. However, ideas of caring for "distant strangers" necessarily sat in tension with instrumental compromises that were to be struck when actually providing support, shoring up funds, or governing those in need.[46] Relief interventions themselves tend to triage the neediest, the poorest, and the most vulnerable against "others" who are not deemed to be suffering just enough to receive aid, revealing not the inviolable value of life but, rather, the "inequality of lives and hierarchies of humanity," as Fassin writes.[47] An array of humanitarian technologies, from English workhouses and Indian famine relief camps in the nineteenth century to modern-day refugee camps, were not only sites for housing recipients of care, enlisting them into (forced) labor or providing welfare, but also of incarceration, stigmatization, and, of course, physical discipline. Rather than proof of a "broken" aid system, the organized violence of penal technologies is—more often than not—simply part of how the humanitarian system "works."

Colonial histories continue to imprint the geographically differentiated manifestation of this violence. Humanitarianism morally justified, underpinned, and propelled colonial conquest of non-Europeans with the aim of "civilizing" or "saving" the colonized from their own cultures and "protecting" them from what was viewed as the destructive onslaught of modernity. Though historically often understood as a dual product of antislavery movements in the eighteenth and nineteenth century and campaigns to give medical aid to wounded soldiers on the battlefields of Europe—notably associated with Henri Dunant's life and his cofounding of the International Committee of the Red Cross (ICRC)—humanitarian reason also deeply shaped the politics and spaces of colonization. A sixteenth-century dispute in the Spanish city of Valladolid saw the missionary Friar Bartolomé de las Casas debate with the theologian

Juan Ginés de Sepúlveda about the "right" treatment of Indigenous populations by Spanish colonizers in the Americas. While both supported colonization, De las Casas contended it should be conducted "justly" and in the spirit of Christian evangelization to save the souls of "natives," rather than as a pure function of worldly imperialist expansion.[48] Similar thinking has since infused British and other European efforts to violently usurp, govern, and "develop" new areas for settlement in the Americas and the Pacific.[49] Though colonizers routinely invoked the trope of "protection" and in this way expressed a will "to govern colonial space humanely," the violence of genocide, dispossession, and capitalist plunder were testimony to the inherent double-edgedness of these superficial claims.[50] Far from concealing the "true" aims of empire, the historian Ann Laura Stoler writes, this liberal rhetoric of compassion was always "based on imperial systems of knowledge production enabled by and enabling coercive practices." "Social hierarchies," she writes rather revealingly, "were produced and nourished by sympathy for empire's downtrodden subjects."[51]

Colonizing the African continent was justified by Europeans with similar humanitarian principles—to suppress the slave trade, advance Christianization, and realize what became known as the "civilizing mission"—while Africans were forced into dependence under a capitalist economy whose levers of power lay in Europe.[52] Feelings of compassion, pity, and piety, though drivers of colonization in their own right, acted as a moral lubricant for all sorts of violent undertakings in the service of white supremacy, land seizures, and extraction. By colonizing the continent and enslaving Africans in Caribbean and North American colonies, Europeans defined the narrow ontological boundaries of "humanity proper" to which colonized Black, Brown, and Indigenous people were not (or were only conditionally) admitted.[53] Liberal humanitarian ideals of protecting "life" and having sympathy for the plight of all of humanity, often thought to have universal appeal, therefore have to be read against the grain of duplicitous moral claims to save *certain* lives while abandoning negatively racialized *others*.[54] Humanitarianism was not opposed to colonial expansionism or racial domination per se but, in many cases, advocated for a "fairer" kind of colonization or simply offered short-term relief to cushion its destructiveness. In a 1932 anticolonial essay, the surrealist André Breton and his collaborators memorably observed that the colonizer, "with his psalms, his speeches, his guarantees of liberty, equality and fraternity . . . seeks to drown the noise of his machine guns."[55]

Achille Mbembe surmises that, because the nature of colonial enterprises was integrally "humanitarian," their violent effects also "could only ever be moral."[56] This articulates the essence of colonial difference: Colonized subjects were "worthy" of charity and salvation when it served the consolidation of colonial power but were deemed expendable when this order came under threat. Thus, empire was the founding act in the emergence of liberal violence that cemented racial order and extractive economies and unleashed physical brutalization while paying mere lip service to equality, democratic rights, and freedom. The civilizing mission, once the ideological bedrock of Europe's rationale for subjugating the non-European world, meanwhile underwent a new crisis of legitimacy between the world wars as colonized people were becoming increasingly disillusioned with their diminishing prospect of ever being considered "modern."[57] After formal decolonization in the mid-twentieth century, the imperial yardstick for improving society based on white superiority had also become more indefensible in a liberal world order, with its normative commitments to equality, making it necessary to reinvent and relegitimize an updated version of the "civilizing mission" through the languages of development, democracy, and, increasingly, aid.[58]

In the present, humanitarianism continues to be troubled by the same tension as it uses a moralizing rhetoric of protection, peacemaking, and psychosocial recovery while authorizing the brutalization of aid recipients. This instates a hierarchy of acceptable harm deployed in the service of the "greater good" of aid delivery: a project of proportionality, if you like, that "uses violence to subdue violence."[59] The history of aid is strewn with attempts not only to reduce suffering ex post facto but also to regulate the kinds of violence deemed legitimate during conflict. The Geneva Conventions were one historic codification of this that formed early building blocks of the nascent international humanitarian order.[60] Humanitarianism has in this way always legitimated *and* mitigated violence by creating codes of moderation by which warring factions could abide, even if this benefit was not extended to colonized or racially subjugated populations. Nevertheless, in establishing a formal rulebook to determine the limits of violence, humanitarianism shed its transformative potential, marking its rise as a liberal technology of rule.[61] Making the use of force acceptable (if not imperative) under particular circumstances turned into a discursive device through which to frame issues as "humanitarian" morally shielded them against critique. Rather than restricting state violence, this boosted the legitimization of force within the bounds of liberal humanitarian laws. Eyal Weizman argues that the merging of humanitarian logics with apparatuses of military or police power since the late 1990s is characteristic of our current politics, which he identifies as the "humanitarian present."[62] One of its unique epochal hallmarks, according to Weizman, is the stipulation that violence supposedly can only be attenuated but never fully ended, rendering aid efforts merely liberal instrumental means "by which the economy of violence is calculated and managed."[63] This has bred a number of practical collusions in the form of military personnel conducting aid work, the militarization of humanitarian search and rescue, humanitarian justifications for armed interventions, military practices that are distinctly "humanitarian," and using aid as an imperial ethic.[64]

Away from active combat zones, however, refugee aid and migration enforcement are the most salient fields in which humanitarian violence is inflicted today. People seeking a better life by embarking on dangerous journeys across the Mediterranean, the US-Mexico border, or Australia's maritime frontiers have overwhelmingly been met with militarized responses aimed at their containment. Border patrols, interceptions at sea, detention, high-tech surveillance, disappearances in offshore prisons, deportations, and the legal shrinking of asylum space each symbolizes a global system that affords unequal access to safe mobility and protection.[65] The coexistence of humanitarian actors and agents of state violence in many of those spaces has indeed created a phenomenon that some call "humanitarian borders."[66] These borders emerge when border crossings along the fringes of global North territories become "a matter of life and death" and provoke humanitarian operations "as a way of governing . . . the social violence embodied in the regime of migration control."[67] The growth of aid infrastructures, multiagency partnerships, and search-and-rescue operations in European border zones in recent years are testimony to this paradoxical condition of aid coinciding with violence. By making migrants' deaths appear as the unfortunate outcome of a well-intentioned aid effort rather than a deliberate deterrent, this violence is profoundly "liberal" in its pretentions to uphold democratic rights, human dignity, and liberty while actively concealing the harm it inflicts on racialized "others."[68]

Nevertheless, once again, the character of humanitarian violence seems to change when it occurs at greater distance from these northern humanitarian borders. Because southern places are *already* imagined as protracted landscapes of "naturalized" crisis, aid here is seen not only as a minimalist stopgap intervention or emergency response but, crucially, as a developmentalist project to foster long-term "progress," prosperity, and protection of racialized "others"—a form of "solidarity as salvation."[69] In the transition from idealistic mission to help suffering strangers to becoming a material system of governance, modern humanitarianism itself took on the contours of a form of colonization in the South. Beginning with the UNHCR's engagement during the Algerian War of Independence and the Congo Crisis in the 1960s, global North–based aid organizations progressively usurped large swaths of land as settlement areas for the displaced populations they vowed to serve. While these humanitarian operations in the twentieth (and twenty-first) century imparted a blend of redemptive ideologies of human rights, peace building, and liberal democracy onto their refugee "beneficiaries," alongside material aid such as food rations, shelter, and education, they simultaneously needed the help of military and police of independent African nation-states to retain "order." In Kakuma, the imposition of this police control is framed as a technical precondition for successfully delivering aid but has itself also become the target of liberal reforms to strengthen police accountability, professionalism, and the "rule of law." While this may not be limited to African, or even to southern, contexts, there the political ground had been so thoroughly prepared by the succession (and effective merging) of the colonial civilizing mission, democratization, and development thinking that their impact has proved disproportionately severe.

While the areas of "friction" between North and South are where contradictions between *restrictive* border control and *productive* aid work are most obvious for Western observers, the violence of refugee aid programs in the global South is often perceived as less intrusive, direct, and spectacular. Jennifer Hyndman and Alison Mountz, for example, claim that in the majority of postcolonial settings, "a quieter, geographically more distant and dispersed war against refugees [is] taking place."[70] Protracted refugee situations hence have seemingly produced conditions in which swaths of refugees are exposed to aid dependence, chronic ill health, sexual and gender-based violence, and ontological insecurity that fuels anxiety about missed life chances and stalled futures.[71] Read in this way, humanitarian violence is not just the product of practical collusions between life-giving aid actors and life-taking agents who enact physical force. It importantly encompasses structural and symbolic forms of violence that filter through governing institutions, strategies, technologies, and discourses, with detrimental effects.[72] Seemingly decoupled from the brutal migration control at the borders of the global North, refugee aid in the South is thereby, above all, seen as productive of "slow violence" in Rob Nixon's sense—namely, "a violence that occurs gradually and out of sight, a violence of delayed destruction that is dispersed across time and space, an attritional violence that is typically not viewed as violence at all."[73] It is akin to what Nancy Scheper-Hughes and Philippe Bourgois called "the routine, ordinary, and normative violence of everyday life" and Johan Galtung famously termed "structural violence" because it lacks clearly attributable harm-inducing action or subject-object relations and instead is "built into structure."[74]

In this book I argue that a binary between slow-moving, invisible, and illegible violence of debilitatingly protracted exile and more spectacular, explosive, and visible forms of death-dealing cruelty unleashed at the global

North's borders does not hold. Again, the marginal position of southern places in global geopolitics not only determines whether slow violence that occurs within them is recognized as destructive or detrimental in the first place; it, in turn, also determines whether harm is automatically relegated to the realm of the structural. Yet it is clear now that "slow forms of violence imbricate with the fast, and the fast inescapably shapes the slow."[75] Even the social production of group-differentiated vulnerability to "premature death," as a key feature of violence, is not tied to a particular speed but can unfold across different timelines, locations, and social sites.[76] What appears as a quieter war against refugees in the global South, then, is only ever truly "quiet" when looked at from the North. Acknowledging this, *Occupied Refuge* goes beyond critiques that render the structural harm of humanitarian refugee aid programs in the global South "illegible" or necessarily "slow" and instead traces the human agents whose actions produce violence in the everyday. Exploring this geography in refugee camps requires attending not only to humanitarianism as a colonizing ideology, system of global governance, and set of imperial legacies, but also to the fact that the authority of aid organizations on the ground—as "governors of people"—is ultimately rooted in their exertion of brute militarized force by proxy. Given Kenya's salience as home to one of Africa's most protracted refugee situations, and two of the continent's largest camps, Kakuma is an especially insightful place from which to consider how humanitarian aid enacts violence by effectively colonizing space, discourses, and people.

Continent of Camps: Policing Black Life

In the opening pages of his book *Managing the Undesirables*, the anthropologist Michel Agier invokes the pitiful sight of hundreds of refugee camps that litter the African continent today. This includes a variety of dwellings commonly subsumed under the label "camp," their physical appearance ranging from clusters of tarpaulin tents with UNHCR branding to quasi-cities built virtually unaided by refugees from scrub, corrugated iron, and brick. For Agier, this proliferation of camps is not so much a forlorn conclusion than a puzzle, "as if Africa had no other option of survival except that of becoming the twenty-first century's continent of camps."[77] As stereotypical as it may be, this characterization captures not only the proliferation of refugee camps today but also the role camps have played historically in African landscapes of aid and colonization: military camps, detention camps, mining camps, sanitary camps, famine relief camps, reeducation camps, labor camps, death camps, and refugee camps. One is even tempted to argue that camps are symbolic of the constraints imposed on the freedoms and mobilities of Black and African life writ large.[78]

Much scholarship on camps has traced their rise as "political technologies" to colonial modernity and attempts by (state) authorities—empires in particular—to exert totalizing control over space, people, and their wayward mobility.[79] As nodes of a power that police, usurp, and racialize, camps seem to mark the spot where "empire touches down in space."[80] Even beyond colonial contexts, camps were deployed to control those who are imagined as threats to state power by containing them in bounded spaces: temporary sites where civic liberties could be summarily suspended.[81] Drawing on the philosopher Giorgio Agamben and his analysis of Nazi concentration camps, scholars have commonly understood the camp as the spatialization of sovereign power where collective identity groups are exposed to extralegal measures by invoking an emergency or "state of exception." This opens up the possibility of arbitrary coercion and dehumanization, effectively blurring the boundary between what actually constitutes "the exception" and what constitutes "the rule."[82] By virtue of exercising this insidious power, Agamben maintains, the camp is capable of stripping people of their "full" personhood in the form of liberal democratic rights, political agency, and legal status, leaving behind but a bodily shell that camp authorities administer as "bare life."[83]

But not all camps are designed to *extinguish* life: Refugee camps in particular are meant to actively foster it. Michel Foucault's writing has offered relevant reflections on this *productive* aspect of government. Departing from mid-eighteenth-century notions of sovereign power that was invested with an unfettered ability "to take life or let live," Foucault diagnoses a broader transformation in the modern workings of sovereignty that is now increasingly aiming "to foster life or disallow it to the point of death."[84] It is what he calls "biopolitics," which is concerned not just with disciplining *individual* bodies but with managing *populations* as a whole and that has, in his understanding, "brought life and its mechanisms into the realm of explicit calculations and made knowledge-power an agent of transformation of human life."[85] It is easy to see the resonance this analytic register has had with contemporary camp studies. Writing on Burundian Hutu refugees in Tanzania, Liisa Malkki uses this Foucauldian frame to characterize refugee camps as a "standardized, generalizable technology of power in the management of mass displacement."[86] In fact, the reliance of aid workers on mobilizing statistics, documents, and headcounts as managerial practices of ordering a perceived "disorder" is now widely recognized and has been noted as one of the key features that mark refugee camps as explicitly biopolitical technologies.[87]

In recent years, however, these conceptualizations have come under fire and have been revised along two lines of critique: First, scholars have noted the insufficiency of Agambenian exegeses of camp geographies that tend to deemphasize, if not preclude, political agency among the encamped and have instead foregrounded the inevitability of politics arising within camps.[88] Empirically, this line of critique goes, camps always contain within them multiple, complex, and ever shifting claims to sovereignty that trouble or challenge the power of camp authorities.[89] Those who inhabit camps are not powerless but appropriate and refashion their topographies, subvert existing power relations, or repurpose resources to meet their own needs. The Christmas party at Abby's, sketched at the beginning of this chapter, speaks to this uncontainable will to carve out life-affirming spaces of joy even when it contravenes official regulations. Second, labeling refugee camps "biopolitical" is based on understanding them as interventions of care or aid that generally are afforded only to white liberal subjects and erase the fact that, within a Western colonial modernity, "racialized subjects are deemed *ineligible* for biopolitics and thus subject to gratuitous, sovereign, or necropolitical violence."[90] In a similar vein, the notion of "bare life" tends to mask the racialization that a priori structures the subject position of those prone to be encamped—namely Black, Brown, Indigenous, and "foreign" populations, whose personhood is questioned or denied even before encampment.[91] Death camps such as Shark Island in German Southwest Africa, *regroupement* camps in French Algeria, the Italian concentration camps for Bedouins in Libya's Cyrenaica, *aldeamentos* in Portuguese-ruled Angola and Mozambique, and the British "pipeline" of detention camps for anticolonial insurgents in Kenya in this sense simply formalized in barbed wire, brick, and mortar what was already a dehumanizing reality of racial apartheid before camps were built.

Obsessed with hygiene, order and segregation, maintaining purity, and preventing leakage against the reality that this was always futile, the camp operates both as a spatial technology to prevent people's motion and as a metaphor for the modern projects of colonization and, later, nation building.[92] In trying to squash insurgencies, contain the spark of resistance, and cut off lifelines of dissent, camps sought spatial solutions to the impossibility of making Africans pliable for empire and, subsequently, colonization by the postcolonial state. In their attempt to "care for" and "control" residents, enact control, reduce social disorder, and reinforce state power, camps were—and continue to be—essentially a technology for policing Blackness and other racially inferiorized bodies.[93] While Africans are seen as sources of productivity (laborers), potential threats to state security (terrorists or insurgents), and survivors of displacement and destruction (famine victims or refugees), their lives, if not contained, are

FIGURE I.I. Entering Kakuma from the AI Highway, 2016. Photograph by the author.

imagined as an unmanageable "excess" and perilous for the rest of society. A colonial observer in Kenya's frontier town of Isiolo who visited British humanitarian camps for the Ethiopians fleeing Italy's invasion of Abyssinia (1935–39) spoke in paternalistic terms about colonial officials, doctors, and nurses who turned the fate of refugees who had "invaded" the colony in a diseased, malnourished, and "verminous" state.[94] Remote spaces of refuge restrict the mobility of the displaced; suspend their lives spatially, legally, and temporally; and prevent any "leakage" or contamination to the outside.[95] Africa as the "continent of camps," then, is best understood not as a purely geographical but also as a racial descriptor that marks the camp as an anti-African technology—a precursor of present-day forms of Black containment.

Fast-forwarding to the present, the geographies of encampment remain unbroken on the continent. South Africa's mining compounds, the famine relief camps in Ethiopia, Rwandan reeducation camps, and Kenya's city-size refugee camps are only some examples that embody an institutional preoccupation of postcolonial states with care and control of African lives.[96] Except, while white European colonizers introduced the camp as a technology to police colonized subjects, it is independent nation-states under African leadership that disproportionately make use of it today to control "non-native" migrants with weaker claims to autochthonous belonging. Eighty percent of African refugees live in camps, compared with only a third outside the continent.[97] Despite a period of "open door policies" during which many displaced Africans enjoyed relatively free mobility until the 1980s, including in Kenya, camps continuously have been put to work on the continent.[98] Postindependence transfers of power extended not only to the police force, military, central bank, and core government bureaucracies but also to the camp as a spatial artifact of colonization to enact compassionate carcerality and capture segments of the populace, especially those deemed "alien." Camps are then, to paraphrase Stoler, in this sense moveable "archives" that join the shifting circuits of power over space and people, and whose legacies of racial othering and immobilization intermittently resurface "here" and "there" as both physical formations as well as logics of rule.[99] The policing of Black life in Africa did therefore not end with decolonization. Alongside ideas about race, ethnicity, culture, and differential capacities for rule, postcolonial African states such as Kenya "nativized" the coercive arms of the colonial state by adopting its tactics of encampment and enclosure to control mobility.[100] It is on this foundation of state violence that contemporary aid programs could build in their quest to discipline, contain, and administer displaced people seeking humanitarian protection.

Humanitarian Colonization Is Not a Metaphor

I sat with Girma and his friend Yerosan in one of the many Ethiopian cafés in Kakuma 1.[101] Both men were in their mid-thirties and had fled Ethiopia during a bout of severe government repression against Oromo dissidents in 2009. Girma was short and slender, with the hint of a beard, and could talk for hours, while Yerosan was tall, lanky, and of much quieter disposition. "If you had asked me before I came here," Yerosan told me as we drank *bunna* (coffee), "I would have imagined the camp to be a place where everybody lives in safety, with enough food, no violence, and prospects for the future, but unfortunately it is not." The two men were unemployed when I met them. Girma had given up his position as a teacher in one of the camp's primary schools because he felt unfairly treated by his Kenyan colleagues, who were paid several times as much for the same job. Yerosan could make ends meet only because he received support from his brother in the United States. When Yerosan spoke, Girma nodded vigorously in agreement, moved closer, lowered his voice, and added, "Some people fled here after having lost all of their family and huge amounts of money and property.... They are still in pain, and the camp worsens their situation. I thought our African neighbors would take care of us in any condition, but that's not true. We are stuck." I could hear the naked despondency in their voices and the sense of betrayal they felt at the turn their lives had taken. As students at Addis Ababa University, they had once dreamed of a family, a career, and a chance to do something with their higher education. This dream was cut short by an Ethiopian police state that relentlessly cracked down on its own youth and, after they fled into exile, a country of asylum that seemed hardly better at realizing the freedoms they desired. "'This is Kenya,' they always say, as if we should be grateful just to be here, and the UNHCR is helping them with their eyes closed," Girma complained. "If you go to the bush outside the camp," he said with a bitter grin, "you won't see wild animals, because even animals don't like this place. We have left our homes, our families, only to be harassed and kept in this camp by the Kenyans. We are not free."

In Girma's and Yerosan's telling, Kenya bore much responsibility for their situation and was colluding with aid organizations to keep them trapped. When I began research in Kakuma, I expected to find what Amy Slaughter and Jeff Crisp, in a much cited article on the UNHCR, have described as "a surrogate state." For them, the UN refugee agency often mimics state power by exerting authority over refugees as quasi-citizens while underpinning its legitimacy with talk of human rights, peace building, and gender equality.[102] In Kenya, this is said to have diminished the role of the *actual* state that supposedly abdicated its responsibility for refugees long ago to foreign aid actors. During the 2000s, Barbara Harrell-Bond and Eftihia Voutira wrote that, in Kenya's camps, "the law of the host country virtually ceased to be applied."[103] Joy Maingi and Kenneth Omeje recently have reinforced this point, arguing that the country has "lost" territorial control and that in Kakuma, and in the northwest as a whole, there was "hardly any state presence."[104] But hearing Yerosan and Girma explain their side of the story raised questions about this humanitarian surrogacy. Was Kakuma really just a place where aid agencies headquartered in Geneva and New York infringed on, and supplanted, the territorial sovereignty of Kenya with their "colonialism of compassion"?[105] While the two Ethiopians spared no criticism for the UNHCR, whose officials they accused of leading a lavish lifestyle while failing to protect their fundamental rights, they were emphatic that their "African neighbors" not only demanded but also *enforced* their encampment.

While colonial metaphors abound in critical scholarship on humanitarianism, their usual focus on the usurpation of sovereign control by foreign aid organizations risks foreclosing a more differentiated analysis of postcolonial orders. Metaphorizing colonialism, Eve Tuck and K. Wayne Yang warn, serves to evade responsibility and forestall justice, and it enables a "move to innocence" that relegates colonization to discursive, epistemic, or wholly abstract domination rather than material control over land, labor, and resources.[106] In short, at the heart of any colonizing project lies a relation of political domination, physical coercion, social stratification, and patterns of economic dispossession. In Kakuma, the Kenyan state has *not* simply been superseded by foreign aid agencies under the leadership of the UNHCR; nor has humanitarianism evolved into a metaphorical empire whose coloniality is reducible to racial paternalism and the biopolitical management of people deemed to be in need of "uplift." In fact, while services in health care, education, food distribution, water supply, and the construction of shelter in the refugee camp have indeed long been outsourced to organizations such as the Lutheran World Federation (LWF), the International Rescue Committee (IRC), the Norwegian Refugee Council (NRC), and the World Food Program (WFP), among others, the Kenyan authorities have actively facilitated the physical growth of camps on their own soil by underwriting aid programs with infrastructures of security to maintain state-defined order. Throughout the book, I use the term *state* alternately to denote both the abstract "idea" of a unitary institution organized around the monopoly over violence and a more disaggregated bundle of people, grounded practices, and social relations that actually "inhabit" this institution in the everyday.[107]

Against unhelpful tropes of "absent" or "weak" African states, the Kenyan authorities are constantly at work through multiple registers, even in the otherwise externally funded domain of humanitarian relief.[108] While the UNHCR held disproportionate sway over Kenya's asylum procedures for almost two decades, the state has slowly reclaimed control over refugee management, especially since the country's first ever Refugee Act was passed in 2006 (see chapter 1). But state involvement had never truly ceased, because street-level agents of the state were always deployed to administer and enforce the law, even in areas under humanitarian stewardship, such as Kakuma. While camps are often thought of as spatial technologies designed to "economize" on actual police officers and guards by virtue of enclosing populations with material barriers rather than manpower, human agents of state violence are indispensable to producing the exclusionary effects of encampment.[109] The UNHCR itself has no jurisdiction or capability to decree laws, enforce laws, or physically sanction refugees. When the refugee agency seeks to prohibit certain kinds of conduct, tackle crime, and restore its idea of "peace," it automatically turns to the Kenyan state in form of the police to enforce its will. This allows humanitarians to sidestep the moral complications of ruling in the name of the displaced while also meting out punitive justice to them. We may infer that a core feature of humanitarian power is not just its financial largesse and an ideological commitment to the "greater good" but, crucially, also its ability to discipline beneficiaries by proxy. Refugees in Kenya have never been solely the UNHCR's responsibility, but Kenyan police officers have always acted as the loyal foot soldiers of the aid regime who are called on when humanitarians struggle to fulfil their role as governors of people. By rendering the state not only an abstract authority but a concrete force of flesh and blood, the "police are," as Micol Seigel writes, "the translation of state violence into human form."[110]

As an institution, the police are essential for states, or any system of rule that is based on organized violence, because they act as armed guarantors for securing property, excluding undesirables, disciplining labor, enforcing territorial integrity, and cementing political power.[111] In colonial regimes, the police as "violence workers," in Seigel's words, also constituted a vital tool for upholding racially differentiated access to space, rights, land, and resources. Frantz Fanon famously charted this geography by writing about the colonial world as divided in two. "The dividing line, the border," he observed, "is represented by the barracks and the police stations."[112] Kenya's colonial police, even during the twilight years of British rule, were hard to distinguish from military garrisons, not least in the thinly populated frontier of the country's north and the "African reserves," where colonized subjects constantly had to be kept in check with military might.[113] By embodying the always partial (and ill-fated) attempts of colonizers to "pacify" and "order" what they conceived of as a dark and anarchic world of African "disorder," the police served as the street-level enforcers of the colonial state: the personification of a foreign occupation. "It is the policeman and the soldier," Fanon opined in this regard, "who are the official, instituted go-betweens, the spokesmen of the settler and his rule of oppression."[114] Therefore, it is helpful, as Lisa Marie Cacho and Jodi Melamed do, to think of them as the "street administration" of colonial racial orders whose normalized discretionary violence challenges the liberal pretension that powers are, or ought to be, separated.[115] At its root, the colonial order was always essentially a police order. In Kenya, as in other parts of the continent, enforcing the law continued to be synonymous with ensuring the survival of ruling elites, privileged minorities, and state organs well into the postindependence era.[116] Even after white-dominated colonial regimes had departed, their African successors continued to fiercely police ethnoracial identities, class divides, and landownership and crack down on threats to private property. But under the cloak of nationhood, the mobility of minoritized citizens and inferiorized noncitizens was increasingly thought of as the new primary peril to state security and "national unity."

However, in writings on humanitarian refugee governance the question of police power is often readily omitted. This is perhaps the result of the uncomfortable tension that arises when policing enters the analytical frame. After all, the purpose of police institutions is to "distribute harm and death according to hierarchies of difference and belonging," while aid work is supposed to achieve its opposite: *alleviate* suffering and *reduce* harm.[117] But this opposition is perplexing only if we think of the Foucauldian shift from "raw" sovereign power inherent in colonial brutality to a more liberal biopolitics as clear-cut. Instead, coercive state power and forms of organized violence have continued to coexist with, and complement, what we can call the "biopolitical empire" of humanitarian aid institutions.[118] It is through this simultaneity of the productive biopolitics of governing refugees and the negative power to police, punish, sequester, and immobilize them that a form of colonial difference comes to be expressed in the present. We know that all liberal orders, including liberal democracies and their aid regimes, tend to allow free movement only for those they consider "proper" subjects or "rational" actors and reserve illiberal techniques of rule for others regarded as "uncivilized" or "unfit" to enjoy those wide-ranging freedoms.[119] While the liberal edifice of international refugee law formally entrusts states such as Kenya with the protection of displaced noncitizens, their overtly hostile policies are reflections of a postcolonial order more broadly in which minoritized or poor populations are hardly considered rights-bearing actors but are "rightless subjects" who are still being treated as if they were colonized. Humanitarian encampment of refugees is in this sense one symptom of a much wider "planetary renewal of colonial relations."[120]

In this book I argue that a key locus of this renewal is humanitarian colonization. Rather than a metaphor for the biopolitical ordering of "disorderly" subjects, or the mere continuation of global North interference in Africa through foreign aid, this colonization is driven by a spatial process of domestic occupation at the hands of postcolonial states that has included land taking, the expansion of camps or settlements, the imposition of extractive economic relations, and the militarized policing of "non-native" migrants who are thus interpellated as a new colonized class. "Colonial occupation," for Mbembe, is quite literally "a matter of seizing, delimiting, and asserting control over a physical geographical area—of writing on the ground a new set of social and spatial relations." A prerequisite for inscribing this colonial geography in space, he writes, is "the production of boundaries and hierarchies, zones and enclaves; the subversion of existing property arrangements; the classification of people according to different categories; resource extraction; and, finally, the manufacturing of a large reservoir of cultural imaginaries."[121] In the past, camps have been put squarely in the service of colonial projects and the control of undesirable mobility under the auspices of empire. After independence, many colonial relations persisted under the mantle of sovereign nationhood by infiltrating economies, institutions, cultures, politics, and mentalities of the formerly colonized.[122] A time-warped "colonizing structure," as the philosopher Valentin-Yves Mudimbe notes, kept the colonial condition partially alive inside the postcolony.[123] Asserting physical control over territories and populations therefore remained a priority for independent African states such as Kenya, not least imposing their national "will" on internal peripheries. Half-hearted reforms meant that while some agricultural land changed hands from white farmers to new Black political elites, the property of many white settlers was simply preserved. Although the quest for self-rule increasingly entailed othering aliens and strangers, who were imagined to be outside the new national polity, this did not affect settlers but was targeted primarily at ethnoracially subjugated citizens and precarious noncitizens from neighboring countries who were deemed a risk to Kenya's stability. Postcolonial nationalism, Nandita Sharma argues, thus often replaced demands for an end to white foreign rule with a demand for an autochthonous national sovereignty: a "right to home rule" that required, at least in theory, a strongly bordered nation in which noncitizens, or those denied full citizenship, were unable to spoil—or even partake in—the national wealth.[124]

Third Colonial Occupation

The arrival of refugees in the 1990s, despite its generally unsettling effects on Kenya's national order, turned out to be an opportunity for the state to shore up support for its unfinished post-*uhuru* project of national integration. Kenyan administrators had been moved into the northern districts but sustained budgetary constraints, and a prioritization of development in the South, had done little to counterbalance a disjointed geography. Colonial policies had left Kenya unevenly integrated, with the fertile southern Rift Valley and the central highlands as centers of political power and infrastructural networks, and the north as a chronically underdeveloped frontier yet to be *fully* occupied by the new state.[125] There was a precedent for this national drive to recolonize the periphery. After World War II, the British colonial government rolled out a suite of policies aimed at rebuilding the Kenyan economy, and those of its other colonies, to reenergize its colonial activities after wartime austerity. Due to the extraordinary influx of funding, material assets, staff, and new developmental schemes at that time, D. A. Low and John Lonsdale describe this period as a "second colonial occupation."[126] Africans, the colonial state reasoned, still required significant investments before they could be truly "ready" for self-government. Urbanization and unending land dispossession further meant that they were thought to "detribalize" at an alarming rate, potentially dissolving the bonds of ethnic solidarity that had served as social glue in the past. Colonial officials regarded the new development plans as a way to penetrate into the farthest corners of their colonial possession and avert unrest through social programs: a self-styled colonialism beyond coercion that proved short-lived until the outbreak of the Kenya Emergency in 1952. Several decades later, the refugee emergencies of the 1990s constituted a similar watershed moment that created the impetus for infrastructural growth and independent Kenya's renewed colonization of its northern hinterland. Expedited by unprecedented levels of foreign aid and a liberal world order intent on reshaping geopolitics after the end of the Cold War, this can be thought of as a *third colonial occupation*.

Colonization is often understood as a process exclusive to empires, imperial companies, or foreign settlers seeking to establish relations of domination over new places with the aim to extract wealth, subjugate "native" peoples, and reorganize social relations based on racialized hierarchies. However, colonial thinking and paradigms have also infused nationalist projects of postcolonial expansion and domination that are frequently omitted from this frame. The third colonial occupation in Kenya took place long *after* independence and used a moment of "crisis" to further incorporate territorial fringes populated by ethnoracial minority populations who, in the eyes of the state, often barely qualified for national citizenship. It was propelled by extraordinary levels of international humanitarian aid mobilized for the benefit of hundreds of thousands of refugees who had newly arrived in Kenya's north. Land was set aside for the construction of internationally funded camps that were settled with refugees, supplied with food by aid organizations, and policed by Kenyan security forces (see chapter 2). Like regular colonial projects, this process was heavily predicated on beliefs in moral progress and superiority, and, given their asylum status, the "rescue" of the colonized. Humanitarian colonization thus created a codependence, a concessionary space of aid, in which the Kenyan state machinery anchored and enforced humanitarian protection by violent means while relief organizations advanced the state's militarized occupation of its own borderlands that hitherto had been beyond its firm reach. It is, in essence, an internal colonial occupation within the national frame that uses a combination of territorial expansion, spatial zoning, segregationist policies, emergency policing, and uneven access to resources in the name of refugee protection, social progress, long-term economic prosperity, and nation building.[127] As part of the imposition of nationalized rule, Kenya folded its territorializing agendas of development, graduated citizenship along ethnoracial lines, and security into what would soon become protracted humanitarian operations.

The camp has turned refugees into occupied subjects who, as noncitizens, are excluded from the power to which they are subject but are also unable to escape from it due to the constraints imposed on them: Their everyday lives are regulated, monitored, criminalized, and disrupted at will.[128] Once it is framed in these terms, we begin to detect Kakuma's family resemblance to other sites of colonization, in which police and paramilitaries act like an "occupying army" on their own national territory, as the Black Panther leader Huey Newton put it.[129] Kashmir, Xinjiang, Palestine, West Papua, Kurdistan, and Western Sahara are among the most recognizable spaces where these colonial paradigms of dispossession, domination, and militarized rule are in action today.[130] Notably, across all these theaters, the camp resurfaces as a means of punishing, concentrating, economically exploiting, protecting, and "reeducating" colonized populations, making it a microcosm of modern colonial relations of rule. "Colony and camp," Stoler therefore notes, structurally "feed off each other" in creating and re-creating enclosures, containment, and systems of ethnoracialized difference that are altered through the course of nonaligned or disparate histories.[131] The end of European empires merely displaced the camp's properties onto new national geographies of colonization aimed at repossessing domestic margins and controlling their minoritized residents. In Kenya, the slippage between occupation, economic development, and humanitarian protection rendered refugees neither "fit" for inclusion in their host society nor fully "eligible" for more humane treatment as liberal citizen-like subjects. They were neither imprisoned nor fully free.

With this in mind, Kakuma camp transpired not as a "safe haven," where refugees could feel protected from the harm they left behind in their countries of origin, but as a place where they were exposed to a new economy of violence. In contrast to scholars who have argued that violence in Kakuma is the result of proliferating crime and "rebel actors," I foreground the originary violence of forced displacement coupled with a militarized occupation that treats refugees as *colonized subjects* forced to live under mobility restrictions, curfews, pass laws, and extractive economic relations, and with threats of imprisonment for daring to dream of a freer and safer life.[132] Aid agencies such as the UNHCR actively bankrolled this system to retain their physical presence in the country and facilitate the delivery of aid. Kenyan nationals and international staff reworked discriminatory imaginaries that organized refugees in colonial fashion as ethnoracial others who are "reticent" to progress or a danger to the national polity. They expressed concerns about the moral fitness of refugees: their capacity to raise children, cultivate loving relationships, engage in peaceful religious practices, or become "modern" members of society who readily disavow "old" cultural beliefs (see chapter 3).

Nonetheless, camp officials also heavily relied on unpaid (and underpaid) refugee labor in health, education, water, sanitation, shelter, and community policing to keep aid programs afloat. This has amounted to a reinvented system of indirect rule in which power was decentralized only when it served the camp's colonial order, always combining "a capacity to implement central directives with one to absorb local shocks," but was left ultimately in the hands of camp authorities (see chapter 4).[133] Refugees were not only deputized as proxies, exposed to physical harm from the police, and robbed of their lifetime by being kept in perpetual "limbo"; they also experienced literal extortion from aid workers, government clerks, and other administrators. This extractive side of encampment became even clearer after cuts to global aid budgets galvanized the introduction of more market-based approaches to humanitarian relief, with a mixture of (neo)liberal policies promoting entrepreneurialism, work schemes, and financial literacy and seeking to "open up" the camp to investors who could capitalize on refugee life and labor. While humanitarianism had long been boosting local economies in Turkana with money and subsidized services, further concessions to capital under the banner of "marketization" were now on the horizon to render the camp and refugees more "productive" (see chapter 5).

Kakuma thus sits at the intersection of claims to protect refugees, harness the forces of racial capitalism, and guarantee planetary mobility control. Rather than acting as "prison guards of the West," the Kenyan authorities are themselves invested in using the camp as a border technology that can separate migrants from its national citizens, address the country's vexatious security question, and create opportunities for rent-seeking from global North donors.[134] Through UNHCR-subsidized salaries for its own security forces and donations in the form of vehicles, materiel, and infrastructure, Nairobi has been able to secure an increasingly strong foothold in—and, in this sense, colonized—the marginalized border areas that historically have slipped away from colonial and, later, postcolonial state control. Encampment, though crippling to the lives of refugees, has nevertheless benefited the state's security ambitions, inflated the power of humanitarian agencies such as the UNHCR, and turned Kenya into a regional bulwark of global mobility apartheid. But like any colonized space, the camp should not be misunderstood as a totalizing form of oppression that produced "bare life" but was marred by profound incongruities, disobedience, and even cracks that sometimes allowed for practices of refusal, manipulation, and defiance to emerge. Rather than outright resistances, these practices were more akin to forms of connivance, opportunism, makeshift maneuvers, non-compliance, and quiet repudiations of life as a confined refugee. If we are indeed at a point where colonial relations are being renewed on a planetary scale, then the story of Kakuma may serve as an urgent warning against putting the movable archive of the camp to work in the service of carceral aid.

Notes on Methods and Ethics

This book is the result of more than fifteen months of ethnographic research conducted between 2015 and 2017, and subsequent engagements over several years with people whose stories lie at the heart of this work. It is part of a long line of scholarship in political geography that has embraced ethnography to use the filigree of everyday life to shed light on processes and structures of power that underpin social relations on a far larger scale.[135] I combined an inductive approach of being immersed in everyday scenes as they unfolded with detailed questions that I asked in follow-up interviews. My study comprised recorded in-depth and semistructured interviews with 110 interlocutors, including official and unofficial "refugee leaders," refugee members of the community police (Community Peace and Protection Teams [CPPTs]), Kenyan police and paramilitary officers, civilian government officials, Kenyan and foreign aid workers working for the UNHCR and its nongovernmental organization (NGO) partners, as well as unaffiliated camp residents. These interviewees were chosen based on their positions within these organizations or their lived experiences (and knowledge) of humanitarian camp rule since the mid-1990s. Depending on each participant's preference, interviews were conducted in English, Kiswahili, or (colloquial) Arabic, sometimes switching between languages as we talked. The book also draws on extensive observations, informal encounters, and what Renato Rosaldo called "deep hanging out," which took place in restaurants, shops, offices, cafés, police stations, markets, and homes, among other places. I met with my interlocutors at roadsides, compounds, roadblocks, and football pitches and accompanied them on security patrols.[136] After these meetings, I usually reconstructed people's narratives, stories, or anecdotes the best as I could and made notes in my journal. While the voices of refugees are always key to this endeavor because they offer us glimpses of humanitarian rule from those at the receiving end of its violence, they are now also increasingly mobilized by aid agencies as "authentic" sources to attest to particular aspects of camp life in the service of institutionalized power. I am more interested in uncovering what the humanitarian system seeks to conceal through applying a "disobedient gaze" that not *only* looks at the lives of refugees—who are usually the subjects of studies on encampment—but, crucially, *also* those authorized to administer them.[137]

This research process was, above all, an exercise in patience—tedious, time-consuming, nonlinear in its course and sometimes taking unexpected turns. Or, as Omod, a young Anuak from Ethiopia, put it when trying to console me during my periodic confusion: "To get a good thing requires a long process; a bad thing you will get immediately."[138] I tried to countervail the paucity of available (and reliable) official information on matters of camp governance, policing, and aid-sponsored militarization in the camp by methodical triangulation with alternative accounts from multiple people, media reports, and internal documents. Due to the sensitivity of the issues discussed, I have withheld the names of respondents or used pseudonyms.

Although the primary focus of my research was Kakuma refugee camp in northwestern Kenya, I also took shorter trips to Nairobi, the Dadaab refugee camps in Garissa County, Ongata Rongai, Lodwar, Murang'a, Nadapal, Lokichoggio, and Kiambu. The purpose of going to these sites was to follow specific research leads, interview former officials, and—in the case of the Dadaab camps—get a cursory sense of how what I later called humanitarian colonization might function differently across aid programs in the country. In Kakuma and Dadaab, the faith-based LWF, which has been working in Kenya since the early 1990s, provided me with accommodation in its compounds, including access to its offices and staff. As I explain in chapter 1, doing this research was a notoriously difficult task at that particular juncture, as Kenya's regional "War on Terror" in Somalia and the domestic front was fresh in the public's mind and shaped people's perceptions of refugees and humanitarian engagements.[139] The high-profile terror attacks on the Westgate Mall in 2013, Mpeketoni town in 2014, and Garissa University College in 2015, and recurring improvised explosive device (IED) explosions in and around Dadaab dominated media headlines and sometimes influenced the kind of access or goodwill I was able to get.

The camp is a peculiar environment for research. Refugees are subject to tight regimes of control, registration, biometrics, spatial organization, enumeration, and distribution of food and shelter. In turn, they are expected to disclose intimate details about their flight history and vulnerabilities to bureaucrats who handle their cases, often from the comfort of air-conditioned offices that are located behind the barbed wire and perimeter fences of securitized aid compounds. This is often done with the understanding that refugees "need someone to speak for them," a role that aid agencies readily assume by treating testimonies, statements, and experiences of refugees in an almost fiduciary capacity.[140] My entry into this world was bumpy, as I was critically eyed by aid workers and government officials who felt that their work had been misrepresented by researchers like me in the past. As a white man affiliated with a prestigious university in the United Kingdom but who spoke fluent Kiswahili and was well versed in the social context, I gained the trust of *some* interlocutors while raising suspicion among *others*. When I first arrived in the camp, one Kenyan official told me point blank that, in his view, "many researchers, especially the whites, have damaged the name of Kakuma refugee camp," an accusation and note of suspicion toward me that I found remarkably difficult to rebut.[141] Among refugees, by contrast, my presence would often "arouse expectations of help or be seen as a way of effecting change."[142] Consultants frequently visited the camp to do studies commissioned by NGOs or the UNHCR that implied a search for technical "fixes" to the problems of camp dwellers. This kind of policy-driven research usually promised an immediate improvement in the lives of refugees and affected the hopes my own work raised. Further, doctoral researchers, as I was at the time, sometimes act "like scavengers searching for hidden treasures," as the late Barbara Harrell-Bond once snidely remarked—an image I was keen to disprove. However, this required honest and difficult conversations with people about the distant (and uncertain) "good" that a critical analysis of the injustice and violence of encampment could potentially do. Whether my work has succeeded in doing so, or whether I have simply become yet another scavenger, remains open for debate.

As a researcher, I occupied a fragile in-between position that allowed me to spend time in the homes of refugees while aid workers were strictly forbidden from doing so under their codes of conduct. However, I was given an agency-issued "gate pass"—a coveted document—that equipped me with comprehensive access to the aid compounds that refugees could enter only with prior permission. This unique position, compounded by my whiteness, afforded me the flexibility to defy at least some of the social "laws of gravity" in the camp by having breakfast at a refugee's house, eating lunch with officers at the police canteen, and having dinner with UNHCR officials, all within one day. Out of all social contacts during fieldwork, Kenyan police officers' openness toward me perhaps surprised me the most. They had never been of direct interest to researchers in Kakuma before, and their responses were often far less polished or cautious than those of aid workers, who were painfully aware of their role in managing not only the camp but also its public relations. The intensity of these day-to-day encounters meant that I was inevitably pulled into emotional force fields, often touched nerves, and stirred anxieties with unpredictable effects.[143] The camp's affective geography differentially structured access, mobility, and social relations for everyone who resided in it. Near the end of my fieldwork, institutional anxieties around my suspiciously long-term stay in the camp boiled over and led to accusations of espionage leveled against me by the Kenyan authorities that subsequently restricted my access. In a last-ditch attempt to regain the trust of these officials, I contacted the German Embassy, which advised me to speak to an officer from Germany's Federal Criminal Investigations Department (Bundeskriminalamt [BKA]) in Nairobi. The irony was not lost on me that, as a scholar passionately critical of the police and state power, I had to bite my tongue in a moment of crisis and seek help from those very institutions. The BKA officer acted as my advocate to try to mend relations with the Kenyan police, who were among my most important interlocutors. The officer eventually wrote a letter to the Directorate of Criminal Investigation (DCI) in Nairobi to underline that I was *not*, in fact, a German spy. Ironically, days after I had overcome the disquiet around this episode, the officer who had intervened on my behalf invited me to a meeting at the German Embassy to ask, now that my rapport with Kenya's police had been restored, whether I would be able to share my "raw data" with his agency—a request I politely, but firmly, declined.

By doing this project, I had to confront the ethical dilemmas of mingling with violence workers *and* the refugees they criminalize. I also had to acknowledge that refugees themselves can become violence workers and local proxies for oppressive systems of rule. As my research progressed, I slowly came to terms with the fact that research can never be "pure" and that my role as a researcher needed to reflect this constant negotiation of muddling through.[144] In fact, the insights I could gain into the violence work that lay beneath the surface of the humanitarian operation could ultimately be useful for its undoing, making my temporary (and comparatively minor) discomfort, trials, and tribulations worthwhile. Although refugees often appear in these pages as *targets* of violence and structural forces outside their control, this is not to suggest a lack of autonomous desires and inaction on their part or, worse still, their reduction to "bare life."[145] In fact, this book illustrates that refugees in Kakuma are simultaneously *surviving*, *resisting*, and *participating in* a system of colonization that is the camp.

Outline of the Book

At its core, *Occupied Refuge* is a study of how humanitarianism and postcolonial nation-states continue to be acutely imbricated with colonial forms of rule. It offers critical insights into the underbelly of humanitarian operations whose existence paradoxically relies on the exertion of militarized force by proxy. Examining specific locations at the global margins provides us with an opportunity to understand the colonial nature of not only displacement, the aid industry, and planetary mobility control, but also of sovereign states seeking to "capture" their own populace and territories. Empirically, the book focuses on Kakuma refugee camp in northwestern Kenya which historically contingent phases of frontier colonization, postcolonial marginalization, and renewed occupation by Kenyan state and aid actors have turned into a contemporary occupied refuge. The empirical chapters each outline one of the four building blocks that underpin this colonial geography of the humanitarian camp: militarized occupation and policing, ethnoracial imaginaries of domination, indirect rule and, last, forms of extraction.

Chapter 1, "Refuge," situates Kakuma in Kenya's political history and geography. As a cosmopolitan refugee camp that has weathered many bouts of securitization, counterterrorism, and militarization over its three decades-long existence, Kakuma has recently become a donors' darling in narratives around refugee resilience, economic opportunities, and entrepreneurialism. The chapter opens with the media spectacle of TEDxKakumaCamp that took place in 2018, throwing Kakuma unexpectedly into the global limelight, and draws out how its polished image as a "poster child" humanitarian camp clashes with the harsh reality of its ruling order.

Chapter 2, "Occupation," traces the everyday geographies of occupation and militarized police control that furnish humanitarian rule in Kakuma. Read against the backdrop of a longer history of frontier colonization in Kenya's northwest, it follows the daily work of police officers in charge of maintaining "public order" in the camp but also hears out the refugees who are exposed to the violence of incarceration, raids, beatings, and curfews. By recounting the stories of both street-level enforcers of the state *and* the refugees they police, the chapter shows that humanitarianism, despite its promises of protection, is made possible only by an architecture of colonial occupation that consists of roadblocks, police stations, a bureaucracy of permits, and the use of collective punishments.

Chapter 3, "Dis/order," moves from this material side of occupation to its cultural text by showing how refugees are routinely subjected to discriminatory discourses that portray them as ethnoracially inferior "others" in need of institutional control. Drawing on my engagements with camp administrators, the chapter illustrates the geographical imaginaries of humanitarian encampment as they transpired in conversations, off-stage behavior, and attitudes that would be deemed unacceptable in more official discourses. It unpacks how racialized tropes of refugees as "criminals and crooks," "sexually deviant," and "uncivilized" not only seemed to validate the urgent moral mission of humanitarianism but inadvertently helped to forge a Kenyan sense of national superiority at the frontier.

Chapter 4, "Community," shifts our gaze to refugees actively recruited by aid and state actors to help administer the camp. Focusing on the lives of these residents tasked with keeping their community "safe," by working for a community policing program called the CPPTs, the chapter reveals how the militarized camp always, and perhaps increasingly, relies on the violence work of refugees themselves. The chapter exposes the contestation over the meaning of "the community" by government officials, aid workers, and refugees, arguing that, rather than strengthening local protection or democratic participation, community policing is a humanitarian iteration of "indirect rule" that effectively undermines the ground on which relations of togetherness, safety, and kinship can flourish.

Chapter 5, "Extraction," focuses on extractive geographies that have emerged through, and structurally underpin, humanitarian colonization. It looks at ordinary inhabitants of Kakuma who feel their lives and resources are slowly draining away and humanitarian workers entangled in the delivery of aid but who are disillusioned at the ineffectiveness and waste of their efforts. The chapter contends that, in contrast to our understanding of camps as institutions that provide resources *to* refugees, they are instead part and parcel of global capitalist circuits through which value is also constantly extracted *from* them in the form of time, wealth, labor, and publicity.

Given the ubiquity of colonizing logics in Kakuma's landscape of humanitarian aid, the conclusion considers what it may mean to *decolonize* such spaces of aid. The book points to the similarities of camps and other places where precaritized citizens also experience state violence, emphasizing a wider quest for reappropriating mobility and the means of a freer life. It grapples with the implications of having normalized the camp as a preferred mechanism for governing minoritized noncitizens in the postcolonial era and the fact that institutionalized aid continues to provide cover for a technology that is so easily weaponized against present and future enemy "others." Linking Kakuma's humanitarian camp order to contemporary demands for mobility and decarceral justice, it concludes by looking toward a radical abolitionist future in which encampment, driven by both colonial and national relations of rule, is dismantled so that more liberatory futures can become a possibility.

Refuge

On June 9, 2018, Kakuma was made the unlikely center of a global media spectacle. It was set to become the first refugee camp in the world to host a TEDx talk that, its United Nations High Commissioner for Refugees (UNHCR) organizers hoped, would help to bring uplifting refugee stories of resilience, recovery, and opportunity to audiences around the globe. "TEDx," a spin-off of the popular TED format that has achieved global following, features carefully scripted talks or performances designed to inspire, educate, and provoke conversations about "big ideas" or novel approaches for tackling humanity's most pressing problems. The choice to host this event in Kakuma was not surprising to those familiar with the industry. The United Nations (UN) refugee agency had promoted the camp as a "poster child" for its humanitarian publicity efforts for some years. "TEDx events are often in privileged settings so we thought about bringing the power of the TED stage to a refugee camp," Melissa Fleming, then the UNHCR's head of communications, told Reuters in an interview.[1] The agency, it seemed, was trying to counterbalance gloomy headlines of terrorism and rampant insecurity in Kenya's other camp, Dadaab, with more wholesome stories about ingenuity, integration, and economic flourishing from Kakuma.[2] In a promotional video released in the run-up to TEDxKakumaCamp, Fleming and her deputy, Dana Hughes, explained with fervor that "Kakuma is a vibrant place. It has nineteen nationalities of people who fled some awful wars, but people managed to rebuild their lives, somehow. And really, it's more than a camp. It's a community. It's a neighborhood. In some cases, some people call it a small city. It's teeming with talent, with dreams, with hopes and even with opportunity."[3]

Kakuma was cast as a tranquil, diverse, and accessible place where humanitarian organizations could feel less "under siege" than in the Dadaab camps, where tighter security measures for aid workers had long become the paralyzing norm.[4] It was also set apart from the security problems that have troubled aid operations around the world in recent decades.[5] To market this new Kakuma "brand," the UNHCR published a glossy visitors information guide to advertise the camp's unique marvels to journalists, researchers, aid workers, and donor delegations, suggesting they "grab a souvenir or two as a reminder of [their] visit," attend cultural dance performances, watch soccer matches, or casually "meet and interact with camel herders at the Kakuma livestock market."[6] The camp was turned into a commercial attraction that could be consumed (and enjoyed!)—one visit at a time—by the most privileged class in the aid industry.

Financed in part by the clothing giant H&M's charitable foundation, TEDx-KakumaCamp took place in a custom-made venue on the premises of a school in the camp. Special equipment and materials were trucked all the way from Nairobi, including a large pop-up event space that re-created the tidy, calm, and slick atmosphere characteristic of other TEDx talks. In the video, Fleming enters the fully assembled venue, which changed the schoolyard beyond recognition. Amazed by this transformation, Fleming asked, "Are we [really] in Kakuma?" to which her colleague replies with a loud laugh: "It says so, so we must [be]." These scenes are bewildering as the organizers seem to congratulate themselves on the fact that they have managed to curate a TEDx space in the unlikeliest of circumstances and keep the "real" camp out. While tens of thousands of viewers from across the world live streamed the event, Kakuma's refugees could watch it on large public screens set up in the camp. The venue itself was reserved for members of aid agencies, local dignitaries, and invited guests. The twelve speakers were handpicked to reflect Kakuma's diversity and help construct a rounded narrative that centered refugees: The activist Riya Yuyada, the filmmaker Aminah Rwimo, and the athlete Pur Biel, who lived in the camp, were joined by celebrity guests such as the Kenyan hip-hop artist "Octopizzo"; the South African actress Nomzamo Mbatha; the American psychologist Paul Slovic; the Somali American fashion model Halima Aden, who spent her early childhood in the camp; Josphat Nanok, then the governor of Turkana County; and, finally, speakers from the World Bank and the UNHCR. While the media coverage was overwhelmingly celebratory, as it literally put African refugees center stage, it strengthened the Kakuma "brand" and legitimized problematic neoliberal visions of a self-help humanitarianism carried by stories of success and resilience.[7] In her talk, Aden—a trailblazer for hijab-wearing women in the fashion industry—divulged, "I'm not afraid to be the first, to step up on my own, to take risks and seek change because that's what being a minority is about. It's about using yourself as *a vessel to create change* and being a human representation for the power of diversity."[8]

The UNHCR country representative in Kenya at the time, Raouf Mazou, reinforced this message of self-making in another video, produced by the International Finance Corporation (IFC) and released around the same time as TEDxKakumaCamp, that celebrated Kakuma's dynamic economy. "What is most important for us in Kakuma now," Mazou said, looking straight into the camera, "is to change the mindset and for all of us to see Kakuma as a *different place*, as a place where there are business opportunities, where people create wealth."[9] Seeking refuge was, in this way, redefined from an experience of interminable loss, sanctuary, and violence to being a springboard into a brighter and potentially more prosperous future in which refugees could, in Aden's words, become "vessels" to create change. Not only refugees but also Kenyans were set to benefit from this changed "mindset" and the material gains that were expected to follow once Kakuma was more widely perceived as a thriving "city in the desert."[10] In fact, a growing body of work has since highlighted the "untapped" potential reflected in the camp's bustling markets and vibrant economic life, which suggest tantalizing opportunities for private investment, entrepreneurship, and wealth creation.[11] The focus on economic productivity, innovation, and reimagining encampment as an incubator for creative solutions has made Kakuma, in the words of Jeff Crisp, the former UNHCR head of policy development who has since become an outspoken critic of the organization, "by far the most intensely and positively written-about camp in the world."[12] TEDxKakumaCamp bore testimony to this perception, which sat uneasily with many of the camp's lived realities that were not represented onstage.

Tucked in the far corner of Turkana County in northwestern Kenya, the camp (*kambi*) was built in July 1992 on an arid stretch of land that was prone to flooding from the seasonal Tarach River. The Tarach, which marks an almost

FIGURE I.I. The cast and organizers of TEDxKakumaCamp, 2018. Photograph by Tobin Jones.

natural separation between town and refugee camp, is a dry riverbed (*lagga*) for much of the year and cyclically turns into a torrential stream during the rainy season. Like many refugee camps on the continent, and elsewhere in the global South, Kakuma is neither fenced in with barbed wire nor surrounded by towering walls but embodies a kind of carcerality that works more subtly through bureaucratic confinement, graduated mobility, and administrative restrictions to enforce the im/mobility of its residents (see chapter 2). With a refugee population of some 213,000, Kakuma dwarfs its more famous European counterparts, such as the now defunct Mória camp in Greece, which housed twenty thousand people at its peak in 2020, or the long-demolished Calais "Jungle" that was once home to eight thousand migrants and refugees.[13] With an average of 11,580 refugees dwelling on each square kilometer, the Kakuma camp's population density is second only to that of the Gaza Strip.[14] Comparable in size to Salt Lake City in the United States or the town of Naivasha in Kenya, Kakuma is now the fourteenth-largest urbanized area in the country.

When looking beyond the gloss of IFC reports and academic studies that hail Kakuma as a place of aspiration, hustling, and economic optimism, the camp remains a geographically remote backwater in Kenya's deprived north, where infrastructure is weak; public investment is low; amenities are poor; and goods from "downcountry" Kenya have to be transported hundreds of miles over long and windy roads to their destination.[15] Despite recent $500 million World Bank–funded roadworks that are expected to raise local living standards, a senior European UNHCR official still dismissed Kakuma as what he pejoratively called "a shithole duty station."[16] Contrasting sharply with the green pastures that financial institutions, their humanitarian partners, and even the TEDx event itself suggested, the camp continues to be widely considered a "hardship mission" where junior aid workers cut their teeth before being rewarded with more comfortable deployments. Among Kenyan government officials, by contrast, this hinterland was a coveted posting that could yield significant financial rewards in the form of cash extorted from refugees to subsidize a lifestyle well above a civil servant's normal means. For refugees (*wakimbizi*), Kakuma is imbued with more conflicting meanings that emerge from their precarious claims to belonging even after decades of staying in Kenya, during which they had to try to foster "a unique lifestyle between permanence and transience."[17] The Sudanese writer and Kakuma resident Kodi Arnu Ngutulu captures this affective ambivalence about life in the camp in one of his poems:

For many it is home, just because they are away from home.
Compared to *home*, it is peaceful—no death brought by slayers.
Unlike *home*, it is segregation—a reminder of not having.
That is how it feels to be in paradise, where you die many times,
    not once.[18]

In Ngutulu's words Kakuma emerges as an oxymoronic abode: a deceptive and uncompromising space that, on the one hand, offers respite from the immediate horrors of displacement and war but, on the other, denies people long-term freedom by truncating their life trajectories—making them metaphorically "die many times"—and foreclosing fulfilled futures beyond humanitarian dispensation. While it may give vital shelter from violence, the camp also creates new carceral conditions and harm that manifest in police crackdowns, security measures, and the colonization of everyday life by aid and state actors, as the chapters that follow show. The twin tales of Kakuma as a "safe haven" in a volatile geopolitical neighborhood and a nursery of opportunity further entrench fears that this imagined calm is at constant risk of subversion and crime from among refugees themselves. TEDxKakumaCamp certainly played into the general sentiment that the fruits of this refuge were hard won and precious, and that any opportunities could arise only when looked after by a strong coalition of aid organizations and the state. Over the years, protecting the camp's "humanitarian and civilian character" had become a political rallying cry to justify infrastructural militarization, expanded police powers, and the mounting of a colonial occupation in the name of peace and protection (see chapter 2). As a sanctuary, cosmopolis, place of hope, hotbed of terror, or makeshift city, Kakuma has invoked contrasting imaginaries that continue to shape what "refuge" might mean to its inhabitants and elicit different strategies for living through encampment.

"Kakuma refugee camp is my home, my future, and my inspiration," began Aminah Rwimo in her TEDx talk. Having lost her family to war in the Democratic Republic of Congo, she emphasized the empowering effect Kakuma has had as a place "where I have learned that *my* dreams are valid, too." Despite her painful memories, she said, "I believe my past is over, I do not live in my past. I focus on my present and my future."[19] While many quite understandably chose to embrace this future-oriented disposition of self-made resilience and optimism to survive in the here and now, others refused to accept the responsibility this placed on them as individuals. Not everyone could thrive in a world of scarcity, and, despite the choices available to those in the camp, much was still outside their control. Ngutulu articulates this more pessimistic outlook when he writes about sorrow, hardship, and lack in Kakuma. For him, the permanent impermanence of camp life, coupled with feelings of not knowing, limbo, and not quite belonging have turned what was a temporary refuge into what he characterizes now, rather ominously, as a "paradise in hell."

A Cosmopolitan Camp

The first residents of Kakuma camp were a now famous group of young refugees from southern Sudan who fled the conflict between Sudan's government in Khartoum and the Sudan People's Liberation Army (SPLA) that had been raging since 1983. Having covered long distances on foot during their flight journeys from refugee camps in Ethiopia via South Sudan and, finally, into Kenya, these young adolescents were given the unflattering but highly memorable epithet "Lost Boys" or "walking boys" by the international press.[20] After arriving in the Kenyan border town of Lokichoggio, where the now defunct humanitarian Operation Lifeline Sudan was based until 2005, these children and young adults were subsequently transported one hundred kilometers inland by the UNHCR to the sleepy frontier town of Kakuma, where a new camp was then being set up—just off the A1 Highway that snakes from Isebania at the Tanzanian border all the way to Nadapal in Kenya's northwest. Elias, whom I met at the Catholic Kakuma Mission Hospital on a sweltering afternoon in August 2016, worked for the UNHCR during this turbulent period in 1992 and was among the first field officers to receive refugees at the Kenya-Sudan border. His superior at the time was the aid worker Kilian Kleinschmidt, who more than twenty years later would achieve global fame as the so-called mayor of

Za'atari (refugee camp) in Jordan.[21] Elias remembers the operational dilemma of this fast-growing emergency in Kenya, where "people were hungry, but you had nearly nothing to give them. They were sick, but there was not a single doctor in sight."[22]

The original section of the camp (Kakuma 1) was constructed in 1991 on a peninsula between the banks of the Tarach in the east and the smaller Lodoket riverbed in the west. This is today the greenest part of the camp, dotted with trees that were planted by the first generation of refugees thirty years ago. The chief of Kakuma recalls this exceptional time of arrival well because he was in secondary school when the camp opened. "Some *wakimbizi* knew how to do business; they opened shops and butcheries where they slaughtered animals. Others came with a sort of 'war hangover,'" he said gravely. But, as if regretting having painted an overly negative picture, he quickly added, "This town wouldn't be the same without refugees. It was very small back then. But now, our Turkana people work in the camp, bring their goats there, their firewood. They benefit."[23] A Dinka elder named Majok was one of the first to settle in the camp when he was a young man. He is slender and of imposing stature, with graying short hair and a distinct limp, and he always holds a walking stick in one hand. As someone who had fought for the SPLA at an early age, he was desperately trying to leave the atrocities of the war behind. "We had nothing on us, but we were happy to be somewhere else. There was nothing here when we stepped off the truck, very little infrastructure, no houses, barely a road. But see how far this place has come. Kakuma has grown so much, but the UNHCR still feeds us," he told me when we meet in the shade of a *Prosopis* tree near his house. "We were once 'Lost Boys,'" he said with an air of melancholy, "but even now I'm not sure we have found our path yet."[24] After this first phase of arrivals, the camp developed infrastructurally with the buzz of what some have called an "accidental city."[25] This founding history has since come to define Kakuma's unique recognizability on the international stage. The story has gained almost legendary status in the competitive environment of the humanitarian industry, in which a high media profile and an inspiring origin story can have tangible funding benefits. It has since been retold many times over in scholarship, memoirs, and fictionalized accounts— immortalized most sensationally in the US author Dave Eggers's book *What Is the What*, based on the life of the "Lost Boy" Valentino Achak Deng.

While the camp started with twelve thousand South Sudanese refugees, it developed throughout the 1990s into a more cosmopolitan space whose makeup increasingly also reflected other displacements that took place concurrently in the region.[26] Upon arrival, refugees were spatially organized into self-identified "groups" that mapped onto their nationalities, ethnic identities (*makabila*), areas of origin, and the like. Thousands of Ethiopians, mostly Amhara and Oromo, were relocated from Walda refugee camp in Kenya's Marsabit to Kakuma in 1993 and were among the first non-Sudanese to join the sizable Dinka, Nuer, and Equatorian communities in the camp.[27] While many of the Ethiopians had originally served in the army of the dictator Mengistu Haile Mariam—and had escaped from persecution as enablers of his former regime—others simply fled the devastation of Ethiopia's civil war (1974–91).[28] Abathun was one of the former military men who had fled to Kenya as the anti-Mengistu forces of the Ethiopian People's Revolutionary Democratic Front (EPRDF) were closing in on his unit in 1991. "I might not look the part now, but I was a navy diver in the Ethiopian armed forces before I came to Kenya. I was in shape," he said, laughing. As a diving instructor, Abathun traveled the world, receiving training in Kim Il Sung's North Korea, where he once parachuted from a plane into the East Sea before being sent to train Muammar Gaddafi's navy divers in Libya, eventually shaking hands with the infamous man himself. Now in his late sixties, Abathun cut an understated figure, steady on his feet but visibly aged, wearing a baseball cap and doing his daily rounds in the neighborhood to stay healthy. "My life is over," he told me, with nostalgia in his voice, "but I'm waiting for resettlement to the United States so my daughter can live hers. Otherwise I would just return to Ethiopia."

Ethiopians have carved out a unique ethnonational enclave in Kakuma that has grown organically around the popular "Ethiopian market" and remains one of the camp's liveliest economic centers. Refugees from all over Kakuma regularly flock here for a taste of coffee at one of the Ethiopian *hoteli* or to purchase high-quality foodstuff sold by retailers in the area. Acholi and Langi refugees from Uganda, many of whom were opposed to the regime of Yoweri Museveni after his rise to power in 1986, settled nearby and founded the so-called Ugandan administration.[29] Further change came when twelve refugee camps, that stretched from the port city of Mombasa up to Kenya's northeastern periphery, were ordered to close between 1997 and 1998. Their fifteen thousand mostly Somali occupants were distributed between the Dadaab and Kakuma camps, which led to a surge in their respective populations.[30] Due to the discrimination that Somali minorities, such as the Bajuni and Barawa, had faced in Somalia and even in their Kenyan exile, the less ethnically homogeneous Kakuma camp became the preferred destination for their relocation and was purposefully expanded in 1998 with a section named Kakuma 2.[31]

Somalis soon emerged as the second most populous national group in the camp after the South Sudanese. Absame, a Bajuni born in Kismayo, lived in Hatimi refugee camp from 1993 until December 1997 before it was shut down

FIGURE 1.2. Entrance to the Ethiopian market in Kakuma 1, 2015. Photograph by the author.

and all residents were moved. "When we left Hatimi camp in Mombasa, we dismantled our tents and loaded them into large containers that were provided by the UNHCR," he said. "We boarded the buses [in January 1998] and the vehicles arrived here [in Kakuma] after seven days. We had our belongings numbered and when the vehicles carrying them arrived everybody took theirs and set up their shelters [again]. We had to start all over."[32] Yet the following year, extremely heavy rains completely submerged one of the relocation zones in Kakuma 2, making it uninhabitable not long after the Somalis had newly settled there. George, a UNHCR official who has worked in Kakuma for twenty years, was one of the people tasked with resolving the crisis. He and his colleagues had to move at least five thousand refugees with trucks to an unoccupied area near the camp entrance in Kakuma 1. While hesitant at first, these relocatees not only adjusted quickly to this new situation but harnessed their business networks to jump-start shops, stalls, and restaurants, eventually giving birth to the "Somali market." "For a long time, the Ethiopian market was the place to be," George recalled, "but soon after the Bajuni and Barawa arrived, the Somali market turned into the primary business hub of the camp."[33] Today the market runs along one of the camp's main transport arteries and, despite occasional flooding, continues to be a vibrant hub of commerce.

In 2003, Kakuma's Somali population surged once again. This time, ten thousand members of another historically marginalized minority, the so-called Somali Bantu, were transferred to the camp from Dadaab, where they had experienced discrimination, to await resettlement to the United States.[34] "We had a difficult life in Dadaab, that's for sure," said Roble, who was one of the refugees moved to Kakuma for protection. He sat comfortably on a plastic chair inside his house, wearing a crisp white kanzu (*thawb*) and spoke with surprising serenity. "We Somali Bantus have been through a lot. We fled Somalia because of discrimination, and in Dadaab it just continued. My first wife was raped there in Dadaab; she was raped by a Warya [majority-clan Somali]. There is a lot of harassment of Somali Bantus, and that's why the UNHCR brought us to Kakuma." As space was becoming scarcer in light of newcomers arriving in such close succession, the UNHCR decided to expand the existing camp by building a new section called Kakuma 3, northwest of Kakuma 2. Roble was initially given a plot in the new section that lay just across from the *lagga*. Gradually, he married his second and then third wife, slowly building homes in other parts of the camp, as well. Life was not easy, he said, but he was determined to make it work. Kakuma town, the adjacent Kenyan settlement from which the refugee camp derives its name, grew in parallel from an insignificant up-country frontier town of five thousand inhabitants in 1991 to forty thousand in 2000, sixty-five thousand in 2009, and, eventually, more than 103,000 in 2019.[35]

The camp's ethnonational makeup would continue to fluctuate over the years. Thanks to a monumental repatriation program for South Sudanese refugees from 2006 to 2008, spurred by the Comprehensive Peace Agreement (CPA) that ended the civil war in 2005 and the steady arrival of further relocatees from Dadaab, Somalis became—if only temporarily—the largest national refugee group in the camp.[36] After civil war broke out once again in newly independent South Sudan in December 2013, thousands of Nuer—many of whom were victimized in sectarian strife between President Salva Kiir Mayardit and Vice President Riek Machar—were forced to flee.[37] Yet for them, Kakuma was by then not an unknown place but had featured extensively in the flight stories relayed by family members and friends who had been displaced to Kenya in preceding decades. At the outermost edge of the camp, where the iron-roofed camp borders the treeless desert plains, this new generation of *wakimbizi* were settled in a so-called New Area, which later would be officially renamed Kakuma 4.[38] While each new settlement meant creating space for newcomers to build a life, it inevitably also distanced some from the main aid agency offices that were clustered near Kakuma 1. Walking from the Ethiopian market to Kakuma 4 could take hours under the best conditions but was often made impossible once the rains started to flood the camp roads. The slow expansion and concomitant diversification of the camp's social geography ushered in a transformative process that dramatically altered not only its infrastructure, ethnonational makeup, and dynamics of everyday life, but also Kakuma's division of labor. People from urban centers such as Mogadishu, Kigali, Addis Ababa, Juba, Khartoum, and Kampala had radically different lifestyles, technical skills, social networks, and financial resources from those who had previously lived in rural pastoralist or agricultural communities. On top of that, large numbers of refugees who were resettled abroad had been sending remittances to relatives who stayed behind, assisting with their livelihoods, increasing their purchasing power and social status and providing some the capital to invest in new businesses that further transformed the look and class dynamics of the camp.[39]

This contributed to the birth of a uniquely multicultural and multiethnic yet class-stratified population in Kakuma that persists to this day. Besides dominant ethnonational groups, there are also a handful of "camp unicorns," such as Saudis, Burkinabés, Yemenis, and, at one point, even an Iranian and a Ukrainian refugee who made the camp their temporary home.[40] Somali shop owners trade in everything from clothes, camel meat, and khat (*miraa* or *veve*) to laptop computers, cell phones, and mobile banking services (*hawala*), while the Ethiopians are among the most successful retailers, wholesalers, and hospitality workers.[41] The camp's streets are replete with restaurants (known as *hoteli*) that sell Ethiopia's national dish—fermented flatbread (*injera*) spiced with different flavors from Oromiya, Tigray, and Amhara—that attract customers from all backgrounds and walks of life. Despite being characterized by prohibiting levels of control by aid and state actors, Kakuma is also a place of unparalleled fusion where Nuer students, Dinka musicians, Darfurian butchers, Rwandese tailors, Congolese hairdressers and barbers, Somali teachers, Burundian motorcyclists, Eritrean chefs, and Turkana firewood traders have built overlapping communities and laid claims to what some have called the "right to the camp."[42]

Drawing on the works of the geographer David Harvey and the social theorist Henri Lefebvre, whose ideas of the "right to the city" have emphasized that an urban politics of justice emerges from spatial acts of creating access, collective dwelling, and political claims making, the analogous right to the camp allows us to make sense in similar ways of the myriad lives lived in the long shadow of humanitarian programs.[43] Asfaw, a lanky Ethiopian journalist in his forties, suggested with a cheeky smile that "Kakuma is a big university"—a place where people learn through lived experiences about the embodied politics of their containment, the aid industry, and their own marginality within it.[44] We sat in a local library in the Ethiopian market, watching the students come and go from their reading rooms. From here, Kakuma truly felt like a "university." On the flip side of his metaphor, however, the camp can be seen as one of the myriad interstitial spaces of circulation, hybridity, and perpetual arrival around the world where notions of "the social" are being constructed a thousandfold through the dreams, lives, and experiences of multitudes of "strangers" into what the anthropologist Michel Agier termed a "little cosmopolitan world."[45] Convivial relations, family life, joy, and everyday solidarities are, in this perspective, as much a feature of life in the camp as the rules that tower over camp dwellers at all times and that narrow the scope for autonomy. Cosmopolitanism, then, is not simply a given; it has to be constantly reclaimed to assert something like the right to the camp. Camp inhabitants do so by defining for themselves, on a daily basis, what it truly means to lead a legitimate and fulfilled life under extreme conditions of immobilization.[46] In Kakuma, isolating feelings of foreignness, nonbelonging, and dislocation, which often mark what Vinh Nguyen calls the temporal, psychological, and political subjectivity of "refugeetude," are shared among the residents and have turned—at least for some—into a source of common identity rather than a point of exclusion.[47] But instead of taking this banal cosmopolitanism as a cause for celebration, Asfaw insisted that refugees in Kakuma, despite being "graduates" of the camp, were also "voluntary prisoners" trapped in a system that endeavors to offer lifesaving support in the short run but, ultimately, inhibits their mobility, privacy, and dignity and even their imagination for living otherwise. "But we agree to that," Asfaw said, resentfully and with a laugh. "What choice do we have?" The contours of the system that he described become clear when we examine the role of aid agencies in funding, building, and ideologically legitimizing Kakuma's aid geographies as part of their attempt to mold camp life as a colonizing endeavor. "Refugee life is the worst," Asfaw finally told me with indignation. "Sometimes it feels like we're here to support the aid agencies and not the other way round."

Making Space for Humanitarianism

A cluster of billboards adorns the entrance to Kakuma, not far from the A1 Highway that links the camp to the world. Emblazoned with bold letters and colorful logos, these road signs display the names of dozens of (mostly) international organizations that advertise their activities in the camp. Some see themselves, as one aid professional in Kakuma remarked in a rather boisterous moment of self-affirmation, as "the lifeline for refugees," without whom "they'd have nowhere to go," while others are more modest and even plagued by occasional self-doubts about their own ability for "doing good."[48] It may also be that Turkana's scraggy, moonlike landscape, with its thorn bushes, shrubs, and infinite meandering dry rivers, lends itself to hyperbole of this kind. When one arrives in Kakuma by road, the camp first comes into sight as rows of iron-roofed houses glimmering on the horizon like a desert mirage. "It looks like an oasis from afar," one humanitarian mused while peering out of the window of a Land Cruiser at the end of a long drive that we shared from the county's capital, Lodwar.[49]

The image of the oasis is seductive, not least because spaces such as Kakuma are conceived of in similar terms—isolated enclaves of fertile land that shelter desperate people on the move from the "harshness" of their surroundings. The geologist Rebecca Lawton writes that "the oasis has beckoned and tantalised us for millennia, offering the weary desert traveller a dip in an open pool, the green shelter of palm fronds and the relief of shade and refuge."[50] Except Kakuma's fertility lay not in its own soil but in the international aid the refugee camp had brought over the previous thirty years. The billboards lining the camp's roads thus signaled a passage from the inhospitable outside into the supposedly rejuvenating and orderly interior of this "humanitarian space." Originally coined by Rony Brauman, the former president of Médecins sans Frontières (MSF), the phrase has weathered some critical debate, gaining currency among aid practitioners and scholars alike to denote a symbolic space of neutrality, impartiality, and civil protection in which humanitarians are—in theory—able to work uninhibited by political interference.[51] The UNHCR's own definition envisions this space as a conducive "social, political and security environment which allows access to protection [and] facilitates the exercise of UNHCR's non-political and humanitarian protection mandate, and within which the prospect of achieving solutions to displacement is optimised."[52] Not unlike the oasis, humanitarian space is said to create favorable conditions for life in environments that are otherwise hostile to it. Critics, however, argue that precisely because such a space cannot ever truly exist in separation from politics, its aspirational language masks the deeply political decisions and actions that it enables.[53] Despite its contested nature, the phrase remains useful not only because of its ubiquity among humanitarian practitioners but also because it makes sense of the ways in which humanitarianism is spatialized in the everyday. Even if they fail to produce a zone that is genuinely devoid of political intrusion, refugee programs quite materially (and lastingly) shape the humanitarian space of intervention through brick, mortar, tarpaulin, and corrugated iron.

Kakuma was etched into Turkana's landscape through the construction of compounds, shelters, an airstrip, and telecommunication towers that form a basic grid along which personnel, information, and things can circulate within a worldwide "aid archipelago."[54] This aspiration to create a nonpolitical domain of protection is therefore both ideologically and materially productive: It lays claims to parcels of land by producing a purposeful built environment and populating it with aid workers and aid recipients who, in turn, legitimize the authority of the specialized agencies that act in the name of a "higher" humanitarian reason. In this sense, the domain is quite literally a colonizing venture that is determined to settle, inhabit, and guard appropriated territories and impose its rule on inferiorized populations, even as it is thought of as benevolent.[55] In other words, "humanitarians travel; humanitarians create economies; and humanitarians settle," as Nisha Toomey writes in her recent work on aid at the Thailand-Myanmar border.[56] Lisa Smirl has used the notion of "auxiliary space" to tease out ways in which aid is spatialized in practice by the production of differential mobilities, out-of-sync temporalities, the settlement of experts, and segregated enclaves of privilege. A key to understanding this is the institutional assumption that aid geographies, just like comparable spaces of colonization, are malleable, blank, and open to being "inscribed" with values, programs, or infrastructures from outside, and that through sleight of hand, "the production of new places can be disconnected from the techniques and processes used to produce it."[57]

Decades of humanitarian programs have left an indelible mark on Kakuma. While it is a node in an expanding archipelago of refugee assistance that spans the globe, the camp's own topography has also become visibly archipelagic. Compounds dot its surface area like fortified islands and dominate its landscape through not only their imposing settler architectures but also the power and resources their occupants are known to command. For aid workers, compounds are tiny, air-conditioned "oases" in themselves that offer welcome respite from the dust, temperature, and buzz of the camp, even as those compounds constitute impenetrable fortresses for those left outside their gates. Agency staff are hermetically sealed off from the very people they supposedly serve by a prohibitive regime of "gate passes" that filters out those without access. Residential compounds are located in close proximity to Kakuma town—its shops, markets, supermarkets, and countrywide transport links—while the "field posts" scattered throughout the camp are, in theory, meant to act as decentralized points for accessing services. Among the forty-two aid organizations in Kakuma there is an (unofficial) pecking order, at the top of which sit UN agencies such as the World Food Program, the International Organization for Migration, and

FIGURE 1.3. Panoramic view from a water tank in Kakuma 4, 2016. Photograph by the author.

the UNHCR itself, whose offices and staff quarters constitute the inner sanctum of this compound world. Years ago, the UN refugee agency mounted an ill-fated attempt to improve the living standards of its staff by building a tennis court and swimming pool inside its walled premises, attracting equal scorn from refugees and the local Turkana in an area chronically hit by drought. Beneath the veneer of humanitarian space as a human-made oasis in a land of scarcity always lie its own internal contradictions, exclusions, and lingering dynamics of segregation.

Meanwhile, the shelters inhabited by *wakimbizi* have also been undergoing constant expansion due to cyclical arrivals of newly displaced people. These houses are constructed from a mix of locally fired bricks, daub, wood, tarpaulins, and corrugated iron sheets and are fenced in with thorny branches from the *Prosopis juliflora* shrub that has become invasive in this part of the Horn of Africa. Kakuma camp covers an area of thirteen-and-a-half square kilometers and is set to grow by five square kilometers more by 2030.[58] Faced with the specter of coming spatial (and social) disorder, humanitarians have therefore tried early on to bring more discipline into the camp's spatial planning, with mixed results. The first system that organized refugees into self-identified "groups" was replaced in 2012, when a UNHCR official proposed to "modernize" and "democratize" the administrative structures of the camp, moving away from a governance model rooted in ethnonational identities to adopt explicitly more multiethnic and multinational constituencies called "blocks" that were again grouped into larger "zones."[59] Inevitably, overhauling the camp's administrative units also precipitated changes in its political and social geography, as aid agencies imposed—in colonial fashion—their own institutional ideals of "order" on the thousands of residents (see chapter 4). While the language of "blocks" and "zones" has since been normalized among the people in Kakuma, some places and neighborhoods have retained their colloquial and idiosyncratic names as "a way of contesting and challenging the allocation of space by humanitarian agencies."[60] Prominent for this toponymic reappropriation are areas such as Zones 3–4 in Kakuma 1, known as "Hong Kong." Now the center of South Sudanese Dinka communities, "Hong Kong" was full of makeshift cinemas that showed Chinese martial arts films when the camp opened in the 1990s, giving rise to the nickname. A cluster of blocks in Zone 2 of Kakuma 1, a hot spot of *chang'aa* (illicit homemade alcohol) production and consumption, is popularly referred to as "Baghdad" due to its association with violence, crime, and frequent police raids.[61]

Notwithstanding the incomplete efforts to create space that is "fit" for humanitarianism and humanitarians, Kakuma came under pressure from funding gaps as donor money began to dry up globally. Every month, refugees queue at one of the distribution centers in the camp to receive food rations. Upon first registering, every head of household is given a ration card indicating the size of her or his family (e.g., Size 1 equals one person; Size 7 equals seven persons). On distribution day, people must line up and confirm their identity through a biometric fingerprinting system before they are allowed to pick up portions of flour, rice, dry beans, cooking oil, soap, and nonfood items according to their family size. The distribution centers resemble cattle pens through which thousands of people are funneled under time pressure by ushers, security guards, and agency workers. Since 2010, the UNHCR in Kenya was forced to progressively downsize its budgets, economizing on lifesaving aid to retain basic humanitarian functions. Food rations were soon permanently cut, never to return to their original levels. When Mazou took over as the UNHCR representative in Kenya, the agency began to court "nontraditional" private actors, including the World Bank, Mastercard, IKEA, the Lego Foundation, and Safaricom in an effort to secure additional funds. This coincided with the rise of the "humanitarian innovation" agenda that had slowly taken root in the industry at the same time and was aiming to free aid work from the "fetters" of established thinking.[62] Kakuma evolved into a hub for innovative projects in all kinds of areas, such as mobile money technology, renewable energy, biometrics, education, financial technology, and even human waste disposal, which were realized largely due to additional funding streams and an organizational willingness to experiment with "new" ideas.[63] While the UNHCR retained its role as the sole gatekeeper for allocating donor funding to partner organizations in Kakuma, it embraced a concept of humanitarian space that was less uniform but resembled more closely what Dorothea Hilhorst and Bram Jansen characterize as "an arena where actors negotiate the outcomes of aid."[64] In this arena, humanitarian principles were supposedly neither preconceived nor dictated from above but were molded from praxis, opening the sector up to diversification on an unprecedented scale. In reality, the collaborative authority of the UNHCR and the Kenyan state provided cover for these experiments that deliberately mobilized corporate and charitable actors. Encampment in this way came to resemble a remake of a colonial concession economy in which non-state actors vied for contracts, agreements, and licenses for their discretionary undertakings in the interest of delivering public services for refugees (see chapter 5).

· Nowhere was this new humanitarian adventurism more palpable than on a patch of land just three miles outside Kakuma. In 2016, the UNHCR and the government of Turkana County (with buy-in from the national government in Nairobi) jointly announced the largest spatial expansion of humanitarian operations in the country since the establishment of Kakuma 4 in 2014, adding 10.51 square kilometers of land to the UNHCR's existing program area.[65] This new Kalobeyei "integrated settlement" was praised as offering an aid model that was fundamentally different from that in Kakuma. Rather than a traditional "care and maintenance" operation, in which a constant supply of donor funding is needed to keep aid flowing, Kalobeyei promised a much more sustainable and less costly approach in which "the market" was envisioned as solving problems of scarcity and allocation.[66] Among the most striking issues about Kalobeyei were the contradictions that soon emerged from planning this new settlement. Though imbued on the surface with ideas nominally at the heart of the humanitarian innovation agenda, the settlement itself ultimately came into being through more established forms of top-down planning that had long earned the UNHCR the title of a "surrogate state" ruling over camps and populations the same way a state governs its citizenry.[67] Kalobeyei was, after all, based on physically encroaching on more areas of communal Turkana land and on erecting large infrastructures for health, education, sanitation, and shelter to house rising numbers of refugees who were arriving almost weekly during the first settlement phase in 2016. The UNHCR was still the prime architect of humanitarian space in Kenya. Despite the agency's benign outlook, the plans to construct a new type of integrated settlement in Kalobeyei—rather than a camp—were always flawed in that they did not reckon with the fact that any usurpation of land by aid actors rested critically on those actors' collaboration with the militarized state. In short, there would simply be no new settlement without violence work.

The UNHCR was never acting unilaterally—neither in Kalobeyei nor in Kakuma. Rather than supplanting the sovereignty of the state in any meaningful sense, the agency was crucially dependent on consent, goodwill, and logistical support from the Government of Kenya. The devolved Turkana County government rose to prominence during this time as a relatively novel stakeholder that could abet land acquisitions and hold local *mabaraza* (public consultations) and was generally more receptive to ideas of refugee integration than the national government in Nairobi. Through this brokerage, Kalobeyei confirmed a lasting truth about humanitarian governance in Kenya: The UNHCR was by no means a stand-in for an absent state but had entered a system of co-rule in which it attended to refugees' welfare, legal protection, and appeals for foreign funds and offered the moral cover of humanitarianism, while Kenya's national government underwrote these functions with the full weight of political sovereignty and its enforcement powers. This was increasingly normalized as the camp "traveled" and continued to suffuse adjoining spaces, infrastructures, and communities, making it a highly adaptable spatial logic through which new projects and innovations could be realized.[68] No matter how noble the intention, establishing a new humanitarian "oasis" on the arid plains of Kalobeyei simply reproduced the carceral effects of encampment found in Kakuma, of which it quickly became an administrative appendage.

Uncertain Refuge

On May 6, 2016, Dr. Karanja Kibicho, principal secretary of Kenya's Ministry of the Interior and National Administration, issued a brief but explosive statement that would quickly circulate on social media and in the international press. He announced that, as a result of hosting refugees, Kenya had "continued to shoulder [a] very heavy economic, security and environmental burden on behalf of the region and international community." Given these circumstances, Kibicho gravely noted that "the Government of the Republic of Kenya, having taken into consideration its security interests, has decided that hosting of refugees has come to an end" and that it was now "working on mechanisms for closure of the two refugee camps within the shortest time possible." Overnight, hundreds of thousands of refugees who had made Kenya their temporary "home" found their safety jeopardized through a mixture of hardball diplomacy and election campaigning by the government of the day, led by Uhuru Kenyatta's Jubilee Party. Gearing up for fieldwork at the time, I was convinced that my research would be conducted in the shadow of this threat, only half-jokingly remarking to colleagues that my project might have to be about chronicling the "end of humanitarianism" in Kenya. Yet the end did not come. Instead, the pronouncement was but one of many the government had made over the years, always carefully (and sometimes less so) weighing its friendly relationships with donors in the global North and its own security interests.

On May 9, 2016, the UNHCR launched a public appeal that was critical of the decision and sought to prevent the closures.[69] Two days later, twelve major humanitarian organizations, including World Vision, Oxfam, the Lutheran World Federation (LWF), the Danish Refugee Council, and the Refugee Consortium of Kenya, also released a joint statement against the closure decision. Although then Cabinet Secretary Ole Nkaissery backtracked shortly after, to clarify that only the Dadaab camps, where the majority of Somali refugees lived, would be closed, the damage had been done. Critics feared that the mixed-message announcement was only the prelude to forced removals. Even the legal challenge brought before the Milimani High Court in February 2017, which ultimately declared a unilateral camp closure unconstitutional, offered only minimal respite from Kenya's renewed onslaught against asylum space.

This was not always so. Although Kenya had received refugees during the colonial era—notably, those fleeing fascist Italy's invasion of Ethiopia in the 1930s, as well as Jews and Poles escaping persecution in Europe in the 1940s—it was not until the second half of the twentieth century that the country was faced with larger numbers of displaced people.[70] Only in 1987 did the number of refugees in Kenya exceed ten thousand.[71] During the 1970s and 1980s, Kenya was granting these refugees a right to choose their place of residence, providing access to its social services, and favoring the economic integration of twelve thousand Ugandans, Ethiopians, Rwandans, and Sudanese into the domestic labor market—a policy that soon would not be seen as desirable in light of the exponentially growing refugee population a mere decade later.[72] Between 1990 and 1992, the modest number of people seeking asylum in Kenya jumped dramatically, to more than 400,000. By 2011, the UNHCR was recording 566,500 displaced people living in Kenya, making it the fifth-largest refugee-hosting country in the world. Lamis Abdelaaty recently argued against the widely accepted narrative that a simple shift took place from a "liberal" to a relatively "closed" refugee policy and noted that national and ethnicized groups of refugees have always

FIGURE 1.4. United Nations plane approaching Kakuma Airstrip, 2016. Photograph by the author.

received differential treatment in Kenya.[73] Even the "laissez-faire" policies that preceded the 1990s were never universally applied to *all* refugees; nor were they internally consistent over time. Instead, Kenya's politics of asylum have always been wedded to the country's security concerns. Fear of foreign armed actors, rebel sympathizers, terrorists, and generally "difficult populations" and Kenya's shifting diplomatic relations with its neighboring countries resulted in particular ethnoracialized refugees being treated with more suspicion than others.[74] Sometimes defined as "freedom from imagined or real danger in present or future," security is a discursive construct that mobilizes collective and individual fear of danger, threat, or harm to set in motion a particular course of action and may even end up reorganizing social life.[75] Since the 1990s, Somalis had been the single largest refugee group in Kenya, making up a striking 85 percent of the country's total. As the civil war in Somalia was driving hundreds of thousands across the country's borders, Kenya became apprehensive not only of the logistical challenges that it faced, but also of the potential threat to postcolonial sovereignty and national cohesion that this movement might portend.

But questions of belonging, ethnoracial identity, and nationalism in contemporary Kenya have their roots in colonial-era anxiety about both the state's territorial borders and its "legitimate" African subjects. Historically, Somalis in Kenya were ambiguously classified as "native aliens" who—despite their racialization as Black Africans—were nevertheless presumed to not fully "belong" ethnically to the Kenya colony.[76] This ambiguity of the Somali presence was compounded by the charge of their alleged disloyalty toward the Kenyan nation in the 1960s and stoked by the irredentist ambitions of the newly independent Somali Republic that sought to unify all Somaliphone polities in the region, including in Kenya's Northern Frontier District. This complicated a crude divide between *foreign* (white) colonizers and *native* Africans because British colonialism had created a liminal class of subjects who were regarded as "native" to Africa but "alien" to Kenya. Within postcolonial Kenya's economy of belonging, in which ethnicity continued to define territorial homelands where some are "Indigenous" and others are foreign "interlopers," this relatively privileged colonial niche of Somalis turned into an unfavorable subject position.[77] The secessionist Shifta Emergency (1963–67) then pitted newly independent Kenya against its Somali minority citizens, who were massacred and forced into "protected villages" by the military.[78] Even after this conflict, the state remained suspicious and decreed that ethnic Somali Kenyans were prohibited from leaving the "closed districts" of the northeast and had to carry a *kipande* (identity card) and undergo screenings to "verify" their claims to citizenship.[79] Violence against Somali Kenyans was normalized but again came to a head when Kenyan forces intervened militarily in the northeast. First, they interned and starved local residents to death in Garissa in 1980, allegedly in an attempt to uproot local "insecurity." Then, in 1984, Kenya's army detained thousands of men and boys on the Wagalla Airstrip in Wajir for days without food or water before executing hundreds.[80] This fraught relationship of Kenya with its own Somali minority was one of the primary reasons the state was so concerned about allowing refugees of the same ethnicity onto its territory. Refugee policy was thus always a "numbers game" and represented a reactionary politics of security.

Camps were a way to deal with these numbers in an "orderly" way. The authoritarian regime of Daniel arap Moi initially avoided the establishment of camps and opted to expedite deportations to discourage the dispersion of displaced foreigners into Kenyan society "proper."[81] Andrew Maina writes that this was due to a deep-seated (and ongoing) disquiet of the Kenyan government that refugees would in effect bring regional conflicts into the country and subsequently destabilize the fragile social, economic, and political order of postcolonial Kenya.[82] But as the logistical and hygienic condition in what was then the only official reception center at Thika deteriorated in 1990, the

UNHCR persuaded the government to allow the construction of larger camps in Kenya's north to relieve the overstretched facility in the south.[83] While Kakuma and the Dadaab camps became the largest of these refugee agglomerations, several smaller camps were scattered across Marsabit, Garissa, Wajir, Mandera, and Kenya's coast, especially Mombasa.[84] This camp expansion drive was broadly in line with the UN refugee agency's 1997 policy on urban refugees, which maintained that humanitarian assistance should be provided only in camps or rural settlements.[85] Despite the fact that a substantial urban refugee program has since been developed and rolled out by nongovernmental organizations—and the UNHCR's own policy has shifted over the years from endorsing camps to explicitly seeking (urban) alternatives—encampment has always remained a de facto feature of Kenya's refugee regime.[86]

Although refugees found much needed sanctuary in the camps, their future in Kenya was insecure. During police swoops in Nairobi and Mombasa in August 1992, two thousand refugees were arrested and forced back to the camps.[87] This dragnet policing tactic would be repeated periodically over the years, especially in the aftermath of the twin bombings at the US Embassy in Nairobi and Dar es Salaam, Tanzania, in 1998 and the terrorist attack on an Israeli-owned hotel in Mombasa in 2002.[88] Security, which had always been key for the Kenyan establishment, now dominated the government's messaging on forced migration outright as the "War on Terror" gained momentum.[89] Even after a return to multiparty democracy under President Mwai Kibaki in 2002, following years of Moi's authoritarian rule, Kenya's state continued to view Somalis in particular through a "security prism."[90] Nonetheless, Kibaki's tenure was also a period of guarded progress during which the country was trying to free itself from some of Moi's antidemocratic legacies by introducing a series of more liberal laws, including Kenya's first refugee legislation: the 2006 Refugee Act. The act was initially thought to signal a new era of asylum politics, enshrining protection for refugees in domestic law and creating special institutions for managing refugees, such as the Department of Refugee Affairs (DRA) that, it was hoped, would replace the organizational maze that preceded it.[91] The act also indicated that Kenya would resume some of the core functions it had ceded to the UNHCR during the 1990s, including refugee status determination (RSD) and camp management. Camp managers were installed to head each of the refugee camps and to oversee the delivery of aid. Although the act formalized the rights of refugees and streamlined the state's administrative powers, it also reinscribed legal restrictions on refugees' mobility and right to work, and allowed their expulsion if national security or public order was at risk.[92]

Upon arrival, refugees in Kenya go through a rigorous registration process. They fill out a "profiling form" for each household that captures such basic information as their names, registration dates, registering officers, photographs, fingerprints, and entry point into Kenya. People are given a temporary asylum-seeker pass that confirms their identity and right to be in Kenya for a period of only six months, after which they rely on a formal RSD process in the ref-ugee camps that can take months or, sometimes, even years.[93] All refugees are required to reside in camps, unless an exception is made on the basis of health or educational needs. All refugees, whether living in a camp or a city, need a "movement pass" that permits them to exit the camps and move around in the country. For the longest time, encampment has been a policy decreed by the executive state rather than by parliamentary legislation, which would eventu-ally be changed years later. Work for refugees is also highly restricted by law, and only in the camps is gainful employment explicitly tolerated, although new legislation promises to widen this right to work in future.

The short "honeymoon phase" between the passing of the Refugee Act and the adoption of Kenya's new reform-oriented constitution in 2010 was brought to an end when two Spanish aid workers from MSF were abducted from the Dadaab camps by Al-Shabaab militants on October 14, 2011. The abduction was taken as hard proof by Kenya's government that "liberal" approaches to providing refuge had failed, and it ordered the military to launch an all-out invasion of Somalia two days later. The invasion, then known as Operation Linda Nchi (Protect the Country), was nominally an act of self-protection and was legitimized by Nairobi as a crucial step in combating terrorism in the re-gion and domestically.[94] Border insecurity and Kenya's ambitions for regional hegemony contributed to the decision to occupy southern Somalia and in this way create a geographical "buffer zone" with Al-Shabaab–held territories.[95] The Kakuma and Dadaab refugee camps, which housed thousands of citizens of the country Kenya was invading, were increasingly portrayed as domestic front lines of this regional "War on Terror": spaces that at once harbored po-tential "terrorists" and represented soft targets for future attacks.[96] The military offensive conducted on the Somali side of the border was also accompanied by intensifying crackdowns on refugees within Kenya itself. Following a series of grenade attacks in Nairobi's Eastleigh neighborhood and across Kenya's north-east, the DRA issued a security directive ordering the "return" of some 100,000 urban refugees to the camps in December 2012.[97] In the next chapter I argue that this invasion of Somalia by Kenya's army was not without precedent but, rather, represented an extraversion of the militarized occupation that had already been underway for years *inside* the refugee camps on the country's own soil.

At the beginning of Uhuru Kenyatta's term as president, the institutional securitization of Somalis reached a boiling point after armed Al-Shabaab fighters staged a high-profile attack on Nairobi's Westgate Shopping Mall on September 21–24, 2013, killing sixty-seven people. "Westgate" became not only a symbol of national unity in the face of adversity but also a byword to justify the escalation of "anti-terror" and, effectively, "anti-refugee" operations.[98] The government claimed, without evidence, that at least one of the attackers, Hassan Abdi Dhuhulow, had previously lived in the Kakuma camp, creating a direct link between refugee hosting and terrorism.[99] Three weeks later, in a move that further proved Kenya's waning hospitality toward refugees, Nairobi signed the "Tripartite Agreement" with the UNHCR and the Federal Government of Somalia to facilitate "voluntary repatriations" of Somalis from Kenya in the months and years to come.[100] In March 2014, then Interior Cabinet Secretary Joseph Ole Lenku renewed the directive for the compulsory return of urban refugees to the camps.[101] A month later, security forces descended on Nairobi's Somali-dominated Eastleigh neighborhood, often dubbed "Little Mogadishu," in what Kenyan authorities named Operation Sanitization of Eastleigh, though it would be more popularly known as Operation Usalama Watch (Operation Security Watch).[102] The operation lasted two harrowing weeks and targeted refugees living in the city while inadvertently also victimizing Kenya's ethnic Somali minority who were caught up in the raids. Thousands of people were imprisoned, abused, humiliated, and "screened" for their legal right to be in Kenya at Kasarani stadium in eastern Nairobi, which was subsequently given the sinister epithet "Kasarani concentration camp."[103] Because encampment was not legally mandated but only a decree at the time, the legal aid clinic Kituo Cha Sheria sued the Kenyatta administration for unlawful detentions. Later that year, the Milimani High Court determined that the government had indeed acted in breach of the law, although this was of little consequence for the survivors seeking justice for their mistreatment.[104]

A deadly attack in June 2014 in the coastal town of Mpeketoni once more emboldened Kenyan authorities in their counterterrorism policies, which continued to limit asylum space gradually. To prevent further legal challenges from refugee rights organizations, the government passed a contested Security Laws Amendment Act that embedded the mandatory encampment of refugees in "designated areas" in law for the first time.[105] On April 2, 2015, gunmen affiliated with Al-Shabaab stormed Garissa University College, in northeastern Kenya, and killed 148 students and staff, making it the deadliest attack in Kenya since 1998. In response, then Vice President William Ruto called for the full closure of the Dadaab refugee camps and vowed that "the same way America never became the same after 9/11, Kenya is going to be different. It's not going to be business as usual. Kenya is going to change for good after Garissa."[106] While Ruto's remarks were understood as a way to vie for increased military and humanitarian funding, State House repeated the closure threat a year later and extended it to Kakuma camp. The closure announcement on May 6, 2016, was given additional weight by the summary disbanding of the government's own DRA. Research for this book began merely a month later and was conducted in an atmosphere of uncertainty about the future of refugee protection in the country. Kenyan authorities added to this confusion by reconstituting the DRA in the form of a new Refugee Affairs Secretariat (RAS) that essentially held the same responsibilities but had been purged of "humanitarian-minded" civil servants; they were replaced with former military officers who could be relied on to prioritize national security. When asked about the balance between the protection of refugees and keeping Kenya "safe," the new RAS commissioner responded: "We know the majority of people here are genuine refugees, but there are a few *elements who use the camps*. They know it's a humanitarian operation, which means they know that the government cannot conduct any major [policing] operation like they would in a Nairobi estate. There could be a few who are pretending to be refugees, those are the *bad elements*."[107] With these institutional changes, sifting through "bad elements" not only became an additional security measure for generating a "safe" environment; it was elevated to being the key purpose of the secretariat, which progressively dropped the liberal humanitarian bearings in its approach to refugee management and advocated for "national security" to always trump "protection."

Refuge in Kenya continues to be uncertain despite the overwhelming praise the country receives from donors in Europe and North America for its generosity. The same logics that are at work along the global North's humanitarian borders, where vows of protection and universal rights meet a sober reality of undignified deaths, disappearances, and the discrimination of those considered "less human," are also fueling state violence against refugees in Kenya. Repeated attacks in the country supplied the necessary justifications to escalate government policies and shaped public opinion. On January 15–16, 2019, another terror attack on an upmarket Nairobi location, the DusitD2 office and hotel complex, deepened the fault lines that had already set the government on a path of narrowing asylum rights. In March 2019, Kenya consequently repeated its by now cyclical calls to close the Dadaab camps and shelved a refugee bill that was originally set to replace the 2006 act.[108] Closure became the haunting thread of Kenya's knee-jerk reactions to emerging security "crises" and was invoked again in March 2021 when the government announced to the press that the Dadaab and Kakuma refugee camps finally would be shut for good by June 2022.[109] We see here that the specter of camp closure was increasingly used as a "disciplinary dispositive"—a tool to render the already dire living conditions of encampment in Kakuma and Dadaab preferable to the bleak prospect of repatriation or dispersal inside the country without institutional support.[110] Although Kenya ultimately passed the new Refugees Act in late 2021, including provisions that theoretically can expedite economic integration and enhance refugees' mobility, restrictions on their basic rights and freedoms still prevail in practice. As evidenced by Kenya's securitized refugee policies of the past decades, there is no end in sight to the precarity of its displaced denizens as long as the state privileges security, policing, and carceral responses to complex issues of inequality, social exclusion, and belonging.

Combating the Violence "Within"

At the heart of Kenya's campaign against terrorism and insecurity was not just the aim to protect its own citizens but also the integrity of humanitarian spaces themselves. Following the closure decision in 2016, the African Union's Peace and Security Council backed Kenya's unpopular stance by publicly declaring that "the camps have been deprived of their humanitarian character and function by the Al-Shabaab terrorist group."[111] A year later, on February 9, 2017, Eric Kiraithe, a spokesman for the Government of Kenya, told the BBC that the Dadaab camp "had lost its humanitarian nature and had become a haven for terrorism and other illegal activities."[112] President Kenyatta himself echoed this rhetoric in his speech at a special summit of the Intergovernmental Authority on Development (IGAD) on March 25, 2017, in which he warned assembled diplomats that "the camp has, over time, lost its humanitarian character. It is not acceptable to us that a space that is supposed to provide safety and assistance, is transformed to facilitate agents of terror and destruction." Although Kakuma was often an afterthought in these statements, Kenya's security agencies had been convinced, since Westgate, that the camp was also a liability. "Especially now that they are closing Dadaab," a Kenyan intelligence officer once confided to me in a hushed voice, "we fear that terror cells might come over and infiltrate Kakuma even further."[113] In the closing document of the summit, the Nairobi Declaration, IGAD heads of state fell in line with Kenyatta's position on insecurity and pledged to "ensure the civilian and humanitarian character of refugee camps and settlements."[114]

Although it is difficult to pinpoint the definitive origin of the phrase "humanitarian character," it came into common usage in the thick circuits of humanitarian organizations during the late 1980s, when a plethora of documents, memos, and reports began to use it. Historically, camps in postcolonial Africa had served as bases for armed liberation struggles and suffered attacks from enemy forces, especially vengeful colonial powers.[115] Debates on how to prevent refugees, host societies, and aid workers from being exposed to this violence continued within the UNHCR until 1987, when an Executive Committee Conclusion finally stipulated that refugee camps and settlements were supposed to have an "exclusively civilian and humanitarian character."[116] This was derived from a mixture of existing international refugee law, human rights law, humanitarian law, national criminal law, and the UN Charter itself and was mobilized to allow for muscular responses to insecurity, including a proposal to deploy international police forces to guard refugee camps that never materialized.[117] The contemporary use of the phrase in Kenya's counterterrorism discourse thus had strategic value as it decentered national security and signaled to donors and humanitarians the country's seemingly more altruistic concern for the safety of *wakimbizi* and the liberal global order on which their protection rested.

Yet the idea of the "humanitarian character" of Kenyan refugee camps being eroded was not rooted exclusively in fear of terrorism. Rather, the congestion of Kakuma and Dadaab has long been thought of as an environment in which interpersonal and intercommunal violence could fester. Violence was a largely elusive category here. Its slipperiness meant that it comprised a spectrum of harm, from kinetic attacks on the body to inflictions of symbolic pain and injury. For Kenya's government and aid agencies, the flip side of banal cosmopolitanism in Kakuma was the camp's proclivity to generate interminable "ethnic" and "ethnonational" strife, a form of violence the state and aid organizations regarded as innate to refugees. Seemingly possessed by this "spirit of violence," camp dwellers were thought to be prone to internalizing rebel violence as a way of life, which tainted the camp itself as a violent space.[118] Far from the image of multiculturalism, mutualism, and peace that TEDxKakumaCamp would later celebrate onstage, the agencies involved in managing the camp were convinced of their duty to perpetually "pacify" a camp that they believed to be infested with crime and hopelessly divided along sectarian lines (see chapter 3). In its *Guide on Operational Protection in Camps and Settlements*, the UNHCR details the kind of activities that are thought to endanger its refugee programs from within:

> Crimes committed in camp settings can range from petty theft of material assistance to physical assault to rape and to murder. Such offences rise

due to the breakdown of traditional community and social structures, impacted by the population density of camps, the limited privacy available, and the cohabitation of people and groups previously unknown to each other. Mechanisms for redress, for victim protection, for fair hearings and appropriate punishment are both necessary but often inadequate.[119]

When I first arrived in Kakuma, I attended an obligatory security briefing by one of the agencies running anti-crime programs: the LWF. Ronald, a stout Kenyan former military officer in his early fifties, delivered the briefing with relish, as he had presumably done for many visitors before me. "We play with lots of things, but we don't play with security here," he declared rather assertively and with rehearsed authority.[120] "Our role is to protect the lives of refugees in the camp and their property," he continued as if reciting a script from an agency manual, before finally ending on his favorite maxim: "Hakuna security nusu; security lazima ni full" (There is no such thing as half security; only full security). Though the camp's inhabitants had escaped unthinkable conditions in their countries of origin, often braving arduous journeys to reach Kenya, Ronald was focused on combating the threat he thought they posed to their hosts, to aid organizations, and to one another. For Ronald and his colleagues, a vital part of "caring" for refugees was to fight against forms of violence and crime in the places they had made their temporary homes and resonated with public calls to ensure the camp's "humanitarian character."[121] During the 2000s, Jeff Crisp had conducted a study to analyze the state of insecurity in Kenyan refugee camps in which he identified a dizzying array of "harmful practices" that he ascribed in part to an understaffed and underfunded Kenyan police force.[122] In these cases, eradicating crime and everyday violence among community members, families, neighbors, and kin in Kakuma was understood to require not a caring hand but, increasingly, the "iron fist" of the law.

In addition to spiraling levels of violence that seemed to neutralize the welfare function of camps, observers deplored their diminishing "civilian character." Sarah Lischer described camps as "dangerous sanctuaries" that risked catalyzing regional conflict by giving refuge to rebels able to spread hateful ideologies and agendas beyond their countries of origin, while others have diagnosed a brewing "crisis of refugee militarization" on the continent.[123] The fear of "refugee warriors" was endemic during the 1990s and early 2000s, when rebel groups were believed to be chipping away at the security of African nation-states; it returned with a vengeance as Al-Shabaab came to notoriety in the region during the 2010s.[124] Again, the UNHCR's *Guide on Operation Protection* is testimony to this long-standing dread of armed refugees:

The militarization of camps constitutes a very serious threat to the security of refugees and host populations. This may include the presence of armed elements residing in refugee camps, taking food and material assistance from camp residents, or using camps as a base for short-term "rest and recuperation." Coercion, intimidation, recruitment (forced or otherwise), combat training and abduction are unacceptable activities that may occur when the civilian and humanitarian character of a refugee camp is compromised.[125]

In Kakuma, this was not hypothetical for much of the 1990s and into the early 2000s. From its birth, the camp was a hub for the armed struggle of the Sudan People's Liberation Army/Movement (SPLA/M) against Sudan's government in Khartoum. Jansen speaks of a "rebelization" of the camp because of the pervasive role active, past, or potential military personnel played in its social life, with SPLA military commanders routinely crossing into Kenya to visit their families or dependents who had settled in the relative safety of the camp.[126] Kakuma was an environment shaped by wars past and present in whose shadows residents continued to live. "Militarization" is thereby more than the ramping up of capabilities for military violence. It also connotes more diffused social, material, and discursive processes that reinforce military cultures, economies, and social hierarchies.[127] Kakuma embodies this in terms of culture and communal memories, as its streetscapes are reminders of the layered histories of war that suffuse the camp's geography, without being the strategic retreat for rebels that it once was. What is left are demobilized former militia members living civilian lives and shops that still bear names associated with these histories of warfare and national liberation, such as Anyanya II, Mai-Mai, and John Garang.[128]

Humanitarian actors nonetheless continued to shift culpability for recurring insecurity onto refugees. For them, as much as for the Kenyan state, the locus of militarization was to be found squarely among camp dwellers, who were cast as either victims of foreign rebels or instigators of armed insurgency. During one of his security trainings, Ronald warned a group of refugee newcomers that Kakuma was an arms-free zone: "We don't want you to build your own weapons like bows, arrows, or spears. Don't arm yourself or you will be arrested."[129] His words struck me as charged with unwarranted suspicion. As they tried to guarantee the integrity of humanitarian space, the UNHCR and its partners, such as the LWF, identified refugees as the primary obstacle in that pursuit while openly welcoming state-led militarization that was unfolding in form of ramped-up police interventions. Dissuading his audience of refugees from engaging in "illegal" activities, Ronald inadvertently acknowledged, not without enjoyment, the threat of premature death that awaited them at the hands of Kenya's police. "There are laws in Kenya," he said with a threatening smile as the room fell silent. "If you get caught, you will be beaten up first and then hurt in other ways. Our policemen are very bad. You would regret it. . . . Even UNHCR can't protect criminals."[130] Preserving the humanitarian character of the camp offered a pretext for entrenching the organized violence that was enshrined in the collaborative rule of the UNHCR and the state. "The presence of police," the UNHCR emphasizes in its guidance on operational protection, "has limited the overt politicization and militarization of the camps."[131] In framing policing as an antidote to the supposed threats emanating from camp inhabitants, the refugee agency foreclosed any prospect of genuine protection. Appeals to the "humanitarian character" of the camp, then, should ultimately be read as shorthand for the claims of sovereign control made over the camp, using humanitarian logics to criminalize refugees and wage slow destruction on their communities with impunity.

Beyond the Brand

For the UNHCR's communications team, TEDxKakumaCamp was a roaring success. The event was lauded not only as a milestone for making the voices of refugees heard, and for putting Kakuma on the global "map," but also as a logistical feat in its own right. "There, in remote Turkana County, a four-day drive from the Kenyan capital Nairobi, our team built a state-of-the-art, fully equipped event space," Fleming marveled, before adding that she was "struck by how important it is for all Kakuma residents that the time they spend here is productive."[132] TEDx even enchanted the seasoned anthropologist Rahul Oka, who, speaking to Al-Jazeera's program *The Stream*, found that it was "a fantastic idea. It's something that has actually plagued me—that we have a conception of refugees as helpless, and yet Kakuma is now one of the most well-studied camps in the world."[133] Oka seemed to repeat the UNHCR's vision of changing the *story* of the camp rather than its material conditions. "What it's gonna do," he emphasized, "is speak about a place that seems to be in despair but it's gonna speak about *success* and it's also gonna talk about *human resilience* and the *human fighting spirit* in the worst of temperatures, sometimes in the biggest of despair."

The fashion model Halima Aden reiterated this belief in self-powered change on the TED stage. "Being a child refugee has taught me that one could be stripped of everything," she told the watchful audience. "Food, shelter, clean drinking water, even friendship. But the one thing that no one could ever take away from you is your education." She regarded her success first in school, and later on the runways of the world, as clear evidence of this. Others spoke with equal sincerity about their experiences of overcoming pain, trauma, and violence and how Kakuma helped them to forge a new life. "We do not choose where to be born," the schoolteacher Mary Maker offered in an emotional address. "We do not choose who our parents are. But we *do* choose how we are going to live our lives." She continued, "Education heals [because] when you're busy solving mathematical equations and you're memorizing poetry, you forget the violence that you witnessed back home, and that is the power of education—it creates this place for peace." Those who attended seemed captivated by these awe-inspiring stories, showing their appreciation with occasional applause or laughter. Despite its inhospitable climate and resource scarcity, Kakuma was depicted by most of the speakers as a place of hope and renewal, where they had finally left the horrors of the past behind.

While this rang true for many whose lives had been in such crisis that any place seemed a welcome retreat, it left unaddressed the violence the camp itself had exerted on them as the years went by. Onstage, Kakuma was a canvas onto which biographies of empowerment could be projected, and that mirrored the image the organizers wanted to create: an imperfect but ultimately benevolent refuge, an oasis. But TEDxKakumaCamp strangely invisibilized the Kenyan state, despite its key role in refugee management in the country. Josphat Nanok, then the governor of Turkana and a former aid worker, was the only state official present in front of the camera because he and his county government more comfortably fit the desired narrative of coexistence and hospitality that the UNHCR hoped to curate to, as Fleming put it, "[kick-start] a conversation that changes the way the world thinks about refugee camps."[134] Nanok had no hand in developing Nairobi's anti-refugee policies that kept Kakuma's inhabitants encamped and excluded over past decades and that the "War on Terror" had only escalated. On the contrary, Turkana county's outlook on hosting refugees was more positive and pragmatic, driven by the knowledge that aid money and jobs in this deprived part of Kenya were closely tied to the continued presence of refugees.

Although the Kenyan state, apart from Nanok, made no formal appearance on the TEDx live feed, giving global audiences the impression of a camp peopled only by humanitarians and their refugee "beneficiaries," its street-level agents were working busily in the background of the event. Police officers and community police were deployed to "control" crowds of refugees who had gathered to follow the proceedings on screens across Kakuma, while foreign guests, celebrities, and local dignitaries received armed escorts to safely traverse the camp in their Land Cruisers. Ironically, for a media event organized "for" and "with" refugees, TEDxKakumaCamp carefully filtered the stories that were allowed to be told on the air while sanitizing the state violence that made the event's smooth running possible.[135] Planned as a turning point to spin a more hopeful narrative of encampment, TEDxKakumaCamp turned out to be a textbook example of the two-faced system of compassionate rule that this book is laying bare. Gripping accounts of resilience, dignity, educational success, and integration that were heard onstage that day could be told only because of the violence work that underpinned the event off camera.

Omitting the state as a source of violence in Kakuma, and its role in making refugee lives more *unsafe*, was a political choice by the organizers, given the uncertainty about the future of Kenya as a refugee host. One allure of jointly administering the camp is that the division of labor between statecraft and aidcraft can obscure when humanitarian logics are marshaled for security purposes and, in turn, when militarized force is unleashed to discipline the very people they are entrusted to protect. This is symptomatic of liberal orders writ large, in which declarative freedoms and ideals are usually presented to global audiences while being undergirded locally by brute force.[136] By looking beyond Kakuma as a "brand," we are tasked with squaring popular imaginations of Kakuma as a place of economic boom, oasis of aid, and launchpad for prosperous futures with the more prosaic realities of securitized and brutalized lives kept in limbo. In so doing, we are able to prize open the contradiction of humanitarianism itself, which presumes that the safety of precaritized populations, as in all systems of "carceral protectionism," requires either denial or restriction of their freedom, ostensibly, for their own good.[137] Kakuma's image as a poster child camp for the UNHCR is therefore dependent on its liberal promises of brighter futures and innovation being quietly upheld through an apparatus of militarized control beneath the surface. This recognition allows us, in the next chapter, to examine in more detail the long-standing colonizing processes through which Kakuma has been made into a space under occupation.

2

Occupation

The Officer Commanding Station (OCS), the official in charge of the police station, was perched behind his desk across from me, filling out paperwork and signing commands. As on most days, Kakuma's central police station was a hive of activity, with dozens of claimants coming and going, hoping to bring their cases to the commander's attention. Despite the power the OCS enjoyed in these parts, his office was furnished sparsely with dusty filing cabinets, stacks of frayed folders, two chairs, and a tattered-looking bench. In the right-hand corner, his secretary was typing up a report on a whirring old computer, occasionally asking his superior for further instructions or clarification. Mounted on the wall behind them were the official portraits of President Uhuru Kenyatta and Inspector General of Police Joseph Kipchirchir Boinett, who were watching sternly over the busy scene. As I waited for my turn to speak with the commander, I heard shouts and loud banging and could smell the sulfuric stench of urine waft over from the overcrowded prison cells next door, where at least two dozen prisoners (*mahabusu*) were locked up under gut-wrenching conditions. The morning roll call was about to start. "Nyamazeni!" (Be quiet!), one of the constables roared as he smacked his baton against the iron bars. Sensing my discomfort, he turned to me and whispered with a hidden smile, "We need to show them who is in charge here. That's why I do this. They need to respect us!" The prisoners filed out of the cell with hands crossed behind their heads as the officers looked on with drawn rifles. "Chini!" (Down!) ordered the constable, and the prisoners immediately obeyed, squatting in the center of the police station's yard, waiting for the day's head count. Concentrating on planning the day's patrols in the camp, the ocs himself was unfazed and took notice neither of me nor of the commotion outside. The clamor of carceral violence had become mere background noise. On the desk in front of him lay a thick red volume entitled *Laws of Kenya*.[1] After a while, he remembered my presence, put his pen and paper aside, turned his gaze toward me, and said:

> In our operations, 70 percent is not by the rule book [tapping with his finger on the volume of Kenyan law]; it's simply by using force. You can't go by the rules all the time in a place like this. People won't listen to you, especially the South Sudanese. There are two things: They are violent by nature, and they aren't used to functioning laws. If you just go and tell them gently, "Please come and do this," they will laugh at you. It's not like in Nairobi or elsewhere. Here, you have to beat and cane them so that they understand what you want. It's not easy.

The commander looked tired and worn but exuded a definitive air of authority. He conducted himself like someone self-assured in his position and of his moral superiority. Only in hindsight did I notice the parallels of his words with the attitudes of colonizers who tend to portray populations in territory they control as ethnoracially inferior, culturally defective, unruly, and needing heavy-handed administration from an external power. Colonial occupation was always tremendously corporeal in that colonizers were convinced that part of their civilizing mission was to dispense "rough justice" against "raw natives."[2] For the ocs, policing the camp was therefore also a matter of peacekeeping on Kenya's home turf. The duty to fulfill this role, and to keep the "peace" among Kakuma's refugees whom he believed to be lawless, had fallen on him and his officers, who fancied themselves embodiments of the "thin blue line": a human bulwark imagined to prevent society's descent into lawlessness and chaos.[3] As I elaborate in this chapter, police officers held the levers of occupation firmly in their hands through a combination of *architecture*, *bureaucracy*, and *physical force* to keep refugees in their place. While this may not be surprising to anyone familiar with cultures of policing generally, it offers a vivid snapshot of the routinized violence that police forces wage in spaces of "care and control" such as the camp. "Violence," Adam Branch writes in reference to displacement camps in in northern Uganda, is "a necessary component of the humanitarian enterprise."[4] The nonchalance with which Kakuma's police chief explained his treatment of refugees was testament to this reality, but it also mirrored more deeply engrained spatial imaginaries of exclusion that coded the camp, and Kenya's north generally, as requiring a special kind of "emergency policing."

Turkana and Kenya's pastoralist northern plains have long been considered a backwater of the country, dating back to British colonial rule and well into the postindependence period. It marked the insecure, unsettled northern boundary of a fecund territory farther south that had been colonized at enormous financial and human expense, and in which resources such as land, labor, and agricultural products were abundant. In contrast, colonial officers based in the capital, Nairobi, described Turkana in the 1930s as being "for the most part desert [of] no value to anyone except the Turkana" and, with the slim prospects of economically exploiting this barren land, dismissed it as the "most worthless district in Kenya."[5] As far as British administrators were concerned, the colony was effectively "divided into Kenya proper, familiar to the tourist and settler, and the Northern Frontier Province, hot, parched, and dusty, to which access is barred unless by special permission"—an imaginary divide that still has import in Kenya today.[6] The Northern Frontier Province was a geographical and political descriptor that signaled the unfinished colonization process at a frontier that on its own constituted 80 percent of Kenya's entire territory and mapped onto the present-day counties of Garissa, Tana River, Marsabit, Samburu, Mandera, Wajir, Isiolo, Kitui, and, not least, parts of Turkana. Cattle raiding, inhospitable terrain, and fierce resistance to colonial encroachments meant that Turkana, unlike other parts of the colony, long remained outside of British control.

British colonizers could retain their foothold in the territory only after commencing its full-on military occupation in 1916 by building administrative outposts (*maboma* [pl.], *boma* [sing.]) that were fortified with permanent garrisons of the King's African Rifles (KAR) in Kacheliba, Kalosia, and Lokiriama.[7] Controlling space was then, and remains today, vital for achieving military goals and colonial conquest. To exert control over a far-flung territory such as Turkana, administrators needed to be seen and develop their capability to intervene militarily outside the southern heartlands of the colony in the Rift Valley and the central highlands. After a series of punitive expeditions in 1917–18 that were aimed at demilitarizing the Turkana communities, and that

FIGURE 2.1. Backyard of Kakuma police station, 2016. Photograph by the author.

were therefore nicknamed the "Turkana Patrol," the entirety of the district was officially "closed" and declared out of bounds for civilians, missionaries, and other (white) foreigners. This special status was legalized with the Closed District Ordinance of 1926 and the Special District Administration Ordinance of 1934, which were in force until independence in 1963.[8] But while the district was off-limits for foreigners, its remoteness and uninviting climate made it the perfect choice as the colony's internal place of exile. Here the colonial authorities could banish dissenters or anticolonial agitators at a safe distance from their political supporters in the south, as they did with the Kapenguria Six in 1953, who were sent to Lokitaung and, later, Lodwar.[9] The most famous of these prisoners was Jomo Kenyatta, who would go on to become the country's first president a decade later and who remembered his banishment in Turkana as "hell on earth."[10] At Kenya's frontiers, space itself was used to break circuits of resistance through isolation of detainees in the north's dusty and desertlike terrain and simultaneously to prepare these areas for state expansion, making carceral institutions such as the prison that held Kenyatta and his fellow inmates a "front-line bastion of colonial power."[11] Dividing territory into manageable sectors, settlements, and military garrisons was a way to impose authority over a seemingly boundless landmass and create concrete anchor points of the state that could "emit" colonial power and "pacify" the frontier and its populations.[12]

Historically, different camps have therefore played a key role in opening Kenya's north to colonization through an extensive carceral network. The Lodwar and Lokitaung prisons were the northernmost points of confinement within a colony-wide system of graduated encampment set up during the Kenya Emergency (1952–60), when the British waged a brutal war against the anticolonial Kenya Land and Freedom Army (Jeshi la Kenya la Ardhi na Ukombozi).[13] This carceral system is often referred to as the "pipeline" because colonial officials conceived of it as a method of sorting and "screening" an estimated 160,000 African inmates according to levels of their involvement in the insurgency and their prospects for rehabilitation.[14] In reality, these camps were places of torture, forced labor, and state-enforced premature death on a massive scale. In addition to detention camps for "hard-core" combatants, this carceral archipelago encompassed transit camps for relocatees, relief camps for families or entire communities with "softer" sympathies for the insurgency, and work camps for those suspected of looser personal associations with the rebellion.[15] Camps were spread out geographically from Turkana in the northwest and Lamu at the Indian Ocean coast to Mageta Island in Lake Victoria. The purpose of the Lodwar prison camp was not only to cut off political detainees from their support bases but also to force them to work, with a view to making their imprisonment "productive." The detainees were forcibly enlisted in labor schemes to construct roads and other public infrastructure that could eventually make this periphery more accessible to the colonial administration. Kenyatta and his fellow inmates thus laid the groundwork for the Lodwar airfield that still exists today. Through such infrastructural outposts at the margins of East African colonies, as Michael Pesek notes, "a more or less close-meshed network of administrative structures was established . . . to bring the presence of the state to the last possible geographic corner."[16]

In his memoirs, the former detainee Josiah M. Kariuki remembers life in the frontier prison at Lodwar. Surrounded by a double barbed-wire perimeter fence, the detention facility consisted of blockhouses with corrugated iron roofs that were parceled off from one another with a further ring of barbed wire and were guarded inside and out by the Kenya Police and Turkana Tribal Police. On arrival, Kariuki and other detainees were "welcomed" by the British camp commander, who sought to demonstrate his total control over their lives with the words, "I am the Camp Officer and the Rehabilitation Officer. I am the Governor and District Commissioner of Lodwar. I am the God of Lodwar. . . . My word is the Law of Lodwar and you must work."[17] This frontier station was bleak and isolated, with dehydration and regular hard labor diminishing the physical and mental health of detainees. It lent itself to the suspension of normal laws or procedures in dealing with routinely dehumanized African detainees. Jomo Kenyatta's firsthand experience of internal exile and encampment, however, did not prevent independent Kenya under his leadership from using similar techniques of carceral immiseration during the Shifta Emergency of the 1960s, when secessionist desires among Somali Kenyans were brutally oppressed. While this frontier served the British not only as an internal desert exile, but also as a natural buffer zone with Ethiopia to the north, postcolonial Kenya largely feared this unincorporated territory that was inhabited by pastoralist communities whose claims to be included in the agrarian nation-state were perceived as tenuous. Now as then, governing this district heavily relied on periodic militarized incursions to defuse emergencies, coupled with the slow but steady construction of fortified outposts as islands of control in areas where the state was otherwise thinly spread.

Colonizing Internal Margins Through Occupation

As much as we think of colonization as an *outward-facing* process that is aimed at conquering new lands and peoples, the establishment of racialized relations of domination and exploitation over "others" is limited neither to such extraverted colonial projects nor to histories of European empires. *Home colonization* was a term originally coined by Vladimir Lenin in 1896 to refer to tsarist plans to settle, and expand into, new areas that were slated for agricultural development in the outer regions of the Russian empire.[18] Colonizing these internal margins was not only a way to accelerate capital accumulation and acquire surplus land but also an attempt to politically "tame" a vast, fraying hinterland that was far away from the metropolitan centers and thus chronically at risk of insurgency, secession, and foreign interference. Instead of venturing beyond its own borders to find new resources, markets, and land, the state sought to more extensively penetrate its existing territory for greater profit and political control. While Russia, Austria-Hungary, the British Isles, and the Ottoman empire are early examples of *internal colonization*, later theorists have also used the concept to analyze the inequitable relations of racial rule over African Americans in the United States and the Black majority in apartheid South Africa.[19]

In the postcolonial era, some countries in the global South have pursued similar projects of internal colonial domination in a quest to consolidate their hard-won national sovereignty or hierarchize the new national body. Liberation did not result in undoing ethnoracial hierarchies, economic exploitation, or infrastructures of control but simply reworked the existing logics of dispossession, racial dominance, and centralized rule through new grammars of nationalism, autochthony, and ethnic supremacy (see chapter 3). This paralleled external forms of colonization in almost all aspects, including settlement building, imposition of political rule, subordination of entire racialized populations, and the use of physical force.[20] The disparities that hitherto had characterized the colony's external relationship with its former metropole were replicated *inside* these postcolonial nation-states. Some governments pushed for the forcible absorption of marginalized peripheries under conditions that clearly favored powerful elites and central administrations. This led to the victimization of ethnoracialized "others" and minorities who inhabited these peripheries. They were sometimes labeled second-class citizens or "alien" noncitizens and denied equal rights or access to citizenship while being targeted in systematic campaigns for assimilation, reeducation, counterinsurgency, forced relocation, segregation, or labor exploitation, as in China's Xinjiang and Tibet; Vietnam's Central Highlands; Mexico's Lerma State; the Moroccan-occupied Western Sahara; Pakistan's Federally Administered Tribal Areas; the Kurdish regions of Turkey, Iran, Iraq and Syria; and Kashmir under Indian occupation.[21]

Far from constituting a peaceful process, these *inward-facing* processes of expansion were (and still are) forcible programs of integration, acculturation, development, and "aid" imposed on marginalized not quite citizens by means of militarized infrastructures that curb their physical and social mobility. In short, militarized occupations form the necessary material backbone of internal colonization. Israel in this way has upheld settler colonial rule over stolen Palestinian land for more than seven decades with a brutal occupation while Morocco has followed a distinct, but not dissimilar, path of coercion in its Saharawi territory. In international law, the term *occupation* refers to temporary military government or custodianship over territories that have been seized by a power through war or conquest.[22] The victor claims the right to rule while recognizing that, at least in theory, the occupied population enjoys basic protections for the duration of this involuntary stewardship. Yet civil liberties are routinely suspended under conditions of occupation, causing executive, judicial, and legislative powers to fuse into one while liberal democratic oversight is annulled so that occupiers are able to rule unchallenged and by decree. What may on the surface be presented as a law-abiding system of pacification is, in fact, often little more than a militarized regime of domination and expansionist rule couched in the mantle of "security" and liberal national development. It is hence useful to look beyond legal definitions alone and focus on everyday manifestations of such relations of rule to identify the "forms of transitivity through which sites of occupation," even those that have emerged through vastly different histories and legal frameworks, "index and refer to each other."[23]

One such point of contact that disparate geographies of militarized rule seem to share are what Eyal Weizman calls "architectures of occupation," through which occupiers mold the built environment in their image and physically drive the process of asserting their territorial claims.[24] Such architectures constitute topographies of enclosure and exception that are materially etched into the landscape in the form of camps, homelands, prisons, restricted zones, no-man's-lands, walls, compounds, enclaves, militarized bases, and police outposts as geopolitical faits accomplis. Road networks, border crossings, and transport corridors splinter local geographies, immobilize occupied peoples, regulate movements, and sometimes stretch across noncontiguous parcels of land that are accessible only through special permits or passes.[25] Apartheid South Africa created nominally "self-governing" but, in fact, unmistakably dependent "homelands," or Bantustans, to segregate Africans and deny them formal citizenship, while Israel pursues analogous policies of separation through pass laws, checkpoints, and practically ineffectual Palestinian authorities.[26] It is precisely these material formations of the built environment and political rule that transform what was once *land* into *occupied territory*.

In much the same way, postcolonial Kenya has a long history of colonizing its internal margins and, with it, its ethnoracialized minorities. Nubians have been subject to systemic discrimination for decades due to their "non-native" legal status in Kenya and have struggled for recognition of their citizenship as a result.[27] Nomadic communities such as the Borana, Gabra, Dassanetch, Samburu, and Turkana at Kenya's northern frontier have been branded interlopers who frustrate the state's pursuit of determining its borders, national citizenship, and land rights.[28] More explicitly still, the Shifta Emergency in the Northern Frontier District, and the enclosure and disenfranchisement of Kenyan Somalis since, bears testimony to such relations of subordination/ superordination in the era of liberation nationalism. In fact, recent counterterrorism operations fueled by the "War on Terror" have escalated the marginalization of Muslim Kenyans generally, leading to forced disappearances and extrajudicial killings on an unprecedented scale.[29] Under these and similar conditions, minority populations the world over are excluded from citizenship and equal rights from the outset, or they are segregated, encamped, and disenfranchised despite possessing nominal rights, making them colonized subjects in all but name. Geography is at the heart of this process of subjectivation because it gives rise to differential regimes of mobility, coded through ethnicity, race, religion, culture, or legal status, which produce "different modes of being" that

FIGURE 2.2. Kenya Police at Jamhuri Day celebrations in Kakuma Town, 2016. Photograph by the author.

reflect the social hierarchies the state imposes.[30] While the historical *kipande* system made visible the racial nature of colonial mobilities—by instituting pass laws for African men and boys aged sixteen and above—later movement restrictions and mandatory citizenship screenings of Kenyan Somalis, which persisted long after independence, illustrated not only the transfer but also the redevelopment of these colonial ideas as part of the national project. The making of Kenyan territory was then a continuous process of defining who, by virtue of their belonging, was allowed to reside within and who would need to endure checks, verifications, or outright detention until proved otherwise.

Kenya's urbanized citizens from (mostly southern) ethnic majorities, such as the Kikuyu, Luo, Luhya, Kalenjin, Kamba, Kisii, and so on, were thus able to move relatively freely in this order while others, marked by their minoritized status, (alleged) noncitizenship, and general socioeconomic marginality, were unable to acquire identity cards (*vipande*) in the first place or were not allowed to leave particular areas or districts without authorization. In distinction to the British colonial order, which pitted the privileged white minority (including the settler class) against a majority of African "native" subjects, postcolonial Kenya reworked these ethnoracial ruling relations in favor of land-based ethnic majorities who were construed as the progenitors and principal drivers of Kenyan nationhood and "modern" development. However, as a matter of fact, it was the ruling strata of middle-class, educated, and propertied professionals or state officials who were at the forefront of imposing this dependence on internal peripheries. Their narrow hegemonic claims to "native" belonging have fueled the state's renewed colonization of the rural interior for the sake of a brighter future with development, security, and revitalized sovereignty. On the flip side, minoritized citizens and noncitizen "others" have invariably been at the receiving end of the criminalization, paternalistic interventions, and containment thought necessary to bring about that future.

Kenya's Postcolonial Frontier

If Kenya's frontiers continued to be colonized after independence, reconfiguring relationships between the central state in the south and its northern peripheries, how was this process brought into motion? The answer lies in the intersections between policing and territorial zoning. When I met a senior official of Kenya's Independent Policing Oversight Authority (IPOA) in a Nairobi café, he explained that postindependence police forces simply adopted colonial classifications for the northern districts with sizable pastoralist populations, including Turkana, as "operational areas." These were essentially cordoned-off militarized zones where rules of civil policing were permanently suspended.[31] Within them, the police and paramilitaries, just like their colonial predecessors, could act as judge, jury, and executioner because residents had few avenues for accessing civilian state institutions or formal justice mechanisms. "This is a troubled geographical area," the IPOA official told me in a grave tone. "When the police are unable to contain crime somewhere, that place can be then classed as an 'operational area' by the inspector general of police, and it means they can get away with committing atrocities such as human rights violations, a lot of them. And they justify this by saying, 'We are in this area, and these people can't be dealt with otherwise.'"

In reality, however, operational areas were almost exclusively located at the northern edges of Kenya, where the risks of pastoralist conflicts, insurgencies, smuggling, and terrorism were considered most acute. In these border spaces, the temporary designation of the operational areas was turned into a permanent mode of rule. "If I am honest," the IPOA official continued, "operational areas are treated as if [their] residents are collectively guilty of something, which is a horrible way of looking at policing in the context of human rights. So when they name a place 'operational area,' [you should] run away, because they will come there: the paramilitary will burn everything down; police will shoot anybody on sight. They can even shoot cows."[32] This internal frontier making re-created strikingly familiar colonial geographies that allowed for exceptional violence to be unleashed on subordinated populations. When officers are deployed to these areas, they usually undergo a visible metamorphosis by swapping their "downcountry" uniforms, consisting of black trousers and blue shirts, for olive green or camouflage uniforms with boonie hats and flak jackets as the sartorial markers of entering into a militarized zone.[33] This is in keeping with geographically differentiated policing in postcolonial Africa writ large, where police officers are often converted into de facto "frontiersmen" responsible for defending and representing the state at its edges.[34]

Since the colonial period, the police have been split into the Kenya Police Force, which operated mostly in urban areas and liaised with public prosecution; the Department of Criminal Investigations; and the paramilitary Administration Police, which has its roots in the colonial "Tribal Police" and was traditionally tasked with public order policing and protecting the colonial state and was deployed predominantly in native reserves with "the specific purpose of beating Africans into submission."[35] Although the distinction between civilian and paramilitary policing measures had always been blurry under the colonial and then the postcolonial state, the use of military-style tactics, weaponry, organizational cultures, paraphernalia, and extraordinary brutality was particularly pronounced along the pastoralist fringes such as Turkana. Due to the sheer vastness of the northern plains, the official police are being reinforced here by a volunteer force known as the National Police Reserves (NPR), formerly known as the Kenya Police Reserves (KPR), who have existed since the mid-twentieth century.[36] Apart from these bands of citizen violence workers, Kenya's central administration often surfaces only under extreme circumstances in these rural reserves, setting up temporary famine relief programs during drought or conducting military-style campaigns to retrieve cattle, disarm rebellious local communities, or mete out punishments. In 1979, following a period of deadly raids, the Kenyan authorities deployed the General Service Unit (GSU), a specialist paramilitary police branch with a reputation for ruthlessness, to disarm Turkana herders and confiscate large numbers of their livelihood-supporting cattle.[37] In 1982, the central government in Nairobi then worked with aid organizations such as Oxfam to provide food aid to eighty thousand Turkana (out of a population of 180,000) in relief camps set up throughout the district, including in Kakuma.[38] Both of these contrary interventions showed that state power tended to coagulate in concrete places where officials appeared in fleeting moments of performative control, before dissipating once again in the barren countryside. This is why, after independence, governing this frontier continued to be defined by the same "paradox" that had structured colonial rule: Every intervention or atrocity against subordinate local communities was declared a necessary act to fulfill the *protective* function of the modern Kenyan state.[39]

This is so despite the fact that constitutional reforms in 2010 initiated major changes in the relationship between Nairobi and its periphery. Proposed in the aftermath of the catastrophic postelection violence of 2007–8, the reforms were touted as bringing "the state" closer to local citizens, leveling imbalances among different parts of Kenya, promoting social cohesion, and ensuring institutions can be accessed from anywhere in the country. Through devolution, Kenya was subdivided anew into forty-seven counties, with a new tier of elected governments that were allocated their own budgets to finance programs in education, health, culture, agriculture, water, transport, and development. In parallel, Kenya embarked on a lengthy process of police reform that, many hoped, would end colonial legacies of repression by uniting the Kenya Police and the Administration Police under the umbrella of a new National Police Service.[40] In this shift from a *force* to a *service*, the police were envisioned to become more effective, democratic, and accountable to ordinary Kenyan citizens and residents. Despite the fanfare with which the process took off, it is now widely acknowledged that key aspects of the reforms have failed.[41] Rather than delivering meaningful change, reforms have instead led to a stabilization of entrenched police structures, cultures, and elite networks. "By establishing new institutions," Anneke Osse observes in this regard, the Kenyan government has simply "adopted 'reform-speak' and taken on the language of accountability and transparency, [while] the actors involved seem highly conscious of the power dynamics in the country and seem wary of disturbing that balance."[42] However, while the failure of the police reforms was predictable, as the brutalization of minorities and poor communities is the raison d'être of any police institution in the world, it also meant that the de facto policing apartheid of "operational areas" was here to stay.[43] In many respects, the north was to remain a "foreign" territory.

Occupying the Refugee Camp

Given the legacy of camps as tools of frontier making in northern Kenya, it requires no stretch of the imagination to envisage their continued use for colonization in the name of humanitarian aid today. Kakuma's location in the northwestern corner of the country is important inasmuch as the surrounding

Turkana countryside itself has, time and again, been depicted as politically, culturally, and territorially outside the nation proper. Colonial imaginaries about this "worthless district" troubled by a hostile climate, native "savagery," foreign intruders, and chronic banditry inspired contemporary perceptions of its interior as an "ungoverned space" with low penetration by the state.[44] Since the 1980s, conflicts in neighboring countries have led not only to mass displacements but also to circulations of small arms and armed groups across the region. This has often served as a convenient justification for Nairobi's heavy-handed approach in these borderlands and strained, already volatile center-periphery relations.

But here I want to point to the dramatic changes Turkana has undergone since the end of the 1980s in particular, when the United Nations (UN) brokered an agreement among Sudan's warring parties to set up a multilateral humanitarian program that could bring aid to Sudanese civilians through Kenya's border. In April 1989, this Operation Lifeline Sudan (OLS) began delivering emergency relief from its new headquarters in the Kenyan border town of Lokichoggio, just one hundred kilometers from Kakuma.[45] With forty international aid agencies involved under the lead of the UN, the northern pockets of Turkana where OLS was most active saw not only an unprecedented influx of money, jobs for local citizens, and infrastructure development, but also increased numbers of Kenyan security personnel being deployed to "safeguard" the flow of aid into Sudan. This collusion between aid actors and armed enforcement was not exceptional to Kenya. Humanitarian assistance anywhere paradoxically relies on infrastructures of violence to be able to operate. For example, the establishment of camps for internally displaced people in Uganda during the 1990s and early 2000s was predicated in large part on the state's synchronized policy of "forcing people into them, preventing people from leaving, and repressing political organization."[46]

Likewise in Kenya, as refugees began to arrive at the border in 1992, and the aid industry gradually shifted its focus from delivering aid *inside* Sudan to tending to the displaced Sudanese in Kakuma camp, police officers were tasked with enforcing the movement restrictions that the government had freshly imposed. Only about fifteen Kenya Police officers and an even smaller unit of Administration Police were stationed in Kakuma at the time to police a geographically vast area that included the town, the refugee camp, and their rural surroundings.[47] While policing in or around Kakuma has always reflected the fragile, episodic, and spatially dispersed modes of state control in this northern interior more broadly, the camp has in fact solidified previously isolated practices of emergency policing in a single location and, over time, turned mobile forms of intervention into a lasting configuration of militarized occupation.[48]

In the early days of the camp, the UNHCR led a relatively laissez-faire administration that looked toward customary leaders to help dispense aid and relied on those elders and on traditional courts for justice and security rather than Kenya's own police and courts (see chapter 4). This changed rapidly after a watershed moment in 1996 when the UNHCR decided that food distribution in the camp should no longer be overseen by customary refugee leaders but henceforth had to be given to each refugee individually from centralized distribution points. The backlash was instant. Discontented with the UNHCR's unilateral decision making and its failure to consult the wishes of camp inhabitants, a group of South Sudanese Lost Boys took matters into their own hands. On the morning that the new distribution system was to be introduced, they held several UNHCR workers hostage at the camp's Social Service Centre, demanding genuine discussions about the way forward. Okelo, who was one of the UNHCR hostages, remembers:

> The police had to come and fired live rounds—at around 6 p.m. we were finally rescued. That very night, the community leaders mobilized the Sudanese youth, and they vandalized everything in the Social Service Centre. . . . And as if that wasn't enough, from there they moved to the half-finished new food distribution center . . . and demolished everything. After that, the government and UNHCR were so annoyed, I think some leaders were arrested and taken to Lodwar [prison]. The government ordered that all services for refugees be suspended until refugees repair the damaged centers and agree for the new system to start operating. We were all sent on temporary leave. It was a government order. Later, UNHCR came back and witnessed the reconstruction of the center; the community members brought back the things they had looted. So that's how they agreed to the new system towards the end of 1996.

In the end, the installation of the distribution center as a humanitarian biopolitical technology, which in itself often enacts violence through surveillance, discipline, and gender discrimination, was possible only through armed enforcement by the Kenya Police. Neither the UNHCR nor the government had any intention to consult refugees but were prepared to manage Kakuma as occupying powers. This came at a time when legitimate urban spaces for refugees were also diminished; all refugees were once again ordered to "return" to the camps in 1998. The standoff at the Social Service Centre showed how fragile the authority of the UNHCR and its partners was and that it irrefutably depended on batons, guns, and the invocation of "emergency" by police to retain a semblance of control.[49] With Kakuma constantly growing in size, its police force followed suit. As it was expanded through the construction of the new subsections—Kakuma 2 in 1997, Kakuma 3 in 2002, and Kakuma 4 in 2014—the face of the refugee camp was refashioned architecturally through the installation of new police outposts and fortifications throughout. From the early 2000s, the much feared GSU, which previously was stationed in Lokichoggio, was called in regularly to "pacify the camp," until an entire platoon was moved permanently to Kakuma in 2008 at the request of the UNHCR.[50] The repeated invocation of pacification to describe the ramping up of police power in the camp meanwhile mirrored an older mode of colonial rule in this border region. In what I have described as the third colonial occupation, Kenya's north was effectively being recolonized with help of international aid actors.

Humanitarianism is often actively implicated in colonization and occupations, claiming a responsibility to protect the "defenseless" citizens of another state. The UN-backed invasions of Somalia and East Timor took Eurocentric standards of human rights and liberal governance as universal blueprints and imposed them on the local populations by force.[51] But muscular aid interventions of this kind are instructive and can broaden our theoretical lens from purely state-driven usurpation of territory to include quasi-sovereign "collaborative" forms of control that are shared by international organizations and state actors. The aim of such kinds of custodial rule over displaced, impoverished, and otherwise suffering populations is the creation of (or return to) a liberal democratic order and preparing conditions for lasting "peace."[52] Through this "secret solidarity" between the forces of aidcraft and statecraft, humanitarians effectively sanction the lives of their beneficiaries being kept under carceral care until decided otherwise.[53] In Kenya, this happened outside a theater of war and without invading a de jure "foreign" territory. Nonetheless, refugee camps grew into colossal holding centers for displaced foreign nationals, which, in turn, reenergized and joined with the state's territorializing ambitions in the north. Kakuma, a space designed for the provision of aid, turned into a modern-day *boma*: a moving threshold of the postcolonial state to assert spatial dominance over its backcountry.

In 2011, the year of Kenya's invasion and occupation of southern Somalia, the UNHCR and Nairobi doubled down on their security collaboration through a Security Partnership Project (SPP) to supply millions of dollars per year for the policing of refugee camps.[54] During the first three years alone, from 2011 to 2014, the UNHCR injected more than $25 million in the form of fuel subsidies, staff housing, and monthly allowances into Kenya's police.[55]

Officers stationed in the refugee camps received a monthly allowance of $50–$140 on top of their salaries. In March 2017, the UNHCR donated an additional forty-three police vehicles to the Kenya Police in Kakuma and the Dadaab camps.[56] Although militarization has been integral to policing Kenya's north since colonial rule, humanitarian sponsorship generated ever newer incentives for the state to intensify its grip over the region. Kenya's entry into the "War on Terror" precipitated the deployment of the specialized Anti-Terrorism Police Unit (ATPU) to deal with antiterrorism and intelligence gathering inside the camp.[57] With more than 196 officers, Kakuma had a disproportionately high police presence for a peripheral subcounty such as Turkana-West. "The irony," a Burundian man called Musa told me when I spoke to him about living standards, "is that they'll cut food rations, they'll reduce Bamba Chakula [a cash transfer program], and they'll tell us there's no money for improving shelters or education. But in the same breath, they don't hesitate to increase the police budget. Never! They buy them new Land Cruisers and take them for trainings. That's the world we live in here."[58] Once again, the UNHCR justified boosting the capacity of an already militarized police by citing Kenya's duty to ensure the "civilian and humanitarian character" of the camp.[59]

This only intensified when the government disbanded its Department of Refugee Affairs (DRA) and replaced its civilian bureaucrats with hard-line military and intelligence officers. Kakuma's new camp managers had little concern for refugee protection, as they doubled as officials for the newly formed Refugee Affairs Secretariat (RAS) and the National Intelligence Service (NIS) who regularly authorized raids and arbitrary arrests in the camp.[60] I was privy to this throughout my stay in the camp. One Friday evening I met Murugi, a senior RAS officer, at a local bar. In his early forties, he was former military, privately educated, and well traveled. Being posted to Kakuma as an intelligence officer was an opportunity for him to prove his worth after a meteoric military career. Twenty minutes into our drinks, Murugi pulled out his mobile phone and called Kakuma's police commander. Covering the phone with the palm of his hand, he mouthed, "Won't be long," to me before greeting the OCS with hearty familiarity. "Habari yako, afande?" (How are you, officer?), he said as he ordered another round of beers with a wave of his hand. His call to the OCS concerned a Somali refugee leader who had allegedly extorted money from community members and, Murugi later told me, needed to be "reined in." Without due process, he decided then and there that the man in question had to be punished. "I'm calling you because I need this *kiongozi* [leader] to sleep in the cell tonight until, let's say, Monday afternoon," he said as he took a sip of his drink. "There was something congested in his head," he continued with a smile, "so a couple of days in the cell will be able to open it up." Having become aware of my presence again, and the exchange I witnessed, Murugi hung up the phone and turned to me. Speaking in a low whisper he said reassuringly, "I'm not a sadist, by the way. I just want him to learn a lesson so that he never takes money from refugees again—we are here to protect these people." Most refugees had little access to formal justice or appeals procedures; nor was there oversight of the discretionary decisions made by camp administrators such as Murugi and the OCS. In the camp, their word was the law.

Through recounting these episodes, the contours of a militarized occupation now begin to solidify. Kakuma resembled other occupied spaces of refuge, such as camps in Palestine, that are also "surrounded by a state, where concentrated and confined populations, often culturally distinct and excluded from the state, are subject to its detailed regulations, which include severe restrictions on and close monitoring of place of residency and, most prominently, the scope and speed of mobility."[61] Kakuma was also populated by displaced foreign citizens who either held refugee status or hoped to receive it and who were subject to a dizzying array of exceptional regulations that forbade them to reside outside designated areas. The exceptional rules laid out by Kenyan authorities and aid organizations, however, had with time congealed into a far more permanent spatial arrangement through which the camp was placed both inside and outside the country's normal order. While in theory, Kenyan laws applied equally throughout the country, including in Kakuma and the north, refugee camps were nevertheless ruled differently, due to the special collaboration between state and international organizations such as the UNHCR, creating what Lucas Oesch, writing about camps in Lebanon, characterized as an "administrative exception."[62] Public services in Kakuma were all funded by international donors and—with the sole exception of policing and security—were delivered only by aid agencies and *not* the Kenyan state. Kakuma was therefore territorially part of Kenya, but it was administratively excluded. It was geographically *in* Kenya but not strictly *of* Kenya, a fact that was also amplified by the whole of Turkana's classification as an "operational area" in which emergency measures were the norm.[63]

Occupation in Kakuma was the product of different convergent forces, spatial processes, and rationalities embedded in both territorialized state power and liberal ideas about what was "necessary" or "legitimate" conduct to ensure refugee protection. It became evident that regular forms of control were dismissed as insufficient, and too limiting, in dealing with refugees. For the purpose of delivering aid, administrators reverted to more drastic measures that ultimately saw the entrenchment of coercive control across three domains: (1) an *architecture* of material barriers and surveillance posts; (2) a restrictive *bureaucracy* to regiment the everyday lives of refugees; and (3) the routinized use of *physical force* to punish and inflict harm on anyone jeopardizing the pretend peace under carceral protectionism.

Architecture: Roadblocks, Patrol Bases, Compounds

The first impression one gets of Kakuma, when driving on the once severely dilapidated (and since overhauled) A1 Highway that leads from Lodwar to Lokichoggio, is an iron-roofed shack and a spike barrier in the middle of the road. Chol Reech, a young poet in Kakuma, described these barriers as "planted thorns" because their barbs appeared to sprout organically from the tarmac surface below.[64] "Lokore" roadblock demarcates the outer border between the camp and the Turkana countryside. Mundane sites such as this constitute a material architecture of occupation inscribed into the landscape of Kakuma that encompassed checkpoints, patrol bases, police stations, and barbed-wire fences, erected for containment and control. Occupiers seek to splinter territories they administer "into a web of intricate internal borders and various isolated cells" in an attempt to regulate the movements of the occupied population.[65] While roadblocks around Kakuma use analog rather than high-tech modes of surveillance, they perform quotidian decision making over the inclusion and exclusion of eligible travelers and enact the asymmetries between police and refugees that emulate military or colonial administrations.

While I passed these roadblocks on countless occasions during my research, I was allowed to spend only two days at Lokore as an official observer. My welcome at the roadblock itself was expectedly cold. The three junior officers staffing the post were apprehensive about having a visitor, but because I had received permission from their superior, they relented. Whenever a vehicle approached the roadblock, one or two of the officers armed with AK-47 rifles got out from under their makeshift shelter to inspect the trunk, check documents, and question the driver and passengers. If they looked or sounded (vaguely) as if they could be refugees of a particular ethnicity, they were asked to show their movement passes and refugee IDs. If they were Kenyan citizens or non-refugee foreigners, a valid national ID or passport was usually sufficient, as long as one was not suspected of being a refugee in disguise. Many Turkana who did not possess identification documents could usually travel without much trouble, as they were considered at home in "their" county.[66] Checkpoints such as this reinforced an ethnoracialized and legal categorization of belonging that was sedimented in such moments of passage. Passengers were scanned for their accents and phenotype, which often could expose someone as South Sudanese, Congolese, Ethiopian, or Somali. Police officers thus became discretionary enforcers of an embodied state order by making personal decisions over who could and could not pass. Bodies themselves in this way were turned into markers of a mobile border.[67]

This rendered Kakuma's roadblocks nodes in a system not of total closure but of selective porosity: Permeability was built into the camp's logics of (im) mobilization.[68] All refugees were required to carry RAS-issued movement passes to exit the camp and needed to produce them at successive roadblocks along the Lodwar-Lokichogio highway if they ventured "downcountry." If they did not have official permits, refugees risked either being taken to jail or paying bribes of sometimes 5,000 Kenyan shillings ($50) to be let through. For a journey from Kakuma to Eldoret, Kitale, or Nairobi, people had to calculate the cumulative bribes they would have to pay in addition to their bus fare and food budget. While forms of micro-accumulation by police officers were common practice on roads across the continent, Kakuma's roadblocks were also distinct as biopolitical technologies for domestic border controls and for categorizing citizens and refugees into ethnoracialized mobility hierarchies.[69] Discrimination and humiliation were therefore a daily occurrence at these transport bottlenecks.

The busiest time of the day was at 4:00 p.m., when two of the main passenger coaches—the Eldoret Express and the Dayah—would pass through the roadblock to travel south toward Nairobi. One of the officers I had spent my day with, a wiry Mombasa-born twenty-five-year-old named Baraka, went to the roadside to check the Eldoret Express. To his delight, he found that some passengers could produce neither valid IDs nor a RAS movement pass that would authorize them to leave the camp. Baraka proudly returned to the shack, where I was waiting, with the ten refugees he had told to exit the bus. They looked increasingly distraught, pleading with Baraka, knowing that if they were unable to bribe him or magically produce the required documentation, their journey would end here. Baraka's colleague, a Somali Kenyan officer named Abdi joined the sorry scene and aggressively shouted at the ten refugees to "sit on the ground!" (*kaa chini!*), which they immediately did. Looking up at the officers with fearful eyes, a young South Sudanese girl who was not older than sixteen explained that she was a high school student studying in Kitale but could provide neither a school ID nor a letter as proof. Uninterested in the girl, Abdi barked at a dark-skinned young boy who was cowering next to her, "Wewe ni kabila gani?" (What tribe are you?) "Mimi ni Mdinka, Afande" (I'm a Dinka, officer), the boy replied and turned his eyes back to the ground. "You are a Dinka, huh? Are you sure?" another officer, who had been waiting in the shade under a nearby tree, asked incredulously. Abdi laughed, patted his colleague on the shoulder, and said, "You know that these Dinka are *kichwa ngumu* [headstrong], don't you?"[70]

My presence complicated the process, as the officers felt unsure whether they could ask for bribes in front of me but clearly also wanted to appear to be acting in accordance with the law. Refugees, by contrast, had often told me that officers were quick to issue threats of beatings and imprisonment and used derogatory language to intimidate, degrade, and dehumanize people who were caught trying to move without documents. Meanwhile, the Dayah coach had arrived and parked behind the Eldoret Express. While Baraka left us to conduct the same checks on the new bus, Abdi turned his attention back to the passengers waiting on the ground. "So, what school do *you* go to?" he finally asked the young Dinka. As the boy remained silent, Abdi looked derisively over to his colleague and said, "You see, he doesn't speak English. What kind of school do you think he goes to?" Just when Abdi seemed to have made up his mind and declared that everyone whose documents were not in order would be "going back to the station in Kakuma," the bus driver ran toward us. He was a short and stocky man with years of experience transporting people across the country. The driver complained that his journey was now being delayed. "I just want to go, *Afande*. Can you help us out here? You don't need to take these kids to the station. They're just going back to school." After a tense minute, Abdi was persuaded but threatened the group of ten that they would go to jail if he found them again without proper documentation. "Now run to the bus and get out of here," he said as they stood up, thanked him, and disappeared.[71]

In symmetry with this coercive policing of the camp's boundaries, the UNHCR also funded the expansion of police bases within Kakuma itself. One of the first was the Administration Police Rajaf post at the edge of Kakuma 1. These police posts manifested a liberal aspiration of bringing police "closer" to refugees while in actual fact decentralizing militarized repression. Most of the posts were enclosed by mesh and barbed-wire fences; some had watchtowers from which the surrounding areas could be surveilled. This architectural fortification of police presence was not accidental but followed the lead of humanitarian agencies in Kakuma that had erected militarized compounds, perimeter fences, barbed wire, and concrete barriers that were reminiscent of settler colonial geographies designed to keep out the colonized and protect their walled-off privileged residents. A type of architecture that is deployed as a protective shield against insurgents and occupied populations the world over has also come to embody the material violence of humanitarian colonization in camps such as Kakuma. Constructing police bases in different sections of the camp eroded possibilities of police oversight and partitioned its geography into smaller police territories, which became virtual islands of control under the command of individual corporals or sergeants with discretionary powers.[72]

On multiple visits to Rajaf and other bases, I witnessed refugees being detained, forced to work for officers to "atone" for their alleged crimes, and humiliated in performances of superordination and control, sometimes for hours on end. On one occasion, two Congolese women were accused of fighting while filling up their jerricans at a water tap and were brought to the police post by a patrol car. Mutua, a middle-aged Kenyan officer wearing a vest and shorts, had emerged from his room and was sitting on a plastic chair outside Rajaf, greeting the two women lazily. As one of them approached to take a seat on a nearby chair, Mutua barked, "Nimekuambia uchukue kiti?" (Did I tell you to take a chair?), followed by the order, "Kaa chini, wewe!" (Sit on the ground, you!) at his feet. Mutua and his subordinate officers were clearly amused by petty cases such as this and enjoyed the power it gave them to break the monotony of their day. After hearing the case, Mutua laughed and then asked the women: "Mbona mnaanza kupigana kama hamna hata nguvu? Washenzi ninyi!" (Why do you start fighting if you aren't strong enough to fight? You savages!). Because he was unable to establish who had started the fight, Mutua decided that both women should be penalized and forced them into several hours of involuntary labor to clean out his offices and private quarters, before eventually sending them home. The architectural network of roadblocks, bases, and compounds had a critical role to play in spatially grounding everyday repression and provided the necessary material infrastructure for that purpose. Architecture thus drove the division of the camp into enclaves as a bridgehead of collaborative control between state and humanitarian actors and marked its external and internal boundaries with "anchor points" of police power that embodied the topography of this occupation.

Bureaucracy: Papers, Permits, Curfews

While roadblocks and patrol bases were infrastructural nodes of occupation designed to discipline and monitor refugees, permits and papers were the bureaucratic currency for the circulation of people *within* and *beyond* the camp. To speak with Michel Foucault, this currency "places individuals in a field of surveillance [and] situates them in a network of writing; it engages them in a whole mass of documents that capture and fix them."[73] The RAS was known to issue movement passes only to refugees they thought to have "legitimate reasons" to leave Kakuma—for example, those seeking specialist medical treatment, secondary schooling, or higher education downcountry.[74] Containment

FIGURE 2.3. Administration Police Patrol Base Rajaf in Kakuma 1, 2016. Photograph by the author.

is framed as a key feature of the protective carcerality inherent to refugee en-campment, as one RAS officer was keen to emphasize during a Security Aware-ness training in the camp neighborhood of Hong Kong. "We give you limited movement for two reasons," he proclaimed to his audience of refugees, "firstly, to make sure that you are protected and provide you with the services here. Secondly, to monitor your activities and make sure you don't get involved in any funny business," he added with a smile.[75]

This bureaucracy that fixed refugees in their only *legitimate* place of residence—namely, the camp—and helped to monitor their every move not only resembled surveillance mechanisms in contemporary occupation regimes elsewhere but also rekindled Kenya's own colonial pass laws, the *kipande* sys-tem, under which African men were forced to carry an ID card (*kipande*) when-ever they left the "native reserves" in search of employment.[76] Such pass laws have a long history, from their origins on slave plantations in the US South and the "reservations" for Native Americans to their later exportation as technologies of control to Britain's colonial territories in Africa. Successive postcolonial regimes in Kenya recognized the efficacy of *kipande* in cementing the servile status of the country's own precarious citizens and prolonged its validity even after independence to monitor the spatial and temporal mobility of Kenya's minorities, especially ethnic Somalis. Kenyan Somalis continued to be restricted in their movements and were segregated in designated districts in an attempt to fix their "alien" identities both territorially and bureaucratically.[77]

In the present, this bureaucracy of difference has reemerged, creating new topographies of ethnoracial hierarchization that once again organized refugees according to their legal status, designated area of residence, and eligibility for movement. Intrinsic to permit regimes and pass laws, then, are also notions of arbitrariness and uncertainty over decision making and the powers individual bureaucrats possessed over each case.[78] During one of my visits to the RAS offices, an elderly Somali Bantu man entered the room to apply for a movement pass. His henna-dyed orange beard, weathered face, and frail stature suggested that he was at least eighty years old. After a courteous greeting, he sat down next to me and addressed one of the RAS officials in rather broken English: "I need a permit to go to Nairobi to see my son. He's sick." The officer behind the desk looked up with steely eyes and responded in Swahili, which the old man did not speak well: "Come back on Thursday, *Mzee*." The man was visibly disappointed and replied angrily, "I talked to the camp manager. He said to come today and pick up my permit." The RAS officer, clearly annoyed, repeated that the elder should come back on Thursday: "Not today. Didn't you hear me, old man?" At this, the elderly man stood up, straightened his back, and stabilized himself with much effort on his walking stick. "I am an elder from the Somali Bantu community, not just anyone. Have a little respect," he said indignantly. "You are just a *kijana mdogo* [young man], so don't treat me like this." The man then walked away from the officers, turned around, and said, "I take it that my travel application was rejected," before exiting through the door.

While only the RAS could issue movement passes, the OCS was in an unparalleled position to grant or withhold permissions of other kinds that refugees required in their daily lives. Murugi, who worked both for the RAS and the NIS, explained to me that "everyone gravitates towards the OCS and his office, [because] that's where the *real* power lies. He makes all those decisions every day, and nobody can appeal."[79] Refugees must apply for authorization from the OCS to organize any wedding, funeral, soccer match, dance, social event, or other festivity.[80] Social life was thus highly bureaucratized and enacted a binary between citizens and refugees that was anchored in the administrative exception of the camp and put the OCS in the position of a "local sovereign" of sorts. For some, this power even conjured the supernatural. One Oromo refugee swore to have seen the OCS engaged in rituals with a peacock: "It made me wonder whether he is actually a *mchawi* [witch doctor]. What a strange man!"[81] But for most, the commander's authority was expressed in more mundane, yet not less life-defining, ways. For a wedding ceremony, the OCS issued the following letter to a South Sudanese Nuer family in 2017:

> Permission has been granted to faithful's of———of mobile no.——— to hold the above-mentioned occasion today—/—/2017 starting from 11:00 a.m. to 6:00 p.m. at his home compound in Kakuma—zone— block 1. Law and order must be maintained all through the ceremony and thereafter. Noise and loud music will not be allowed. All participants to the ceremony must be confined within the specified venue. The stipulated time frame must be observed. Contravention or failure to observe the conditions given herewith will lead to arrest and subsequent prosecution. Signed———, O.C.S. Kakuma Police Station

This permission letter showed how the Kenyan state and its police activated what Foucault calls the "power of writing" to diminish the dignity of refugee subjects with bureaucratic procedures.[82] Minor wrongdoing, such as unauthorized socialization, loud noise, or breaches of stipulated time limits were considered acts of insubordination against the police-enforced camp regime and became punishable crimes. In conjunction with movement passes, permits not only placed spatial restrictions on refugees but also curtailed and suspended autonomous forms of sociality and spaciotemporal freedoms. During a training with newly arrived refugees, Ronald, the LWF's security chief, stressed that permissions from the police were absolutely vital to living in the camp if people wanted to enjoy a modicum of sociality. "Otherwise," he cautioned his listeners, "the police will come, arrest you, and throw out your food and drinks. It will be very embarrassing for you in the presence of your in-laws."[83] Ronald rationalized and normalized these exceptional rules as a simple fact of camp life but did not acknowledge that this de facto state of emergency did *not* extend to the rest of the country. "Kenyan law is [just] very different from wherever you come from," he said when asked by a refugee why these laws were in place.[84]

While it had become habitual for the Kenyan state to declare localized emergencies and curfews following sporadic terror attacks in counties such as Wajir, Mandera, Garissa, and Lamu, Kakuma camp has been subjected to such exceptional measures uninterruptedly for more than a decade.[85] Curfews in camps often serve as "artificial markers of nightfall" that induce an "automatic

FIGURE 2.4. Police checking passengers at Lokore roadblock, 2017. Photograph by the author.

shift of practical authority on a quotidian basis."[86] Even though the administrative separation of responsibilities between the Kenyan state and aid agencies was a cornerstone of camp rule, the daily curfews always signaled a temporary contraction of humanitarian influence during which all power was in the hands of the police. No vehicles other than police vehicles were allowed to enter the camp at night, and even RAS officials had to notify the police of their movements in advance.[87] Refugees were strictly required to remain in the camp between 6:00 p.m. and 6.00 a.m. and were expected to stay inside their residential homes after 8:00 p.m. The enforcement of these rules was asymmetrical and selective, affording more leniency to the Turkana or to refugees with good connections to the police.

This permanent curfew, normally a last-resort measure by state security forces, stood in contradiction to the fact that even the official "crime rates" in Kakuma were not unusually high for an urban area of its size, as the subcounty police chief confirmed.[88] Nonetheless, during a security meeting in December 2016, the UNHCR's security liaison officer handed a list of "special security measures" to be implemented by the police in the run-up to Christmas because the refugee agency expected increased levels of crime around the holidays.[89] As the vignette at the start of this book showed, this request in effect provided carte blanche to the police and led to the arrest and extortion of more than a hundred refugees at Abby's bar. When the police were asked to conduct additional patrols, the UNHCR usually offered further fuel allowances and logistical support to ensure the "compliance" of the refugees while keeping the police content. Although refugees always tried to resist and circumvent regulations, permits, and curfews—through bribes, personal relationships with officials, or simply breaking what are unjust laws—these bureaucratic technologies remained highly invasive in determining the cadence and spatiotemporality of everyday life in the camp and were both disciplinary and biopolitical in their effects. In the absence of separation walls, this bureaucracy of exclusion wrapped like a paper-thin membrane around Kakuma and complemented visible architectures of occupation with the power of documents that at any point could be denied or revoked.

Physical Force: Incarceration and Collective Punishment

The refugee camp is one of many contemporary spaces that hinge on a "diffuse field of forces" that "surrounds, immerses and embeds" its colonized subjects in a mix of seemingly benign, rationalized, but—in reality—highly coercive forms of ordering.[90] As under most occupations, the exercise of unrestrained physical force (or threat thereof) in Kakuma was invariably part of wider strategies of domination and found their expression most tangibly in carceral microgeographies that underpinned police practices with roundups, raids, torture of detainees, and collective punishment. Along with nightly intrusions into the homes of refugees, soccer matches were some of the most common arenas of police intervention. They drew large crowds and therefore were, in the eyes of camp authorities, especially prone to violence that needed to be put down. In early October 2016, the referee prematurely terminated a match at the Bafana Bafana soccer field between the Congolese team Lamassia and the South Sudanese Dinka team All Stars FC due to a dispute over the score, which ended in a minor scuffle among the players. In response, LWF security officers alerted the police commander, who called on the GSU to "calm" the situation. In what was a common scenario, rather than having a calming effect on the situation, the GSU arrived with loaded guns and batons drawn, giving out warning shots into the air before dispersing crowds by driving through them at speed with their Land Cruisers. Those who were not fast enough to outrun the vehicles were arrested, taken to the station, and jailed. This incident was not unique; it followed a common script by which refugees were officially put in cells for breaking one law or another but with the goal of extorting money from them (see chapter 5).[91]

Although much has been written about the carcerality of camps generally, relatively little attention has been paid so far to incarceration as a strategy of rule *within* them.[92] Prisons are local microcosms of a racialized system of carceral violence on a wider scale. The homogenizing containment of the refugee population in Kakuma camp, and refugees' targeted detention in cells, has fostered a system of graduated carceralization. Diverging from Foucauldian understandings of prisons as technologies of reform or discipline, however, the camp's carceral microgeographies were indicative of more brute and necropolitical forms of population control that are characteristic of colonial rule, aimed at disrupting joy and social lives and suppressing the existence of hospitable refugee spaces by militarized means.[93] In a particularly sinister episode, following a series of shootings in the camp, three South Sudanese suspects were detained by police and subjected to torture, which one government administrator euphemistically described as "special interrogation techniques." With their hands cuffed behind their backs, the three suspects were hung upside down over a wooden pole that was propped up between two tables inside the police interrogation room. After being forced to remain in this excruciating position, suspended in the air, they eventually confessed to the crimes of which they were accused.[94]

In addition to the criminalization of individual refugees, the police meted out collective punishments to whole communities that were deemed particularly "disruptive" to the running of the camp. In late October 2014, a series of events led to intercommunal violence in which almost twenty people were killed and several hundred people were displaced inside Kakuma. The catalysts were reports of an attempted rape of a Nuer girl that sparked local infighting among some South Sudanese youth, leading to the death originally of one person. Soon the police were accused of failing to investigate the case properly, causing one Nuer leader to publicly state that he had visited the police post in the Hong Kong neighborhood to follow up on the rape case, but that the police had been unresponsive. Tensions ran high and quickly spread from Hong Kong in Kakuma 1 to many other parts of the camp. Further conflict ensued the following weekend, when a Burundian *boda boda* (motorcycle taxi) driver accidentally hit a South Sudanese child and was set on by camp residents who injured him with a machete, burned his motorbike, and subsequently attacked other Burundian and Congolese drivers in the area. In the following days, several refugees were killed under unknown circumstances, their corpses appearing in the dry riverbed. The refugee-led news outlet Kakuma News Reflector (KANERE) estimated at the time that almost twenty people were killed during the violence and eight thousand refugees left their homes to seek temporary shelter outside the police station and the UNHCR's main compound.[95] Following this fighting and the UNHCR's pleas to the police to restore order, senior officers were convinced that the Nuer community was to blame for the unrest and therefore should be punished. As the subcounty commander of Turkana-West explained to me:

> It was [difficult], but I just sat down and thought, "What I should do?" And I realized the main culprits of this issue are the Nuer. You know, they are very tough-headed, the Nuer. Very tough-headed. So we decided to go after them. The head of UNHCR cried, "What am I going to tell the people of Geneva?" So I called the officers and told them we should do an operation. We had to go from house to house in the New Area [Kakuma 4], . . . getting boys, taking them out and beating them seriously, indiscriminately. And then we brought them here to the police station, all of them. The cells were full, even in Lodwar. Those who could run away went to South Sudan, by foot. We really disciplined those people, and since that time, nobody has ever died. And, of course, we did this having received affirmation from the HSO [the UNHCR's head of sub-office].

Although it is uncertain whether the UNHCR endorsed this indiscriminate violence in explicit terms, it is likely that its leadership was more than happy to leave the responsibility for the crackdown with the Kenya Police. At least, the UNHCR's collaboration and financial support for the police suggested quiet toleration of punitive policing, while the agency could publicly disavow the damaging effects these operations undoubtedly had on refugees. This episode not only brought to mind the collective attribution of guilt to occupied populations in other parts of the world, but also conjured up Kenya's own colonial and postcolonial histories of violence in which entire ethnoracialized minorities, such as Kenyan Somalis, have been forced into "protected villages," displaced, and executed at will.[96] Even though these events of 2014 were extraordinary in scale, such spectacular forms of organized violence to "pacify" the camp were anything but unusual. They followed familiar patterns of policing colonized people and occupied territories that dictated that only a decisive show of force could rein in people portrayed as unruly and incapable of dialogue. Earlier that year, the police had staged a mass raid in the South Sudanese Equatoria community after an Administration Police officer, who was accused of raping a refugee woman, had been repelled by her neighbors.[97] Hence, occupation not only violently respatialized the camp neighborhoods through sporadic police incursions, roundups, and bouts of imprisonment, but also willfully ruptured the cohesion of entire communities while etching feelings of subjugation and dehumanization into refugees' bodies. Recognizing the irony of the brutality of the police, which mirrored the kinds of violence from which Kakuma's residents had fled in their countries of origin, a Congolese refugee named Bosco, who had lived in the camp for a decade, remarked with cynical amusement: "Polisi hapa ni kama waasi wakija kushambulia kijiji" (The police here are like rebels when they attack a village).[98] Intermittent pacification campaigns were lucid reminders of the assaults and coercion that undergirded the mundane and, perhaps, less conspicuous forms of domination that otherwise saturate this occupied refuge. Invocations of emergency and exception laid bare that, underneath a thin veneer of humanitarian civility, physical force was always an ultimate possibility.

A Labyrinth of Forces

As I stood up to leave the police commander's office, which had become too noisy and crowded for any meaningful conversation to be had, he grabbed my arm and said, as if to reassure both me and himself, "When you are the commander, you'll handle situations the way they come to you, not the way it's written in a manual." My face must have betrayed my consternation and dislike of the dehumanization he afforded the very people he was in charge of "protecting." As he shook my hand to say goodbye, he added rather hastily, "There is no training on how to cope with some of the people we have here."[99] Deep down, so it seemed, even the police regarded the drive for liberal reforms, professionalization, and accountability as meaningless. In fact, the commander and his subordinates felt increasingly besieged by the large numbers of refugees who not only spoke foreign tongues and were culturally "other" but hardly qualified, at least in the officer's view, for inclusion in Kenyan society or a right to basic human dignity. This chapter reveals a shift from viewing the camp as a place of resilience, opportunity, and economic optimism, as laid out in chapter 1, toward recognizing it as an instrument of territorial state control amid protracted humanitarian efforts to house and protect refugees. It allows us to see how global circuits of aid and national territorial state politics can reinforce one another to produce a blend of colonial and postcolonial modes of unfreedom through which ethnoracialized refugee "others" are ruled.

Refugee aid operations inevitably exert violence through biopolitical technologies that are deemed a pragmatic necessity. As key sites where the aid industry touches down in space, they attract enormous resources, mobilize global compassion, and become entangled with the dilemmas of territorial statehood.

At the same time, they produce spatial formations such as camps, aid archipelagos, and enclaves whose microgeographies are reminiscent of the way in which colonial occupations past and present were spatialized. For Achille Mbembe, as for Fanon, colonization is thus, above all. "a labyrinth of forces at work" that is physically incised into the spaces that colonizers seek to usurp, civilize, dominate, and order.[100] The creation of this labyrinthine geography, however, has so far featured only marginally in scholarship on refugee encampment, although its role as a coordinate system of control warrants more detailed attention. Occupation, as I have described it, represented the material foundation that made humanitarian colonization possible and was articulated through the settling of land, the molding of the built environment, and the imposition of rule over a foreign populace. In Kakuma, police bases and roadblocks operated in tandem with circuitous bureaucratic procedures that created permanent uncertainty about the denial or approval of refugees' movement into, out of, and within the camp. This was augmented through police roundups that resembled military incursions into an enemy territory rather than the liberal law enforcement that humanitarian organizations propagated, funded, and praised. As one of Kenya's internal margins, Turkana provided the perfect backdrop against which state and aid officials could impose their vision of rule: a colonized geography perennially awaiting the enforcement of "order."

Yet the refugee camp is far from an Agambenian "pure space of exception," where vulnerable life is totally exposed to the whims of organized violence.[101] We have seen that the camp exists only as far as its exceptional rules are enforced by violence workers: state oppression in human form. It is not reducible to an abstract reified "thing" within, against, or beyond which life unfolds but is itself constituted of innumerable "prosaic practices" that reveal its heterogeneous, unfinished, and relational nature as a space.[102] Although the police officers in Kakuma were small cogs in a system, who executed orders and bided their time, the cumulative effects of their daily actions and discretionary decisions were what made the containment of refugees possible. In turn, *wakimbizi* mediated this environment by varyingly keeping their heads down, paying bribes, forging alliances, and flouting rules. Protests were uncommon, but when they did occur, they were directed both at the state and at humanitarian organizations that were held accountable for their failed promises of protection. Due to the intersecting injustices they suffered, LGBTQI+ refugees in particular were a force to be reckoned with in pushing back against institutionalized power in the camp.[103] Though small in actual numbers, theirs were some of the most visible challenges to the camp's normalized violence. By sending letters to UNHCR headquarters in Geneva, petitioning foreign embassies, and camping outside the UN field posts in defiance of police orders, these demonstrations were embodied struggles for inclusive asylum space under occupation. This underlined that the camp was totalizing space not only of exception but also of "potentiality," where refusals could arise.[104] The "labyrinth of forces" at work, we might then conclude, does not only refer to architectures of occupation alone but may also gesture to the quotidian counterforces that incessantly refuse, resist, and evade its grip from within the camp. But rather than romanticizing these political acts as heroic standoffs with this carceral technology, it is worth reminding ourselves that they often simply modify the ways in which power works on people, and that most refugees are entangled in more contradictory webs of connivance, compromise, and collaboration.

Finally, these insights on Kakuma's local occupation lead to a more nuanced view of the global politics of asylum and carceral migration control. They enable us to trace analytical lines among interlocking systems of mobility control, hierarchization of ethnoracial identities, labor exploitation, and policing that span the planet, which Catherine Besteman has collectively described as "militarized global apartheid," and instances of aid intervention that often revitalize, subsidize, and sanitize projects of internal colonization in the global South.[105] It is thus imperative that we venture into "the margins" to clearly see the fallout not just from the global North's direct imperial meddling through warfare, counterterrorism, and armament, but also from more benign-looking policies of relief. There is value in recognizing the ongoing transmissions of violent logics and colonial repertoires both from empire to nation-state and from global boardrooms to local camps.

3
———

Dis/order

"We ensure that the camp is running smoothly and that both refugees and Kenyan citizens are safe and at peace," said Alfred cheerfully as I settled down on a chair in his office at Kakuma's airstrip.[1] His desk was almost empty, save for a few scattered files that he hastily shoved into one of his drawers upon my arrival. I could still hear the deep humming sound of the United Nations Humanitarian Air Service (UNHAS) aircraft outside that had landed just minutes earlier, before it finally reached its parking position and its propellers fell silent. A small crowd of people had gathered outside the fenced office block, some of whom were squatting on the concrete veranda, fixed in agitated conversation, while yet others were waiting patiently a few feet away in the shade of an acacia tree.

Alfred, who is Turkana-born, worked as the security liaison officer for Kenya's Refugee Affairs Secretariat (RAS). His original role had expanded over the years to include mediation with local Turkana communities, making him a de facto go-between for the camp manager and many of the refugees. "In a camp like this," he stated matter-of-factly as he folded his hands in his lap, "we sometimes have problems understanding each other, since we have got people from fifteen or even twenty countries living side by side. Honestly, it's a bit like Babylon [laughs]. I often call meetings between different tribes in the [camp] blocks and speak with their elders to hear about the challenges they face. As you can imagine, there is no lack of problems to discuss." Every morning and afternoon, this compound came alive with scores of refugees flocking to the RAS offices to apply for one of the coveted movement passes for a trip down south, request new housing, file complaints, or try to get the camp manager's attention in any other kind of administrative matter. In moments such as these it became clear that the refugee camp was, above all, a gigantic bureaucratic machine, well oiled at times but more often creaky and in need of repairs. "Yes, refugees need protection," Alfred said, pausing briefly to contemplate his next words. "But the most important thing is that there is *order*. Without that, there *can* be no peace, no safety, and no protection. So you could say we are here to bring order to life in the camp. That is our mission."

This was hardly the first time a camp official voiced their concerns about the supposedly wayward lives of Kakuma's residents. Indeed, many in the employ of aid organizations and the Kenyan state made their exasperation about the "disorderliness" of the refugees openly known. Essential to successful camp management, or so it seemed, was to remain steadfast, undeterred, and forward-looking in a quixotic pursuit of an "order" that seemed to be constantly slipping away. The longer I spent in Kakuma, the more I became convinced that the colonial occupation it represented was not only founded on exerting brute force through police and paramilitaries but could be sustained long term only by weaving a wealth of imaginaries into an ethnoracial cultural text that also kept camp dwellers socially "in their place." This text remained, for the most part, unspoken but was thought self-evident by those engaged in its everyday production. Like older colonial tropes, this present-day discursive text served as a living repository of folk knowledge about the ruled—their habits, cultures, and presumed (im)moralities—that were used as explanatory frames to make sense of camp life and one's own role within it. Nowadays, its authors were primarily Kenyan officials and aid workers who belong to ethnic majorities from the country's south for whom the camp, and the arid north generally, had come to symbolize a domestic otherworld and a visceral reminder of the "backwardness" from which the rest of modern Kenya is said to have long since progressed. These camp officials tended to conceive of themselves, if not explicitly then definitely through their actions, as educators sent to "discipline" and "teach" refugees how to behave properly in a "rule of law–based" liberal society such as Kenya, in an attempt to make them into reformed human subjects.

What I am interested in here is tracing this imaginative construction of Kakuma camp as a pre- or even antimodern space through the banal discourses and exchanges of knowledge about the encamped in which administrators participated and the effects they had on legitimating humanitarian colonization. Street-level actors tasked with managing, protecting, and assisting subject populations often also most actively voice and circulate the parochial culturalist beliefs and sensibilities that arise from their work. I found that administrators, including aid workers, police officers, and civilian government officials, devised regimes of knowledge that stigmatized both the spaces and the refugees under their care/authority and that were shot through with power asymmetries. They often cast themselves as protagonists in the social advancement of refugees whose lives they spoke of as if they were mere canvasses on which goodwill, progress dreams, and feelings of compassion could be projected. The camp was thus made into a staging ground of self-actualization for a multitude of actors to lay their own claims and be seen to empower, educate, and colonize the indigent. In Kakuma, this interplay between imaginations of difference and power hierarchies was reminiscent of colonial renderings of the world, in which colonizers portray the colonized in paradoxical fashion as childlike and dangerous, erotic and savage, and loyal and capricious, as well as in need of civilizing reforms.[2]

This archive of colonial phantasms had filtered into postcolonial Kenyan society, which remained closely structured around ethnoracial hierarchies and essentialisms. Though officials in Kakuma shared certain preconceptions, their respective subject positions—as police officers or humanitarians, foreigners or citizens—and their own ethnoracial identity inevitably colored their views and the stories they spun. While there was a small minority of (frequently white) Europeans and Americans, Asians, and aid workers from other parts of Africa, most employees of aid and state agencies were Kenyan. In my search for racializing interpretations of camp life, I had to attend to subliminal forms of knowledge, often expressed in offhand remarks, that digressed from what was usually deemed acceptable for representatives of their organizations to utter in public. By spending down time with officials, I was able to glance behind this hard institutional façade to gain more unabridged insights into the self-conception of camp staff and their understandings of refugee "others." By excavating this knowledge, I started to disentangle the thickening web of fantasies and facts that often characterize postcolonial social worlds in their irreducible suspension "between the imaginary and the real."[3]

During an outreach event for newly arrived refugees, a Kenyan humanitarian called Wafula, with several years of experience working in the camp, articulated his fixation with the imagined (im)morality of camp residents. Setting aside the Kenyan state's preoccupation with threats of terrorism and the appeals of aid agencies for more robust humanitarian solutions, he was worried first and foremost about what he understood as the camp's state of moral disorder. "Here in this camp," he lectured to the hundreds of refugees who were huddled together under a crowded tarpaulin tent, "we have madmen, womanizers, and thieves, so beware and don't get involved in any funny business as you start your new life here."[4] I found that similar tropes recurred in conversation with other officials, many of whom envisioned encampment as a moral civilizing project. First, they depicted refugees as cunning "crooks" whose presumed dishonesty and proclivity to crime had to be carefully monitored and contained. Second, they often spoke of the eclectic dangers of hypersexuality, promiscuity, homosexuality, and "deviance" among refugees that were feared to gradually unravel Kenya's more "virtuous" social fabric. With the third trope they pathologized *wakimbizi* as "mad" subjects whose erratic, uncontrollable, and "uncivilized" behaviors were thought to stem from displacement-induced trauma and a cultural disposition towards anarchy and lawlessness.

Over the years, these cognitive frames normalized an understanding of refugees in Kakuma as shrewd and dishonest, requiring both heavy-handed enforcement and caring pedagogical interventions while being spatially isolated from the rest of society. Rather than denying the agency of refugees altogether, imaginaries such as these alleged that they possessed a surfeit of the wrong *kind* of agency—one that was corroding the fictitious ideals of Kenyan orderliness, morality, peace, and social cohesion. In contrast, the chaos that the camp and its denizens embodied was seen by many administrators as a dormant threat that would soon enough "spill over" into the entire country, if left wantonly unchecked. In addition to being a place of last resort and emergency aid, the camp doubled as a social buffer that could—at least, it was hoped—contain the excesses of a wicked populace.

Ethnoracial Imaginaries of Space

Representations of spaces and populations typically serve to legitimize the methods of their rule. Refugee camps therefore have invited vivid imaginaries, ranging from their depiction as "dangerous sanctuaries" and "hotbed[s] of intrigue" to sites of humanitarian crisis with a "lack of normal social structures."[5] In Kenya, the specter of terrorist infiltration created a toxic additional layer of fear over insecurity, territorial disintegration, and impending loss of state control inside the camps. In public opinion, Somalis in particular have been chastised for supposedly destabilizing the peace and cohesion of their country of asylum, despite Kenya's very own, long histories of social division and discrimination against various ethnoracialized minorities.[6] Kenyans from all walks of life, especially those from southern ethnic majorities, were quick to regurgitate the xenophobic sound bites that some politicians had broadcast in the past, including populist claims that the "camps shelter terrorists" or that the "refugees can't expect hospitality while killing Kenyans."[7] Although these beliefs were not representative of society as a whole, there was a noticeable proliferation of this language immediately after the Westgate Mall attack in 2013. Ordinary citizens (*wananchi*) recognized the need to relieve human suffering but were also worried about the economic, social, and security fallout from hosting refugees.[8]

However, behind this contemporary anxiety about terrorism and lawlessness lurked not only familiar spatial but distinctly ethnoracial imaginaries that have their origins in the colonial era. Such imaginaries were socially held "spatial stories" by means of which people, spaces, or places were made sense of and talked about in everyday life.[9] Doreen Massey argued that, rather than constituting mere descriptions of our world, such spatial stories are in fact the "image[s] in which the world is being made."[10] By actively spinning taken-for-granted knowledge about places and people, these imaginaries often go beyond the realm of the discursive and have a direct material impact on social relations as people begin to "act in relation to, and through, [them]."[11] Far from a fixed set of ideas, imaginaries constitute a dynamic repertoire of shared understandings about the world, social collectives, cultural belonging, and the self that are constantly reworked in practice.[12] The crux of spatial storytelling are performative repetitions and the reactivation of certain beliefs in quotidian interactions that translate abstract ideas of "otherness" into the concrete realm of the ordinary. Instead of displaying a given social reality, these sensibilities influence how people think, act, or feel in the first place, which means they ultimately "produce the effect they name."[13]

In colonial and postcolonial societies, these imaginaries are often distinctly racial. The colonial world order, in which countries such as Kenya struggled for formal independence, has left behind a host of dehumanizing inheritances that haunt them to this day. In his magisterial treatise on white supremacy, Charles Mills argues that logics of racial domination find their expression not only in the legal, economic, and political structures that categorize, or differentially privilege, racialized humans, but also in imaginations that demarcate the world's "civil and wild spaces."[14] Predictably, civilized spaces are associated with Europeanness through the master signifier of whiteness, while former colonies are simply folded into the "wild" sphere of savagery imagined to stretch across a whole tapestry of "uninhabitable" geographies—such as slums, camps, ghettos, and occupied territories—that are deemed incongruous with "proper" humanness and human habitation.[15] Those who dwell in such emblematic places of crime, poverty, underdevelopment, and "chaos" are automatically devalued, by association, in their own claims to full humanity and are thought to be trapped in an anachronistic state of nature. Through a "temporal alteration," in the words of Aníbal Quijano, the colonized and racially inferioritized populations who live in those geographies are construed chronotopically as belonging to the past, seemingly giving credence to evolutionary hierarchies of civilization and culture.[16] Worse still, negative imaginaries tend to "stick" to, and follow, the bodies of racially subjugated people, producing a form of "circular indictment": The moral properties of a space "taint" its inhabitants as a priori immoral beings while space itself is imprinted with the presumed depravity of racial "others" who people it.[17] Space in this way is "raced" through geographical projections of racial inferiority, while race is simultaneously "spaced" once it is tied to particular ontologies of risk, underdevelopment, and vice. Negatively raced spaces the world over, as Mills makes clear, are set apart from their "civilized" outsides by a fundamentally different moral topography.[18] In the uninhabitable geographies such as the camp, the civilizing mission is believed to be not yet complete.

Since formal colonial rule, racialization in African societies has often been expressed through notions of ethnicity and "nativeness." While American slavery homogenized Africans into a Black collectivity in diametrical opposition to European whiteness, the institution of racial apartheid throughout much of colonial Africa also created ethnocultural differentiations among the colonized. Racialization on the continent, though part of white supremacy on a global scale, was articulated through a decentralized "colonial policy [that] racialized the African as native."[19]

A shift from direct to "indirect rule," especially explicit in British colonies, meant that the racial divide between white European colonizers and colonized Africans morphed into new grammars of nativeness that extended sociocultural hierarchies to local identities that were portrayed as primordial, mutually exclusive, and immutably "tribal." Colonial space was thus organized into a nested hierarchy of identities: an overarching binary between Africans (or natives) versus Europeans (or non-natives), which conferred (or withheld) collective rights according to their imagined proximity to whiteness, and a secondary layer of competing native identities. The figure of the native here was far from simply a token of political subjection; it was always also an essentialized ethnological category that tied imaginaries about people's "physiological, emotional, and mental character to, ultimately, capacity for rule."[20] In this way, colonized Africans underwent a dual process of racialization as natives living under the thumb of Europeans and as members of their "tribes" who were purportedly beholden to fixed cultural practices and administratively confined to designated ethnoracialized spaces. Nothing seemed to jeopardize this order more than "detribalized" Africans who left their homes and migrated to the colony's cities, where the indirect rule of "tribes" was minimized.

In Kenya, one key structural legacy of British rule were the ethnoracial vernaculars that outlived empire. As I have mentioned, in the eyes of colonial officials the colony was divided between an agrarian south with (semi)sedentary populations and a sparsely populated, nomadic north with an "unproductive" pastoralist economy. Within each of these domains, the British further distinguished an ethnoracialized cultural patchwork of "tribal" entities that formed the bedrock of a decentralized administration. The colonial territory was partitioned into various "native reserves" that served as pools of exploitable labor for white agricultural production and as forms of racial segregation, and that ostensibly protected Africans from the vices of modern life.[21] To this day, the hinterland of Turkana that lies beyond the handful of urban areas in the county is colloquially referred to as "the reserve." The resulting quilt of ethnic microterritories had a strong imaginative pull, as each ethnic collectivity became associated with its own unique set of sociocultural, moral, and physical traits that rendered it, at least in the minds of the colonial authorities, either eligible or ineligible for cooptation and civilizational uplift.[22] Somalis were paradoxically categorized as "native aliens": Although racialized as Black Africans, they were constructed as nomadic migrants and interlopers in Kenya. Even after the end of colonial rule, they have remained in an ambiguous and delicate in-between position that at times can enhance or destabilize their collective rights to national belonging.[23]

This vernacularization of ethnoracial politics still suffuses how conceptions of ethnoracial belonging shape Kenyan society today. The far north has long occupied an "alien" place in the mental mappings of most Kenyans and retellings of their national history. Geographically inaccessible, politically indomitable, and beset by so-called *shifta* (bandits) activities, these areas are often quickly dismissed by southern Kenyans as not quite Kenyan due to unresolved border disputes, histories of secessionism, pastoralist conflict, and the fraught loyalties of local citizens, who, often rightfully, view Kenya's central

FIGURE 3.1. Funeral dance of South Sudanese refugees from Equatoria in Kakuma 1, 2016. Photograph by the author.

state with healthy suspicion.[24] When traveling south from towns such as Lodwar, Garissa, or Isiolo, it is not uncommon to hear this imaginative divide being reinforced even today, with passengers casually asking one another, "Unaenda Kenya?" (Are you going to Kenya?). Kakuma refugee camp itself has been inserted into these ethnoracial geographies since its inception thirty years ago. Its location alone fuses popular panics about foreign refugees with more deep-rooted misgivings directed at Kenya's historically marginalized Turkana population as not-quite-equal citizen "others." As the next section shows, recent anxiety about insecurity, terrorism, and fragile citizenship were compounded, if not eclipsed, by the idea that Kakuma's refugees have become harbingers of a looming "moral disorder."

Moral Disorder

When I asked Michael, a Kenyan protection officer with the United Nations High Commissioner for Refugees (UNHCR), about security in Kakuma, he leaned back in his leather office chair, sighed with frustration, and then cautioned me sternly that "the camp is another jungle altogether; it's another jungle."[25] Perhaps sensing my perplexity, he continued, without needing any further prompts, to explain: "We are dealing with refugees here—one, people that do not understand the law; two, people that do not understand order, you see?" Different shades of this sentiment were ubiquitous among camp administrators such as Michael. But what he articulated was not just his concrete fear of crime, terrorist forays, or the decline of social cohesion that have been common talking points in political debates since the start of the country's "War on Terror." Instead, his remarks suggested a more deep-seated unease about the imagined "otherness" of refugees, whose "primitive" and impulsive behavior he saw as the root of the camp's recurrent operational challenges and wider moral decay.

Questions of morality permeate life in refugee camps, and many scholars have described the emergence of place-specific codes of piety, virtue, and transgression among the displaced. In Lukole camp in Tanzania, for example, Simon Turner noted that refugees employed a moral vocabulary to make sense of changing class, gender, and intergenerational dynamics that accompanied their displacement.[26] Liisa Malkki showed how Hutu refugees resisted their local integration by reimagining their camp as a place of moral purity in which "refugeeness" had become a unique identity that could positively set camp dwellers apart from surrounding communities.[27] Due to Kakuma's extraordinary ethnocultural diversity, comparable visions of the camp as a unifying moral community are harder to discern there. But the officials working for aid agencies and the Kenyan government have internalized their *own* cognitive foils through which they interpret the social landscape of the camp while situating themselves within it. In the same way that refugees use rumors, conspiracy theories, and fictive rationalities to make sense of their lives in exile, camp officials rationalize their work with the help of such imaginative repertoires.[28] Instead of being attributable to a single author or origin, however, these cognitive frames were produced as part of a diffuse discursive field and hinged on the illusion of their own validity as simple facts. And it is, first and foremost, this imaginative thinking that I examine in an attempt to comprehend the logics and motivations of humanitarian colonization.

As Michael illustrated in his characterization of Kakuma, the camp was being imagined as a cesspit of vice and an antipode to its more "orderly" outside. Its political designation as an area where exceptional administrative powers applied heightened a sense of the cultural, social, and moral boundaries that were drawn around it. By demarcating a micro-territory of exception and cultural nonbelonging, these political logics "reproduce[d] orientalist mappings of the world that deem some people incapable or unworthy of citizenship."[29]

Given that humanitarianism is driven by Enlightenment ideas, including an irrefutable belief in engineering social progress and spreading civilization, it has always required the colonized, slaves, refugees, and other principal objects of its compassion to be yet unincorporated "people out of place in the spatial organisation of modernity."[30] Aid is a vehicle that can, at least in theory, redeem the wretched of the earth from the ills of their squalor, want, and racial ineptitude. As others have pointed out, the biocentric figure of "the human"—which was always at the heart of humanitarianism—was itself modeled on white bourgeois Man as a stand-in for all of humanity and thus reproduced a distinctly racialized understanding of lifesaving.[31] In this thinking, some were predisposed to indefinite ameliorative care while others would be abandoned on the road to colonial modernity.

Camps in this sense rearticulated a well-rehearsed institutional-cum-imaginative divide that also separated colonial native reserves and colonized subjects from proper citizens of the colonial state. Spaces of civility were defined in opposition to the contorted mirror images of their supposedly uncivilized and inferior "other."[32] "Otherness," as Zygmunt Bauman writes, is nothing but shorthand for socially constructed dichotomies that are key for "the practice and the vision of social order."[33] Order and disorder are pictured as mutually exclusive domains, whereby "the other of order" is associated not only with Africanness or nativeness but, more fundamentally, also with "ambiguity, chaos and indeterminability."[34] Refugees embody this imagined lack of order. Like the "detribalized native" who spurred popular panic around moral degeneracy in colonial cities, refugees have been forcibly severed from their places of origin, unmoored from what was understood as a cohesive traditional order and therefore represented its "constitutive outside."[35] Elisabeth Olivius notes how camps are sometimes depicted as "anarchical, primitive and precivilizational context[s] where refugees act in a purely self-interested way."[36] As physical incarnations of a diffused planetary apartheid, they are designed to hold captive the human detritus that is not only displaced and impoverished but also attributed a whole host of moral flaws. Globally, camps have come to symbolize microcosms of "otherness," humanitarian containers for the human "cost" of disasters and wars, onto which fears, fantasies, and disreputable desires can be readily projected.

As far as Kakuma was concerned, these imaginations were not just abstract but infused the work of officials on the ground. During a verification exercise, a head count of all refugees, a Congolese senior UNHCR official called Denis vented his frustration at how disruptive the refugees had been to his task. He was convinced that if nobody had the courage to "organize these people, they [would] disturb the whole process."[37] Denis was a kind and soft-spoken man whom I had socialized with in my free time. But his managerial position, and the pressure to process hundreds of refugees every day, had changed his demeanor and turned a considerate man into a cold administrator. After I arrived at the UNHCR field post, where the verification was taking place, I saw Denis barking orders at a group of middle-aged Somali men who had been waiting in the blazing sun for hours to be finally let into the compound. Having lost patience, two of the men started pushing against the field's fence posts in an act of bitter frustration. Denis was enraged and asked security personnel to disperse the small crowd with wooden sticks and whips. He himself rushed outside to push the men away from the fence while threatening to confiscate the food ration cards of anybody found to be causing further trouble. "If we didn't have these fences here," he said as he turned toward me, in exasperation and short of breath, "we wouldn't be able to manage these people. I knew that from day one. I have never seen a place quite like this. These people are incredibly chaotic and lazy, I'm sorry to say, but it's the truth." Sentiments such as this were clearly heartfelt and, perhaps, therefore sometimes contradicted the expectations Denis had of his own outlook as a humanitarian. They rendered the camp a site of pedagogical intervention and helped to naturalize the notion that refugees were unruly and anti-civilizational.

A number of officials spoke about refugees as if they were not the primary purpose of the aid operation but, rather, a mere nuisance they had to monitor and discipline. This delegitimization of refugees' claims to equal humanity, bodily inviolability, and dignity was not just a byproduct of the segregative process of encampment: Ideas of ethnoracial difference rationalized the power hierarchies that actively *produced* the camp's geography. Kakuma's *wakimbizi* were, at best, framed as moral strangers who required paternalistic support for the management of their lives and, at worst, incendiaries who willfully undermined the professed "good" that aid actors were trying to do on their behalf. Positioned as subordinate subjects, camp residents were in this way disqualified from "liberal" means of ordering and required the whip. This did not mean that the camp officials denied refugees their agency. Instead, many were convinced that those living in Kakuma were endowed with a negative agency that warranted extraordinary measures of social and geographical containment. Spiraling criminality, devious sexuality, and overall "madness" were the ways in which this negative agency was thought to be most clearly expressed.

Street-Smart Criminals and Crooks

There was an unspoken understanding among officials that anybody who worked in Kakuma for long enough would become attuned to the "disingenuous" behavior of refugees. Diplomats, senior UN officials, rights advocates, academics, and anyone who had only fleeting experience inside the camp were considered too naïve and trusting toward refugees, with their judgment clouded by well-wishing humanitarian sentiments. One day, as I was about to join a meeting in one of the camp's local security offices, an official with the Lutheran World Federation (LWF) took me aside to warn me about the powers of deception that he ascribed to the refugees. "If you are not smart [enough], you can't manage the Somalis," he pronounced authoritatively as his gaze sought mine. The same official wore his own ability to apparently "see through" the supposed trickery and charades of the encamped as a badge of honor that, for him, was naturally beyond doubt.[38]

The list of undesirable activities in which Kakuma's *wakimbizi* were engaged was accordingly long and included informal trade in corrugated iron, illicit housing sales, fabrication of insecurity claims for boosting their resettlement cases, bootlegging home-brewed alcohol (*chang'aa*), and systematically pilfering food. Some refugees had been found to be collaborating with aid workers in sporadic theft from the World Food Program's warehouse. The unauthorized buying and selling of ration cards alarmed camp authorities and donors enough to spur the introduction of biometric technology in 2016 to verify people's identities at food distribution. The causes of these illicit activities are both obvious and obscure, with some explaining them as a way for refugees to cope with the perpetual resource scarcity and the harshness of camp life or as reactions to humanitarian bureaucracies that show little to no accountability toward those living under their rule.[39] Bram Jansen describes "cheating" in Kakuma as acts of "impression management" that are born from a system that is already premised on strategic representations of the self for accessing resources.[40] Eligibility for resettlement in a third country, for example, was usually determined using hierarchized criteria of protection need and, with it, deservingness that enticed some to amend their cases to conform more legibly to institutionally recognized categories of suffering. Kakuma's police commander routinely lamented the profusion of "self-inflicted crimes in which someone decides to stage-manage an offence with the intention to get resettlement."[41]

Perpetuating ideas of crookedness and criminality among refugees is discursively useful to underpin humanitarian colonization. Cindy Horst argues that the seemingly opposing images of refugees as "cunning crooks" and "vulnerable victims" shape the ways in which aid workers are able to interact with them.[42] Camp bureaucracies are far from unprejudiced or impartial apparatuses for distributing aid. One senior UNHCR official joked to me, as we began to discuss corruption within the agency, that "some believe humanitarians are people of a different kind, with higher morals and ethical standards. Of course, sometimes the opposite is true."[43] Government officials and police officers in particular believed that a large portion of refugees in Kakuma were essentially fraudsters who took advantage of both international aid and Kenyan hospitality. Among Kenyan administrators, this often led to attempts at "saming" refugees with the aim of relativizing the hardship on which their claims of resettlement and protection were made. As Naomi Schor explains: "If othering involves attributing to the objectified other a difference that serves to legitimate her oppression, saming denies the objectified other the right to her difference."[44] In Kakuma, however, "saming" was intimately tied up with, and even existed alongside, processes of "othering." Many police officers and national staff of aid agencies showed misgivings about the supposed ease with which refugees, especially Somalis, not only seemed to invite Western sympathy and access resources, but were also subsequently able to gain residence in wealthy countries of the global North. As a former camp manager, Mr. Kamau, put it: "What I can say is, when it comes to the Somalis, they are very difficult. Somalis are very difficult to deal with, because they are very cunning. It is easy for them to hold citizenship of even five countries at the same time." This cunning was a source of mistrust among the camp officials. Kenyan administrators regarded their country as more closely aligned economically and geopolitically to Europe and North America than were the countries from which Kakuma's refugees had come, but they felt they were unfairly denied the same advantages of prospective lives abroad. Further, the transnational connections that many refugees cultivated as a result of global displacement were taken as a cause of concern to question their "genuine" vulnerability and eligibility for generous aid. Neatly woven into this imaginary was the enduring suspicion toward Kenya's own Somali minority, whose precarious belonging has long put their claims to citizenship and loyalty to Kenya in doubt. Mr. Kamau continued: "They are very opportunistic—they are very opportunistic! Immediately when you start resettling them [from Kakuma camp], you will [also] inevitably end up resettling [Kenyan] Somalis from even Garissa."

And yet Somalis were not the only refugees who were viewed negatively. When interacting with humanitarian staff, it was commonplace to hear generalizing indictments that suggested "few Somalis will tell you the truth" or equally problematic proclamations that "the [South] Sudanese are absolute criminals."[45] In fact, distrust and suspicion have long existed in Kenyan camps, where the UNHCR itself has considered Somalis and South Sudanese "difficult populations."[46] Based on these widely held sets of beliefs, police officers in Kakuma felt concerned that refugees were playing a double game of appealing to white donors and well-meaning advocates, on the one hand, while revealing their "true" (often) criminal nature only to Kenyan aid workers and government officials, on the other. Conversely, some refugees were convinced that the camp's African bureaucrats, whether Kenyan or otherwise, could not be trusted. A refugee from Burundi named Sylvestre deplored that the "whites are more humane than Africans. Africans don't love each other. I'm unable to express in words the type of indignity they [have] shown me."[47] When I pressed Sylvestre on this point, asking him whether his asylum in Kenya was not a sign of solidarity, he waved his hand dismissively and said, "That does not automatically make us safe." Marcus, a thirty-year-old policeman who had been stationed in the camp for years, illustrated how the presumed "double game" of refugees played out in Kakuma's majority-Dinka area of Hong Kong:

> There is no good or bad youth in Hong Kong. They are all bad, thieves and thugs. When the *wazungu* [white people] show up in their Land Cruisers, refugees shout, "Our rights! Our rights!" But for us Africans, there is no such thing. When we [the police] come to Hong Kong, they throw stones at our cars and officers. That's how they *really* are.[48]

Murugi, the senior RAS officer, shared this general sentiment and was keen to let me know that "97 percent of refugees here are not genuine but look for resettlement or opportunities for crime. Only the remaining 3 percent have *actual* refugee claims."[49] The pro-asylum arguments I could muster in response were met with sly amusement or derided as revealing white naïveté and my "soft spot for refugees." Sustained international aid for Kakuma's refugees was often received locally with a mixture of incomprehension and gratitude. Although the causal relationship between refugees and crime was accepted by many beyond doubt, the presence of aid agencies also secured livelihoods for thousands of Kenyans. Moral duplicity and surreptitious scheming were understood as the crux of the matter. Refugees were not only believed to be defrauding a complaisant and naïvely benevolent "international community" but were also imagined to be deliberately souring Kenya's geopolitical alliances with Europe and the United States by repeatedly putting Nairobi in a diplomatic quandary over the sensitive question of camp closures.

Although crookedness was predominantly ascribed to refugees in their interactions with relief organizations and state officials, this was accompanied by a fear that their immorality could eventually "rub off" on the local Turkana community, whom many middle-class Kenyan officials, especially those from the south, regarded as their "backward" compatriot protégés.[50] During a joint meeting with refugee leaders, state representatives, and the UNHCR, a Turkana elder struck an equally paternalistic tone in describing the impressionable nature—and, thus, the perceived susceptibility to bad influences—of the Turkana in Kakuma: "I pity my own Turkana people. Most alcohol that the refugees brew in the camp is sold to the Turkana, who finish it all. We are the best customers for alcohol from refugees, and it's ruining our people." Despite these pronouncements, the relationship between the refugees and Turkana communities in reality was more socially complex. While sharing some of the reservations about refugees as interlopers and competitors for resources, many Turkana saw their own historically unfinished inclusion in Kenya's nation-building project as reason enough to embrace a contingent cultural identification with Somali, Dinka, and Nuer refugees as fellow pastoralists. At the same meeting, the chief of Kakuma referred to these communities as his "next of kin," with whom the Turkana shared unbreakable cultural ties despite being formally divided by citizenship, borders, and national belonging. "We Turkana," he reiterated boldly, "are their grandmother's leg. We need each other; we are one people."[51] Identities and imaginaries in Kakuma therefore were never fully fixed, as well as highly contextual and subject to reinterpretation.

Sexual Deviance and Idleness

Another trope that fired the popular imagination in Kakuma was presumed sexual deviance and idleness among the encamped. Cultural differences and a conflict-related breakdown of familial bonds were said to be responsible not only for a spread of highly promiscuous and extramarital relationships, but also for the soaring number of defilements and rapes. Humanitarians have a history of being deeply invested in policing the health, bodies, and sexuality of their beneficiary populations, which emulates the intimate biopolitics and moral order making of white colonial regimes.[52] Of particular concern to aid organizations in Kakuma were various bodily functions of refugees, which were monitored and targeted to be rectified through campaigns for improved hygiene, HIV/AIDS prevention, bans on early marriages, and sensitization about sexual- and gender-based violence.[53] Kakuma was one of the first refugee camps in the world in which "gender programing" was comprehensively rolled out.[54] Billboards along Kakuma's roads conveyed educational messages warning against public health risks such as open defecation, domestic abuse, and unwanted pregnancies, as well as the detrimental effects of female circumcision. At the same time, gender identity and sexual orientation have become increasingly potent, yet also contested, grounds on which to base asylum claims.[55] Even though the establishment of a specialized "gender desk" in Kakuma's police station, funded by foreign donors, signaled a growing sensitivity toward gender-based violence, there was little to indicate that this went beyond a performative embrace of liberal ideals. Wanjiku, the police officer in charge of the desk, was sometimes caught between following "official" procedures and applying a more lenient "common sense" in her policing duties. While legally required to press for carceral solutions, and to prosecute abusive parents and partners, she sometimes decided that the occasional caning of children was more appropriate parenting, especially for refugees, who in any case, she insisted, suffered from a lack of self-control.

Yet this institutional focus on sexual health and reproductive rights masked the fascination some officials harbored for the intimate lives of refugees. Sexuality and desire were structurally embedded in the exercise of power within the camp. Here, too, any societal preoccupations with sexuality worked as "a subtle network of discourses, special knowledges, pleasures, and powers" that were the organizing principles of public morality.[56] Subliminal knowledge about refugees in this way coproduced and upheld a fictive moral order. Not unlike exoticized and sexualized subjects in prior colonial discourses, the figure of the refugee hence became "at once an object of desire and derision" that was always judged against the fiction of a superior morality and civilization, but nonetheless spurred the fleshly fantasies of those exerting power over them.[57] Wilson, an inspector who had formerly been stationed in Kakuma, was both troubled and titillated by what he viewed as indecent and hypersexual behavior on display in the camp:

> In Kakuma, those people are especially idle. And when they are idle they tend to fuck a lot, or to be fucked. I talked even to Somali ladies, asking "Why do you really [get] involve[d] in these things?" They told me, "You know, once I've eaten, there's no work that I do. I'm being fed, so my [only] work is to fuck," you see. These are the things—Actually, I stayed [in Kakuma] and got a good knowledge so that if today I would go to serve there again, I know their ways. The climate also contributes to this immorality. Because I find that those people who live in warm places like Kakuma or even Mombasa, they like fucking, and they also commit similar crimes.[58]

For Wilson, the blanket provision of humanitarian aid—which takes care of the basic livelihood needs of refugees—is one of the main reasons for this inflation in promiscuity, while the hot climate of Turkana and the cultural diversity of the camp were interpreted as equally conducive to immoral behavior.[59] Accordingly, the imagined moral decline of camp life was understood to be partly due to the refugees' "keeping their old habits," as well as the result of aid programs that had inadvertently destabilized more "durable" patriarchal gender relations, an explanation that Turner also heard in Tanzania.[60] Tropes of refugee idleness and sexual deviance were therefore inextricably linked in accounting for Kakuma's moral deficit. The thought that aid actors were literally fostering population growth by unconditionally feeding camp residents was a matter of controversy among Kenyan administrators—the demographic threat of a "refugee bulge"—but was ultimately looked on with quiet complacency because the bill was being footed largely by wealthy donor countries.

Often cited among the "old habits" of refugees was their expected ignorance of women's rights and gender equality. Kenyan aid workers tended to warn refugees about their country's progressive laws and cultural values, which, they insisted, looked unfavorably on some practices, such as early marriage.[61] Erastus, a young police sergeant, voiced similar concerns and stated that refugees "marr[ied] off small girls, and that's how women's rights are violated."[62] The fact is that Western humanitarian discourses are quick to assign these refugee women the role of victims of "regressive" cultures who require the protection of aid workers as their enlightened saviors. Refugee men, in contrast, are represented as the bearers of "uncivilized masculinities" that endanger women's lives.[63] Hegemonic and subaltern masculinities are thus pitted against each other over the protection of marginalized women, which has historical resonance with colonial societies. The bulk of sexual panic and imagining around Africans in colonial Kenya were similarly the result of social and cultural frictions that arose in moments of intimate encounters and were laced with racial inequalities.[64]

Hypersexualizing imaginaries of violently virile refugee men likewise circulate incredibly freely through banter and storytelling. Rashid, a young policeman, recounted with horror a story he had heard about a Somali truck driver who, on a trip through South Sudan, was allegedly raped by soldiers blocking the road. Rashid had been in Kakuma for only four months, but the telling and retelling of such horror stories among officers had already affected his view of the world. When I asked him how that kind of narrative made him feel about his work in the camp, he concluded, "It's quite simple: They [refugees] aren't good people."[65]

The negative impact of "Western" humanitarians on the moral and cultural lives of refugees was believed to go even a step further than allegedly boosting fertility rates. The presence of the few white aid workers in particular, with their presumed inclination to espouse the rights of sexual minorities, was decried as undermining decency and "promoting homosexuality" outright in Kenya, where sexual acts between same-sex individuals were prohibited. Again, Wilson explained:

> That is also a clip of the problem. Some refugees were even protesting, making it known that it is their right [to be homosexual]. Because there are those people from Belgium, France, they have legalized same-sex marriages. So, you find those people are also here in the camp because the European community has an interest in the refugee camp. That's why you find them forcing those bad morals onto refugees.[66]

This put refugees into an impossible double bind of being either seen as far too susceptible to a more permissive "Western" sexual morality or, alternatively, as not yet "developed" enough to become fully part of modern Kenyan society and enjoy the protection of their human rights. Humanitarian colonization was therefore a way for the state to leverage international aid in situ while being able to keep the immorality of refugees from "leaking out."

The tension between desire and disavowal was constant, causing some administrators to portray refugees as "depraved" while secretly engaging in their sexual exploitation. It was common knowledge that a substantial number of children in Kakuma had been fathered by police officers and that casual sex between refugees and aid workers—though officially prohibited by codes of conduct—was widespread. Murugi, the RAS and intelligence officer who had shown contempt for refugees on multiple occasions, openly recounted his sexual affairs with Somali women whom he fetishized as "exotic" objects of desire. During one of our conversations at a local bar, he boasted about his sexual exploits and the ease with which he was able to find "willing" refugee women due to his influence. "They might need a movement pass, or a new plot and I make it happen, so we help each other," he said with a laugh. "By the way, if you were wondering, they all look the same with the hijab, but when they take it off, their hair is long and curly!"[67] The flip side of publicly performed disdain for the immorality of refugees was this exploitative and sexualizing gaze that reproduced structural power asymmetries on an intimate microscale. "Disavowal," if we invoke the words of the social theorist Stuart Hall, is therefore nothing but a "strategy by means of which a powerful fascination or desire is both *indulged* and at the same time *denied*."[68]

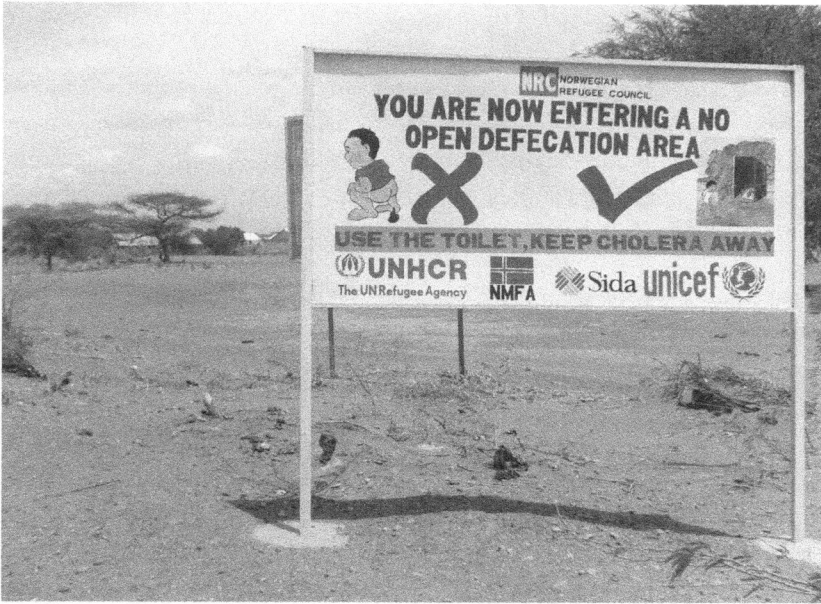

FIGURE 3.2. Public hygiene billboard in the camp, 2015. Photograph by the author.

Madness and Uncivilization

A third pervasive trope encompassed the other two and imagined refugees as inherently "mad" and "uncivilized." Despite internal differentiations that labeled certain refugees as more unruly than others, often along ethnoracial lines, this perspective acted as a blanket explanation for the violence, insecurity, and "chaos" that typically features in journalistic and scholarly writing on camps.[69] John, a mid-career police sergeant from western Kenya, was convinced that his time in the camp had given him irrefutable ethnological knowledge about the habits of his subjects. As we sat in his office at a police post in Kakuma 3, he looked at me with a stoic demeanor and offered his psychological analysis of those he was sworn to protect: "I always say that most refugees have had terrible experiences in their home countries, so now they are 'don't-carers.' They don't care about how their actions affect Kenya or their fellow refugees."[70] Displacement and war-related trauma, which *wakimbizi* undoubtedly have suffered, were among the most commonly cited reasons for their perceived unpredictability and enduring state of "madness." John continued: "Refugees don't respect the police. When we disperse a crowd, they come after you and even insult you. In Kakamega [County, in western Kenya], you won't see that a policeman is being insulted or that someone resists an arrest. Here, if you aren't careful, they can even snatch the gun from you."[71]

Invoking insubordination of refugees toward the police was not just a way to confirm their "otherness" for John. It also reenvisioned Kenyans as imaginary, and improbable, model citizens. Unlike public discourses in which refugees are sometimes depicted as would-be terrorists with a hidden, conspiratorial anti-Kenyan agenda, this characterizes them first and foremost as a pathologized category of humanity. "Even killing," an inspector observed with great confidence on an afternoon in the police canteen, "is not a problem for them at all."[72] This pathologization was hardly surprising considering the imaginative power that disease, infection, and trauma have persistently had in colonial discourses and continued to have in more contemporary debates on migration.[73] Vanessa Pupavac notes that deterministic traits are often casually embedded in humanitarian operational culture and thus "[construct] war-affected populations as traumatized and subject to psychosocial dysfunctionalism."[74] This particular madness imputed to refugees in Kakuma went beyond what we might call "ordinary" predicaments and everyday frustration and was pictured as far more existential, seemingly dislodging the refugees' being in and from the world.[75] It is therefore only fitting that refugee camps in Kenya have sometimes been described as "highly dysfunctional entities."[76] However, while ascribing antisocial and "immoral" behavior to war-related trauma was widespread, notions of social dysfunctionality were replete with ethnoracial and culturalist overtones. When I asked John about this, he said, without hesitation: "I think it's because of the laws they are used to. *Their* laws are different from *our* laws. Also, they were brought up fighting with wars raging around them. Culture is another factor—*our* culture is different from *theirs*."[77]

Although experiences of war and conflict were rationalized as the psychological causes of social and moral disorder, culture in its most essentialized form was constructed as the "natural" spring from which this lawlessness flowed. The police chief's insistence that South Sudanese refugees were violent by nature and that they had no comprehension of functioning laws, which I described in chapter 2, was also telling in this regard.[78] I became convinced that camp officials were, knowingly or not, projecting their interpretation of the Enlightenment's twin figures of the "barbarian" and the "savage" onto Kakuma's refugees. A product of modern society and, in this case, mass displacement and the humanitarian intervention that followed in its wake, the barbarian is an antagonist to "Western" civilization that he "despises, covets and constantly fights."[79] Invoked throughout European political thought—from ancient Greece to Thomas Hobbes, John Locke, and John Stuart Mill—in relation to the figure of the "savage," who is imagined as innocent but precivilizational, the barbarian embodies a treacherous and subversive force. In Michel Foucault's terms, the barbarian "does not make his entrance into history by founding a society, but by penetrating a civilization, setting it ablaze and destroying it."[80]

In Kakuma, the attributes of both the "savage" and the "barbarian" notably surfaced in popular narrations of refugees' behavior. Officials, in contrast, often cast themselves in the role of cultural envoys sent to deliver *wakimbizi* from evil and colonize their hearts and minds with the progressive ideals of gender equality, human rights, public health, and reproductive rights. As the "custodians of the values of civilization and history," as Albert Memmi famously wrote about European colonizers in North Africa, these administrators inside the camp were likewise thought to have the "immense merit of bringing light to the colonized's ignominious darkness."[81] Murugi subscribed to similarly disparaging imaginings and contended that the camp was simply being governed by what he called the "politics of the head bone." In his rendering, the refugees were following basic instinct in their interactions with one another and officials, which threw them into a Hobbesian fight for survival. "If you want to make it here, you need to knock people down with your head first, before you start thinking," he explained to me. This incapacity of refugees to live cooperatively was attributed not only to resource scarcity but also, especially, to their premodern dispositions. Informing this racial "othering" was the sly reproduction of colonial stereotypes about African impulsivity, immaturity, and sheer monstrousness that pervaded the reasoning of camp officials, some of whom had also accused refugees of engaging in cannibalism, sodomy, and witchcraft.

Even though Kenyan government officials and humanitarians were predominant in shaping this discursive field, white and other foreign humanitarians could thrive at least as much on the spectacular stories that affirmed their preexisting racialized fears about "darkest" Africa. The cultural predispositions of African refugees presented a convenient explanation for the recurrent managerial challenges they faced, exonerating aid workers of responsibility while locating shortcomings in the disagreeable lives of the displaced. Katie, a white American humanitarian in her early thirties, invited me for dinner after a long day at the office. "Current arrival numbers [of new refugees] are just too much, we're really stretched, and the workload is so high," she said as she started to cook. "And the ones that *are* coming, excuse my language, but they are a difficult lot, if you know what I mean." I said that I did not and asked her to explain. "Well, they are undermining a lot of what we are trying to do here," she said. "You tell them one thing, and they do another. I don't mean this in a derogatory way, but the Lotukos are fucking bush people that don't even know how to use a toilet. There are all sorts of innovative projects, but we can't even fucking make them stop FGM-ing [a reference to female circumcision, also known as female genital mutilation] themselves, so how are they going to learn more complex stuff?"[82] Clearly, she felt comfortable enough around another white person to share her racist views about South Sudanese refugees, who, in her opinion, were one of the main obstacles to the smooth delivery of aid in Kakuma.

While refugee "crooks" supposedly undermined the success of humanitarian assistance out of ill will or for personal profit, this racist account singled out the Lotuko as uncivilized agents of disorder who were seen as unworthy even of receiving aid. Supposedly irrepressible, less than human, and outright animalized behavior of refugees, in the words of a veteran aid worker I met around the same time as Katie, rendered Kakuma simply "the worst location for white UNHCR staff."[83] Thrown into this miniature heart of darkness, "expat" humanitarians felt they were up against not only "corrupt" African government officials and an unfamiliar hot climate, but also a beneficiary population that seemed inexplicably to be resisting the civilizing influences of humanitarianism. Their subjectivation as mad or uncivilized was inseparable from imaginings of sexual deviance and crookedness as markers of their infrahumanity. Together, these forms of disorder that refugees were thought to bring about legitimized the organizational and moral foundations of humanitarian colonization. It was through the civilizing effects of aid, and the unabashed saviorism of its agents, that officials ultimately hoped to uplift refugees from a putative "barbarism" or "savagery" and bring about social and cultural transformations that could propel them into a modern future.

Encampment and Frontier Nation Building

The construction of the camp as a cultural antithesis to its outside is part of a wider conversation about Kenya's own nation building. While humanitarianism has always been a civilizationist endeavor, guided by the gold standards of Euro-American piety and compassion, it was also being coopted by the Kenyan state to justify the colonization of its own northern hinterland. As far as the camp symbolized a pedagogical space of aid intervention, aimed at the social improvement of its "beneficiaries," it was also consigned to a unique place in Kenya's national cosmology. When I met Lemuya, a special adviser to the governor of Turkana, he was keen to share his views on Kakuma's position in the wider political geography of Kenya. With his piercing gaze and exaggeratedly upright posture, he was ever the military man, even after leaving his previous job with the Kenya Defence Forces (KDF). Sitting across from me at one of Lodwar's up-and-coming bars, he explained:

> By nature of Kakuma's geostrategic location in Turkana—at the crossroad of Kenya, South Sudan, and Ethiopia—we are looking at many security and cultural problems. The national government holds many fears surrounding security, and so does the county government that I serve. Civil war in South Sudan is, of course, a big factor. War then manifests in Kakuma from time to time because refugees are often the same people who are also fighting across the border. They bring war with them. That leads to a breakdown of order, not only in the camp, but also in the surrounding areas. At the same time, banditry is normal and culturally engrained in Turkana and even the places where some of the refugees come from. It might be stereotypes, but it's important we acknowledge that the camp is quite exceptional.[84]

The exceptionality that Lemuya conjured here was not dissimilar to what I had often been told by officials in Kakuma itself. They, too, insisted that the camp was an almost valve-like border space, an exceptional zone of contact and separation, through which all kinds of foreign goods, people, customs, and hazards could enter Kenya. It was therefore treated with the same caution as any external border, making the camp a minuscule enclave of "alien" territory that the Kenyan nation-state continuously had to claim, secure, and occupy with all of its might.

Although "foreign" in these respects, Kakuma was nonetheless incorporated squarely into recognizably Kenyan grammars of belonging. Ethnicized identities in the country were usually invoked most strongly in the service of political campaigns that hinged on claiming autochthony and privileged relationships to the land to devalue converse claims made by opponents.[85] Kenya's fragmented ethnic geography often presented itself as a tightly knit "system of moral meaning and ethical reputation within a more or less imagined community" that distinguished *insiders* of particular identity groups from those on the *outside*.[86] Moral belonging in this context was spatialized through mapping popular cultural boundaries onto the country's patchwork of ethnic territoriality.[87] On this mental map of Kenya, each ethnoracialized identity grouping was accordingly allocated a place of belonging that it called "home" and where the legitimacy of its presence was the most secure. The process of devolution—and, with it, the creation of more fine-grained and de facto ethnically defined "counties" after 2013—formalized parts of the political map to bring it in line with this imagination.[88] But refugees remained uniquely "out of place" in this essentializing organization of Kenya's political cartography and were not only excluded from formal citizenship but also had no claims to a designated "homeland" within the borders of their long-term country of asylum.

Notwithstanding the political disputes over national belonging among Kenyan citizens themselves, the discursive positioning of refugees as "moral strangers" or "foreign interlopers" had the effect of reinforcing a provisionary, but shared, Kenyan identity among the citizens who were employed in the camp. The moral disorder contained in the camp constituted a conducive foil through which Kenyan administrators—whether they were aid workers, civil servants, or police officers—could express negative imaginings about "others" while inadvertently mending the vestiges of a chronically fractured sense of "Kenyanness," if only ever temporarily and contingently. In the country's national order of things, Kakuma thus became a kind of *surrogate homeland* to which refugees were legally bound (through mobility restrictions) but without being protected through sociocultural inclusion in the nation. This surrogate homeland therefore anchored its denizens in a place where their residence was partially accepted and not outright criminalized. as in larger cities, but that nonetheless afforded no privileges or prospects for enabling a more permanent social belonging. Addressing a gathering of refugees and humanitarians, a government official left no doubt as to the ownership of the land (*ardhi*) on which refugees were settled, even after spending decades in the country: "Some refugees who come here think that the compounds they live in are theirs. This land is community property of the Turkana, not private property. No refugee holds his own land as property. The land is *ours* here." His insistence on this issue was no accident; it evinced the postcolonial anxieties that continued to haunt Kenya because of its history of land dispossession. Meanwhile, the categorical exclusion of refugees from Kenya's ethnoterritorial map was also articulated by a Kenyan humanitarian who cautioned a group of refugee youth not to confuse their country of asylum with their homes.

The humanitarian had called a meeting to discuss recent reports of criminal activity in a camp neighborhood and sensitize community members to keep one another safe but quickly began to castigate them for the actions of unknown assailants. "Hakuna Kongo ama Sudan hapa" (This is not Congo or Sudan), he warned his listeners. "Hapa ni Kenya!" (This is Kenya!). This sense of Kenyanness inverted the tropes used to racialize refugees. It was performed through quotidian assertions of cultural supremacy and Kenya's alignment with Western ideals such as progress, development, and modernization. Through this, the raced space of the camp seemed to contain not only the "human consequence" of foreign wars but, with them, also what appeared to be the contagion of "failed" statehood and calamitous disorder itself. Administrators liked to think of themselves as modern Kenyan citizens, who had long tempered their ethnocultural loyalty and moved up the imagined development ladder to embrace a more civic national identity, which distinguished them from the toxic ethnic parochialism they understood to still prevail among refugees.

Paul Gilroy analyzes the camp as both a material political technology and a metaphor that marks fault lines between the inside and outside of identities. In fact, it is through examples of such "camp thinking," he insists, that "shared patterns of thought about self and other" are reinforced and spread, creating mental images of cultural and ethnoracialized collectivities to which one may or may not belong.[89] Kakuma was therefore not only a holding space for a motley crew of displaced foreigners, whose only commonality was their exclusion—in one way or another—from Kenya proper, but it also became a backdrop against which a localized form of nation building could take effect. Here, *wananchi* could reinvent themselves as benign humanitarian settlers, frontiersmen (and women) operating along the fringes of Kenya's north and driving the country's adopted values, ideals, and civilizational achievements of democracy, rule of law, civic nationalism, and human rights into a hitherto unincorporated hinterland. This kind of frontier nation building shared much with the expansionist colonial projects that preceded it but differed in that it was not white colonial officers securing the edges of the colony but experts and administrators from southern ethnic majorities who were bringing knowledge, development, and civility to this margin. By effectively recolonizing the Turkana countryside, this time under the guise of delivering aid with the help of international agencies, Kenyan authorities and their ordinary officials mobilized conspicuously colonial techniques of differentiated mobility, dehumanization, and illusions of order to reframe themselves as envoys of a modern nation justly strengthening its control over a vast, and yet untamed, periphery.

The Cultural Text of Colonization

The rise of hegemonic discourses around security and antiterrorism have exacerbated sectarian tendencies in Kenyan society that often pit identity groups against one another. While historical linkages to "the land" as agriculturalists, workers, pastoralists and, more generally, "autochthones" are important ways for some to make sense of what are in essence exclusionary *political* dynamics, religious difference over the years has become another embattled terrain on which politicized identities were forged. The proliferation of ethnoracializing imaginaries gave shape to what I call the *cultural text of colonization*, which has had a profound impact on the conduct of the Kenyan state and aid actors in their dealings with refugees. This is so because prejudices and sensibilities are more than just a socially problematic or hurtful discursive field. They are registers through which deep-seated ethnoracialized colonial hierarchies of power are performed and legitimated, with consequences for the material lives of those who are being ruled. Rather than mere remnants of a racist past, colonial representations of difference in this way are continually being "mobilized, reworked and mediated through ideologies, individuals and institutions in the postindependence period."[90] Thievery, sexual peril, and pathological madness have continued to be projected onto Africans long after independence and have been particularly instrumental in ostracizing new "non-native" and migrant others in countries such as Kenya.[91]

Acknowledging this enduring exchange between the imaginary and the real, the fanciful and the material, offers useful vistas into the lived ordinariness of this occupied refuge. At the street level, administrators performed the banal labor of aid and state power and were naturally at the forefront of reworking grammars of racial belonging and culture in practice. Yet the knowledge they produced as an everyday cultural text was by no means uniform or unchanging. Rather, the imaginative framings of the administrators perpetually reformulate a discursive field that was sensitive to both local events and geopolitical shifts that were endlessly incorporated into a growing textual repertoire. For refugees, the vagaries of camp life necessitated a similar search for meaning, but one that centered their plight as an important touchstone of international politics and tended to overestimate, if anything, the interest that global players ultimately had, for better or for worse, in their lives. As colonized subjects, Kakuma's refugees interpreted the world through local realities in the camp and imaginative frames that afford them some degree of "ontological surety" in a world that was otherwise full of speculation, hope, and existential fear.[92] "Living in uncertainty, having their symbolic order crumble due to violence and flight," Turner writes about refugees in Tanzania, "they attempted to create some sort of order through rumours."[93] The same could be said about Kakuma's residents whose lives might be on hold indefinitely and outside their control, but who refused to see themselves automatically as marginal actors in world affairs.

By inverting this gaze and seeing the camp through the eyes of officials administering it, we are made acutely aware of their attempts—and often heartfelt obligation—to create "order" where they suspect none exists. The moral condemnation of refugees was part of the same contiguous process of control as containment that imposed spatial restrictions on their mobility. This cultural text had far-reaching effects on the psychosocial lives of the encamped, influencing their encounters with those in charge of security, food, health, and social protection, fragmenting communities and corroding their collective sense of self-worth while inadvertently validating stereotypes by triggering socially unwanted coping strategies. The preoccupation of officials with upholding a virtuous sense of morality and fighting disorder was disconcerting not least because it contradicted equalizing tales of a "common humanity" that humanitarianism itself professed. We know well that humanitarian projects often fall short of these high-minded aspirations and in practice are wedded to the narrowly defined abstracted "human" subject who alone is considered worth saving.[94] As a result, the morally disagreeable lives of those ethnoracialized "others" excised from this category are devalued and stripped of their claims to compassion. For that reason, the cultural text I have described in the camp was not an aberration of, or even a departure from, humanitarian principles but, in fact, pointed toward their differential application and selective violence.

These insights force us to reconsider the texture of encampment as a material political technology alone. More than an assemblage of policemen and aid workers, of checkpoints and databases, permits and patrols, the camp's imaginative geography was at least as significant for policies of containment. During an interview, one nongovernmental organization worker summarized this circumstance quite well when he concluded: "At the end of the day, they are *just* refugees. *That's why* they are contained in a camp."[95] The specter of moral disorder was instrumental for rationalizing the enduring immobilization of refugees and, at the same time, conjured strikingly familiar colonial fears about contamination, ethnoracial violence, sexual desire, and social deterioration. Images and anxieties about these foreign refugee "others" circulated through conversations, innuendos, and casual remarks, making grand narratives about the world's moral geography a very intimate part of ordinary camp life. Kakuma camp was ultimately reimagined not only as stopping the "leakage" of immoral lifestyles but also as a space of moral probation where refugees learned to progress socially. The next chapter shows how this translated into granting provisional and partial responsibilities to refugees to govern their own "communities."

4

———

Community

In the afternoon of Friday, July 22, 2016, the sun was bearing down on us with more ferocity than usual. I had decided to join a community policing patrol scheduled to set off from a security office in Kakuma's South Sudanese–majority Equatoria Community.[1] Surrounded on all sides by residential compounds, the office block consisted of an administration building, a shaded meeting area under a *Prosopis* tree, and a makeshift cell. The small group of refugees on patrol duty that day gathered at the main office building, constructed from corrugated iron and mud bricks, wearing blue reflector vests emblazoned in large letters with the abbreviation "CPPT," for Community Peace and Protection Teams. The CPPTs were a community policing program funded by the United Nations High Commissioner for Refugees (UNHCR) and managed in the camp by the Lutheran World Federation (LWF). Although the CPPTs were supposed to be unarmed, some of their members were wielding crude batons and metal pipes. One was holding an archaic-looking club with rusty nails protruding at the end.

Lucy, a stout forty-plus-year-old South Sudanese woman, was in charge of this motley crew of Didinga, Acholi, Lopit, Lotuko, Dinka, Nuer, Tennet, and Somali refugees clad in light-blue uniforms, ready to comb through this neighborhood of the camp in search of drug users, thieves, and "suspicious characters."[2] As a young woman in the early 2000s growing up in a poverty-stricken border town, where jobs were hard to come by, Lucy joined the Sudan People's Liberation Army (SPLA) in pursuit of a stable career, respect, and a better life. But only a few years passed before she abandoned the SPLA and fled to Kakuma, marking the beginning of an unsettled life, moving back and forth several times across the border as the fortunes of newly independent South Sudan waxed and waned. Even in exile, Lucy retained her soldierly composure and fostered the commanding tone she had acquired during her youth in the rebel army. She was no stranger to harsh discipline or drill and could easily join the banter with the military men around her. When the LWF first recruited refugees who would be willing (and able) to help police Kakuma camp, Lucy volunteered, sensing both an opportunity to make a living and use her training for the good of "the community."

Wherever the gaze of humanitarian organizations could not reach, they resorted to hiring refugee staff as their "eyes and ears." The CPPTs were expected to report security incidents, control crowds during sports matches and food distribution, settle petty disputes, and act as intelligence gatherers for the Kenyan police. By September 2016, the LWF had enlisted more than 330 people into the program—roughly one CPPT officer for every six hundred ordinary camp residents.[3] For several years, Kenya's government itself had been eyeing CPPTs as potential proxies to support its security and counterterrorism operations among refugees. By virtue of being embedded in camp neighborhoods, able to translate the foreign languages spoken in mosques, markets, and churches, and often desperate for a shred of authority, community police members had become an invaluable human resource.

The state's growing interest in the CPPTs coincided with the countrywide rolling out of Nyumba Kumi, another community policing initiative specifically designed to delegate responsibility for information gathering and surveillance in the fight against terrorism and crime to ordinary Kenyan citizens (*wananchi*). If Nyumba Kumi diffused police power among the citizenry—making it felt in every aspect of their lives—then the CPPTs extended this logic to camps such as Kakuma, where the close-knit social fabric of refugees rendered the grip of state authority even more tenuous. In effect, the "community" was touted as the preferred terrain on which security and protection work should be realized. Inside the camp, where a multiethnic and culturally diverse population lived under the joint carceral care of the UNHCR and the Kenyan state, community policing was developed into a technology of government: an instrumental vehicle for reorganizing violence work through, and ostensibly in the interest of, local residents.[4]

Despite channeling exceptional powers into a demarcated space of institutional control, camps are typically home to a multiplicity of formal and informal institutions, dynamics, social logics, and everyday sovereignties.[5] Due to this heterogeneity, they also abound with educational and social programs that target refugees as objects of reform, rehabilitation, and governmental control. This makes community both the scale of existing sociality and a domain onto which particular ideologies are projected to help manage displaced populations.[6] If refugees are considered "unruly" quasi-colonial subjects to be tamed, then the level of community is the key battleground where their "hearts and minds" are to be won. In Kakuma, this involved actively enrolling *wakimbizi* into everyday camp governance by way of democratic elections, civic education, human rights trainings, peace-building programs and, not least, community policing schemes through which they would, it was anticipated, learn to conform to the prescribed institutionalized conducts that over time had congealed into a kind of "camp governmentality." In theory, refugees were to be molded in the image of lofty principles such as liberal democracy, gender equality, humanitarian compassion, free market capitalism, crime control, and counterextremism while preparing for the day when they would stand on their own feet once again. This place-based governmentality was, in a Foucauldian sense, an eclectic ensemble of logics, procedures, techniques, institutions, and programs geared to ensure the smooth running of the camp, which meant trying to regulate minutely the personal conduct of refugees.[7] Camp residents were expected to live up to the conditions and behavior that "orderly" encampment required of them, although this did not preclude their frequent refusal to conform.

It might therefore be tempting to see the governmental mobilization of the "community" as another way to scale back state control, divest from public services, or even devolve enforcement powers to refugees. As scholars have done, we might conclude that governing the camp "through community" follows a distinctly neoliberal logic, in which bonds forged through kinship, labor solidarity, mutual aid, and shared social status are dissolved into a community of individuals as entrepreneurs of their own existence.[8] While this may indeed offer cues for analyzing current aid policies that emphasize self-reliance, choice, and liberal empowerment, there is potency to the idea that this camp governmentality—and community policing specifically—has unmistakable roots in colonial technologies of indirect rule that are repurposed in the present.

As I demonstrate in this chapter, community policing in Kakuma was an attempt to achieve multiple contradictory aims: localize the levers of humanitarian protection, domesticate existing autonomous justice systems, and harness the dense social networks of refugees in the service of Kenya's expanding security state. Community policing therefore came in two parallel guises: as a liberal technology of government that in theory hinged on the *limitation of force and democratic self-regulation*, and as a more illiberal colonial technology of proxy rule based on *discipline and violence* against "dangerous" subjects deemed unworthy of restraint.[9] By examining the relationship between community-level governance and humanitarian colonization, we begin to understand Kakuma camp as a hybridized space in which colonial and (neo)liberal methods of postcolonial rule were fused over decades, opening up fault lines around questions of authority, sovereignty, and the nature of humanitarian power. Finally, while aid and state agencies espoused competing visions of how the "community" should be mobilized, refugees were pushing against this governmental control, at times below and often above the surface, with homegrown forms of counterorganization that arose from a loosely structured and more fractured "deep community."

A Genealogy of Indirect Rule

The notion of community-based or decentralized refugee governance is hardly new. For years, humanitarian agencies and advocates have stressed the need to "localize" protection activities, foster "participatory" decision-making tools to enhance the local legitimacy of aid, and create room for specifically "refugee-led" solutions.[10] Refugee communities, living in camps as well as in cities, have often been framed as convenient surrogates who are able to strengthen the humanitarian system—arguably "from below"—not least by availing themselves as "first and last providers of protection."[11]

Seeing the inklings of neoliberalism in this trend is valid insofar as sustained budget cuts have created an institutional push to communize the costs of social protection by inadvertently increasing reliance on remittances, kinship networks, and self-improvement while inhibiting genuinely democratic accountability. The UNHCR and its nongovernmental organization (NGO) partners have pursued this agenda more or less explicitly, following the changing tides of global refugee policy that resulted in the Global Compact on Refugees and the

Comprehensive Refugee Response Framework (CRRF). At the core of these plans, and of others that preceded them, lies a liberal politics of responsibilization and self-reliance that aims to create "self-governing" refugee subjects and, accordingly, develop "camps into spaces of community and skill-building."[12] Late liberalism, arguably, promoted the decline of "the social" as a category of collective organization in favor of "the community" as a heterogeneous, disjointed and, ultimately, more governable domain.[13] The community, we may surmise, always acts as an ambivalent force: It can be the glue that binds its constituent networks together or the very medium that casts social relations into a rigidly predefined mold. Akin to how ideas of democratic citizenship have shaped the governance of liberal society, invoking *the community* as the most relevant scale of camp administration is less about solving problems than prescribing a strategy of government.[14]

Beyond the charge of neoliberalization, in what Suzan Ilcan and Kim Rygiel call "resiliency humanitarianism," refugee camps in Africa offer additional insights for analyzing the theory and practice of localization as communitization through the longue durée of colonial forms of indirect rule that persist on the continent.[15] Camps are rarely managed in line with the self-defined needs of refugees; instead, they are managed according to "supralocal understandings of local needs."[16] This means, in practice, that aid agencies and the state construct a fictive alignment between their own governmental priorities and the aspirations of their refugee subjects. This conjuncture between a moral paternalism and political supremacy over the lives of camp dwellers has given further credence to refugees as colonized subjects who are "not perceived to be fit to enjoy the full rights of citizenship."[17] In the context of Kakuma, this genealogy of "the community" as a technology of indirect rule brings into view the ways in which humanitarian colonization hitherto has been able to unfold. Far from authority being redistributed, communities were continually colonized and *remade* to fit the logics of encampment that emphasize social uplift, moral probation, and perpetual apprenticeship for refugees that, in turn, echoed the auxiliary power of colonial-era "native administrations."

In the early twentieth century, Europe's colonization of Africa shifted from a conquest model fueled by its hunger for resources and land, and legitimized by the racist "civilizing mission," to a phase of power consolidation. There was little doubt that long-term occupation of territories on the continent was financially costly and required sizable deployments of colonial administrators on the ground. Further, colonized Africans were resistant to the imposition of external rule and could, arguably, be governed more efficiently if political authority was at least partly vested (if only nominally) in already established political systems. Based on earlier experiments in India and Natal, the British championed such an approach to colonialism that, "rather than building from the ground up wholly new forms of government in colonized territories," saw European colonial sovereignty "layered atop existing indigenous institutions."[18] Shortly after becoming independent from Britain in 1910, the Union of South Africa sent a fact-finding mission to the United States to learn from its experiments to confine Indigenous peoples in nominally self-governing, but de facto dependent, "reservations."[19] The roots of "native reserves" on the continent, or what would later become South Africa's "Bantustans," are therefore to be found in global knowledge transfers in colonial technologies of rule. Lord Frederick Lugard, however, was ultimately credited as the principal architect and proponent of this system that became widely known as "indirect rule." As the governor of Northern Nigeria (1914–19), Lugard assumed the mantle of a colonialist humanitarian who, through "pacification" campaigns, aimed to root out Indigenous "despotism" and the slave trade while breaking the anti-British spirit of those who resisted colonization. His vision of colonialism was that of paternalistic protectionism, not unlike similar sensibilities that survive in humanitarian operations today. By thwarting genuine political autonomy among Africans, indirect rule rested on the belief that it was the task of Europeans "to conserve what was good in indigenous institutions and assist them to develop on their own lines."[20] This created a blueprint for many later forms of racial apartheid. Only by authorizing *certain* institutions and individuals, and disempowering *others*, could the colonial state ensure that its interests were lastingly secured.

In any case, colonial administrators retained a final say over decisions taken by "native administrations." Europeans conceived of colonialism as a fiduciary duty to prevent supposedly "despotic" powers being accumulated in the hands of self-minded African rulers. In Lugard's own writing, he leaves no doubt as to where the ultimate sovereignty of the colonial state should lie—namely, in the hands of Europeans—even if its influence was to be exercised with caution to preserve a veneer of "native" legitimacy.[21] That said, indirect rule formalized the kinds of local arrangements that colonizers had always drawn on when deputizing African *askaris* (soldiers), interpreters, cultural brokers, and intermediaries, without whom colonization was impossible to realize.[22] Although these liminal professions held little official power, their occupants were able to accrue relative social status and authority in their own localities and thus functioned as "hidden linchpins of colonial rule."[23] When the multiple layers of racial civilizationism woven into indirect rule as a technology of power are peeled back, a simple political disappearing trick lies at their core that could "costume an act of state coercion as an independent expression of community sentiment."[24]

In his landmark book *Citizen and Subject*, Mahmood Mamdani theorized the growth of indirect rule as the bifurcation of the colonial state into a "European" and a "native" sphere, in which modern (white) urban "citizens" and colonized (Black) African rural "subjects" were to be governed by different laws, each according to their own station within the colonial hierarchy. African customary laws not only acted to "localize" European domination but were thought of as a means to "guide" the colonized along a developmental ladder toward modernization. Europeans overwhelmingly relied on local tools of administrative repression to enforce colonial laws, safeguard supplies of labor, and oversee the day-to-day workings of the state bureaucracy through what Mamdani calls "decentralized despotism." By flattening the differences among variegated political traditions, colonial anthropology meanwhile elevated chieftaincies to be the only legitimate rulers over "tribal" societies. Where colonial officials could not find the type of African institutions they required, they simply resorted to manufacturing them; but where they did exist, they were to "be re-created or modified to align with colonial interests and agendas."[25] In Kenya, a series of "Native Authorities" ordinances formalized the role of the "chief" as the lead African administrator in each location in Kenya after 1902. While chiefs received only meager salaries, they were vested with the symbolic prestige of the colonial state that tasked them with tax collection, public order maintenance, labor discipline, and the administration of "justice" to those living under their tutelage.[26]

By tying each colonized subject by default to a "tribe" and a "chief," the European colonial state not only reconfigured political orders but altered the very ground of African subjecthood. Mamdani notes how the prescriptive nature of "custom" progressively restructured the contours of the "tribe" as a "more or less self-contained community" that was acting to some degree autonomously but not independently of the colonial state. "Encased by custom, frozen into so many tribes, each under the fist of its own Native Authority," he writes, "the subject population was, as it were, containerized."[27] In this way, Africans were not only excluded from citizenship proper, but indirect rule actively negated alternative Indigenous claims to "community" that exceeded a subordinate identity. It was a moving relation of power organized around governmental control that aimed to decentralize violence work, mask colonial power, colonize the minds of African subjects, and enlist them into the machinery of their own subjection. This left the colonized with only simulated responsibilities: They were allowed to perform certain roles as part of native administrations but always remained necessarily fixed in a subsidiary position devoid of independent authority.

Decentralizing Violence Work in Kenya

During the Kenya Emergency (1952–60), native administrations set up "home guards" as loyalist community defense forces against the insurgents of the Kenya Land and Freedom Army (the so-called Mau Mau). In the process, the idea of community was increasingly weaponized as home guards became the African faces of a violent colonial campaign to brutalize, encamp, and detain their kith and kin as would-be insurgents.[28] Violence work had always also been the domain of "native" soldiers, or *askaris*, given the vast areas that colonizers had to administer and the notoriously scarce resources available for it (see chapter 2). Appointed by colonizers to enforce foreign laws, these surrogate troops were paradoxically "both wielders and subjects of colonial power" and embodied a double bind of colonization: the European dependence on recruits from among the colonized to administer, conquer, and punish.[29] This militarized caste of "violent intermediaries" was at the front line of colonial order making, equipped with a "flexible combination of linguistic facility, literacy, local knowledge, and of course, the ability to threaten and use violence."[30]

Soon after independence, the home guards were disbanded and partially integrated into what became the Administration Police. But community-based violence work continued to exist in the form of the Kenya Police Reserves (KPR), originally a white settler vigilante organization that was later turned into a proxy force for policing the rural peripheries, as well as a cacophony of unaffiliated local self-defense groups such as the Sungusungu.[31] Since the 1990s, however, community policing has become a formalized paradigm for organizing local anti-crime activities throughout Africa in tandem with the state. At this juncture, it subsumed liberal reformist strategies and initiatives imported from Anglo-American contexts to improve police-public relations and foster accountability in the spirit of "democratic policing," especially in societies deemed "fragile" or "conflict-ridden."[32] This latest iteration of community policing was driven by a liberal desire to affirm links between formal security actors and local denizens, as well as to mend rifts among socially "fragmented" populations. In Africa, programs of this kind were a corollary of neoliberal policies infused with local sociocultural symbolism; importantly, they also formed a key "part of state repressive arsenals."[33]

As Kenya's political ground shifted, different forms of governing and policing "through community" took shape. Speaking to me in an interview, an official of the Independent Policing Oversight Authority (IPOA) was clearly exasperated that "community policing has had so many forms and faces that we aren't really sure anymore where the head and [where] the tail is."[34] Under the authoritarian regime of President Daniel arap Moi, "security committees" served as vehicles for the surveillance of citizens.[35] With the dawn of multi-party politics in the 1990s, the committees were mobilized by the incumbent government to retain its stranglehold on power. After defeating Moi in the 2002 elections, incoming President Mwai Kibaki promised a far more partici-patory policing approach and launched a National Community Policing Policy in April 2005, which was short-lived because both the police and the political elites were ill-disposed toward reforms.[36] In the aftermath of the 2007–8 post-election violence, community policing was revived to catalyze change in the security sector, despite its hitherto doubtful record.[37] New laws led to the proliferation of citizen-police forums throughout Kenya, which remained unimplemented even when Uhuru Kenyatta took office in 2013 and intro-duced Nyumba Kumi, yet another community policing scheme in which ten households form a local neighborhood security cluster.[38] In its 2015 guidelines for the Nyumba Kumi initiative, the government postulated that "it is incum-bent on citizens to participate in matters of their security not only as part of their civic duty but also in the spirit of patriotism to their country."[39] Illustrat-ing this nationalist drive was a promotional video released in 2014 with the slo-gan *Ulinzi unaanza na mimi, Ulinzi unaanza na wewe* (Vigilance starts with me, Vigilance starts with you) in which a beady-eyed President Kenyatta walks toward the camera and issues a warning to "terrorists, criminals, and thugs," who he urges to "run and hide, because there will be thousands of cameras and millions of pairs of eyes watching you."[40]

Despite these public relations efforts, Nyumba Kumi faced tremendous challenges because of low levels of public participation, insufficient funding, and the tendency of the authorities to "crush" citizen-led initiatives.[41] How-ever, its governmental value lay arguably less in its efficiency as an organizing platform than in its capacity to reinforce "security as an imagined community" in Kenya.[42] Especially *wakimbizi* and other ethnoracialized minorities were in this way at risk of being tarnished as a fifth column of terrorists and portrayed as a suspect community of outsiders. State-organized community policing played a significant role in cascading police powers into neighborhoods and in stoking popular fears about the presence of "foreigners," giving impetus to police operations that targeted those read as noncitizens across Kenya's urban centers and camps.[43] Mirroring the ways in which indirect rule reformulated African subjecthood during the colonial era, this postcolonial localization of

FIGURE 4.1. Makeshift cell at Equatoria Security Office in Kakuma 1, 2015. Photograph by the author.

policing sharpened the boundaries between rights-bearing *national citizens* and rightless *non-native subjects*. Humanitarian camps crystallized perhaps more clearly than other spaces how minoritized populations were subjected to systematic containerization through physical encampment and their sorting into ethnoracial communities to make them pliable for domination.

Community Rule in Kakuma

The wind lashed fine dust into our eyes as we approached a shallow ditch a few hundred meters from the last houses in Kakuma 4. The lifeless body of Lorot, one of many Turkana who came into the camp every day, had been dumped here the previous night. I was with Michael and Gai, two Nuer CPPTs working in this neighborhood. When we arrived, Lorot's corpse had already been removed by the police, leaving a hole and bloodstained sand as sole traces of his murder. We were joined by Michael and Gai's Kenyan supervisors and a CPPT I did not recognize but who introduced himself as Yual. For them the case was clear: Lorot must have been killed inside the refugee community and temporarily hidden in a well or a house, before being taken to this bushland around the camp under cover of darkness. "My name is Yual," said the third CPPT as he stepped closer. "Lorot was my best friend. I am shocked. We were eating together from one plate on most days. Unfortunately, we are still trying to follow up what has happened. I want to find the person who did this and—" At this point, Yual stopped, snapped his fingers, and gestured as if administering beatings to an imaginary criminal. Yet there was nothing left for Yual and the other CPPTs to do. The Kenya Police took over serious cases such as this, and the refugee officers often learned about the outcome only days later. Lorot's killer was never found, and the circumstances of his death remained shrouded in mystery.[44] "That is normal," Yual told me with frustration. "We do our best, but once it goes to the police, there is no justice for anyone."

Shortly after Kakuma was established in the 1990s, the LWF launched a community policing program called "refugee guards" to tackle crime in the camp. To learn about this early phase of security governance, I met with Selomon, a stocky and graying Ethiopian man who had lived in the camp for nearly twenty-five years. As he took a sip of *bunna*, Selomon recounted that in 1997 two refugee guards were allocated to each of the ethnically defined communities at the time—namely, Ethiopians, Somalis, Ugandans, Nuer, Dinka and Equatorians—in an effort "to maintain public order." According to him, Kenyan police presence was scant in those days, and refugees like him were frequently asked to "help out" with managing their own encampment, creating structures of "participatory confinement."[45] The UNHCR administered Kakuma at first by categorizing refugees such as Selomon into ethnic and national communities with which they identified on arrival. Each community was given a separate plot of land on which to settle, and that later shaped the contours of the nascent camp neighborhoods. In those early days, Selomon tells me, *wakimbizi* ran their own political administrations, so-called councils of elders, which convened to administer customary justice through "bench courts."[46] Likely because they lacked alternatives, aid agencies celebrated rather than penalized this regulatory plurality until the early 2000s, when this parallel justice system was banned due to concerns that the decisions taken could violate human rights standards or contradict Kenyan law. Unsurprisingly, the reputation of the refugee guards, who drew their legitimacy from the councils of elders, was infamous not least because they "often received inadequate training, and some of them were known to beat up other refugees with impunity."[47]

Meanwhile, Kenyan citizens were hired to supervise a small number of refugee guards under the auspices of community administrations. Until 2005, the LWF's Kenyan staff sometimes outnumbered the refugees they formally supervised, and it was the citizens who conducted most nightly patrols in partnership with the KPR. Since independence, the KPR had evolved into an unpaid paramilitary equipped by Nairobi with guns and ammunition to project state power in the rural peripheries, where official police presence was thin. The KPRs were established on the premise that the rural margins of Kenya, plagued by cattle rustling and banditry, could only be governed effectively by using local defense forces. Kenyan police often had ambiguous and strained relationships with both KPRs and refugee guards due to biases and favoritism that had taken shape through friendships, ethnic ties, or simply the dispensation of *kitu kidogo*.[48] Asked about this period, a senior police officer named Wekesa insisted that the refugee guards "were *actually* assisting, the[se] refugees were *actually* assisting in relaying information, but it reached a time when they wanted to take over the duties of the *real police*—our duties." Wekesa paused here and looked at me, seeking my affirmation, before continuing to explain, "If they arrest[ed] someone, they [usually] wanted to assume authority. So that became a form of extortion. But actually, they were giving us support and information."[49] It was telling that Wekesa emphatically distinguished between refugee guards and the "real" police, which spoke to an underlying fear of the Kenyan authorities that international aid agencies were actively cultivating parallel security structures among refugees that bypassed the state. As the camp grew in size, official crime rates expectedly soared, prompting the LWF to accelerate its recruitment of refugee guards in 2006.[50]

But the "camp community" remained a double-edged sword. While it could offer some form of diasporic belonging through communal resource distribution, kinship networks, and religious solidarities, it also risked reproducing forms of exclusion. Even though Selomon had foregrounded the positive qualities of a strong community through which refugees were able to retain their cultural identities and achieve safety in numbers, this disproportionately favored refugees like him who were overwhelmingly well connected, reasonably educated, and, usually, male. We know that camp inhabitants often draw strength from multiple communities that are simultaneously ethnonational, religious, or more situational in nature. But the ambivalence of these communities meant that they could equally become conduits that exacerbated existing power hierarchies, negating their benefits in creating belonging and safety and instead adding another layer of repression that was difficult to escape.[51] In this sense, community rule provided not a "solution" to the social problems of patriarchal oppression, social marginalization, and imposition of humanitarian government, but, in fact, simply displaced structural inequalities into a different, more local domain.

This became especially clear when aid agencies sought to co-opt community as a form of social and political life. In 2011, the UNHCR began to reform Kakuma's old identity-based governance structure as it advocated for greater democratization. The refugee camp was to be redivided into multiethnic "blocks" and "zones" to replace previous administrations based entirely on ethnic and national identity. All councils of elders were to be disbanded and to give way to block and zone leaders who would stand in democratic camp elections and were deemed more "inclusive" and attuned to the procedural expectations of humanitarians. This was in line with the UNHCR's long-standing efforts to transform the socialities of refugees by offering training in democratic governance and peace building as part of its Peace Education Program. Peace education was championed as a core humanitarian pedagogy that tended to prioritize harmony over social justice and was deployed in a variety of contexts as "a form of pacification."[52] As a governmental intervention in refugee environments, it aimed to "transform collectivist attitudes [and] wishe[d] to replace community enforcement with self-enforcement."[53] Indeed, peace rhetoric was still ubiquitous in Kakuma as part of a standard repertoire of measures that sought to prevent social fragmentation and conflict, appearing in the name of not only the LWF's Peacebuilding Unit but also a defunct Peace and Cultural Centre outside of town.[54] This liberal search for peace and democracy also prompted the UNHCR to draft a "constitution" for the camp in late 2011, which signaled a shift toward institutional capture of refugee-run governance structures and delegitimized any forms of unauthorized community leadership that defied this transition.[55]

Community policing was again made a priority in this restructuring of power. The country director of the LWF at the time explained that, because his NGO was responsible for community policing not only in Kakuma but also in the Dadaab camps, there was more at stake in the way that refugee guards were presented publicly. In Dadaab, refugee guards had faced more animosity from the general refugee population, and several of their members were killed or injured or resigned from duty within a short period of time.[56] The LWF felt compelled to boost the popular legitimacy of community policing, and in an attempt to display professionalism, it decided to rename the ill-reputed refugee guards CPPTs. Although the head of the LWF was adamant that the name change had improved the safety of his employees, there was little to suggest that it meaningfully changed negative perceptions of community-based violence work that refugees were recruited to do under the humanitarian banner.[57]

The UNHCR and its partner organizations rode the popular wave of crime-prevention programs that started to spread across Africa with the aim to anchor humanitarian protection directly "within communities."[58] Invoking "peace and protection" in the name of CPPTs was meant to signal the program's rooted-ness in humanitarian protectionism that underpins refugee encampment more generally. In a strategic paper, the UNHCR had argued that refugees "harbor a wealth of social and cultural traditions or religious practices, neighborhood associations, work experiences and political experience" that agencies should uti-lize.[59] The contemporary aid regime was using language that was analogous to that of the former colonial state that had justified carceral repression of colonized Africans with the aim to "protect" their customs and rights while ostensibly set-ting them on a path of progress and development. But colonial ideas were now interlaced with neoliberal principles that venerated economic efficiency, individ-ual responsibility, "community" rather than "the social" as a territory of govern-ment, and forms of self-regulation that did not require overt disciplinary force.[60]

Community policing became an experiment in which the UNHCR and the LWF could tap into the existing competencies of refugees to maintain public order almost effortlessly, at least in theory. Recruits such as Lucy and Selomon were cast as willing foot soldiers of the aid machinery, a new kind of *humani-tarian askaris*, tasked with minimizing disruptions to the camp operation, even as they faced the same limitations on their freedom as ordinary refugees. A large number of recruits, such as Lucy, had been employed by the military, po-lice, or rebel groups in their countries of origin and were eager to reuse those skills in exile. James, a South Sudanese CPPT, had been one of the personal bodyguards of John Garang, the legendary founding leader of the SPLA, and was redeployed to guard his mausoleum in Juba after the leader's death in a helicopter crash in July 2005. But the vast majority of CPPTs were simply look-ing for any opportunity to find work, without prior experience. In the course of expanding the ranks of the CPPTs, the very idea of community was nar-rowed to a vessel with innate cultural legitimacy that could be reconstructed and "fixed" to become conducive to humanitarian power. In contrast to the colonial era, however, community governance in twenty-first-century aid oper-ations was a more mundane affair. When CPPTs were not controlling crowds at sporting events, guarding schools, or patrolling during food distribution, they were mostly left to solve petty quarrels among refugees.

When I returned to the Equatoria security office, I saw that Lucy and her officers had detained two middle-aged mothers, their infants, and a teenage girl and were holding them in a makeshift cell. The two women, I was told, had been caught fighting at the water tap in the morning and had been arrested for disturbing the peace by a local CPPT named Mark. "We will try and solve the case here first," replied Mark when I asked what would become of the detainees, "and if that's not possible, we can refer it to the police, but that will depend on how willingly they cooperate." Mark unlocked the cell door and led the prisoners into a nearby room. It was small with mud-plastered walls and was outfitted with three long benches, a rickety table, and several notebooks. A CPPT duty schedule was pinned to the door. Speaking in Arabic Juba, the lingua franca in South Sudan's Equatorian states, Mark began first to record the women's names, ages, and ration card numbers, before he asked them, each in turn, to narrate their version of events. One of the women, Esther, had visited her friend Ruth the previous night. She had been drinking *chang'aa* and was inebriated when she arrived at Ruth's house and demanded that Ruth give her food. When Ruth refused, admonishing her friend for her drunkenness, an altercation broke out during which Ruth chased Esther away. But while leaving, Esther tripped and fell, incurring a minor injury to her right arm. When she returned to her home, she called her daughter and claimed that Ruth had caused the injury. Esther's seventeen-year-old daughter then rushed to Ruth's house, hurling insults at first and then stones in the belief that Ruth had abused her mother. The next morning, Ruth met Esther again at the communal water tap where refugees queue to receive their daily water ration. Ruth grabbed Esther's jerrycan and threw it at her, leading to a fistfight until bystanders intervened and called the community police. In the conversation, the CPPTs were able to piece this story together and urged the parties to settle the dispute amicably to avoid police involvement, which often resulted in more harm. Esther apologized for being drunk that first night, and her daughter expressed regret about having assaulted Ruth without knowing the full truth. After shaking hands, the two women were dismissed, and the case was closed.

While community policing promoted the idea of refugees' setting the security agenda, in reality this happened under close supervision by the LWF and, by extension, the UNHCR. The refugee agency claimed, using circular logic, that "working through community mechanisms enhances protection, and enhanced protection strengthens communities."[61] The CPPTs were placed in pseudo-managerial roles that were meant to consolidate the refugee community not as an autonomous form of social existence with a life of its own, but as what Michel Foucault has called a mechanism of security: a highly domesticated sociality forged in the image of institutional needs. The CPPTs were effectively simulating self-regulation and community protection, which was desirable only as long as it occurred within a narrow "field of action" delimited by humanitarian organizations.[62] Performing communal duties was part of the conduct of camp governmentality, but this did not mean that the CPPTs were always content with their role. When I brought this up with Nimco, a thirty-one-year-old Somali CPPT, she opened her eyes wide and exclaimed: "We are like goats to them [aid workers]. If we are called, we'll come. If not, we just stay where we are, in our blocks or at home waiting for instructions from above. I'll look for a different job soon. I don't see a purpose anymore."[63] Nimco was not alone in her disillusionment with this kind of local security work and the disdain she felt that not only agencies but also the general refugee population harbored toward the CPPTs. Many thought they were simply exploited for their labor to create safety "on the cheap" while being expected to show the highest level of ideological commitment to the cause of humanitarianism, despite being a precarious and underpaid refugee workforce.

This became evident when a meeting was called by the LWF's Youth Department to voice the agency's dissatisfaction with CPPTs during a recent soccer match. To make matters worse, a Kenyan staff member stood up and claimed that the CPPTs were not only shying away from coming to work but, even when they were present, they were sometimes drunk or chewed the stimulant *miraa* (khat). This enraged the CPPTs, most of all Celestine, a middle-aged Burundian woman who retorted, with fingers pointed at the LWF official, "My soul hurts a lot listening to what you're saying. I don't like that you are accusing us of not working. We work 24/7, and not everyone can go to these matches. Who will then guard the community?" While most of the men sat quietly through the meeting, Lucy also seized the opportunity to voice her frustration without mincing her words: "You have a lot of disrespect for us. For you there is nothing like 'thank you.' Your mouths are very bad" (*Midomo yenu ni mibaya sana*). This revealed the tensions that arose from the humanitarian attempt to micromanage community protection. Although a narrow definition of community was represented as the primary object of policing, it had little empirical foundation beyond the shared spaces in which refugees resided. Instead, strategic myths about the value and cohesion of "community" legitimized continuing tutelage from the aid agencies. Keeping this community under close supervision produced subjectivities that were not foreseen to have the capacity for autonomous decision making or responsibility. At a training session, a senior program manager for the LWF told CPPTs: "Sometimes people don't appreciate the work you do or realize that cases are being solved because of your work." Trying to spark a positive sense of togetherness between employer and employees, he then declared: "I want to emphasize that because of you, people see the LWF as a *big army* that is present in every corner of the camp." Ironically, the idea that the CPPTs were, indeed, a "big army" in the service of a higher humanitarianism was precisely the hallmark of this hollowed-out community, one that was reduced to being the "eyes and ears" of aid actors with limited accountability to their own refugee constituents. In this sense, the fear of the Kenyan police that humanitarian agencies were building parallel structures in the community was not far-fetched.

The CPPT uniforms of light-blue shirts and dark-blue trousers were material reminders not only of this governmental control but also of its contestation. Foucault famously theorized the uniform as a paradigmatic item through which governmentality is enacted on the body.[64] The CPPTs' clothes emulated Kenyan police uniforms as worn downcountry (though notably not in "operational areas" such as Turkana); however, they were issued by the LWF, paid for by the UNHCR, and intended to strengthen ties to the agencies. Police-style shoulder marks that differentiated among ranks were introduced to incentivize work ethics and a sense of career progression, instill discipline, and, above all, foster a sense of loyalty to the LWF.[65] Kenyan supervisors therefore reprimanded individual CPPTs for their unwillingness to wear uniforms, resulting in wrangles over authority and the minor politics of dress. Maryam, a young Somali CPPT explained:

> Maybe you arrive at work late and a Kenyan [supervisor] tells you, "Why have you done that? Don't you know that's wrong? You think we are here to laugh or entertain you? Do you know where your salary comes from?" You hear others telling you, "Why are you not wearing [your] uniform? [Do] you think this uniform was not bought with donor money?" But you fail to understand. You cannot spend the whole week in [one] uniform. The uniform is supposed to be washed, but you are simply told, "Wash it in the evening and wear it in the morning." It's undignified.[66]

Kenyan supervisors (CPPAs) were a key to the implementation of localized policing in Kakuma camp; officially, they ensured compliance with human rights and humanitarian principles, but more important, they were supposed to bring CPPTs "back in line," even when such efforts failed. Each CPPA was responsible for overseeing a security office in one zone of the camp, which was headed by a subordinated refugee supervisor. This doubling of responsibility was interpreted by the CPPTs as a lack of trust in their work and contributed to a lingering sense of frustration with excessive control. The CPPAs were often, whether rightly or wrongly, accused of arriving late at the office in the morning, taking attendance, and exiting the camp shortly after, leaving refugee staff to do the bulk of their daily tasks. During an LWF meeting, a South Sudanese CPPT named Nhial lamented, "If there is misconduct on the part of the LWF office we should also be able to blame the Kenyan national staff, not always us *wakimbizi*. We report to you, but you Kenyans are required to take action, too." Complaints such as this frequently reached the agency and were symptomatic of the built-in hierarchies of the camp operations. Although "local ownership" was a stated goal of community policing, the privileging of Kenyan staff, and the one-way accountability to the superstructure of aid organizations that sidelined local camp residents, put this logic in doubt.

In 2015, humanitarian agencies poured 52 million Kenya shillings ($500,000) annually into community policing in Kakuma.[67] But recruiting refugees as "employees" on the payroll of the LWF and the UNHCR was also a gamble. On the one hand, their average salary of 3,800 Kenya shillings ($38) a month offered a meager yet welcome income in addition to the free food rations given to every refugee. On the other, the transactional nature of this employment contravened claims to their "embeddedness" in the community and produced further friction over payments and duties, not least because the Kenyan supervisors, on average, earned no less than seven times more than refugees. It may seem ironic, then, that the LWF and the UNHCR have cultivated a kind of *ownership from above* through which they felt entitled not only to information from within communities but also to the loyalty of refugees. At one morning roll call, Ekai, a Kenyan supervisor, appealed to the CPPTs to honor this chain of command, emphasizing: "You have to report to the LWF. Remember that the police chief is not your boss. We are *not* employed by the government. We work for the LWF. Only if the case is serious, we call the police for reinforcement, but that's it."[68] Ekai's admonishment encapsulated the schizophrenic position in which the CPPTs often found themselves. As humanitarian *askaris*, they had to feign deference to their aid agency employers and, by extension, the donors who funded them; profess their staunch commitment to a prescribed but always elusive notion of "peace"; and perform a mock version of community that was more concerned with the needs of the aid regime than the protection of refugees.

State Proxies

Although the CPPTs were financed and administered by humanitarian actors, sustaining a workable relationship with Kenyan state authorities was critical. As early as 2014, Kenya's Department of Refugee Affairs (which later became the Refugee Affairs Secretariat [RAS]) assumed direct control over the CPPTs in the Dadaab refugee camps, and LWF officials sensed that it was but a matter of time until Kakuma followed suit, which it did not long after I finished my initial research.[69] If the government's wider promotion of Nyumba Kumi for counterterrorism was any indication, the refugee camps were considered linchpins where national security was at risk. But while Nyumba Kumi pitted citizens against external threats, especially from a suspect community of "foreign" refugees and migrants, community policing in the camps used refugees *themselves* to protect the Kenyan state. After unsubstantiated reports claimed that the Westgate and Garissa attacks were planned in Kakuma and Dadaab, respectively, the regime decided to build its networks of refugee informants. In broad strokes, this resembled the British government's counterterror Prevent initiative launched in 2006, which expected Muslim communities to self-police and conduct surveillance among friends, neighbors, and colleagues.[70] By virtue of their status, economic hardship, and limited freedom, the CPPTs were pressured by circumstance into becoming collaborators with a state that regarded them with collective suspicion. To rationalize this strategy, the authorities drew a perfunctory distinction between "real refugees" and "bad refugees" with which the CPPTs could selectively (and precariously) be included in Kenya's imagined security community, while at other times facing summary exclusion.[71] Reinforcing this sentiment, a security officer from Kenya's refugee affairs agency addressed a group of CPPTs and asserted:

> When you as refugees have problems, we also have problems. We are in this together. We know you have fled your countries for many reasons, and that your governments may send people to track you down even here in the camp. So, if you see someone who you suspect of being a foreign spy, hitman, or terrorist, please let us know. Not all refugees *are* refugees. We have to pray to God to give us maximum security.[72]

But policing the camp was based not just on commitments to human rights, democracy, peace, and self-regulation but also on more illiberal methods of control. Tension between the CPPTs and police led Kenyan supervisors to remind the CPPTs frequently of their "place" in the camp. One of them, David, beseeched the CPPTs to "please find a respectful way of talking to the police, even if they disrespect you. We are working for the LWF; the police work for the government. Who do you think has more power? The government, that's it!" David briefly paused and added, "You know how it works: Security *inaanza na wewe*," mimicking the Kenyatta government's security campaign slogan. But this was easier said than done, not least when the CPPTs themselves were targeted by security forces. David recognized this, and his admonition was meant

FIGURE 4.2. CPPTs on patrol in the dry Tarach River bed (*lagga*), 2015. Photograph by the author.

to prevent future conflicts with the police that had sometimes left the CPPTs ridiculed by local residents as powerless henchmen who could not protect even themselves. "When CPPTs are being caned by the police in front of other refugees, it gives a bad picture," David continued. "Who in the community will respect you after that? No one."

For Kenyan security actors, the distinction between friend and foe was blurry when it came to noncitizens who were thought to hold a grudge against the very state that not only meddled in regional politics, prolonging the conflicts that had caused them to flee, but also kept them encamped. Pierre, a Congolese CPPT, remembered a Kenyan intelligence officer addressing an LWF meeting that was called to discuss "the Somali question." The agent instructed CPPTs to relay any information they might have on fellow refugees—not least, Somalis, who were considered most prone to religious extremism. Pierre told me that he was frightened, knowing that Kenyan spies were likely everywhere and that anyone could be accused of terrorism. The intelligence officer, Pierre recalled, emphasized that if information was not forthcoming, the CPPTs would face severe consequences for their right to stay in Kenya: "We will come back, arrest the CPPTs who refused to give us information, close the camp and deport all of you immediately!"[73] This was no empty threat, as Kenya's Anti-Terrorism Police Unit (ATPU), which was notorious for having conducted dozens of extrajudicial killings of Muslim leaders in the country, arrested two Somali CPPTs on suspicion of supporting Al-Shabaab shortly after. Abducted from their homes at night by masked men and transported to Nairobi, the two suspects were held in a high-security jail and charged in Milimani High Court for terrorism. One them was the seniormost CPPT in Kakuma, a fiercely outspoken man called Sharmaake, who commanded tremendous respect in the camp. Although the prosecution had little evidence of his wrongdoing, Sharmaake was forced to accept a deal and pay 300,000 Kenya shillings ($3,000) for the charges to be dropped, allowing him eventually to return to Kakuma and resume his position as refugee leader of the community policing program.[74] Many CPPTs were likewise forced into impossible in-between positions that put them in constant fear of "double stigmatization"—namely, being treated simultaneously as "suspects" by Kenyan authorities and as loyalist "government spies" by fellow refugees.[75]

Community rule in Kakuma thus contradicted the notion that refugee camps today are increasingly managed through liberal governmentality alone. Kenyan authorities, in fact, often capitalized on securitizing refugees as enemies of the state to secure their own hegemony over the camp's policing operations. Humanitarian visions of CPPTs as a "big army" for democratic governance, protection of human rights, and peace building were therefore called into question by the constant possibility of state interference, criminalization, threats of violence, and expulsion of refugees from Kenya. The liberal imagination has never conceived of "dangerous" colonized subjects, as opposed to rights-bearing citizens, as equally deserving persons but, instead, coerced them into submission.[76] Uniformed refugees in Kakuma were therefore deployed as state proxies at the behest of Kenyan police to arrest fellow refugees and extort money, and they embodied this contemporary iteration of "decentralized despotism." Their standing with ordinary refugees suffered, as they were seen as enacting violence for the Kenyan state.

Some CPPTs received threats from neighbors for passing information to the LWF, the UNHCR, or the police. Maryam, a Somali CPPT in her early twenties, had reported her neighbor's children, who had accidentally shattered the windows of a parked NGO vehicle while playing. When the police arrived, she remembered, they simply "beat up the children until they admitted who was guilty; then it was concluded that their mothers had to repay the damage. It was awful." Maryam was distraught and had second thoughts about her role as a CPPT because ordinary refugees distrusted her and threatened her with retaliation. "Whenever I go to the market," Maryam said, "these people stare at me and say, 'This lady is bad. She can have our children arrested. Let's show her that we can hurt her, too.'"[77] An Acholi colleague of Maryam's, Rebecca, experienced similar threats. After doing her duty to organize the queues at food distribution, her neighbors felt wronged by her actions and started to insult her as a "whore" and a "spy" whom they did not want to see near their homes. When she returned home, one of her neighbors appeared at her house, slapped her, spat in her face, and said, "Now you are here, but wait until we get back to South Sudan. I'll kill you."[78]

Viewed in this light, the CPPTs were not so much an initiative to cultivate horizontal cohesion among refugees or a strategy of localizing humanitarian protection as a vehicle for violence work that reinforced a hierarchical dependence on the Kenyan state. To uphold this dependence, Kenya's RAS decided to cleanse the ranks of CPPTs from what were considered "disloyal elements" through a vetting exercise that began in 2017.[79] Many CPPTs feared that "vetting" was no more than an attempt to handpick the most compliant individuals who did not "rock the boat" at a time when Kenya was keen to accelerate voluntary refugee repatriations to Somalia. Yet even with this looming threat, aid workers from the UNHCR and the LWF seemed more worried about their own waning influence over security funding than the erosion of refugee protection. A senior LWF administrator in Kakuma warned regretfully that the government was "now setting the stage for fully absorbing the CPPTs, and that'll be it for us. We'll be pushed out."[80]

Deep Community

One afternoon, I found myself in a dimly lit and smoke-filled establishment located just off one of Kakuma's markets. A beaded curtain hid the muddy steps that led down into this makeshift bar that was filled with short tables and plastic chairs. I had stumbled on this place by accident while trying to shelter from the bustle of motorbikes, hawkers, and marketgoers outside. Those who wished to hide from the prying eyes of their pious relatives, friends, and the police could find sanctuary in this den, where no judgment would be cast. Once my eyes had adjusted to the dark, I could see that the place was peopled with "outcasts"—women and men indulging in gambling, secret dates, and drinking. My accidental intrusion felt voyeuristic but also intimate, as it gave me a glimpse of the camp's underbelly. As I settled down, a bulky Somali man dressed in a *macaawis* (sarong) approached me with a broad smile. "I'm Big Fish," he announced, "but many call me 'Big Man in a small house' because I've been in this refugee camp for too long." Big Fish seemed like a larger-than-life character, loudmouthed and fueled by illicit *chang'aa*. He described himself as a "survivor of aid" who had lived through war, bereavement, inadequate food, and police brutality. When I explained what had brought me to the camp, including my interest in policing and security, he laughed. Looking around the room at his audience, Big Fish stepped onto one of the tables, raised his hands up high, and screamed, "Ah, there are so many *wonderful* rules in this camp, but 70 percent of refugees don't follow them at all. The other 30 percent occasionally try." His performance, and the underground venue in which it was staged, showed that something smoldered beneath the camp's surface, an undiminished dignity that neither heavy policing nor stricter rules could undo. Big Fish's gallows humor in the face of encampment, and his determination not to take it seriously, were expressions of this defiant spirit that rehumanized those whom Kakuma held captive for so long.

This subtle defiance also surfaced from within the two competing visions of community policing imposed on camp residents. Like any technology of government, community policing in Kakuma generated "practices that form in, around, through or against the plan."[81] Less institutionally scripted, these actions were intrinsically pluralistic and incongruous and followed not one logic but a diversity of logics. Whereas aid agencies subscribed to a particular myth of community most serviceable to their administrative needs, and Kenyan authorities clung to the notion of refugees as an exploitable "suspect community," miscellaneous forms of counter-organization emerged in the cracks of these top-down governance strategies and that I here conceptualize as the "deep community." Not cohesive in a meaningful sense, this loosely structured community, if it can be described as such, was made up of a mosaic of customary and religious authorities, business networks, kin relations, exile organizations, savings societies, and "liminal experts" who were the authors of practices that manipulated and diverted local policing efforts from their institutionally prescribed path.[82] Speaking of a deep community is hence a convenient catchall for different sites of counter-conducts in which the idea of a unified "refugee community" was contested and instead gave way to the vicissitudes of a more uncontainable expression of camp life.

Tom, a Nuer CPPT in his mid-forties, embodied these overlapping forms of social organization exceptionally well. Like many of his compatriots, he had been an SPLA soldier before escaping the war to Kenya. In addition to being a CPPT supervisor, he was a respected Nuer elder, an evangelical pastor in a local church, and a private counselor for family matters. When I first met Tom, he had recently been at the center of a scandal involving the Nuer council of

FIGURE 4.3. CPPTs at the reception center in Kakuma 3, 2015. Photograph by the author.

elders, which continued to exist even after it had been stripped of its official status by the UNHCR. Tom had accused the elders of sponsoring a Kakuma chapter of the Sudan People's Liberation Movement–In Opposition (SPLM-IO), Riek Machar's rival faction that was fighting President Salva Kiir's incumbent government at the time. He subsequently reported the council to the Kenyan criminal investigations police to make them aware of potential "rebel activity" in the camp but then used this opportunity to consolidate his own power base among Nuer residents. Though going on patrol with him risked embroiling me in this scandal by association, it gave me a sense of how inseparable his multiple roles were. Depending on who we encountered, people amiably addressed Tom as "commander," "counselor," or "pastor," while yet others preferred to call him by his given Nuer name. He carried these roles as he strode through the camp, blurring whose authority he was acting under at any given time.

The LWF obligated the CPPTs to ensure that community policing remained a locally grounded peacemaking endeavor but also set limits on what *kinds* of justice and enforcement it deemed acceptable. Despite the official ban on traditional "bench courts," and attempts to diminish the influence of "councils of elders," CPPTs had gradually assumed some of their responsibilities and even employed former bench court personnel as their own. Tom explained:

The cooperation between CPPTs and the Nuer council of elders is very close. If we get a case that belongs to the elders, like adultery, which is not punishable by law in Kenya, we call upon customary law and hand the suspects over to the elders. If a person does not want to listen to us in the [CPPT] office, we work together with the elders and the parents and ask them, "Come and see the way your child has behaved in the office here: Is this the way you should behave?" If the accused still does not understand, we can also take them to the police, so that they will eventually come back [to the community] as a normal person.

Despite the official delegitimization of customary justice, it remained CPPT policy to refer noncriminal cases to councils of elders that sometimes claimed jurisdiction beyond this. Given our knowledge on everyday policing across African societies, it is not entirely unexpected that existing social-ordering practices should mediate external governmental programs in Kakuma in such a way. A thirty-five-year-old South Sudanese man named Riek, dressed in an official CPPT uniform, explained why he thought bench courts should continue to be in charge of administering justice even in criminal cases such as rape, instead of relying on the Kenyan police and justice system, which many people regarded as inefficient, biased, and broken:

Maybe a girl has been impregnated or raped. After arrests are made, [the elders] sit down and hear the case, because whenever we would forward those cases to the police, nothing would be solved. So the bench court is there to reduce hatred between communities, to ensure dialogue and compensation. Whenever people were arrested, they would sit down, agree, and compensate one another.

The way Riek and Tom navigated their respective in-between positions as CPPTs and members of their local communities illustrates the kind of acumen and social skills they developed under occupation. Ethnoreligious networks often unsettled the procedural, nonpartisan conducts that the LWF and the UNHCR prescribed. This became especially clear while I was spending time with CPPTs in an ethnically diverse security office. One day, an elderly Somali man came into the office and inquired about one of the Somali supervisors, Ali. The CPPTs on duty that day were a young Nuer man, along with a Burundian woman and a Congolese woman, who rebuffed him with the words, "This is not Ali's personal office. It's the security office. If you have a problem, we can receive you, too." Angered at this, the man insisted on returning the following day for a second attempt to see Ali. Once he had left, Feza, the Congolese

CPPT, explained that this kind of pick-and-choose behavior was a common occurrence in their office. Their two refugee supervisors, Ali and Barre, were known to interpret the rules of their work quite liberally, often bypassing procedures if a case demanded it. "When they get cases, it's only in their language [Somali]," Feza said, "and then they disappear with the clients into a back room or their own homes." The Nuer CPPT agreed with this and deplored that his colleagues were secretive when they handled cases. "Once they take over a case," he told us, "they just solve it here and there, without any traces or written records."[83]

Although community policing functioned as a reinvention of indirect rule, it was always contested and demonstrably limited. However, we know that any plan introduced into the social world, despite contestation, necessarily changes it.[84] It is therefore too easy to dismiss the two competing technologies of government in Kakuma as simply failing at managing social dynamics. In fact, like many localized forms of rule on the continent, CPPTs often explicitly drew on the financial resources and symbolic capital of the Kenyan state or international aid agencies to legitimize their actions while also distancing themselves from them when necessary.[85] The language and symbols of humanitarian governmentality were incorporated into prevailing social repertoires and daily practices without fully determining them. Thus, community policing in Kakuma was not simply an organizational shell furnished with practices that contradict their original intent; it has equally produced new hierarchies, relationships, and sources of symbolic authority that redefined the camp order. For instance, business associations or market committees sometimes harnessed the symbolism of CPPTs for their own purposes. The Ethiopian wholesaler Mesfin, who had become famous through global news coverage as the camp's dollar millionaire, employed CPPTs to guard his property at night and had personally funded the construction of a security office in the Ethiopian market, thus blurring the lines between privatized security and humanitarian-sponsored protection of "the community" as a public good.[86]

The Kenyan state's vision of local security governance, in contrast, was less concerned with imparting a set of idealistic goals toward which refugees would aspire than with imposing discipline and strengthening state control. Yet, counterintuitively, this command structure animated CPPTs to defy institutional attempts to dictate their conduct even more. Pierre, who had been threatened with deportation if he failed to act as a state informer, remained steadfast in the face of intimidation. He looked at me defiantly and asked, "How can you report something to someone who threatens you like that? It's simple. You don't, because you cannot trust them, and that's the issue." The CPPT program therefore had limited success in mobilizing refugees for counterterrorism or protecting other state interests. The CPPTs had no incentive to cooperate with security forces beyond getting short-term personal gains because they remained, above all, precariously included in Kenya's security community and felt their own disposability. Omitting information, bypassing procedures, and defying orders could sometimes be tactics to save one's own life. Abdelhaq, a Somali CPPT, recalled that a police officer once complained to him that "the CPPTs aren't working hard enough, even though there is Al-Shabaab in the camp, and [they] just aren't telling us." Abdelhaq was proud to have challenged the officer on that day: Eyeing the Kenyan officer, Abdelhaq had straightened his posture and replied, "I cannot tell you whether I see Al-Shabaab [in the camp], because you take bribes, and tomorrow you might say that I myself was a terrorist all along. I can't risk it. I value my life."[87]

This disobedience manifested differently across Kakuma. The Ethiopian market was a walled-off area with its own community-run gates, a camp within the camp, notorious for its lively business activities and two popular bars: Red Hotel and Electric.[88] After curfew, Kenyan policemen would sometimes knock on the gates and demand entry, as the bars also attracted sex workers and drugs. Bekele, an Ethiopian CPPT, told me that he refused them entry once, knowing that allowing the police to enter would mean trouble. "Don't worry; we'll call you if we need assistance," he told the officers through the locked gate before wishing them a good night. Even when the police officers protested, reminding Bekele of his position, he stood his ground and said, "Please don't come again. We don't need your services. Why do you disturb us at night without good reason?"[89] Similar acts of refusal were not uncommon among CPPTs and epitomized a fractious sense of obligation toward communities that lay deeper than those prescribed by aid actors or the state. Like indirect rule generally, community policing was here precariously "layered atop" existing social institutions in a balancing act among the interests of aid organizations, the Kenyan state, and the refugees who were recruited to perform violence work on their behalf. This left the community as unstable terrain where governmental control touched down among refugees to enforce compliance, but where it also inevitably provoked everyday acts of refusal.

Protecting the System

My shadowing of Lucy's patrol with her CPPTs in Kakuma 1 went by without major incidents, save for a few warnings they issued for public drunkenness. "We need to show ourselves, walk around the blocks regularly so that people see we're around," Maryam whispered to me as we traversed the *lagga*. "But honestly," she continued, "we rarely encounter crime unless someone brings it to our attention. Patrols like this are mostly for show." Indeed, there was an internalized belief in "broken windows" policing, whereby the slightest signs of social disorder had to be dealt with decisively to discourage spiraling further crime.[90] But because of this punitive outlook on society, the idea that community policing strengthened democratic participation of refugees in protection appeared even more questionable. The LWF and the UNHCR tried to convince donors of their credentials in refugee-led protection, although they promoted an image of "community" that reproduced liberal conceptions of empowerment, self-regulation, and human rights rather than considering the needs of residents. Likewise, the state sought to use community-based security to filter compliant (or "good") refugees, some of whom would help to police the camp, from those it deemed dangerous and who might threaten national security. In both cases, community was a malleable foil through which institutionalized power could be expressed locally and that, in a sense, containerized the independent social forces of refugees. When I asked Maryam about the purpose of her work, she made no effort to hide her disillusionment: "Of course, we sometimes make peace in the community, but on the whole, we are protecting the people in UNHCR, LWF, and those in the government. We are protecting the system."

Maryam articulated the inner contradictions of community policing as a way to secure a system that considered people disposable pawns. If we understand indirect rule as a recurring relation of power that is not transfixed in history but continues to act in the world today, then the camp is one of the spaces where it is most pronounced. In Kakuma, essentialized ideas about ethnonational identity and liberal notions of community as a civic "force for good" converged and set the stage for community-based governmental interventions. A key parallel between indirect rule generally and community policing were their built-in hierarchies in which violence ultimately was imagined to be delegated "downward" to the street level while local legitimacy flowed "upward" in return. During a meeting at a UNHCR office, Kakuma's RAS camp manager conveyed this dynamic well when addressing refugee leaders: "Your mother is UNHCR, your father is the Government of the Republic of Kenya. You must respect your parents!"[91] Focusing on the mutable object of the community also complicates our grasp of humanitarian colonization by revealing how its structures of domination are not only inevitably partial and shot through with contestation, refusals, and resistance but are also *facilitated* by those who collaborate with power, often for their own survival. Community rule put some *wakimbizi* in a position to benefit from occupation, while others worked through its cracks to manipulate its local effects. The presence of a deep community therefore did not just delineate the limits of official authority but validated the urgency felt by those in charge of the camp to domesticate or ban autonomous forms of grassroot organizing among the encamped.

The forays of community policing into Kakuma can also tell us something about indirect rule as a general political technology of governing the poor, the colonized, and the displaced. Thinking about the camp as a colonized space makes us question the meanings of the term *community*—not only its pitfalls in reproducing violence, but also its transformative potentials that frequently remain unfulfilled. Indirect rule always cuts both ways, and despite large quantities of resources being expended in the interest of consolidating power, it opens up an unpredictable space of possibility. In Kakuma and elsewhere, community rule was not a local "fix" to the diminished legitimacy of a political order. Instead, it intervened irreversibly in particular social worlds by reformulating the grounds on which subjecthood and community rested, thus colonizing not only a stretch of land on which refugees could settle but also reconfiguring their bonds of kinship, identity, and belonging. This, in turn, exacerbated and brought to the fore various forms of extractivism in the camp, which is the focus of the next chapter.

5

———

Extraction

It is easy to forget the logistical feats that large relief operations require. While aid programs in cities can make use of parts of the existing urban infrastructure, remote camps such as Kakuma are usually more cut off from established transport routes, communication lines, and public service networks. The A1 Highway, which was once the main artery for aid destined to reach Kenya's troubled northwestern neighbor during Operation Lifeline Sudan (1989–2005), has also become vital for the upkeep of thousands of refugees in Kakuma since the camp was opened some three decades ago. On a dusty afternoon, I sat in the office of the Refugee Affairs Secretariat, where Kakuma's camp manager leaned back in his leather chair and explained to me that the resource question was central to the planning of both the government and the United Nations High Commissioner for Refugees (UNHCR). "Land has become very expensive and competitive," he told me as we sat facing each other at his large and shiny mahogany desk. "Acquisitioning land for camp expansion to house more refugees may become a challenge soon, but other resources are equally scarce. At this time of the year, we are experiencing drought, and there is rivalry about the extraction of water between the host community and refugees." To manage this chronic scarcity, Kakuma had always been a destination terminal for extraordinary resource flows from outside, intended to reanimate the precarious lives of refugee residents. Key to these logistical efforts were humanitarian supply chains that spanned the entire globe and through which myriad items, such as food, medicine, building materials, personnel, vehicles, water, information, and other life-supporting necessities, were constantly circulated, transported, distributed, and stored.

During my fieldwork, not a day went by without the arrival of trucks carrying essential goods from downcountry Kenya or the Port of Mombasa. The metaphor of the "oasis" of aid, which humanitarian workers occasionally invoked, was in this sense not so far-fetched because the continuous stream of aid deliveries helped to defy an otherwise hostile natural environment and could artificially create micro-conditions for life in the Turkana desert. But it also risked misrepresenting Kakuma as a nurturing space, where relief was available in great abundance. In reality, food rations were cut year by year as donor money was either not forthcoming or drying up, despite generous pledges to the contrary made by donor governments during funding appeals. Between 2016 and 2022, expenditures for the UNHCR's Kenya operation steadily decreased from $124.3 million to $84.4 million per year, a reduction of more than 32 percent, while the number of refugees kept rising.[1] Like many *wakimbizi*, Ngabo, a middle-aged Rwandan, was incredulous about this trend. He could not fathom that countries as rich and powerful on the world stage as the United States, the United Kingdom, and Germany, and that provided much of the UNHCR's funding, were purposely cutting aid that sometimes was barely enough to feed his family for a single week. Sitting with me in the courtyard of his tiny house, his hands folded almost clerically in his lap, Ngabo asked sharply, "Why do they keep doing this? I have lived here for decades, and it's always pretty much the same. Big lorries arrive, offload their *magunia* [sacks of food], petrol, and *mabati* [corrugated iron], but for us life does not change apart from our time ticking away. So why are they doing it? We are just looking for a life here (Sisi tunatafuta maisha tu hapa)."

Michael, the UNHCR official I had befriended during my stay in Kakuma, expressed a similar sense of bewilderment. He deplored that aid was injected into the camp around the clock, and on an enormous scale, but that there was ultimately little to show for. "In theory, *the state*—and I want to stress this—is supposed to provide the bulk of protection, and the UNHCR just supplements that," he told me with a rather mischievous smile that suggested he realized his breach of the common script to which many aid workers adhere when speaking to researchers or journalists. "But that's not how it goes, as you well know," he continued. "If you ask me, I don't think the UNHCR is getting a fair deal for all the resources they keep pumping into this place." Michael looked around his office, as if to check for eavesdroppers, before turning back to me and saying, "With these millions of dollars it costs to keep Kakuma running every year, we are trying to kill a fly while there is a snake waiting for us. Do you understand? We should be focusing on killing the snake instead. But that's my personal view."

Michael's disillusionment with his employers, and the aid industry more generally, was not unique among field staff like him. They were usually the first to bear the brunt of any ill-conceived policy, budget cut, or managerial mishap in Geneva or Nairobi. The insight that emergency aid was unable to address the root causes of displacement ("the snake," in his words), and remained ineffective even after decades of costly intervention ("killing the fly"), was therefore neither original nor surprising. However, I could not help but think that, despite his understandable frustration with the sector's inability to make transformative change, he was still missing a fundamental point about the political economy of the camp and humanitarianism writ large.

In contrast to both Michael's and Ngabo's observations, the collaborative colonization of this micro-territory by humanitarian and state actors was by no means a one-way street: As much as financial aid, material supplies, and a rotating workforce were brought *into* the camp, there was an equally steady flow of resources being extracted *from* it. On first inspection, this may seem puzzling, especially in the context of humanitarianism that prides itself on aiming to replenish resources, restore diminished capacities, and revive threatened life chances rather than further draining them. But what bears noting here is that "killing the fly" was a far more lucrative and achievable goal in the short term than attempting to slay "the snake." Of course, aid agencies were first and foremost concerned with managing the delivery of services, which also dictated their funding and workforce structure and limited their everyday operational conduct. Yet the resources that were poured into Kakuma did not simply disappear into nothingness; they yielded relative economic and geopolitical returns for the countries, agencies, and institutions that supplied them. In much the same way as colonialism generally, humanitarian colonization in Kakuma pivoted markedly on a capacity to incessantly capitalize on the lives, land, and labor of subordinate populations. Their physical presence as living, breathing human beings was the basis on which the extractive operations of the aid machinery ultimately could proceed.

To understand how and why the refugee camp was turned into a site from which wealth, profit, and value could systematically be derived, I find it necessary to trace the different forms of extraction at play. In Kakuma, extraction came in multiple guises and was hardly reducible to, though it always included, the outright plunder of material resources. But encampment also invited more imperceptible forms of micro-extractivism that targeted people's remittances, savings, unpaid labor, and aggregated data, as well as the slow but persistent depletion of their very life time. By placing these seemingly disparate forms of extraction in relation to one another, we see that the camp is in fact less an oasis than a contemporary type of colonial concession: a frontier territory where prospecting, investment, infrastructural projects, humanitarianism, and foreign contractors coexist to create both subtle and explicit modes of dispossession and economic exploitation. This analytic enables us to think of this occupied refuge not only as a militarized geography in which refugees are contained, policed, and segregated but also as an extractive frontier. By attending to these questions, I place Kakuma more firmly within recent debates on humanitarian extraction while showing that the siphoning of assets, money, labor, and life time from refugees follows a familiar colonial logic but with contemporary features. While colonial occupations are never reducible to control over resources, control over resources is often woven into their original legitimation or the agenda behind their continuation.[2] Ultimately, cognate processes of extraction are key to understanding how this colonized micro-territory has come to endure and proliferate in our world, in spite of its consistent failures to fulfil liberal promises of protection and care.

Of Extractive Frontiers and Concessions

Living and working in Kakuma, whether as a career choice or by virtue of seeking asylum, meant inhabiting a frontier. As I argued more fully in previous chapters, the camp's location lent itself to all sorts of imaginaries that exceptionalized both it and its residents. In settler colonial imaginations, frontiers loom particularly large and have sometimes gained cultural significance through expansionist mythico-histories such as Manifest Destiny in the United States, Battlers in Australia, and the heroized journeys of white Boer Vortrekkers in South Africa. Until now, frontiers have been not just physical lines of expansion but imaginative projects that conjure a form of pioneering governmentality steeped in the virtues of overcoming environmental hardship, peril, and adversity in the pursuit of progress, ethnoracial supremacy, and "civilization." Since the Turkana countryside was historically one of the places in Kenya where British control was weakest and that epitomized the frayed boundaries of Kenyan nationhood, sovereignty, and ethnic belonging even after independence, it also represented a geographical frontier where foreign interventions, prospecting activities, and extraction could take place without restraint. While the aid-induced third occupation facilitated the growth of vital infrastructure for the delivery of humanitarian assistance, it did so proclaiming that opening up hitherto inaccessible borderlands would also ensure the safety, protection, and prosperity of *wakimbizi* in the years to come.

"Frontiers," as the anthropologist Anna Tsing notes, typically demarcate the "edge of space and time: a zone of not yet—not yet mapped, 'not yet' regulated."[3] It is from this supposed clean-slate environment that sundry opportunities are said to emerge precisely because of its still unregulated or unsubdued nature. Building a refugee camp in this periphery, though at first an emergency response to displacement, almost immediately also presented new opportunities for the militarization, dispossession, and usurpation of land. In fact, frontiers tend to attract an eclectic host of actors who may be openly predatory or ostensibly benign; who rally around processes of raw accumulation, claims making, and territorial conquest. Through what seem to be contradictory acts of plunder and pacification, as well as care and commerce, Tsing argues, these actors ultimately "confuse the boundaries of law and theft, governance and violence, use and destruction"—and, as we might usefully add, aid and extraction.[4] Drawing on the foundational work of Rosa Luxemburg, Sandro Mezzadra and Brett Neilson conceptualize this relationship between capitalism and its "outsides," where given resources are to be perpetually unearthed, appropriated, and exploited, as "frontiers of extraction."[5] For capitalism to reproduce itself, it demands constant prospecting for new areas into which it can expand with operations of accumulation.[6]

However, rather than exclusively deriving surpluses from the organized depletion of material reserves, such as oil, coal, minerals, water, timber and the like, Mezzadra and Neilson insist that frontiers equally rely on alternative, nonliteral forms of extractivism, including processes that exploit, monetize, and "cut through patterns of human cooperation and social activity."[7] Capital, hence, always pursues the lasting reorganization of "the whole social fabric according to the logics and imperative of its valorization," and it is for that reason that any notions of humanitarian aid, welfare, or social protection that communitize the costs of services based on principles of solidarity or compassion become the targets for structural adjustments.[8] Interpreted in this way, extractive frontiers represent both physical and figurative thresholds where an array of noncapitalist practices, value forms, life forces, and social relations are continuously being translated into potential and actual profit.

So far, we have seen that "the camp" historically has served as the frontier architecture par excellence that has always aided colonizers to settle land, secure their property, and project militarized power (see chapter 2). Camp outposts were logistically linked via transport routes to ports and larger cities from which goods or armed reinforcements could be requested. But while camps constituted a temporary measure of spatial control over people and land, through fences, barbed wire, or manipulated earthworks, logics of economic extraction remained secondary to their political subjugation. Yet frontier colonization also stimulated the emergence of a cognate and coeval space that was more explicitly designed for economic control over resources in a given territory: the concession. Concessions are territorial enclaves carved out through special legal and political arrangements among states, private corporations, and other ruling agencies to ease the extraction of resources and feed them into the circuits of global capitalism. But just like camps, concessions are more than physically delineated brick-and-mortar (or tent-and-tarpaulin) institutions. They manifest larger "social processes" and political projects of economic organization based on social relations of patronage, a racialized economy of difference, and exclusive access to the means of extraction/ production that are made material through concessionary geographies as territorial units.[9]

During the European colonization of Africa, concessionary zones sprouted up across the continent as circumscribed fiefdoms of exploitation that were isolated from the territories that surrounded them but, ironically, were closely integrated into world markets.[10] Early imperial ventures in India, China, and West Africa were almost entirely organized by forcing preferential and exclusive access for Europeans through nodal trading posts (or *factories*) for transshipment rather than more expansive dominion over vast areas of territory.[11] However, the demise of formal colonialism did not bring these concessionary geographies to an end. The concession as a model of fragmented economic ordering continued to flourish in a variety of contexts during the postcolonial era and into the present. Until now, states have granted private corporations and other juridical entities privileged access to stretches of land and resources through special concessionary agreements in the hope of profitable returns from economic activities for which the state itself incurs little to no direct costs.[12] Typically, a concession will have a laxer tax regime; bypass or waive vexatious land and labor rights; provide security to protect the interests of capital;

and create extralegal administrative structures to favor foreign entities, maximize their profits, and minimize responsibility toward local denizens and ecosystems.

Given these circumstances, it is the more surprising that humanitarian camps have not been analyzed as concessionary zones in their own right. They, too, are the products of special arrangements among states and foreign donors, nongovernmental organizations (NGOs), aid agencies, and now, increasingly, the private sector. While not sites of extractivism in the conventional sense, camps have come to be imagined as new frontiers of late capitalism where market forces are able to generate profits by inserting themselves into aid structures, systems of welfare, and humanitarianism that previously were somewhat "shielded" from naked logics of accumulation.[13] In Kenya's north, the humanitarian industry has been one of the largest, most lucrative, and steadiest streams of income and employment over the years. Since Operation Lifeline Sudan and the advent of refugee operations in Kakuma and Dadaab, the infrastructural development that has taken place in these marginal areas is immense, even though they have remained highly localized. Recently, more typical concessions began to develop throughout the country, especially oilfields, wind farms, forestry conservation projects, and special economic zones for literal extraction.[14] Since 2011, Turkana itself has become a hot spot for exploratory oil drilling conducted by the British company Tullow Oil around the small town of Lokichar, which was also expected to benefit from the eventual construction of the Lamu Port-South Sudan-Ethiopia-Transport (LAPSSET) corridor. Protests by disaffected Turkana citizens were repeatedly met with crackdowns from Kenyan police forces and private security contractors, highlighting the pitfalls of petroleum-fueled concessionary projects in marginalized areas.

The concession as an adaptable frontier geography enables us to reflect more critically on the extractive operations that occur in Kakuma. Humanitarian colonization is not just a mode of political rule but is centrally predicated on appropriating wealth and value in the form of money, labor, public relations, and lifetime. This chapter traces how the enclavic spaces of the camp and the concession become entwined through processes of micro-accumulation among police officers, aid workers, other camp officials, as well as the aid system's macro-predations on refugee labor, legal statuses, and refugees' value as incipient capitalist subjects. Even though some of this is specific to humanitarian rule in northwestern Kenya, it also reveals much larger trends in capital's militarized search for new frontiers on the continent and the colonial undercurrents of this ongoing despoliation globally.

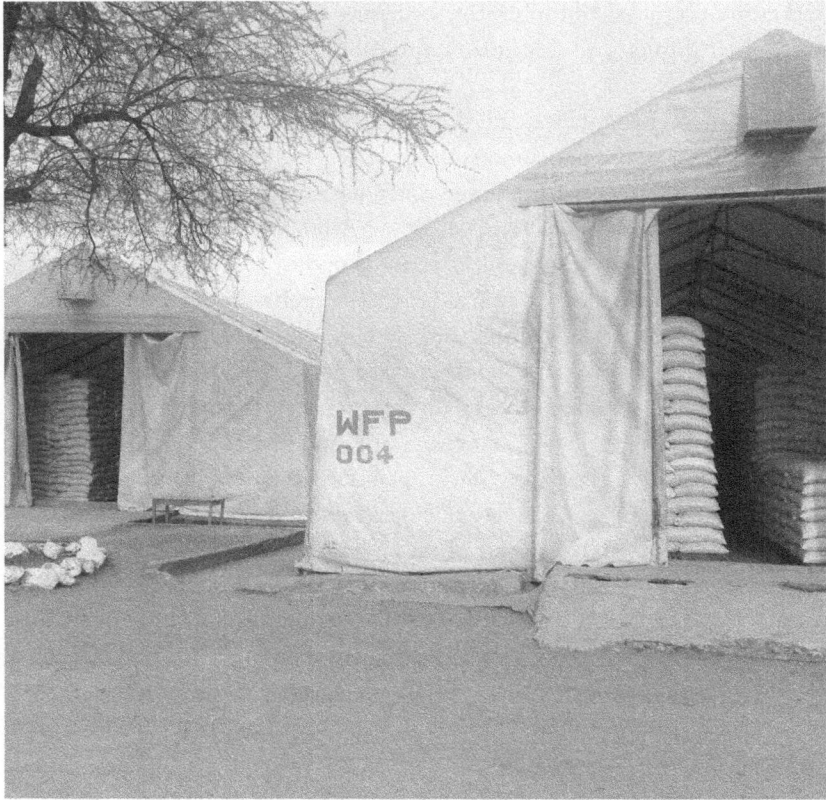

FIGURE 5.1. World Food Program warehouse in Kakuma, 2016. Photograph by the author.

Mining for Bribes

I now focus more closely on the circulation of material resources in the camp economy through everyday extraction. Overall, Kakuma camp represents not only a place of refuge from the conflicts in people's countries of origin, but also a major livelihood option and opportunity for refugees to virtually "dig aid" in their search for a more prosperous future.[15] For many, the camp—despite its carceral nature—was still a rudimentary safety net to fall back on if they wanted to try their luck in a Kenyan city without recourse to institutional aid, or even dared to contemplate the possibility of repatriation. Nyabeel, a South Sudanese woman in her late thirties, was one of those daring people. She told me about her short-lived attempt to return to her former life in Juba during a period of relative calm in the civil war in mid-2015. She had left Kakuma in the hope of being able to rebuild her urban existence in what had since become a tumultuous city. But when she arrived in the South Sudanese capital, she found that the small retail shop that she used to manage before fleeing to Kenya had now been taken over by another woman who had taken Nyabeel's long absence as license to occupy the property. "There was nothing I could do, no one to appeal to. The war changed everything," Nyabeel told me in a breaking voice. But despite intense feelings of loss and injustice she did not want to give up. Her status as a refugee enabled Nyabeel to return to Kenya, unpack her bags again, and resume her life in the camp where she could wait for the next chance of return to Juba.

While international aid played a huge role in keeping Kakuma running, life in the camp was not completely at the behest of humanitarian agencies alone but relied in no small part on remittances that many refugees received from friends or family abroad and the livelihoods they pursued locally. This flow of money into the pockets of residents, however, also created fertile conditions for predatory forms of micro-accumulation. Regardless of the large billboards that proclaimed that all services in the camp were free of charge, many officials took advantage of people's desperate circumstances and extorted money at every turn. While material extraction is typically imagined as excavating resources from the earth, Kakuma's extractive geographies were based on the figurative "mining" for bribes. The fact that this unfolded in a humanitarian space in Kenya's periphery was not a coincidence but spoke to the ways in which resource extraction throughout Africa has often occurred in economic enclaves or concessions, where accumulation could more easily materialize, be managed, and be protected. Aristide, a forty-year-old Congolese refugee who had lived in Kakuma for years, was a self-proclaimed critic of the aid industry, although he worked for one of the agencies. Fearless on the outside and with a jovial facial expression, he often joked about the futility of his job, the cynicism of life in the camp, and the ways in which ordinary refugees were preyed on. While sitting at a local restaurant, Aristide explained how Kenyan police officers practically "mined" for bribes:

> Every little criminal they get their hands on makes money. I've seen endless cases of people entering and leaving the cells—500, 1000, 1,500 Kenya shillings and you're out, depending on what you have done. If you're in the right, it doesn't mean that you will get away. People pay good money for "being in the right." Once you've paid 3,000 or 5,000 shillings, they'll shout at the other person: "Why are you making this guy's life so difficult, what's your problem?"

Aristide's description not only situated resource control in the broader context of incarceration and spatial control in the camp but also recognized that refugees can at times exert agency by deploying corruption in their favor. Perceptions among police officers and humanitarians alike that certain refugees, such as Somalis, were particularly "business-savvy" and had easy access to remittances exacerbated these predations and made them objects of envy among poorly paid Kenyan officers.[16] While the extortion of citizens by police across Kenya is equally common, the legal frameworks and material architectures that spatially fix refugees in the camps have made them especially susceptible to this exploitation.[17] Marthe Achtnich has aptly termed such strategies of monetary extraction by means of detention, incarceration, and encampment "accumulation by immobilization."[18]

The prospect of resettlement to a third country, usually a chance to begin a new life in the global North, aggravated this predation in Kakuma. In 2001, a United Nations (UN) report uncovered crimes committed by UNHCR staff who, together with police officers and other NGO workers, engaged in smuggling and systematic extortion in the camp.[19] Again, although this reflected prevalent malpractices in Kenya and among its police more generally, it affected a spatially secluded, forcibly immobilized, and noncitizen population that was nominally under the joint protection of the UNHCR and the state.[20] More recent investigations by the UNHCR's Inspector General's Office (IGO), the refugee agency's internal investigations unit, indicated that criminal networks continued to pervade the aid operation—most prominently, the UNHCR and Kenya's police. While a sizable number of officers regularly extort petty amounts of cash, others are part of more organized networks that orchestrate monetary extraction from refugees on a larger scale. The Burundian refugee Hakizimana explained,

> There are refugees who have family abroad that make phone calls and transfer money. During the UNHCR interviews for resettlement, the agency uses fellow refugees as interpreters. Now, the [refugee] interpreter then connects the person calling from abroad with a senior staff inside the UNHCR. They negotiate the terms of assistance, and the people part with cash in the process. That's it.[21]

However, even after paying bribes in the hope of fast-tracking their resettlement claims, most of them would eventually fail. By paying more than $2,500, refugees who fell outside the official criteria for resettlement, which prioritized people at risk, survivors of torture, and those in need of specialist medical procedures, could be considered for (and sometimes be granted) flights to third countries in the global North. A UNHCR insider with in-depth knowledge of the investigations of extortion in Kakuma referred to these links between Kenyan police and aid workers bluntly as the "humanitarian aid cartel."[22]

On multiple occasions, officials from the UNHCR, NGOs, and the government recalled having been approached and urged by police officers to come "into the fold" and being lured with promises of a share in the prospective spoils.[23] A former magistrate sent to preside over Kakuma's court was even threatened by the police chief to either join the "cartel" or face severe repercussions. Fearing for their life, the judge decided to relocate from Kakuma town to one of the compounds that are usually reserved for aid workers. In May 2017, five UNHCR staff were suspended on suspicion of fraud, while the cases were (ironically) transferred to Kenya's police for further investigation.[24] For years, Hakizimana had worked as a community police officer for the Lutheran World Federation (LWF) and heard regular complaints from fellow refugees about their failed attempts to gain resettlement by paying bribes. One day, he recounted to me, the IGO contacted him during a visit to Kakuma, and he arranged for the investigators to speak with witnesses who could testify against the police. When the police found out Hakizimana had helped an anticorruption investigation, they detained and questioned him at the Kakuma police station. "They slapped me in the face and asked me, 'In what capacity are you following up on those bribe cases?' because they thought I was out to spoil their business," he said. "They showed me several photographs of refugees—my neighbors, in fact—who I had put in touch with the IGO directly. But I denied everything, even to know their names or have anything to do with them." According to Hakizimana, the interrogating officer lost his patience and repeatedly asked, "Why are you taking us as fools? We have full information to prove that you provided the IGO with witnesses so that some UN staff will be losing their jobs. Tell the truth!"

In the weeks that followed, Hakizimana could not sleep in his own house for fear of being detained again, or worse. The Directorate of Criminal Investigations (DCI) demanded he report to its office every week to ensure he did not leave the camp. One day, a white DCI vehicle was parked outside Hakizimana's house, and a junior police officer called for him to come out. "The officer just said, 'The boss needs to see you,' and I knew this meant trouble," Hakizimana remembered. When Hakizimana entered the vehicle, the DCI commander, clearly drunk, flung his arm around his shoulders and asked him why he was causing the police such headaches. When Hakizimana denied any wrongdoing, the officer simply slapped him and drew his gun. "This is when I lost it, I didn't know what to do," Hakizimana told me. He recalled that the junior officer intervened at this point and told his superior, "This is too much." However, the commander accidentally released a shot from the gun, at which time Hakizimana was pushed out of the police vehicle, which drove off in haste.

Hakizimana knew that he had to act quickly. He packed his essential belongings in a backpack and hid at a friend's home for the night. From there he contacted the IGO. Days later, the UNHCR's inspector general took Hakizimana into his witness protection program in Nairobi, where he was put up in a safe house. But even the safe house was often not enough to protect witnesses. Both UNHCR officials and Hakizimana talked about instances when refugees were abducted by unmarked vehicles, lured by phone calls from fake UNHCR officers informing them of a "meeting" they had to attend. Some weeks later, Hakizimana eventually left Kenya to be resettled in Canada to protect him from his police pursuers. Although the UN refugee agency had consistently signaled its willingness to dispel the allegations of misconduct and review its operations, likely under pressure from its donor countries, extortion existed not only as the opportunistic "violence of *kitu kidogo*" but formed part and parcel of a larger system of occupation through which state and aid workers exercised control over the refugees' lives, movements, and financial resources.[25] Months after Hakizimana left the camp, Kakuma's police chief faced possible disciplinary action over his conduct, as more and more cases of extortion, intimidation, and physical violence against refugees came to light. But before criminal charges could be brought against him, he was transferred to another location in Kenya, never to set foot in Kakuma again. It was clear that the colonial occupation of the camp and the state-authorized dispossession of refugee wealth that underwrote it held fast and would not be challenged in the courts. And even if they did, there was little doubt that the accused would walk free as part of a system that usually protected its own.

Exploiting Labor

Labor has so far played an almost understated role in my analysis of humanitarian colonization. While aid operations across the world have had to cut their budget lines, compromising shelter and minimum quantities of food made available to refugees, so-called incentive work has often flourished in this artificially produced economy of scarcity. By invoking *incentive work*, I use a common umbrella term for distinct semi-voluntary labor relations among aid organizations, states, or private actors and the recipients of institutional aid in camps and cities.[26] While refugees have long been closely incorporated into aid delivery, their work in this capacity is at times understood as a form of "volunteering," for which remuneration can only ever be paid as an incentive that "is intended to acknowledge the volunteer's effort but not provide full compensation for their labor."[27] As I showed in chapter 4, community policing was one of the most direct iterations of voluntarized labor performed by refugees to uphold the camp's regime, but it was certainly not the only one.

In fact, thousands of Kakuma residents were on the payroll of aid agencies as teachers, security officers, nurses, builders, mechanics, gardeners, interpreters, or casual laborers of one kind or another. These jobs were notoriously underpaid, precarious, and low in status, despite their importance for humanitarian actors to keep the aid operation financially and logistically afloat. "Without them," a recent report found, "there would be almost no face-to-face contact with refugee households around issues of survival, rights and wellbeing."[28] For years, journalists from the Kakuma News Reflector (KANERE), an independent refugee-run news outlet, have reported on potential labor rights violations and the exploitative nature of incentive work. Refugees are, for example, employed as teachers in schools alongside Kenyan colleagues but with notable differences in pay. "This is what they call free education," one Kakuma resident remarked derisively when speaking to a KANERE reporter, highlighting the absurdity of refugee workers subsidizing an aid system meant to protect them through their own time and labor power.

According to a refugee health-care worker, an international NGO in charge of hospitals in the camp responded to demands for better wages by terminating the contracts of "many of our colleagues and [giving] us the money through these cutbacks," before deciding to double the workload to offset this loss of employees.[29] If anything, this was common practice, especially when funding was axed or donors' priorities suddenly changed, forcing employers to reorganize their refugee workforce by issuing new and, usually, more unfavorable contracts. Mercy, a Congolese incentive worker for a major NGO in Kakuma, was first laid off before being asked to reapply for a job she had been doing for years but with the dire prospect of receiving only two-thirds of her original pay. Sitting in her living room, she looked angry and betrayed. "They told me up front that I will keep my job but would have to do it for much less because donors were not able to pay us properly anymore," she said. In Kakuma, incentive work forms the subsoil of a system of aid and protection that is cynically propped up through the extraction of surplus value from un(der)paid and encamped workers, essentially creating a hyper-marginalized "captive labor market" as the unacknowledged economic backbone of what Elisa Pascucci has poignantly called "actually existing humanitarianism."[30]

Community policing officers (CPPTs) were among the lowest rungs of refugee laborers even by camp standards. Many were disillusioned by what they felt was unfair treatment from the LWF's head office, compared with their Kenyan colleagues, whose income was an average of five to ten times higher and who were afforded more job security. A meeting with a senior manager became unexpectedly heated when Gakuoth, a Nuer CPPT, addressed the thorny question of labor rights, workload, and equal compensation. "Boss, let me tell you," he began with palpable irritation, "we on our side are doing our job. But the office has problems. We always put reports on the table, but the cases aren't followed up by our Kenyan colleagues. What are they doing to deserve the money they get paid? Some national staff aren't even working at all. I have two children and work full time, sometimes both day and night. Is that fair?" Instead of taking Gakuoth's concerns seriously, however, the manager minimized them, responding dismissively that "the message I'm getting here is that your work has become too difficult for you to handle. It's not a blame game."[31]

Despite the disparities on display between refugee staff and their Kenyan counterparts, the "privilege" of the Kenyans was itself rather minimal. The stratification of the humanitarian economy meant that downcountry staff from Nairobi or southern Kenya were predominantly hired in managerial roles, usually at higher rates of compensation, while smaller administrative roles, which required no university degree, went to the local Turkana, who were also poorly paid. Citizenship merely elevated these "local staff" above a threshold that distinguished between a low-income citizen workforce and outright impoverished refugee incentive workers. Akin to workfare or comparably punitive neoliberal policies of mobilizing poor and socially excluded groups for labor, aid agencies had succeeded in "reframing work as a benefit" that was offered to refugees as part of their humanitarian package.[32] People such as Mercy and Gakuoth not only acted as the front line of humanitarian services but often carried the full weight of the entire system on their shoulders. While colonization is always driven, at least in part, by the prospect of resource extraction, the incentive labor of Kakuma's refugees was a surreptitious byproduct of the aid industry's forays into this area. After all, aid agencies had not come to Kenya's rural hinterland to deny refugees proper wages for their work, but as time went by, they recognized that the surplus they could skim off this productive labor was, in fact, essential to the survival of the humanitarian camp itself and became a hallmark of its concessionary geography.

Value, Markets, and Publicity

Recent years have seen significant shifts in the ways in which the UNHCR and the Government of Kenya have framed refugee hosting in Kenya. Security concerns and counterterrorism, although still high on Kenya's list of political priorities, were now increasingly mentioned in the same breath as economic development and the benefits of enhancing refugees' access to employment and markets. TEDxKakumaCamp in June 2018, discussed in more detail in chapter 1, was a publicity gig organized partly to celebrate this wider trajectory toward self-reliance, public-private partnerships, marketization, and entrepreneurial "solutions" to forced displacement that had already long been underway in the entire sector. After decades of providing life-supporting aid to refugees as a matter of welfare, aid agencies and their donors started to question whether such prolonged interventions were economically unsustainable and perhaps even inhibited the desired self-reliance of refugees.[33]

In an interview, Raouf Mazou, the UNHCR's former Kenya country representative, noted that in the early 2010s the UN refugee agency had essentially reached a "dead end" with its care-and-maintenance approach to encampment.[34] On the one hand, refugee camps such as Kakuma have always been outlets for "fixing" the surpluses in donor money, aid workers, material aid, technology, and logistical services "in place" to try to manage emerging crises of the capitalist system in situ by reinvesting resources into camps that could at once balance state budgets and help contain negatively racialized refugees.[35] Some private companies, such as Kenya's telecommunication giant Safaricom and Equity Bank, have long made high profits in Kakuma, not least due to the vital services they have provided, which gave them a quasi-monopoly. On the other hand, there also has been a push to extract value more directly by incorporating refugees and asylum seekers more closely into the circuits of capitalist markets, consumption, financial services, and commodification of data. Planetary containment, it became clear, could yield not only political but also economic returns if a niche was created for the encamped as subordinate market actors.

Accordingly, critical (forced) migration scholars have noted an emerging trend in state and aid policy toward valuing refugee and migrant life in a way that makes it commensurable, ready for circulation, and, therefore, more exploitable.[36] While refugees, unlike slaves or indentured laborers, are not themselves commodified as property, camps and other carceral spaces used for containment have facilitated the marketization of their biological existence itself, "render[ing] actual, living migrants as abstract migrant life."[37] The abstract value of migrants and refugees, Lauren Martin writes, thus "rests in their potential in/voluntary labour, revenue for service contractors, transaction data and waiting time."[38] In Kakuma, abstract refugee life became precisely valuable first and foremost through the basic services deemed necessary for its reproduction. The UNHCR usually subcontracted with NGOs in essential sectors such as health, housing, water, sanitation, and hygiene (WASH); education; security; and protection. More than forty NGOs worked as so-called implementing partners under the lead of the UN refugee agency and Kenya's Department of Refugee Services to physically sustain the life of refugees. This created an extremely lucrative market for aid money, expertise, and professional employment across various pay scales. For decades, the legal prohibition of work and unauthorized movements by refugees within and outside the camp has ensured the conversion of immobilization, refugee status, material scarcity, and impoverishment into valuable shares in the aid economy. As long as refugees were unable to move, work for a wage, or farm to subsist autonomously, there was a need for the humanitarian industry to exist, intervene, and expand.

However, in most conversations this side of humanitarianism's "destitution economy" was muted.[39] Michael, the UNHCR staff member who felt that the "international community" has not gotten its money's worth from funding Kakuma over the past three decades, said the persistence of aid flows is a result of misplaced goodwill from global North donors who do not care that their money is lost. This sense of inefficiency and waste was echoed by a UNHCR Livelihoods officer who compared aid work in Kakuma to the supposed sluggishness of a one-party socialist state. "You get free handouts; you get free in kind [aid]," he said with iron conviction during an interview. "Everything is very structured and planned, and everything is free. You've got all these little signs, saying all services in this camp are free. Very much like a communist kind of [system]. . . . [But] that creates this dearth or lack of private activity to some extent."[40] The camp, in this reading, constituted a "frontier" of the free market, a moving threshold of capitalist ways of thinking, producing, and working that seemingly were always progressing toward a teleological end point prefigured by Euro-American neoliberalism.[41]

In these imagined futures that were often shared among aid professionals and managers, the concessionary logic of the refugee camp was particularly pronounced. For them, Kakuma represented a "test case" to prize open a field of human cooperation, sociality, solidarity, and nonprofit activities that hitherto had managed to avoid the fate of welfare provisions and social protections in much of the world, which, since the 1980s, had slowly been dismantled, privatized, or deregulated. As a concession with reasonably controlled conditions, a forcibly immobilized population, and administrative regulations that set it apart from Kenya proper, Kakuma provided potent conditions for this economic experimentation. To fulfill what neoliberal models dictated, however, the camp would have to be subjected to a belated round of structural adjustments on a micro scale to allow for renewed extraction to take place. "In the end," Ngabo, the Rwandan who had wondered about the reasons for the tenacity of humanitarians even after years of failing to transform the lives of camp dwellers, explained as he poured me another cup of tea in the yard of his tin-roofed house. "They are self-interested, like everybody else. That's what I have learned here."[42]

At the heart of the new plans to open up the camp to private investors and streamline its supposedly sluggish processes were collaborations among aid actors, the state, and private businesses that were thought to bring a new dynamism to old structures of encampment. The chief executive of a multinational company's foundation that was funding aid projects around the world was clear that private businesses could "provide some innovation or some new thinking in a humanitarian setting to get to a point where we can provide better quality for less money."[43] "Maybe the design of those [traditional humanitarian] programs wasn't such that it would allow for longer-term impacts," he surmised while emphasizing that, normally, "as soon as the donor funding leaves, it falls apart."[44] "You need to have good partners that look at this as a commercial venture, and not some sort of an aid structure," he continued with the authority of a man who had rehearsed his argument many times and remained unimpressed by his critics. "It needs to be profitable. It needs to be set up in a way that you can make a profit every year, because otherwise, at least it needs to be self-carrying.... You can't make it dependent on constant aid money every year." To achieve this and reduce the reliance on external funding, it was thought necessary to extract more value from refugees as laborers, consumers, and potential borrowers. In short, profitability and market solutions hinged on transforming the camp's refugees into "good" capitalist subjects who would graciously be allowed "to embrace the forces of free-market capitalism."[45]

A World Bank economist who had worked for years assessing the size and profitability of Kakuma as a market diagnosed that refugees first needed to become better market actors, sufficiently versed in management, business administration, the ins and outs of investment, and financial literacy, to fully benefit from capitalist markets. For her it was not the free market that endangered the welfare and livelihoods of refugees but their inability to *operate effectively* within it. Refugees, she argued, by virtue of their status as chronic recipients of aid, found themselves "in a very vulnerable position" that, for her, raised the ultimate question of whether one could somehow help them to "*actually* use their capital, their human capital, to make something out of it." In her calls for refugees to develop themselves, or be remade into more successful market actors, the World Bank official casually reproduced colonial ideas of an evolutionary ladder of capitalist productivity that negatively ethnoracialized populations would have to "climb" for their full humanity to be recognized.[46]

In proposing solutions to make Kakuma more profitable, self-sustaining, and livable, a coalition of aid organizations, state authorities, and private investors inadvertently normalized the camp's violence. The unfreedom of encampment was framed no longer as the main problem that needed addressing but as a factor that held back the right "mindset" of refugees. The Kakuma Kalobeyei Challenge Fund was a five-year program set up in 2020 by the International Finance Corporation (IFC) to invite private companies, social enterprises, and local businesses to bid for startup funding along different investment tiers and enroll in tailored trainings to boost their "business mindset" and skills.[47] Mastercard and Western Union started to offer similar financial literacy programs, no doubt equally anticipating a growing client base for more profitable transactions through their networks. Safaricom, itself already well established in Kakuma's telecommunication market, received a further contract from the World Food Program to run its mobile e-voucher food system, Bamba Chakula ("Get your food" in Swahili), through which refugees were able to buy items of their choice rather than being given standard in-kind donations. The IKEA Foundation had tested its investment in humanitarian projects in the Dollo Ado camps of Ethiopia and decided to finance a number of projects and partnerships in Kakuma camp as a result. While many companies were happily "prospecting" for profits or future opportunities for accumulation, cheered on by humanitarian actors desperate to demonstrate the productivity and benefit of refugees, the nuts and bolts of encampment itself were never truly questioned. Even if marketization seemed to offer a way out of impoverishment or securitization, it so far has not delivered on those bold promises. In fact, the praise for *more* markets and *less* material aid seemed to follow first and foremost the funding fatigue of donors and to suit their shifting geopolitical priorities. But it could hardly camouflage the complicity of those states, corporations, and financial institutions in reinforcing the unequal global operations of capital that catalyzed forced displacement in the first place.

Finally, in addition to seeking to stimulate homegrown economic activities among refugees and producing fertile conditions for investors who would normally avoid "risky" environments, the marketization agenda created returns from global publicity. As I point out in chapter 1, TEDxKakumaCamp boosted Kakuma's reputation and visibility on the world stage and reinforced an existing image of the camp as a hub for humanitarian experiments. For decades, the refugee camp had been a stage from which to orchestrate philanthropic campaigns. Its multiethnic and multicultural population, and its charm as an underdeveloped but relatively "safe" rural backwater in the borderlands, offered the perfect conditions for the public relations exploits. Now, Kakuma is among the most visited camps in the world; diplomats, celebrities, and high-profile politicians from global North "donor states" all make appearances, including Germany's President Frank-Walter Steinmeier, the UN High Commissioner for Refugees Filippo Grandi, the British athlete Mo Farah, and Switzerland's President Alain Berset. In 2002, the Hollywood star and UNHCR goodwill ambassador Angelina Jolie used a break from filming the sequel to her blockbuster movie *Tomb Raider* in Kenya to visit the camp and establish a primary school for girls with a personal donation of $200,000.[48] "With this help, and the construction of this school," Kofi Mable, the head of the UNHCR's Kakuma office at the time, is quoted as saying during Jolie's televised visit, "future generations of girls will be saved." Kakuma may be a place of everyday extortion, precarious labor, and racial markets that position refugees unfavorably in the global economy, but for the circuits of humanitarian publicity, it was the gift that kept on giving. The potential to profit from refugees in this occupied refuge seemed simply to have no bounds.

Draining Lifetime

"The camp is not a forever place. There's nothing here for me. Inshallah, I will leave one day if I can. But everybody says so—I know that."[49] Fawzia and I sat inside one of Kakuma's popular coffee shops, drinking *makyato* and discussing our hopes for the future. Her family had fled Somalia in the early 2000s. When I met her, she was twenty-six. Fawzia's memories of her childhood in Mogadishu were understandably faint because she came of age in Kakuma, where most of her friends and family had rebuilt their lives as much as they possibly could, themselves "looking for a life" (*kutafuta maisha*). She was one of thousands of young refugees who knew neither a life outside the camp nor free from the aid system that housed, fed, and supported them. "Life," Fawzia once told me wisely, "moves more slowly here in the camp. Sometimes it can feel like it chokes you and will make you gasp for air." The ubiquity of social media among her agemates meant that those who stayed behind in Kenya could follow, almost in real time, the lives of peers who had been resettled abroad in the United States,

Canada, Europe, and Australia. Facebook and Instagram became windows into an alternative future—one in which Fawzia and her friends were not bound by the rules of encampment; were not fazed by sporadic sandstorms on the desert plains; and did not suffer from the indignity of dwindling food rations but could simply pose for a selfie at a Wendy's restaurant or picnic in a Minneapolis city park.

In addition to sustaining a militarized architecture and extractive operations of micro-accumulation, encampment had severe debilitating effects on the life chances, well-being, and health of camp dwellers, truncating their aspirations and grinding them into an oppressive mold of forced waiting. The operations of capital not only sought to invade new geographical areas and unravel any social relations of solidarity for material gain, but time itself had become one of the multiple frontiers into which logics of capitalist accumulation have increasingly expanded. Refugee humanitarianism was, in figurative terms, "choking" people's lifetime.[50] It is through strategic contractions, suspensions, dilations, and outright annihilations of time that extractive activities thus can proceed and feed on the life force of its human subjects. Inasmuch as Karl Marx used a vampire metaphor to describe capital's irrepressible thirst for "living labor," which it needs to reproduce itself by means of the surplus it sucks from laborers during working hours, vampiric predation on lifetime is more universal and, arguably, extends into the realm of humanitarianism.[51] Fawzia was painfully aware of this bleeding away of her opportunities and was not alone in her deferred dreams of a life beyond Turkana. Anyone who had spent considerable periods living here could attest that lifetime was an invaluable resource in itself, which the camp was constantly seeking to drain from *wakimbizis'* veins. The South Sudanese poet Mary Aluel, who grew up in Kakuma, gloomily but tenderly articulated this slipping away of time when she wrote:

Despondence and disappointments creep in,
Futility of life it is.
The fiction of being an unknown in an unknown land,
Paralyses the thoughts of going for it, making it, taking it
Grim persistence it is,
But the wait is eternity,
Fate remains,
Everyday.[52]

Exasperation at this eternal waiting was a grueling sentiment shared among many of Kakuma's inhabitants. With their "grim persistence," refugees had to queue in the blazing sun during food distribution and head counts; while awaiting appointments with humanitarian staff; to gain access to aid compounds; or to simply see a doctor at one of the camp's hospitals. Then, of course, there was the existential waiting for one of the UN refugee agency's "durable solutions": repatriation, resettlement, or local integration. For places such as Kakuma, where integration has long been blocked by Kenyan authorities and where a return to Somalia or South Sudan has, for decades, been nothing but a distant fantasy, resettlement to a "third country" was many people's only hope for a future after the camp. Yet only a vanishingly small number of refugees with specific protection needs were airlifted each year to Europe, North America, and Australia, which typically admitted them only after strict health and security screenings.

Kakuma gained fame as a launch pad for these resettlement futures. Few camps in Eastern Africa resettled more refugees abroad, although even in a peak departure year not even 1 percent of camp residents were able to embark on this life-changing journey. Camp residents would pride themselves of "having a process," a turn of phrase that indicated being somewhere in the pipeline for resettlement, though few would actually reach the end of this process.[53] As some of their friends started life afresh in Melbourne or Minnesota, Mary Aluel's and Fawzia's generation felt overwhelmingly stuck and left behind, abandoned in a place that was marginal even within Kenya itself. "Time in the refugee camp," Melissa Gatter argues in her book on Azraq camp in Jordan, "is endless and unwanted."[54] For Fawzia and Mary, time inside the camp moved with glacial slowness, leaving its residents to their own thoughts, regrets, trauma, and reverie while, in turn, their chances of ever enjoying a full life, outside the camp, seemed to be getting smaller by the day.

"The camp is a time more than it is a place," writes the scholar-poet Yousif M. Qasmiyeh.[55] The futility of life lived in cyclical encampment has the effect that even unborn life, eventually, has to abide by its rules and is quickly absorbed into its endless rhythms of stasis. Encamped existence, in recognizably colonial fashion, can therefore be productive of a life as "living dead," "stolen time," or "dead time" or as representing what some have even called "social death" of those deemed ineligible for personhood and willfully left in limbo, unable to graduate to a complete and dignified existence.[56] This is not to suggest that lives are not lived passionately, with love, friendships, and community flourishing in Kakuma. But it means that life in the camp remains always haunted by the specter of lost potential—of what might have been; of what never will be; and of the chances that were never given or seized. No matter how promising humanitarianism may be, in its entrepreneurial guises that promise investments, new opportunities, economic integration, and greener pastures, Aluel ultimately reminds us that often "there is no relief for the vulnerable, fate is the only motto—everyday." While Kakuma stretched time elastically within its perimeters, trapping refugees in holding patterns of forced waiting without recourse, it also seemed to drain their long-held optimism for change or an end to their plight, making the camp, in Qasmiyeh's words, "the incinerator of time."[57]

The aporic invocation of the camp's deathliness—its negation of life, so to speak—even as it aims to replenish it, is not a coincidence. It arises from two distinct understandings of life as biological (*zoe*), on the one hand, and biographical (*bios*), on the other.[58] Biological life comprises cyclical life processes that have to do with (human) biology, cellular reproduction, and physical existence, while biographical life refers to the course of a (human) life—its unique events, actions, and future-oriented projects that form a biography. This has the effect that, even as humanitarian interventions foster the former through nutritional programs, shelter provision, or emergency health that keep the body alive, they tend inadvertently to hinder the prospects of the latter the longer a camp endures. Self-directed biographical life projects, replete with personal dreams and hopes for a fulfilled existence, are thus frustrated and grind to a halt as they are slowly drained of their liveliness and possibility. Encamped refugees, like other carceral subjects in prisons and detention centers, which Ruth Wilson Gilmore evokes in her theorization, in this way also become "tiny territories primed for extractive activity to unfold."[59] By arresting their development, exacting an emotional toll, and putting refugees' lives on hold, camps such as Kakuma are similarly "extracting and extracting again time from the territories of selves."[60]

While refugee encampment reinforced feelings of "stuckness," domination, and control, the purpose of extracting lifetime from Kakuma's denizens did not stop there. Draining lifetime from refugees was, crucially, a geopolitical calculation to create economies of waiting in the global South. Without financial resources, unable to migrate to Europe on their own volition, and hoping that one day they might be chosen for resettlement if they could only endure one of the world's countless waiting rooms, Kakuma's refugees were kept in their place through the promise of a life that for most would never be. Their containment in the Turkana desert is precisely the value that can be derived from refugees in a global system of racialized borders and buffering. The immobilization of refugees through spatial exclusion, temporal suspension of their life cycles, and delay is one crucial form of return for the investments that global North donors have made by bankrolling humanitarian camps at the global margins.

Concessionary Encampment

The meteoric rise of the marketization agenda in refugee humanitarianism over the past decade, although not entirely new, signaled the recognition that economic rationalities are key to logics of encampment. "You don't [usually] see a refugee camp as a place that is actually creating wealth, even if it's the case. You don't see [it]. It is counterintuitive," said Mazou during an interview in which he tried to highlight the innovative nature of the UN refugee agency's recent shifts to market-based solutions. The agency was proud not to inadvertently present refugee populations as dependent, inept, and burdensome any longer but, instead, as "assets" or "resources." Yet the rhetoric of resources, Yolanda Weima has rightly argued, "is a way of knowing and valuing that which is other than human."[61] It strips people of their claims to full humanity and reduces them to their abstract value as flesh, bones, labor, and data that are ready to be circulated, monetized, exploited, or otherwise rendered available for accumulation. In contrast to those who see in this a departure from a previous humanitarian reason that stayed aloof from capitalist ways of valorizing human life, an examination of disparate processes of extortion, voluntarized labor, market adjustments, and forced waiting reveals that Kakuma camp always served as an exceptionalized site of extractivism.

This observation opens a fresh window into the economic and political geographies of Kakuma as an occupied refuge. It shows that refugee encampment in Africa, although on its surface a spatial technology primarily geared toward facilitating mobility control and delivery of aid, shares many properties of the concession. As co-articulations of colonization, or colonial formations, they symbolize an unbroken will to subdue land, labor, and populations to the laws of capitalist accumulation and capture, push forward frontiers of civilization, and capitalize on human and nonhuman riches. If colony and camp generally feed off each other, as Ann Laura Stoler poignantly noted, then the concession marks another key component of this political matrix of spatial domination.[62] Concessions historically have served as bridgeheads to expedite expansion and economically anchor emerging colonial claims in unsettled frontier zones. They work by prospecting for, enclosing, and securitizing resources primed for export or circulation, as well as by disciplining and confining the workforce necessary to extract them. By theorizing Kakuma as a concession within the process of humanitarian colonization, I draw attention to these analytical parallels without suggesting their absolute determinacy. Since the refugee camp is a spatialization of relief work, its extractivist underpinnings appear more subdued than those found in mining compounds, logging concessions, or colonial trading posts, whose justification is often accumulation alone. However, what emerges through these contradictions is a modality of humanitarian rule that we can refer to as *concessionary encampment*, which mobilizes legal and extralegal mechanisms to derive value from biological processes and from sociality, life time, and material wealth. I am therefore persuaded by Stoler's claim that the camp and colony exist in a "deadly embrace" that reproduces the social deformations of enclosure, containment, and coercive architecture, but argue that this embrace can be felt most tightly in the concession, which transforms refugees into both *concrete* governable subjects and *abstract* value for capital.

This not only demands that we come to terms with the extractive logics of humanitarian aid alongside its more curative, compassionate, and life-supporting purposes, but it also has implications for our understanding of camp geographies writ large as productive of a specific concessionary politics. Regimes of colonial occupation are generally driven by overlapping aims of territorial control, political domination, and appropriation of resources. In the case of Kakuma, however, the extraction of resources is articulated quite differently from more conventional sites, where material wealth is literally unearthed from the ground beneath. In contrast, operations of capital within the camp are multiple, and their extractive mechanisms routinely predate on the bodies and labor power of inhabitants and hew the years left of their lifetime. While these extractions may seem to dampen any hopes for a better tomorrow, camp dwellers have become attuned to them and sometimes have found ways—momentarily, at least—to defy or manipulate these concessionary arrangements. Time, labor, and money, while prime objects of desire for capital accumulation, are then equally resources at the disposal of refugees awaiting their turn to "seek a life" by any means necessary. Kakuma's position as a humanitarian safety net from which riskier life projects could be launched therefore did not contradict its extractive character. It simply showed that such nodes of capital accumulation also offer room and resources for ordinary refugees to maneuver. For many, it was not just about withstanding the extractive operations of the camp, which tend to grind hopes and dreams into fine dust, but about using the camp's structures to realize or adapt as much of one's own life plans as possible.

Conclusion

Kakuma, a desolate wilderness,
a blazing fire, an earthly furnace,
venue of day darkness.
Don't shut your eyes blind!
Speak the truth loudly!

Disclose yourself thoroughly!
You are a storehouse of whirlwinds,
abominable dust and a heap of sand.
Home of the undernourished,
a graveyard, never satisfied.
  —Fantaye Agaro, "Rise Kakuma!"

On June 20, 2023, World Refugee Day, the Kenyan government and United Nations High Commissioner for Refugees (UNHCR) jointly announced that, after decades of mandatory encampment, the country was now finally shifting its approach to refugee management by turning the Kakuma and Dadaab camps into integrated settlements. This signature policy came to be widely known as the Shirika Plan and received a substantial funding pledge of 28 billion Kenyan shillings ($200 million) from international partners. The policy's name was carefully chosen to express a broader aspiration to get the state, donors, humanitarian agencies, refugees, and local citizens to all work together.[1] After all, invoking a spirit of togetherness has had long-standing popular appeal throughout Kenya's postindependence history, in which self-help fundraisers and community-level political mobilization to unite the country were led with the rallying cry "Harambee!" (Let us all pull together!) under President Jomo Kenyatta. The multiyear Shirika Plan tapped into the existing imaginations of this national spirit. Shirika, it was claimed, would not only ease pressure on "host communities" living in areas around the refugee camps, foster self-reliance among refugees, and transition from largely humanitarian to government-led service provision but also turn the camps themselves into future-oriented and more "robust economic hubs."[2]

Kalobeyei, the UNHCR's first attempt at humanitarian urban planning seven years earlier, has served as the model for this more comprehensive transformation process of "moving from encampment to empowerment," as one Kenya Broadcasting Corporation (KBC) television presenter put it.[3] Just like the previous schemes on which it built—notably, the Kalobeyei Integrated Socio-Economic Development Plan (KISEDP) and Support for Host Community and Refugee Empowerment (SHARE)—the Shirika Plan sought to make encampment politically palatable, despite its demonstrably adverse effects on the lives of refugees. Kakuma and Kalobeyei in particular were touted as test cases to show that a more financially sustainable, livable, and more "productive" camp environment was possible, even without granting refugees substantive freedom or admitting that many, if not most, would likely stay in Kenya indefinitely. "By promoting the socio-economic inclusion of refugees," Kenya's Prime Cabinet Secretary Musalia Mudavadi said during the High-Level Dialogue at which Shirika was announced, "we are collectively preparing them for their eventual voluntary repatriation to their home countries."[4] Until then, funders, aid organizations, and liberal academics agreed that Kenya would do well to recognize the considerable economic potential of refugees and camps as hubs of future investment and labor reserves that could make substantial contributions to the country's national economy. "Over the years," Mudavadi noted in this regard, "the government has endeavored to ensure that refugees participate in nation-building."

But months later, when John Burugu, Kenya's commissioner for refugee affairs, was asked live on the air whether Shirika would grant refugees freedom of movement, he rebuked the presenter with a resolute "No." "Empowerment," Burugu warned during the interview, "does not necessary result to [*sic*] free movement for refugees."[5] The right to move, he insisted, would be granted only if and when needed, with the Kenyan government remaining the arbiter of said need. And since refugees could already access health care, education, and protection in the camps, Burugu reminded KBC viewers, they simply "don't need to come [out] from wherever they are [currently residing]." In short, no matter the efforts that were being put into promoting the new reform plan, the encampment policy would ultimately remain intact. Noah, a forty-plus year-old Burundian refugee and father of three in Kakuma, was therefore reluctant to believe that he and his family would move anytime soon from being encamped to being "empowered." "I haven't seen any improvements whatsoever in Kakuma so far. If anything, the conditions are only getting worse by the year," he told me as we sat in his home drinking tea and eating fresh *maandazi* (sweet fried bread). When I inquired about his hopes for the future, Noah struck a melancholic tone and said, "I would like my children to enjoy the freedoms we currently don't have, I want them to study, to live in peace, and not to be stuck here forever." Noah had spent the previous thirteen years building a largely precarious life in Kakuma camp, taking on incentive jobs for aid agencies whenever he could and driving a *boda boda* (motorcycle taxi) to make ends meet. His oldest daughter, he told me with pride, had recently been accepted to a Kenyan secondary school in Eldoret and came back to Kakuma only during school holidays. Noah's skepticism toward the Shirika Plan was thus born of years of firsthand experiences seeing policy after policy that promised to change life in the camp ultimately fail.

These contrasting outlooks on refuge, freedom, belonging, and mobility give a glimpse of the debates on encampment in Kenya (and beyond). Although some public figures, such as Burugu and Mudavadi, continued to espouse the paradoxical view that refugees needed to prove their worth as "guests" of the Kenyan nation and were expected to boost the economy without ever putting down permanent roots, this was challenged by many refugees who felt they had already endured a difficult life in limbo, inertia, and scarcity for too long and deserved to pursue their own aspirations. Even though Shirika promised to move away from a care-and-maintenance paradigm of humanitarian aid by promoting market-based service delivery, a more investment-friendly environment, and the sharing of natural resources between refugees and local citizens, it offered no credible prospect of lifting the draconian laws that had long kept Kakuma's and Kalobeyei's refugees physically in place. If anything, the liberal ideas underpinning Shirika, with its prioritization of free markets, empowerment, entrepreneurial solutions, and leaner aid structures, successfully masked that the policy risked entrenching the status of the refugee camp as a colonial microterritory within Kenya—a precarious homeland for displaced noncitizens, where people's fundamental rights were always partial and revocable and where their very personhood was thrown into question.

The story of Kakuma refugee camp as an occupied refuge thus challenges some false assumptions about the nature of humanitarianism and refugee protection in the global South, particularly Africa. First, providing emergency aid in former colonies such as Kenya is never a "nonviolent" or cleaner alternative to border enforcement that brutally kills thousands of people on Europe's doorstep each year. While the harm caused by forced encampment across the African continent on some levels may seem less publicly visible or even direct, especially when viewed from the comfort of European capitals, refugee camps such as Kakuma are never innocent institutions of civil protection. They have always required the forces of militarized occupation to subject refugees to exceptional regimes of control that are anathema to promises of dignity, humanity, protection, and care. Second, what I have described as humanitarian colonization is not a project just of global North interventionism, in which "white saviors" bypass local sovereignty to rescue indigent African refugees. From the beginning, Kakuma relied heavily on Kenya's willingness to deploy its own police and paramilitary forces as armed guarantors of this foreign-funded humanitarian order. "Nation building," as invoked by Mudavadi during the Shirika dialogue, is, for this reason, not just a question of refugees creating economic wealth that benefits the Kenyan "host nation." It also represents a distinctly colonial project in its own right through which the Kenyan state, over decades and with the help of international aid money, has been able to physically "anchor" itself in (and exercise control over) larger swaths of the country's northern territory than it otherwise could. Viewed from Turkana, although the arrival of aid professionals, experts, materiel, and police and the concerted expansion of camp infrastructures over the years has brought welcome economic development for many, it is also a form of internal colonization. Predominantly middle-class Kenyan officials from downcountry ethnic majorities turned into gatekeepers for international aid organizations and temporarily settled in what they, to this day, consider a backwater of their nation. Thus, for both international actors and this strata of Kenyan staff, the camp, its refugee inhabitants, and its environs have always been a somewhat "foreign" territory that not only elicits feelings of compassion but also has required their firm-handed patronage.

Given these circumstances, the popular excitement about the Shirika Plan's capacity to not only "fix" refugee encampment in Kenya, but also become an example of how to offset the serious cuts in global aid budgets, obscures the reactionary nature of such developmental pipe dreams. When asked how the transition from camp to settlement might change how Kakuma will be policed in the future, the camp's police commander offered a much more sobering prospect. "As part of the Shirika Plan," he said, "we have asked for the construction of at least three additional police stations. Currently, there is only one in Kakuma, with small police posts in key locations throughout the camp. Once the new stations have been built, each can in turn support another five police patrol bases so that we can reach deeper than before into the refugee community."[6] Rather than reversing the militarized occupation that is physically embodied in the camp by defunding institutions of state violence in exchange for credible civic inclusion, Shirika seemed simply to offer more of the same: a horizon of colonial consolidation under the mantle of nation building and regional development, with the unapologetic backing of donors, humanitarian actors, government officials, and liberal scholars.

Decolonizing Spaces of Aid

What future is there for refugee camps such as Kakuma? If one is to believe aid advocates, policymakers, and certain academics, humanitarian camps are already an outdated, inelegant, or even offensive way to deal with survivors of global displacement and disasters: suboptimal and temporary stopgap mechanisms put in place until more durable solutions can, eventually, be found. The UN refugee agency's own search for "alternatives to encampment" and the rise to prominence of urban refugees on global policy agendas have reinforced this perception.[7] In fact, the "camp" label itself has become contentious in aid circles, describing a supposedly anachronistic spatial technology that sits uneasily with liberal humanitarian ideals of human rights, equality, care, nonviolence, and universal compassion. This is ironic because the history of colonization and liberal empire, from which refugee camps were originally born, was itself permeated with such philanthropic beliefs that legitimized, rather than challenged, carceral protectionism as a moral and even "civilizing" force. In short, the liberal distaste for refugee camps as *in theory* objectionable but *in practice* unavoidable architectures of aid hitherto has failed to bring about their categorical delegitimization, let alone dismantlement. To the present day, Kutupalong,

Za'atari, Ain al-Hilweh, Dollo Ado, Mae La, Dadaab, Bidi Bidi, Kakuma, and Nyarugusu are household names in the humanitarian geography of the world, metonyms for a planetary archipelago of encampment in which the wretched of the earth are held. While academic debates on forced migration are sometimes alleged to have "moved on" from camps to center emerging topics such as digital technology, urban asylum, and self-sufficiency, millions of camp inhabitants themselves have not had the luxury of this subterfuge. Their lives are as bound up with the space of the camp as ever.

Although humanitarian colonization refers to a system of collaborative control, wielded jointly by aid and state actors who are backed by private capital and responsible for entrenching militarized camps in the global South, we must also acknowledge the "cracks" in this edifice of containment. Hope for decolonization can be found in the underbelly of such aid operations, where ordinary refugees chart new ways to create solidarities, intentionally inhabiting spaces of control, and are chipping away at confining geographies through unauthorized, "fugitive" movements in, out, and around the camp. Because I have argued, in allusion to Eve Tuck and K. Wayne Yang, that colonization in Kakuma is not a metaphor but a regime of domination that is based on concrete spatial practices and architectures, any decolonizing moves must reflect this reality.[8] Attempts to decolonize spaces of aid cannot be content with pursuing liberal solutions that simply pledge more empowerment, investment, authentic voices, entrepreneurship, improvement, or rebranding of camps overnight as "settlements." When I asked a young South Sudanese man called Majok about the Shirika Plan, he was certain that it would "have a lot of negative impacts for those living in Kakuma." Majok did not suggest that this was due to ill intent by the donors or agencies; rather, he believed that the plan simply downplayed the material need of refugees for free movement and secure housing and disregarded the autonomous life goals of the thousands stranded in the camp. They "neither want to stay in Kenya nor go back to their homeland," he said. Instead, they are "hoping to be resettled to Western countries."[9] Though Kakuma was officially given the status of a municipality in 2023 to create a more amenable climate for private investors, in anticipation of more comprehensive changes in the wake of Shirika, it remained unclear whether turning the camp into a settlement would even work without freeing refugees from the segregative violence of movement passes and forced enclosure. It was far more likely that this new initiative, like others before it, would eventually result in the continued denial of the wages of citizenship to refugees, as well as the obstruction of more hopeful and life-affirming futures beyond the camp.

This is why even the well-intentioned analytical reframing of Kakuma as an accidental urban formation, or "city-camp"—though laudable for recognizing acts of place making by refugees—risks detracting from the uneven, militarized, and colonial ground on which this camp urbanism is built.[10] The camp is not just a "naked city," or a city of lack born from haphazard policies. It is a deliberate technology of population control that is imposed on, and can reshape, urbanized spaces while exceptionalizing the lives of their residents.[11] While many camps increasingly have become sprawling hubs, with city-like looks, dynamics, amenities, and social infrastructures, they have not lost the restrictive features of their campness. On the contrary, cities and certain neighborhoods within them that are exposed to over-policing, raids, curfews, state-authorized premature death, and ethnoracial discrimination may, in turn, gradually have assumed the characteristics of camps. Clampdowns on poverty, the militarization of urban zones, and extrajudicial killings of precarious urban citizens in Nairobi's "slums," such as Mathare, Dandora, and Kibra, show that what Mike Davis once called the "carceral city" in North America may have found its analogue in the "occupied city" of the global South today.[12] The question therefore is not whether Kakuma is a camp, city, or town, or whether it is becoming an integrated settlement, but how carceral or police power is purposely deployed across its unequal geography to mete out death-dealing violence and reorganize life. Explicitly labeling a camp "not a camp" therefore is nothing but a move designed to mask the widening chasm between defending the status quo and imagining liberatory, decarceral, and decolonial futures. In short, the "integrated settlement" is to *the camp* what the "informal settlement" is to *the slum*: a sly euphemism that sugarcoats the liberal violence continuously waged in these places.

Despite the inflation of decolonizing ambitions in recent years, there is much value in their continued pursuit. The scholar and revolutionary Walter Rodney, in fact, reminds us that in Africa (and beyond), the aim ultimately is not "freedom from formal colonial rule," something that was arguably won more than half a century ago, "but the enlargement of freedom within the states which are juridically independent."[13] Kenya gained independence from British rule in 1963, but its society and politics remain tethered to colonial logics of land enclosure, policing of mobility, ethnoracial territoriality, criminalization of poverty, and the permanent violence of dispossession. A decolonial reckoning would mean undoing such durative relations of power and domination that still dictate hierarchies of race, ethnicity, gender, ability, class, knowledge, and ownership, as well as perpetuate a highly reductive notion of "humanity."[14] While we are aware, as Sylvia Tamale reminds us, that "the colonial machinery never goes to sleep," it bears noting that neither do the embodied struggles for decolonization that seek to reorder the world in the search for equality and justice by fighting against borders, carceral violence, and racial apartheid.[15] Humanitarianism, which historically defined the moral bedrock of European colonialization, increasingly has become a prime target for these demands today. Hiring practices, institutional racism, unequal resource allocation, the geopolitical interests of donors, and the imposition of solutions from above all have received criticism. More fundamentally, there has been a growing sense that, to decolonize humanitarianism, we must not only abandon its intellectual foundations and liberal discourses and dismantle the colonial hierarchies of race that are encoded in its mandate, but we should expect in the future to call for more radical, reparatory forms of justice that will shake the system to its core.[16]

Here I want to suggest that, as we strive toward decolonization by rethinking the moral grounding of aid and the fight against racial capitalism and toward reevaluating our relationship with the figure of "the human" that lies at the heart of white supremacist humanitarianism, we must not forget the urgency of abolishing spaces through which its coloniality is ultimately reproduced, made material, and enabled to touch down in space. In Frantz Fanon's anticolonial writing, *decolonization* is shorthand for subverting cruel divisions, racial zoning, and immobilization foisted onto the colonized by colonizers who in this way purport to rightfully hold them captive, segregated, protected, and "in place."[17] Only by reappropriating the means of a free life as fully autonomous people capable of determining their own locomotion and social identity, and by making choices geared toward liberation, can colonized people carve out places of freedom. Decolonization hence is only thinkable, if you like, as an uncompromising "disenclosure of the world" through which partitions and borders of racial homelands, ghettos, reservations, plantations, and encampments are lifted, disallowed, and, ultimately, abolished.[18] In Kakuma, as anywhere, decolonization as disenclosure is not a one-off event; rather, it includes multiple routes of freedom seeking. Even without official movement passes issued by the Department of Refugee Services, people traveled to Kenya's downcountry cities and simply bribed their way through police checkpoints along the way. Clandestine movements in and out of the camp are autonomous political acts by refugees who are deciding to appropriate the space of the camp, to breach its geographical confines, and thus to reject its carceral power. While realizing immediate, short-lived freedoms in this way, most never gave up on their resettlement dreams that would see them ultimately leaving the country that has colonized, and held them in carceral care, for so long. In this spirit, if people are to live happy, healthy, and safe lives in which they denounce colonial subjugation and embrace their desired freedoms, there is no other option but to ensure that their enclosure in camps comes to an end.

Disobedient Futurity

During a visit to Kakuma several years after my original research ended, I sat down with Yusuf. He was a respected elder and businessman in his late fifties wearing immaculately white attire, despite the dust that swirled outside his shop in the Somali market in Kakuma 1. While a lot had changed in Turkana, including the construction of a brand-new tarmac road to link this periphery to Kenya's urban centers farther south, much in the camp remained the same. Developing public infrastructure for the benefit of refugees, until recently, had not been desirable because it was thought of as (quite literally) cementing the notion that they were in Kenya to stay. Yusuf had escaped Somalia during the unfolding horrors of the civil war in 1991. Displaced from his home and unable to continue working as a cook, he walked across the border carrying nothing more than a backpack, his prayer mat, and a bottle of water. When he arrived in a coastal fishing village that was home to Kenya's Bajuni community, Yusuf negotiated his clandestine passage south. "From that Bajuni village I took a boat to Mombasa, where I had heard I could find safety, food, and a place to sleep," he said. "We were temporarily put up in the city's International Show Ground, in the middle of the city. We were on display like animals in a zoo for everyone to see."[19] Yusuf was subsequently moved from one refugee camp to another during the course of his life while trying to start and sustain small businesses to help him get by. From the International Show Ground, where he originally landed, he was first relocated to Mombasa's Utange, then to a camp in the Swaleh Nguru neighborhood, before he and other camp residents were eventually moved by truck to Kakuma in late 1997. "I have seen more of this country than most Kenyans," Yusuf told me with a bitter laugh that spoke of his lifelong travails. "But we aren't citizen of this country." He smiled sourly: "That I want to tell you: We are citizens of the camp."

Yusuf and I were still sitting behind the counter of his shop as the heat of the day began to wane. "Having lived here for so long," I asked cautiously, "do you feel like you are leading a dignified life?" Yusuf looked at me in slight bewilderment. "Dignity," he slowly repeated after me:

> Dignity means to lead a life without abuse, trouble, or needing to fight for scraps of food. But it's so much more than that. It's about building something better, being able to make your own plans, having a family,

maybe children, moving up in the world. Thank God, I was able to have a lot of children who are now in school, although we are still here in the camp.

I wanted to know what he made of the recent promises of empowerment, the talk of economic transformation in Kakuma, and the idea of further integrating refugees like him into Kenyan society. He replied:

> I told you, we are citizens of the camp. First of all, the word *refugee* itself implies a lack of freedom. As refugees, we cannot move freely. Wherever we want to go, we can't without a document or at least some struggle. We are not like Kenyans. Most Kenyans can travel from one corner of the country to another without being questioned, without disturbances. But [for] us refugees? It's always "Where are you going?" "What are you doing?" "Who are you?" "Where are you coming from?" "Do you have permission?" And if you don't have the right documents, [they say,] "Just go back." There is no dignity in that.

Yusuf paused to take a sip of *bunna* (coffee). His graying hair, glassy eyes, and frail stature suddenly made him appear much older than when we began our conversation. He had tolerated life as a refugee, made the best of it for many decades, and seized opportunities when they arose, but he had never really made peace with his displacement or with the camp itself. "I know one thing for sure," Yusuf eventually told me as I stood up to bid him farewell. "Whichever country I will go to next, I will not miss Kenya."

As a byproduct of encampment, this self-made "citizenship" of the encamped fostered a feeling of defiance and collective knowledge born from struggle under a colonial occupation that humanitarianism had imposed. Importantly, it also projected a sense of *disobedient futurity* that went beyond the limits of what the liberal aid regime considered feasible or desirable for refugees in places such as Kakuma. The acceptable futures charted by the UNHCR, especially the horizon of durable solutions, prescribed a form of obedient subjecthood that required refugees to sacrifice personal life goals and ambitions for the sake of a "rules-based" humanitarian order. Patience, fairness, and deservingness were turned into weapons to discipline the autonomist desires, hopes, and actions of those whose happiness and fulfillment was perpetually deferred.[20] Even the many years Yusuf had spent in Kakuma did not quash his belief in a future that would come to pass *after* the camp. For him, the camp, despite the stranglehold it had on his life and the lives of his loved ones, was ultimately a transitory space: a waystation he needed to transit through if he were to gain a life of his own design at the other end. After all, outside Kakuma there was a whole world to be won. While Yusuf knew that his resettlement "process" was at the mercy of the UNHCR and whatever country in Europe or North America was sympathetic to his case, he—like many other citizens of the camp—was not defeatist but disobedient in his resolve to move on. No regulation would deter him from pursuing what he had set his mind on all along. Certainly, humanitarian colonization was not enough to crush his freedom dreams and could deny neither him nor his children their future. He would make sure of that.

Of Camp and Nation

The story of Kakuma as an occupied refuge, where global humanitarianism physically anchors and reproduces itself, is incomplete without also broadening our gaze to the societal context in which the camp was created. As all geographers know, place matters. In this sense, despite signaling an exceptional politics, camps reveal something profound about the societies that deemed them a necessary solution.[21] To this day, Kenya's postcolonial nation-state remains a zombified colonial tool of ethnoracial, gender, and class oppression—a ravenous administrative machinery that feeds not only on the precarity and life force of refugees, asylum seekers, and other "foreigners" but, crucially, also on its own disenfranchised and marginalized citizenry. While independent Kenya was born in the throes of Britain's counterinsurgency against the Mau Mau, during which tens of thousands of people were held in camps and tortured, the new nation—shortly after—deployed the same systematic violence against those it branded as aliens, not quite Kenyans, terrorists, or "Shifta." Inside the skin of the sovereign Kenyan nation still dwelled the undead soul of the colony. Against this backdrop, the refugee camp as it exists today is not an anomaly or a mere remnant of colonial governmentality but the logical result of the country's postcolonial nation building. Postindependence, the camp is no longer primarily a technology to hold captive African subjects who threaten the imperial order but has been repurposed to curtail the rights of non-nationals to stay, move, belong, and live freely. It has become a carceral border technology to contain large swaths of "non-native" migrants in Kenya on humanitarian grounds. It pits *wakimbizi* against *wananchi*, with dire effects. Humanitarian colonization in the Kakuma camp thus ultimately troubles the divide between the logics of colonial rule and those of postcolonial Kenyan nationalism.

This begs the question of what rights can be realized, and what futures imagined, for those who are *not* recognized members of Kenya's "autochthonous" political community if even the lives of the country's own *wananchi* are so casually devalued, rendered disposable, or put at risk. What does it mean for citizenship and belonging if poor Kenyan youth in the urban slums can be abducted, displaced from home, tortured, and killed with the same impunity as Somali or South Sudanese refugees in a camp? Finally, what does it tell us about the nature of borders and global mobility apartheid if the indisputably colonial logics of walling, segregating, and encamping are now being universalized, sanitized with liberal language, and rendered so ordinary and benign that they appear, at least to many, as "common sense" even long after empire has ended?

The point of studying refugees and encampment is not to dwell on the particularities of a unique cruelty. Rather, it helps to open a window into the substratum of the postcolonial state: its self-reproduction by means of colonial territoriality; its continued deferential relationship to former colonizing countries in the global North; and its internal ethnoracial rule over unwanted subject populations. Kenya's postcolonial nationhood was built, in large part, on foundations very similar to those of the previous colonial order: a belief in centralized administrative power, private property and land (dis)possession, and territorialized ethnic belonging and the necessity to police the mobility of precarious citizens and noncitizens presumed to be incorrigibly "out of place."

For much of Kenya's history, camps have been used to discipline anticolonial uprisings and quell the centrifugal forces of competing forms of domestic nationalism. Since the 1990s, however, they have become a more fixed feature of the country's political landscape. No longer fleeting sites for disappearing unruly "native" subjects, they metamorphosed into surrogate homelands for Kenya's permanent "foreign" minorities of refugees against which the nation could reliably position itself. This demonstrated that camps were not only concrete institutions of control but also living symbols for the divisive ethnoracial matrix of nationalism and autochthony.[22] Just like the national borders that give them their meaning, camps always already constituted material "conduits for the realization of postcolonial power."[23] Their boundaries trace imaginary lines that separate the nation from its internally colonized "others" who may have sought *refuge* within its borders but are not allowed to be *at home*. Rather than negating the violence of colonial rule, Nairobi turned its colonizing tendencies inward in a quest to reestablish, once and for all, control over both its body politic and its vast northern hinterland. Encampment has been an opportune technology to segregate hundreds of thousands of refugees with the help of aid funding, and to perpetuate a nationalist narrative around the perils of their indefinite presence, while building militarized capacity for the police to curb this alleged territorial "encroachment." Read in this way, humanitarian colonization is a spatial symptom of the more widespread disease of renewed colonial relations that continue to haunt the Kenyan postcolony today. A society in which the camp is an accepted method for dealing with minoritized and ethnoracially "othered" populations will always also reserve it as a conceivable possibility for the policing and dehumanization of future domestic "others."

In Kakuma, and Kenya more broadly, encampment has wreaked tremendous havoc over the years. The social, psychological, and physical ruination it has caused in the lives of displaced people has been immeasurable. But the key question will be how to exit from these normalized politics of containment that have severely stifled the imaginations of civil society, state agents, and international bodies for so long and to enter into a future of disenclosure in which mobility justice, solidarity, and liberation are put front and center of a radically remade Kenyan society. After all, rather than living in a surrogate "country of UNHCR," refugees in Kenya are tethered to the colonial structures of their host state.[24] Reformist proposals such as the Shirika Plan thus offer little hope for reaching toward the horizon of decolonization. They foresee a future in which refugees, asylum seekers, and other people on the move continue to be subjected to the liberal violence(s) of aid, neoliberal capitalism, and a global rights-based order that demands from those who seldom benefit from its protection that they patiently "wait" for their turn to be free. Liberal policies such as this are designed to deflect any radical momentum that risks dismantling carceral humanitarianism while taking the whole edifice of the bordered nation-state with it. Insights from Kakuma encourage us to look for alternative pathways and freedom dreams that are not beholden to a narrow catechism of nations, borders, and citizenship. In acts of defiant world making and everyday abolitionism, refugees and migrants themselves are already ushering in a world they want to see by jumping fences, defying unjust immigration laws, evading capture, or simply speaking their truth so that they can claim freedoms that the camp continues to withhold. In the postcolonial world, these are not only vernacular forms of anticolonial but also anti-national "world making" that dispute borders, camps, and nations through autonomous actions, dreams, and manifold disobedience.[25] At the same time, there are parallel movements among precarious citizens—in particular, those living in urban slums whom the state has long targeted, abandoned, displaced, maimed, and discarded as rightless refuse equally "alien" to the body politic.

Lifting the occupation by abolishing the camp, hence, is not a limited localized struggle. It requires remaking nothing less than the fabric of postcolonial Kenya. Anti-camp thinking and organizing is meaningful only if it recognizes that, unless debilitating carceral powers, state violence, coloniality, and nationalism are uprooted *inside* as well as *outside* the camp, its logics of exclusion are bound to return. What victory is won by rejecting refugee encampment as a physical institution of mobility policing if police forces are set to continue their violence work unimpeded after the camp's physical demise? This book has brought the violence that humanitarianism routinely enacts at the planet's margins back to the center of the analysis of global apartheid. Its task has been to unpick the layers of a carceral protectionism that has turned large numbers of refugees into populations under militarized occupation and to generate critical insights that may encourage the emergence of more just futures. Without doubt, only refugees and other migrants themselves will spearhead that liberation.

Notes

INTRODUCTION

1. Janmyr and Knudsen, "Introduction," 391.

2. Dyke, "Public Health Aspects of a Refugee Camp"; Easton-Calabria and Herson, "In Praise of Dependencies"; Hyndman, "Refugee Camps as Conflict Zones"; Kibreab, "Myth of Dependency Among Camp Refugees in Somalia 1979–1989"; Krause, *Difficult Life in a Refugee Camp*; Lischer, *Dangerous Sanctuaries*; Milton et al., "Radicalism of the Hopeless"; Mogire, "Refugee Realities"; Muggah, *No Refuge*; Noji, "Public Health in the Aftermath of Disasters."

3. United Nations High Commissioner for Refugees, *Operational Protection in Camps and Settlements*, 38.

4. De Genova, "Spectacles of Migrant 'Illegality.'"

5. Besteman, *Militarized Global Apartheid*; Tesfahuney, "Mobility, Racism and Geopolitics"; Walia, *Border and Rule*.

6. Agier, *Managing the Undesirables*; Duffield, "Governing the Borderlands"; Gazzotti, *Immigration Nation*, 11; Hyndman, "To Help or Not to Help?"

7. Andersson, *Illegality, Inc.*; Lemberg-Pedersen, "Manufacturing Displacement"; Zaiotti, *Externalizing Migration Management*.

8. Lowe, *The Intimacies of Four Continents*.

9. Mbembe, *On the Postcolony*, 13.

10. Gilmore, *Golden Gulag*, 28.

11. This was true for many emerging postcolonial nation-states around the world. I borrow this phrase from Dirik, *The Kurdish Women's Movement*, 5.

12. Mbembe, *On the Postcolony*; Ndlovu-Gatsheni, *Coloniality of Power in Postcolonial Africa*; Stoler, *Duress*; Ngũgĩ wa Thiong'o, *Decolonising the Mind*.

13. Pfingst and Kimari, "Carcerality and the Legacies of Settler Colonial Punishment in Nairobi," 699.

14. Besteman, *Militarized Global Apartheid*; Nevins, "Policing Mobility."

15. Sharma, *Home Rule*.

16. Jenkins, "Ethnicity, Violence, and the Immigrant-Guest Metaphor in Kenya."

17. Mountz, *The Death of Asylum*, xix.

18. Das and Poole, *Anthropology in the Margins of the State*; Cons and Sanyal, "Geographies at the Margins"; hooks, *Feminist Theory*; Tsing, "From the Margins."

19. Comaroff and Comaroff, "Theory from the South," 114; Connell, *Southern Theory*; Santos, *Epistemologies of the South*.

20. De Genova, *The Borders of "Europe"*; Jones, *Violent Borders*; Mainwaring, *At Europe's Edge*; Squire, *The Contested Politics of Mobility*; Tazzioli, *The Making of Migration*; Vaughan-Williams, *Europe's Border Crisis*; Vradis et al., *New Borders*.

21. Albahari, *Crimes of Peace*; Boochani, *No Friend but the Mountains*; De León, *The Land of Open Graves*.

22. Benton, "African Expatriates and Race in the Anthropology of Humanitarianism"; Daley, "Towards an Anti-Racist Humanitarianism in a Post-Liberal World," 360.

23. Lemberg-Pedersen et al., *Postcoloniality and Forced Migration*; Picozza, *The Coloniality of Asylum*; Rodríguez, "The Coloniality of Migration and the 'Refugee Crisis'"; Tascón, "Refugees and the Coloniality of Power."

24. Dragsbaek Schmidt et al., *Refugees and Forced Migration in the Horn and Eastern Africa*; Falola and Yacob-Haliso, *African Refugees*; Fiddian-Qasmiyeh, "Introduction"; Nawyn, "New Directions for Research on Migration in the Global South"; Pasquetti and Sanyal, *Displacement*.

Although the binary of "global North" and "global South" is an imperfect, if not problematic, signifier that may seem discursively to cement rather than reduce global disparities, it serves as useful shorthand for recognizing the politically, socially, economically, and epistemically unequal global distribution of power that was largely produced (and continues to be shaped) by global geographies of colonization, empire, and capitalist exploitation. See Besteman, *Militarized Global Apartheid*; Sud and Sánchez-Ancochea, "Southern Discomfort."

25. Daley, "Refugees and Underdevelopment in Africa"; Harrell-Bond, *Imposing Aid*; Hyndman, *Managing Displacement*; Kibreab, *Refugees and Development in Africa*; Landau, *The Humanitarian Hangover*; Malkki, *Purity and Exile*.

26. Estroff, "Identity, Disability and Schizophrenia," 250. See also Vigh, "Crisis and Chronicity."

27. Jumbert and Pascucci, *Citizen Humanitarianism at European Borders*; Papada et al., "Pop-Up Governance."

28. Loescher and Milner, "Protracted Refugee Situations and State and Regional Insecurity," 4.

29. United Nations High Commissioner for Refugees, *Global Trends in Forced Displacement in 2021*, 20.

30. Barnett, *Empire of Humanity*; Mudimbe, *The Invention of Africa*; Skinner and Lester, "Humanitarianism and Empire."

31. Chimni, "The Geopolitics of Refugee Studies"; Gatrell, *The Making of the Modern Refugee*.

32. Anderson et al., "Slow Emergencies," 623.

33. McKittrick, "Plantation Futures," 7.

34. Betts et al., *UNHCR*, 32.

35. Mangala, *Africa and the New World Era*, 7.

36. Rostis, *Organizing Disaster*, 69.

37. Betts, "International Cooperation Between North and South to Enhance Refugee Protection in Regions of Origin"; European Council on Refugees and Exiles, *Guarding Refugee Protection Standards in Regions of Origin*; Milner, *Refugees, the State and the Politics of Asylum in Africa*.

38. Active Learning Network for Accountability and Performance, "The State of the Humanitarian System," 37; Glasman, *Humanitarianism and the Quantification of Human Needs*.

39. United Nations High Commissioner for Refugees, *Global Trends in Forced Displacement in 2021*; UNHCR Budget and Expenditure, accessed October 28, 2022, https://reporting.unhcr.org/budget-expenditure.

40. Chakrabarty, *Provincializing Europe*.

41. Hyndman and Giles, *Refugees in Extended Exile*.

42. Landau, "A Chronotope of Containment Development."

43. Reid-Henry, "On the Politics of Our Humanitarian Present," 757; Weiss and Barnett, *Humanitarianism in Question*, 6.

44. Feldman and Ticktin, *In the Name of Humanity*.

45. Fassin, *Humanitarian Reason*.

46. Calhoun, "The Imperative to Reduce Suffering."

47. Fassin, "Inequality of Lives, Hierarchies of Humanity," 239.

48. Wynter, "Unsettling the Coloniality of Being/Power/Truth/Freedom," 269.

49. Barnett, *Empire of Humanity*; Lester and Dussart, *Colonization and the Origins of Humanitarian Governance*.

50. Lester and Dussart, *Colonization and the Origins of Humanitarian Governance*, 14.

51. Stoler, *Duress*, 188.

52. Mudimbe, *The Invention of Africa*, 33; Ndlovu-Gatsheni, *Coloniality of Power in Postcolonial Africa*; Rodney, *How Europe Underdeveloped Africa*; Ngũgĩ wa Thiong'o, *Decolonising the Mind*.

53. Walcott, "The Problem of the Human"; Wynter, "Unsettling the Coloniality of Being/Power/Truth/ Freedom."

54. Daley, "Towards an Anti-Racist Humanitarianism in a Post-Liberal World"; Pallister-Wilkins, "HuManitarianism."

55. Breton et al., "Murderous Humanitarianism."

56. Mbembe, *Critique of Black Reason*, 12.

57. Barth and Hobson, *Civilizing Missions in the Twentieth Century*.

58. Barth and Hobson, *Civilizing Missions in the Twentieth Century*, 11.

59. Asad, "Reflections on Violence, Law, and Humanitarianism," 394.

60. Crawford and Pert, *International Humanitarian Law*; International Committee of the Red Cross, *The Geneva Conventions of 12 August 1949*.

61. Reid-Henry, "Humanitarianism as Liberal Diagnostic."

62. Fassin and Pandolfi, "Introduction"; Weizman, *The Least of All Possible Evils*, 4.

63. Weizman, *The Least of All Possible Evils*, 3–4.

64. Atanasoski, *Humanitarian Violence*; Garelli and Tazzioli, "Military-Humanitarianism"; McCormack and Gilbert, "The Geopolitics of Militarism and

Humanitarianism"; Nunan, *Humanitarian Invasion*; Weiss and Campbell, "Military Humanitarianism."

65. De Genova, *The Borders of "Europe"*; Loyd et al., *Beyond Walls and Cages*; Mountz, *The Death of Asylum*.

66. Pallister-Wilkins, *Humanitarian Borders*; Walters, "Foucault and Frontiers"; Williams, "From Humanitarian Exceptionalism to Contingent Care."

67. Walters, "Foucault and Frontiers," 138.

68. Isakjee et al., "Liberal Violence and the Racial Borders of the European Union"; Neu, *Just Liberal Violence*.

69. Chouliaraki, *The Ironic Spectator*, 11.

70. Hyndman and Mountz, "Refuge or Refusal," 85–86.

71. Dyke, "Public Health Aspects of a Refugee Camp"; Harrell-Bond, *Imposing Aid*; Hyndman and Giles, *Refugees in Extended Exile*; Krause, *Difficult Life in a Refugee Camp*; Noji, "Public Health in the Aftermath of Disasters"; Priddy et al., "Gender-Based Violence in a Complex Humanitarian Context."

72. Lopez et al., "Geographies of Humanitarian Violence," 2233.

73. Davis and Isakjee, "Ruins of Empire"; Mayblin et al., "Necropolitics and the Slow Violence of the Everyday"; Nixon, *Slow Violence and the Environmentalism of the Poor*, 2.

74. Galtung, "Violence, Peace, and Peace Research," 171; Scheper-Hughes and Bourgois, "Introduction."

75. Christian and Dowler, "Slow and Fast Violence," 1072.

76. Gilmore, *Golden Gulag*.

77. Agier, *Managing the Undesirables*, 3.

78. Gilroy, *Between Camps*.

79. Diken and Laustsen, "The Camp"; Edkins, "Sovereign Power, Zones of Indistinction, and the Camp"; Minca, "Geographies of the Camp."

80. Hom, *Empire's Mobius Strip*, 7.

81. Ek, "Giorgio Agamben and the Spatialities of the Camp."

82. Agamben, *Homo Sacer*; Agamben, *State of Exception*; Minca, "Giorgio Agamben and the New Biopolitical Nomos."

83. Agamben, *Homo Sacer*.

84. Foucault, *The History of Sexuality, Volume 1*, 138.

85. Foucault, *The History of Sexuality, Volume 1*, 143; Foucault, *Security, Territory, Population*.

86. Malkki, "Refugees and Exile," 498.

87. Bulley, "Inside the Tent"; Glasman, *Humanitarianism and the Quantification of Human Needs*; Hyndman, *Managing Displacement*; Jaji, "Social Technology and Refugee Encampment in Kenya."

88. Kallio et al., "Refugeeness as Political Subjectivity"; Rygiel, "Politicizing Camps"; Sigona, "Campzenship."

89. Martin, "From Spaces of Exception to 'Campscapes'"; Oesch, "The Refugee Camp as a Space of Multiple Ambiguities and Subjectivities"; Ramadan, "Spatialising the Refugee Camp."

90. Howell and Richter-Montpetit, "Racism in Foucauldian Security Studies," 6 (emphasis added).

91. Weheliye, *Habeas Viscus*.

92. Gilroy, *Between Camps*, 88; Netz, *Barbed Wire*.

93. Forth, *Barbed-Wire Imperialism*; Herbert, *Policing Space*; Khalili, *Time in the Shadows*; Mbembe, *Necropolitics*; Weheliye, *Habeas Viscus*.

94. Sequeira, "The Ethiopian Refugees in Kenya."

95. Turner, "What Is a Refugee Camp?"

96. Crush, "Scripting the Compound"; Edkins, "Sovereign Power, Zones of Indistinction, and the Camp"; Purdeková, *Making Ubumwe*.

97. United Nations High Commissioner for Refugees, *Global Report 2018*.

98. Chaulia, "The Politics of Refugee Hosting in Tanzania"; Milner, *Refugees, the State and the Politics of Asylum in Africa*; Rutinwa, "The End of Asylum?"; Verdirame and Harrell-Bond, *Rights in Exile*.

99. Stoler, *Duress*, 74.

100. Mamdani, *Citizen and Subject*; Mbembe, *On the Postcolony*; Pierre, *The Predicament of Blackness*.

101. Interview, Kakuma, March 8, 2015.

102. Slaughter and Crisp, "A Surrogate State?" 8.

103. Verdirame and Harrell-Bond, *Rights in Exile*, 15.

104. Maingi and Omeje, "Policing Refugees in Fragile States," 75.

105. Hyndman, *Managing Displacement*, xvi.

106. Tuck and Yang, "Decolonization Is Not a Metaphor."

107. Abrams, "Notes on the Difficulty of Studying the State"; Aretxaga, "Maddening States"; Gupta, *Red Tape*; Mitchell, "Society, Economy and the State Effect"; Painter, "Prosaic Geographies of Stateness."

108. Bierschenk and Olivier de Sardan, *States at Work*; Chalfin, *Neoliberal Frontiers*.

109. Netz, *Barbed Wire*, 136.

110. Seigel, *Violence Work*, 14.

111. Bhandar, *Colonial Lives of Property*; Neocleous, *A Critical Theory of Police Power*.

112. Fanon, *The Wretched of the Earth*, 3.

113. Anderson and Killingray, "Consent, Coercion and Colonial Control"; Throup, "Crime, Politics and the Police in Colonial Kenya, 1939–63"; Waller, "Towards a Contextualisation of Policing in Colonial Kenya."

114. Fanon, *The Wretched of the Earth*, 38.

115. Cacho and Melamed, "'Don't Arrest Me, Arrest the Police,'" 159.

116. Beek et al., *Police in Africa*; Hills, *Policing Africa*.

117. LeBrón, *Policing Life and Death*.

118. Chouliaraki, *The Ironic Spectator*, 40; Foucault, "The Birth of Biopolitics"; Mbembe, *Necropolitics*.

119. Kotef, *Movement and the Ordering of Freedom*.

120. Mbembe, *Necropolitics*, 4; Mwangi, "Refugees and the State in Kenya."

121. Mbembe, *Necropolitics*, 79.

122. Maldonado-Torres, "On the Coloniality of Being"; Memmi, *The Colonizer and the Colonized*; Quijano, "Coloniality of Power and Eurocentrism in Latin America."

123. Mudimbe, *The Invention of Africa*, 14.

124. Sharma, *Home Rule*, 13.

125. Berman, *Control and Crisis in Colonial Kenya*; Lind, "Devolution, Shifting Centre-Periphery Relationships and Conflict in Northern Kenya."

126. Low and Lonsdale, "East Africa."

127. Blauner, "Internal Colonialism and Ghetto Revolt"; Calvert, "Internal Colonisation, Development and Environment"; Wolpe, *The Theory of Internal Colonization*.

128. Kotef, *Movement and the Ordering of Freedom*, 38.

129. Newton, "A Functional Definition of Politics."

130. Junaid, "Death and Life Under Occupation"; Shelley, *Endgame in the Western Sahara*; Weizman, *The Least of All Possible Evils*.

131. Stoler, *Duress*, 77.

132. Crisp, "A State of Insecurity"; Jansen, "The Refugee Camp as Warscape."

133. Mamdani, *Citizen and Subject*, 60.

134. Mbembe, *Necropolitics*, 98.

135. Ghoddousi and Page, "Using Ethnography and Assemblage Theory in Political Geography"; Herbert, "For Ethnography"; Megoran, "For Ethnography in Political Geography"; Mountz, *Seeking Asylum*.

136. Clifford, "Anthropology and/as Travel," 5; Rodgers, "'Hanging Out' with Forced Migrants."

137. Pezzani and Heller, "A Disobedient Gaze," 294.

138. Conversation, Kakuma, July 30, 2017.

139. Anderson and McKnight, "Kenya at War"; Lind et al., "Killing a Mosquito with a Hammer"; Mogire and Mkutu, "Counter-Terrorism in Kenya."

140. Malkki, "Speechless Emissaries," 388.

141. Brankamp, "Feeling the Refugee Camp," 387.

142. Harrell-Bond and Voutira, "In Search of 'Invisible' Actors," 291; Krause, "Researching Forced Migration"; Pittaway et al., "Stop Stealing Our Stories."

143. Brankamp, "Feeling the Refugee Camp," 388.

144. Van Maanen, "Epilogue," 346.

145. Agamben, *Homo Sacer*.

CHAPTER 1. REFUGE

1. Bhalla, "Poets and Models Star at World's First Refugee Camp TEDx Event in Kenya."

2. Brankamp, "The Cynical Recasting of Refugees as Raconteurs Can't Mask the Grim Reality."

3. "Behind The Scenes—The Making of TEDx Kakuma Camp," video, posted February 13, 2019, accessed November 23, 2022, https://www.youtube.com/watch?v=vwxRrubJfpQ&t=523s.

4. The Dadaab refugee camp complex is composed of four separate camps: Dagahaley, Hagadera, Ifo, and Ifo II.

5. Duffield, "Challenging Environments"; Hoffmann, "Humanitarian Security in Jordan's Azraq Camp."

6. United Nations High Commissioner for Refugees, *Visitor's Guide*, 8.

7. Brankamp, "The Cynical Recasting of Refugees as Raconteurs Can't Mask the Grim Reality"; Daley, "Rescuing African Bodies"; Ilcan and Rygiel, "Resiliency Humanitarianism"; Turner, "#Refugees Can Be Entrepreneurs Too!"

8. Halima Aden, "A Place of Hope: From Refugee Camp to International Fashion Model," TEDxKakumaCamp, June 9, 2018, YouTube, 7 min., 39 sec., https://www.youtube.com/watch?v=roe-STL8JxI&t=53s.

9. International Finance Corporation, "Kakuma: A Refugee Camp with Its Own Informal Economy," video, posted May 3, 2018, accessed January 12, 2023, https://www.youtube.com/watch?v=oXLpweEIA1E.

10. Jansen, *Kakuma Refugee Camp*; Oka, "Unlikely Cities in the Desert."

11. Betts, *The Wealth of Refugees*; Betts et al., *Refugee Economies*; International Finance Corporation, *Kakuma as a Marketplace*; Sanghi et al., *"Yes" in My Backyard?*

12. Jeff Crisp (@JFCrisp), tweet dated February 5, 2019.

13. Agier et al., *The Jungle*; International Rescue Committee, "Moria Refugee Camp During the Coronavirus Pandemic"; UNHCR data, accessed November 23, 2022, https://data.unhcr.org/en/country/ken/796.

14. United Nations Human Settlements Program, *Kakuma and Kalobeyei Spatial Profile*, 76.

15. Betts, *The Wealth of Refugees*; International Finance Corporation, *Kakuma as a Marketplace*. *Downcountry* is a term commonly used to describe Kenya's south-central heartland around Nairobi.

16. Conversation, Nairobi, July 6, 2022.

17. *Wakimbizi* is from the Kiswahili root *-kimbia* (to run or flee). Teferra, "Kakuma Refugee Camp," 164.

18. Ngutulu, "Paradise in Hell."

19. Aminah Rwimo, "Telling Our Own Stories: Finding Hope Through Film," TEDxKakumaCamp, June 9, 2018, YouTube, 10 min., 35 sec., https://www.youtube.com/watch?v=ouy23z9BS3I&t=10s.

20. Schechter, "Governing 'Lost Boys'"; Verdirame and Harrell-Bond, *Rights in Exile*.

21. Rudoren, "Calm Boss Overseeing a Syrian Refugee Camp's Chaos."

22. Field notes, August 25, 2016.

23. Interview, Kakuma, November 26, 2016.

24. Interview, Kakuma, October 30, 2016.

25. Jansen, *Kakuma Refugee Camp*.

26. Only after independence on July 9, 2011, would these refugees be known as "South Sudanese."

27. The geographical and administrative term *Equatoria* originated in the early period of the Anglo-Egyptian Sudan. Since January 2017, this region has been subdivided into nine states (Tambura, Gbudwe, Maridi, Amadi, Terekeka, Yei River, Jubek, Imatong, Kapoeta). Many of the region's local communities are agrarian, as opposed to the predominantly pastoralist and numerically larger Nuer and Dinka. During the civil war that started in 2013, the Equatorian states have become the scenes of some of the worst violence against civilian populations: see Jok, "Diversity, Unity, and Nation Building in

South Sudan"; Justin and Van Leeuven, "The Politics of Conflict in Yei River County, South Sudan." Interview with an Ethiopian refugee from that period, February 24, 2017.

28. I have interviewed numerous Ethiopians from that generation, all of whom were former military officers. Interviews were conducted in Kakuma on August 1, 2016, and February 14, 2017.

29. Jansen, *Kakuma Refugee Camp*.

30. Grayson, *Children of the Camp*; Schechter, "Governing 'Lost Boys,'" 91; Verdirame, "Human Rights and Refugees."

31. The Bajuni are a coastal fishing community with low social status in Somalia's clan system. The Barawa are an urban coastal community with origins in the ethnically diverse mercantile classes in the city of Brava. For more in-depth information, see Hill, *No Redress*. Interview, Kakuma, July 21, 2017.

32. Interview, Kakuma, May 19, 2017.

33. Interview, Kakuma, July 21, 2017.

34. "Somali Bantu" populations are the descendants of slaves who were taken from the East African coast during the Indian Ocean slave trade, mostly from present-day Tanzania, to work in agriculture in the riverine area between the Juba and Shabelle rivers in Somalia. Catherine Besteman provides a superb account of the ethnogenesis of "Somali Bantu" identity and its operationalization for humanitarian purposes since the start of the Somali civil war: see Besteman, *Making Refuge*; Iazzolino, "Power Geometries of Encampment"; Schechter, "Governing 'Lost Boys,'" 91.

35. Jamal, "Minimum Standards and Essential Needs in a Protracted Refugee Situation"; Kenya National Bureau of Statistics, *The 2009 Kenya Population and Housing Census*; Kenya National Bureau of Statistics, *The 2019 Kenya Population and Housing Census*.

36. Grayson, *Children of the Camp*.

37. President Salva Kiir Mayardit belongs to the Dinka Bahr al-Ghazal, whereas former Vice President Riek Machar is a Nuer and has a history of collaboration with the Khartoum government during the second Sudanese civil war.

38. The population size of each camp section differs greatly: Kakuma 1 (62,115), Kakuma 2 (18,768), Kakuma 3 (42,097), and Kakuma 4 (21,634), statistics were provided by the UNHCR's Kakuma Head of Sub-Office on August 7, 2017.

39. Horst, *Transnational Nomads*; Ikanda, "Animating 'Refugeeness' Through Vulnerabilities"; Jansen, "Between Vulnerability and Assertiveness."

40. While two Saudis and one Burkinabé were still in the camp at the time this was written, the Iranian and Ukrainian refugees had been resettled and repatriated, respectively, before I arrived in Kakuma.

41. Khat (or *qat, miraa, veve*) is a stimulant plant that is popular across the Horn of Africa.

42. Woroniecka-Krzyzanowska, "The Right to the Camp."

43. Harvey, "The Right to the City"; Lefebvre, *Writings on Cities*.

44. Interview, March 18, 2015.

45. Agier, *Borderlands*, 61.

46. Feldman, "What Is a Camp?"

47. Nguyen, "Refugeetude."

48. Conversation with humanitarian in the UNHCR compound, March 5, 2015; Malkki, *The Need to Help*.

49. Conversation, January 21, 2017.

50. Lawton, "Midnight at the Oasis."

51. Audet, "Humanitarian Space"; Thürer, "Dunant's Pyramid"; Yamashita, *Humanitarian Space and International Politics.*

52. Tennant et al., "Safeguarding Humanitarian Space," 4.

53. Hyndman, "To Help or Not to Help?"; Kleinfeld, "Misreading the Post-Tsunami Political Landscape in Sri Lanka"; Slim, "Violence and Humanitarianism."

54. Duffield, "Risk-Management and the Fortified Aid Compound," 457; Scott-Smith and Breeze, *Structures of Protection?*

55. *Oxford English Dictionary*, 3d ed. (Oxford: Oxford University Press, 2022), s.v. "colonization."

56. Toomey, "Aid and Development at the Thailand-Myanmar Border."

57. Smirl, *Spaces of Aid*, 16.

58. United Nations Human Settlements Program, *Kakuma and Kalobeyei Spatial Profile*, 76.

59. Interview with UNHCR field unit officer who has been stationed in Kakuma since 1996, July 21, 2017.

60. Jansen, "The Accidental City," 122.

61. For more on this, see Jansen, "The Accidental City"; Schechter, "Governing 'Lost Boys.'"

62. Betts and Bloom, *Humanitarian Innovation*; Sandvik, "Now Is the Time to Deliver."

63. For example, between 2016 and 2019 the start-up Sanivation conducted a trial program in which the feces of Kakuma's refugee residents were recycled into usable briquettes for cooking in the camp: Bhagat and Roderick, "Banking on Refugees"; Global System for Mobile Communications Association, *Mobile-Enabled Energy for Humanitarian Contexts*; Scott-Smith, "Humanitarian Neophilia"; Thomas et al., "Moving Beyond Informal Action."

64. Hilhorst and Jansen, "Humanitarian Space as Arena," 1120.

65. United Nations Human Settlements Program, *Kakuma and Kalobeyei Spatial Profile*, 76.

66. Betts et al., "The Kalobeyei Settlement"; United Nations High Commissioner for Refugees, *Kalobeyei Integrated Socio-Economic Development Plan in Turkana West.*

67. Miller, *UNHCR as a Surrogate State*; Slaughter and Crisp, "A Surrogate State?"

68. Brankamp, "Camp Abolition," 109; Jansen and de Bruijne, "Humanitarian Spill-Over."

69. UNHCR data, accessed January 10, 2023, http://www.unhcr.org/57308e616.html.

70. Lingelbach, *On the Edges of Whiteness*; Shadle, "Reluctant Humanitarians."

71. Abdelaaty, *Discrimination and Delegation*, 135.

72. Milner, *Refugees, the State and the Politics of Asylum in Africa*; Veney, *Forced Migration in Eastern Africa*; Verdirame and Harrell-Bond, *Rights in Exile*, 31.

73. Abdelaaty, *Discrimination and Delegation.*

74. Brankamp and Daley, "Laborers, Migrants, Refugees"; Hyndman, *Managing Displacement*, 130; Mwangi, "Refugees and the State in Kenya"; Nyaoro, "Refugee Hosting and Conflict Resolution"; Schechter, "Governing 'Lost Boys.'"

75. Buzan et al., *Security*; Graham and Gregory, "Security," 672; Neocleous, *Critique of Security.*

76. Weitzberg, *We Do Not Have Borders*, 41–42.

77. Schlee, "Territorializing Ethnicity."

78. Whittaker, *Insurgency and Counterinsurgency*.

79. Lochery, "Rendering Difference Visible"; Scharrer, "Ambiguous Citizens."

80. Anderson, "Remembering Wagalla."

81. Hyndman and Nylund, "UNHCR and the Status of Prima Facie Refugees in Kenya."

82. Maina, "Securitization of Kenya's Asylum Space."

83. Campbell, "Urban Refugees in Nairobi"; Verdirame and Harrell-Bond, *Rights in Exile*, 33.

84. These additional camps included Habasweine, Rhamu, Liboi, Mandera, Banessa, El Wak, Walda, Swaleh Nguru, Utange, Marafa, Hatimi, and Jomvu.

85. United Nations High Commissioner for Refugees, *UNHCR Comprehensive Policy on Urban Refugees*, 10.

86. Crawford, *The Urbanization of Forced Displacement*; United Nations High Commissioner for Refugee, *UNHCR Policy on Alternatives to Camps*; United Nations High Commissioner for Refugee, *UNHCR Policy on Refugee Protection and Solutions in Urban Areas*.

87. Human Rights Watch, *Human Rights Watch World Report 1993—Kenya*.

88. Abdelaaty, *Discrimination and Delegation*; Veney, *Forced Migration in Eastern Africa*.

89. Glück, "Security Urbanism and the Counterterror State in Kenya"; Maina, "Securitization of Kenya's Asylum Space."

90. Kagwanja and Juma, "Somali Refugees," 219.

91. Maina, "Development of Refugee Law in Kenya."

92. Government of Kenya, *The Refugee Act 2006*.

93. Claire Walkey has done an excellent in-depth study of refugee registration in Kenya: see Walkey, "Building a Bureaucracy."

94. Kenya Defense Forces, *Operation Linda Nchi*.

95. Anderson and McKnight, "Kenya at War."

96. Al-Bulushi, "Race, Space, and 'Terror'"; Brankamp and Glück, "Camps and Counterterrorism," 530.

97. Yarnell and Thomas, *Between a Rock and a Hard Place*.

98. Bachmann, "Governmentality and Counterterrorism"; Glück, "Security Urbanism and the Counterterror State in Kenya"; Mwangi, "The 'Somalinisation' of Terrorism."

99. Straziuso and Odula, "One of Westgate Mall Attackers Lived in Kenyan Refugee Camp."

100. Government of Kenya et al., *Tripartite Agreement Between the Government of the Republic of Kenya, the Government of the Federal Republic of Somalia and the United Nations High Commissioner for Refugees Governing the Voluntary Repatriation of Somali Refugees Living in Kenya*.

101. Ombati, "Refugees Ordered to Relocate to Kakuma, Dadaab Camps as Urban Registration Centres Shut."

102. Some observers in Eastleigh jokingly referred to it as "Operation Osama Watch," an allusion to the former Saudi-born head of Al-Qaida.

103. Balakian, "Money Is Your Government"; Brankamp and Glück, "Camps and Counterterrorism"; Independent Policing Oversight Authority, *Monitoring Report on Operation Sanitization Eastleigh Publicly Known as "Usalama Watch"*; Kenya National Commission on Human Rights, *Return of the Gulag*.

104. Wirth, "Reflections from the Encampment Decision in the High Court of Kenya."

105. Government of Kenya, *The Security Laws (Amendment) Act.*

106. Canadian Broadcasting Corporation, "Inside Dadaab"; Mutambo, "In Wake of Garissa Attack, Kenya Frustrated by Dadaab Issue."

107. Brankamp and Glück, "Camps and Counterterrorism," 535–36 (emphasis added).

108. Bhalla, "Kenya Orders Closure Dadaab Refugee Camp This Year."

109. Wambui, "Kenya to Close Kakuma, Dadaab Refugee Camps by June 2022."

110. Weima and Minca, "Closing Camps," 272.

111. Government of Kenya, "Kenya: P[rincipal] S[ecretary] Karanja Kibicho Explains Why the Government Is Shutting Down Refugee Camps," press release, May 11, 2016, accessed January 25, 2025, https://reliefweb.int/report/kenya/kenya-ps-karanja-kibicho -explains-why-government-shutting-down-refugee-camps.

112. BBC, February 9, 2017, accessed January 25, 2023, https://www.bbc.co.uk/news /world-africa-38917681.

113. Conversation, December 14, 2016.

114. "Nairobi Declaration on Durable Solutions for Somali Refugees and Reintegration of Returnees in Somalia," Intergovernmental Authority on Development, March 25, 2017, https://igad.int/communique-special-summit-of-the-igad-assembly-of-heads-of -state-and-government-on-durable-solutions-for-somali-refugees.

115. Janmyr, "Revisiting the Civilian and Humanitarian Character of Refugee Camps," 227.

116. United Nations High Commissioner for Refugees, *Conclusion No. 48 (XXXVIII).*

117. Da Costa, *Maintaining the Civilian and Humanitarian Character of Asylum*; Janmyr, "Revisiting the Civilian and Humanitarian Character of Refugee Camps"; United Nations High Commissioner for Refugees, *Guidance Note on Maintaining the Civilian and Humanitarian Character of Asylum*, 10.

118. Mbembe, *On the Postcolony*, 175.

119. United Nations High Commissioner for Refugees, *Operational Protection in Camps and Settlement*, 27.

120. Interview, Kakuma, March 2, 2015.

121. This is based on an interview with a senior UNHCR protection officer in Nairobi on March 30, 2017, and email correspondence with another senior protection officer on January 21, 2017.

122. Crisp, "A State of Insecurity."

123. Lischer, *Dangerous Sanctuaries*; Muggah, *No Refuge.*

124. Okech, "Asymmetrical Conflict and Human Security"; Zolberg et al., *Escape from Violence.*

125. United Nations High Commissioner for Refugees, *Operational Protection in Camps and Settlement*, 42.

126. Jansen, *Kakuma Refugee Camp.*

127. Graham, *Cities Under Siege*; Lutz, "Making War at Home in the United States"; Masco, *The Theater of Operations.*

128. Anyanya II were a group of mutineers during the early phase (1978–89) of the Second Sudanese Civil War. *Mai-Mai* is a broad term used to describe community-based militias and defense groups that have sprung up in the Democratic Republic of the

Congo. John Garang was the legendary leader of the SPLA until 2005, when he was killed in a helicopter crash.

129. Security Awareness training, August 19, 2016.

130. Security Awareness training, August 19, 2016.

131. United Nations High Commissioner for Refugees, *Operational Protection in Camps and Settlement*, B8.

132. Fleming, "Let's Change the Way We Think About Refugee Camps."

133. Al-Jazeera English, "Can #TEDxKakumaCamp Change How Refugee Camps Are Seen?" video, streamed June 7, 2018, https://www.youtube.com/watch?v=S3nj38zTQKs.

134. Al-Jazeera English, "Can #TEDxKakumaCamp Change How Refugee Camps Are Seen?"

135. See the TEDxKakumaCamp website, accessed January 21, 2023, https://www.ted.com/tedx/events/21032.

136. Kotef, *Movement and the Ordering of Freedom*; Lowe, *The Intimacies of Four Continents*.

137. Rodriguez et al., "Carceral Protectionism."

CHAPTER 2. OCCUPATION

Parts of chapter 2 previously appeared as "'Occupied Enclave': Policing and the Underbelly of Humanitarian Governance in Kakuma Refugee Camp, Kenya," *Political Geography* 71 (2019): 67–77. Reprinted with permission from Elsevier.

1. Brankamp, "Occupied Enclave," 67.

2. Anderson, "Punishment, Race and 'the Raw Native,'" 479; Pfingst and Kimari, "Carcerality and the Legacies of Settler Colonial Punishment in Nairobi," 710.

3. Steinberg, *Thin Blue*.

4. Branch, "Humanitarianism, Violence, and the Camp in Northern Uganda," 495.

5. Lamphear, "Aspects of Turkana Leadership During the Era of Primary Resistance," 226.

6. Parkinson, "Notes on the Northern Frontier Province, Kenya," 162.

7. Collins, "The Turkana Patrol of 1918 Reconsidered," 109.

8. McCabe, "The Failure to Encapsulate"; Shanguhyia, "Insecure Borderlands, Marginalization, and Local Perceptions of the State in Turkana, Kenya, Circa 1920–2014."

9. The "Kapenguria Six"—Jomo Kenyatta (who would become the country's first president), Bildad Kaggia, Kung'u Karumba, Fred Kubai, Paul Ngei, and Achieng Oneko—were charged with sedition in the context of the colonial Mau emergency (1952–60) and were sentenced to imprisonment and internal exile. The anticolonial activist Harry Thuku (1895–1970) was exiled to Kismayu in modern-day Somalia in 1922–25, from which he was relocated to Lamu, Witu and, finally, Marsabit.

10. Maciel, "Memoirs of a Frontier Man," 25.

11. Bernault, "The Politics of Enclosure in Colonial and Post-Colonial Africa," 15.

12. Netz, *Barbed Wire*.

13. The colonial regime referred to the Kenya Land and Freedom Army as the Mau Mau.

14. Anderson, *Histories of the Hanged*; Elkins, *Imperial Reckoning*; Kariuki, *"Mau Mau" Detainee*.

15. Elkins, *Imperial Reckoning*, 129.

16. Pesek, "The Boma and the Peripatetic Ruler," 234.

17. Kariuki, *"Mau Mau" Detainee*, 136–37.

18. Lenin, *Lenin Collected Works, Volume 3*, 562.

19. Blauner, "Internal Colonialism and Ghetto Revolt"; Ture and Hamilton, *Black Power*; Wolpe, *The Theory of Internal Colonization*.

20. Calvert, "Internal Colonisation, Development and Environment," 53.

21. Anand, "Colonization with Chinese Characteristics"; Byler, *Terror Capitalism*; De Coss-Corzo, "The Infrastructures of Internal Colonialism"; Evans, "Internal Colonialism in the Central Highlands of Vietnam"; Gonzalez Casanova, "Internal Colonialism and National Development."

22. Duschinski, *Resisting Occupation in Kashmir*; Stirk, *The Politics of Military Occupation*.

23. Junaid, "Death and Life Under Occupation"; Makdisi, *Palestine Inside Out*; Visweswaran, "Introduction," 7.

24. Weizman, *Hollow Land*.

25. Amir, "The Making of a Void Sovereignty"; Loizides, "Contested Migration and Settler Politics in Cyprus"; Mbembe, *Necropolitics*, 81; Ophir et al., *The Power of Inclusive Exclusion*.

26. Gordon, "From Colonization to Separation"; Legassick and Wolpe, "The Bantustans and Capital Accumulation in South Africa"; Peteet, *Space and Mobility in Palestine*.

27. Balaton-Chrimes, "Statelessness, Identity Cards and Citizenship as Status in the Case of the Nubians of Kenya."

28. Galaty, "Boundary-Making and Pastoral Conflict along the Kenyan-Ethiopian Borderlands"; Wario Arero, "Coming to Kenya."

29. Ndzovu, *Muslims in Kenyan Politics*.

30. Kotef, *Movement and the Ordering of Freedom*, 15.

31. Hogg, "The New Pastoralism"; Waller, "Towards a Contextualisation of Policing in Colonial Kenya."

32. Interview, Nairobi, August 15, 2017.

33. Interview with senior Kenya Police officer, Kakuma, February 5, 2017.

34. Göpfert, *Policing the Frontier*.

35. Nyabola, "Decolonise da Police."

36. The National Police Reserves were formerly known as Kenya Police Reserves: Mkutu and Wandera, "Policing the Periphery," 20.

37. McCabe, *Cattle Bring Us to Our Enemies*.

38. Hogg, "Destitution and Development."

39. Mbembe, *On the Postcolony*, 34.

40. The Kenya Police Service and the Administration Police Service have retained their parallel institutional structures, with each being headed by an assistant inspector-general of police.

41. Amnesty International, *Police Reform in Kenya*; Diphoorn, "The 'Pure Apples'"; Osse, "Police Reform in Kenya."

42. Osse, "Police Reform in Kenya," 919.

43. LeBrón, *Policing Life and Death*; Seigel, *Violence Work*; Vitale, *The End of Policing*.

44. Mkutu and Wander, "Policing the Periphery."

45. Efuk, "Operation Lifeline Sudan."

46. Branch, "Humanitarianism, Violence, and the Camp in Northern Uganda," 478.

47. Interviews with, among others, an Ethiopian refugee who arrived in 1993, Kakuma, February 24, 2017, and an Administration Police officer who served in Kakuma in the 1990s, September 6, 2018.

48. Maingi and Omeje, "Policing Refugees in Fragile States."

49. Punitive interventions were common practice—for example, in 1996, 2003, 2014, and during my research between 2016 and 2017: based on interviews in Kakuma with refugees, May 18, 2017, June 1, 2017; with LWF staff, April 3, 2017; and with UNHCR staff, July 20, 2017.

50. The GSU is frequently used against urban protesters and for special operations in liaison with the Kenya Defence Forces along the northern frontier: interview with the UNHCR's Kakuma security chief who formulated the request to the government, Kakuma, January 27, 2017.

51. Fox, *Humanitarian Occupation*, 3–4.

52. Anderson et al., "Slow Emergencies."

53. Agamben, *Homo Sacer*, 78.

54. United Nations High Commissioner for Refugees, *Kenya*.

55. Communication with UNHCR security adviser, Kakuma, August 18, 2017; United Nations High Commissioner for Refugees, *Kenya Comprehensive Refugee Programme 2016*.

56. Muraya, "Mobility of Cops in Kakuma, Dadaab Camps Enhanced."

57. Interview with police commander, Kakuma, March 2, 2017.

58. Conversation, Kakuma, October 27, 2023.

59. United Nations High Commissioner for Refugees, *UNHCR Kenya Planning Summary 2017*.

60. Interview with senior LWF staff, Kakuma, July 21, 2017; conversation with senior RAS official involved in the reshuffle, Kakuma, December 14, 2016. The author was present when RAS managers ordered arrests of refugees on multiple occasions.

61. Peteet, "Camps and Enclaves," 225.

62. Oesch, "The Refugee Camp as a Space of Multiple Ambiguities and Subjectivities," 111.

63. Ramadan, "Spatialising the Refugee Camp," 73.

64. The poem, "Planted Thorns" is by Chol Reech: see Brankamp and Ngutulu, "Poetry on the Run."

65. Mbembe, "Necropolitics," 28.

66. Taken from my field notes about the Lokore roadblock, February 10, 2017.

67. Khosravi, *"Illegal" Traveller*; Mbembe, "Bodies as Borders."

68. Newhouse, "More than Mere Survival," 2298.

69. Beek, "Money, Morals and Law"; Hope, "Police Corruption and the Security Challenge in Kenya"; Schouten, *Roadblock Politics*.

70. *Kichwaa ngumu* is a racializing term that literally means "hard head." It implies a particular kind of stubbornness and stupidity.

71. Taken from my field notes about the Lokore roadblock, February 10, 2017.

72. Herbert, *Policing Space*.

73. Foucault, *Discipline and Punish*, 189.

74. Based on a series of documents released by a self-proclaimed Refugee Research Team (RRT) on January 16, 2017. The RRT aimed to make public institutional misconduct in the UNHCR, RAS, nongovernmental organizations, and the police in Kakuma.

75. Security Awareness training, Kakuma I, Zone 2/3, "Hong Kong," August 18, 2016.

76. Berman, *Control and Crisis in Colonial Kenya*, 147.

77. Lochery, "Rendering Difference Visible," 620–23.

78. Berda, *Living Emergency*; Rijke and Minca, "Checkpoint 300."

79. Conversation, Kakuma, February 17, 2017.

80. Interview with head of LWF security, August 18, 2016.

81. Conversation, August 9, 2017.

82. Foucault, *Discipline and Punish*, 189.

83. Security Awareness training, August 19, 2016.

84. LWF Security Awareness training, Kakuma 1, August 18, 2016.

85. The Government of Kenya has repeatedly imposed curfews on Mandera, Lamu, Waji, and other counties since 2014 via public notifications in the *Kenya Gazette* (http://kenyalaw.org/kenya_gazette).

86. Jolliffe, "Night-Time and Refugees," 4.

87. The RAS deputy camp manager called the OCS to ask for permission, Kakuma, February 17, 2017.

88. Interview, Kakuma, March 2, 2017.

89. Conversations with two Kenyan police officers who have served in the camp for six years, November 21, 2016, and an interview with the UNHCR's security chief, January 27, 2017.

90. Weizman, *The Least of All Possible Evils*, 23.

91. Interviews with two UNHCR protection staff, Kakuma, July 20, 2017; July 28, 2017. The incident at the football match was recounted to me by two refugee community policing officers (CPPTs) who were present, October 9, 2016.

92. Minca, "Geographies of the Camp"; Moran et al., *Carceral Spaces*.

93. Foucault, *Discipline and Punish*; Mbembe, *Necropolitics*.

94. Conversation, February 17, 2017.

95. KANERE, "Violence in Kakuma Kills 20."

96. Anderson, "Remembering Wagalla"; Duschinski, "Introduction"; Weizman, *Hollow Land*; Whittaker, "Legacies of Empire."

97. Group meeting with LWF refugee local security staff, July 31, 2017.

98. Interview, Kakuma, August 10, 2017.

99. Conversation, December 8, 2016.

100. Mbembe, *On the Postcolony*, 174.

101. Agamben, *Homo Sacer*, 78.

102. Painter, "Prosaic Geographies of Stateness," 754.

103. Camminga, "Encamped Within a Camp."

104. Martin, "From Spaces of Exception to 'Campscapes.'"

105. Besteman, *Militarized Global Apartheid*.

An earlier version of chapter 3 was published as "'Madmen, Womanisers, and Thieves': Moral Disorder and the Cultural Text of Refugee Encampment in Kenya," *Africa* 91, no. 1 (2021): 153–76. Reprinted with permission.

1. Interview, August 17, 2017.

2. Kothari, "Spatial Practices and Imaginaries"; Mudimbe, *The Invention of Africa*; Sander, *Difference and Pathology*.

3. Mbembe, *Critique of Black Reason*, 130.

4. Kakuma, August 19, 2016.

5. Bartolomei, "Who Am I?" 87; Crisp, "A State of Insecurity," 619; Lischer, *Dangerous Sanctuaries*.

6. Mwangi, "The 'Somalinisation' of Terrorism and Counterterrorism in Kenya," 7.

7. Taken from conversations with a hairdresser and an information technology consultant, respectively, Nairobi, June 2016.

8. International Rescue Committee and Twaweza, *Kenya*.

9. Gregory, "Imaginative Geographies"; Watkins, "Spatial Imaginaries Research in Geography," 509.

10. Massey, *For Space*, 84.

11. Watkins, "Spatial Imaginaries Research in Geography," 509.

12. Hall and Lamont, "Why Social Relations Matter for Politics and Successful Societies"; Taylor, "Modern Social Imaginaries."

13. Bialasiewicz et al., "Performing Security," 406; Wacquant et al., "Territorial Stigmatization in Action," 1275.

14. Mills, *The Racial Contract*, 41.

15. McKittrick, "Plantation Futures," 6; Wynter, "1492."

16. Quijano, "Coloniality of Power and Eurocentrism in Latin America," 221.

17. Mills, *The Racial Contract*, 42.

18. Mills, *The Racial Contract*, 46.

19. Mamdani, *Citizen and Subject*; Pierre, *The Predicament of Blackness*, 13.

20. Pierre, *The Predicament of Blackness*, 14.

21. MacArthur, *Cartography and the Political Imagination*; Overton, "Social Control and Social Engineering."

22. Schlee, "Territorializing Ethnicity."

23. Weitzberg, *We Do Not Have Borders*, 41–42.

24. Lind, "Devolution, Shifting Centre-Periphery Relationships and Conflict in Northern Kenya"; Meiu, "Who Are the New Natives?"; Weitzberg, *We Do Not Have Borders*.

25. Interview with UNHCR protection officer, Kakuma, July 20, 2017.

26. Turner, *Politics of Innocence*, 83.

27. Malkki, *Purity and Exile*.

28. Turner, "Under the Gaze of the 'Big Nations,'" 239.

29. Rygiel, "Politicizing Camps," 808.

30. Barnett, *Empire of Humanity*; Mayblin, *Asylum After Empire*, 37.

31. Benton, "Risky Business"; Pallister-Wilkins, "HuManitarianism."

32. Mudimbe, *The Invention of Africa*; Said, *Orientalism*.

33. Bauman, *Modernity and Ambivalence*, 14.

34. Nyers, *Rethinking Refugees*; Turner, "Under the Gaze of the 'Big Nations,'" 230.

35. Soguk, *States and Strangers*.

36. Olivius, "Constructing Humanitarian Selves and Refugee Others," 284.

37. Kakuma, October 4, 2016.

38. Conversation, Kakuma, March 2, 2015.

39. Harrell-Bond, *Imposing Aid*; Ikanda, "Animating 'Refugeeness' Through Vulnerabilities"; Jansen, "Between Vulnerability and Assertiveness"; Kibreab, "Pulling the Wool over the Eyes of the Strangers."

40. Jansen, "Between Vulnerability and Assertiveness," 577.

41. Interview, Kakuma, March 2, 2017.

42. Horst, *Transnational Nomads*, 93–94.

43. Informal conversation, Nairobi, June 16, 2017.

44. Schor, "This Essentialism Which Is Not One," 45.

45. Conversation with Kenyan aid worker, Kakuma, March 2, 2015.

46. Hyndman, *Managing Displacement*, 130.

47. Interview, April 6, 2017.

48. Conversation, Kakuma police station, November 21, 2016.

49. Senior RAS official, Kakuma, December 14, 2016.

50. This repeatedly came to the fore through a blend of overt assertions and offhand remarks about the supposed "cultural underdevelopment" of the Turkana and their need to abandon "traditional" ways of life.

51. Kakuma, Turkana Cafeteria, December 14, 2016.

52. Mbembe, *On the Postcolony*; Stoler, *Race and the Education of Desire*.

53. Horn, "Exploring the Impact of Displacement and Encampment on Domestic Violence in Kakuma Refugee Camp"; Kiura, "Constrained Agency on Contraceptive Use Among Somali Refugee Women in the Kakuma Refugee Camp in Kenya."

54. Ensor, "Lost Boys, Invisible Girls," 206.

55. Camminga, "Encamped Within a Camp"; Lewis and Naples, "Introduction"; Spijkerboer, *Fleeing Homophobia*.

56. Foucault, *The History of Sexuality, Volume 1*, 71; Stoler, *Carnal Knowledge and Imperial Power*.

57. Bhabha, "The Other Question," 96.

58. Interview, Nairobi, January 14, 2017

59. Interview, Nairobi, January 14, 2017.

60. Interview, Kenyan LWF staff, Kakuma, 23 May 2017; Turner, *Politics of Innocence*.

61. Gender Awareness meeting, Kakuma, August 19, 2016.

62. Interview, February 7, 2017.

63. Ngo and Hansen, "Constructing Identities in UN Refugee Camps"; Olivius, "Constructing Humanitarian Selves and Refugee Others," 272.

64. Anderson, "Sexual Threat and Settler Society," 66.

65. Conversation, February 10, 2017.

66. Interview, Nairobi, January 14, 2017.

67. Conversation, Kakuma, February 10, 2017.

68. Hall, "The Spectacle of the 'Other,'" 267 (emphasis in original).

69. Crisp, "A State of Insecurity."

70. Conversation, Kakuma, February 7, 2017.

71. Conversation, Kakuma, February 7, 2017.

72. Interview, Nairobi, January 14, 2017.

73. Fanon, *The Wretched of the Earth*; Harper and Raman, "Less than Human?"; Taylor, "The Politics of Securing Borders and the Identities of Disease"; Vaughan, "Madness and Colonialism, Colonialism as Madness."

74. Pupavac, "Pathologizing Populations and Colonizing Minds," 489.

75. Jackson, "The Shock of the New," 58; Sander, *Difference and Pathology*.

76. Crisp, "A State of Insecurity," 624.

77. Conversation, Kakuma, February 7, 2017.

78. Conversation, Kakuma, December 8, 2016.

79. Duffield, "Getting Savages to Fight Barbarians," 148.

80. Foucault, *Society Must Be Defended*, 195.

81. Memmi, *The Colonizer and the Colonized*, 119.

82. Conversation, Kakuma, August 15, 2016.

83. Conversation, Kakuma, January 17, 2017.

84. Interview, Lodwar, May 15, 2017.

85. Lonsdale, "Soil, Work, Civilisation, and Citizenship in Kenya"; Lynch, "Kenya's New Indigenes."

86. Lonsdale, "Moral Ethnicity and Political Tribalism," 132.

87. Jenkins, "Ethnicity, Violence, and the Immigrant-Guest Metaphor in Kenya."

88. D'Arcy and Cornell, "Devolution and Corruption in Kenya"; Ghai, "Devolution."

89. Gilroy, *Between Camps*, 82.

90. Kothari, "Spatial Practices and Imaginaries," 238.

91. Amoko, "The 'Missionary Position' and the Postcolonial Polity."

92. Turner, "Under the Gaze of the 'Big Nations,'" 227.

93. Turner, "Under the Gaze of the 'Big Nations,'" 237.

94. Pallister-Wilkins, "HuManitarianism."

95. Interview, Nairobi, July 12, 2017.

CHAPTER 4. COMMUNITY

Elements of chapter 4 were based on "Refugees in Uniform: Community Policing as a Technology of Government in Kakuma Refugee Camp, Kenya," *Journal of Eastern African Studies* 14, no. 2 (2020): 270–90.

1. The term *Equatoria* itself is a colonial construct: a catchall first used by the Ottoman Egyptian government of Khedive Ismail Pasha to designate the peoples and territories of its southernmost Sudanese province during the nineteenth century. Until today, South Sudan counts Equatoria among its three principal administrative areas. When people fled Sudan's civil wars in the early 1990s, the term continued to be used to identify refugees in exile with their places of origin.

2. The phrase "suspicious characters" is frequently used during LWF and police training for CPPTs.

3. Brankamp, "Community Policing in Kakuma Camp, Kenya"; Brankamp, "Refugees in Uniform."

4. Stenson, "Community Policing as a Governmental Technology."

5. McConnachie, *Governing Refugees*; Minca, "Geographies of the Camp"; Ramadan, "Spatialising the Refugee Camp."

6. Brankamp, "Refugees in Uniform"; Bulley, "Inside the Tent."

7. Foucault, "Governmentality," 102.

8. Brankamp et al., "The Camp as Market Frontier"; Ilcan and Rygiel, "Resiliency Humanitarianism."

9. Mbembe, *On the Postcolony*; Opitz, "Government Unlimited."

10. Milner et al., "Meaningful Refugee Participation"; Pincock et al., "The Rhetoric and Reality of Localisation."

11. Russell, "Challenging the Established Order."

12. Ilcan and Rygiel, "Resiliency Humanitarianism," 344.

13. Brown, *Undoing the Demos*; Rose, "The Death of the Social?"

14. Cruikshank, *The Will to Empower*, 1.

15. Ilcan and Rygiel, "Resiliency Humanitarianism."

16. Hyndman, *Managing Displacement*, 88.

17. Turner, "The Barriers of Innocence," 8.

18. Myers, *Indirect Rule in South Africa*, 1.

19. Mamdani, *Neither Settler nor Native*, 98.

20. Crowder, "Indirect Rule," 198.

21. Lugard, *The Dual Mandate in British Tropical Africa*.

22. Moyd, *Violent Intermediaries*; Yannakakis, *The Art of Being In-Between*.

23. Lawrence et al., *Intermediaries, Interpreters, and Clerks*, 4.

24. Myers, *Indirect Rule in South Africa*, 42.

25. Myers, *Indirect Rule in South Africa*, 2–3.

26. Berman, *Control and Crisis in Colonial Kenya*; Bogonko, "Colonial Chiefs and African Development in Kenya with Special Reference to Secular Education"; Tignor, "Colonial Chiefs in Chiefless Societies."

27. Mamdani, *Citizen and Subject*, 51.

28. Branch, *Defeating Mau Mau, Creating Kenya*.

29. Moyd, *Violent Intermediaries*, 22.

30. Moyd, *Violent Intermediaries*, 205.

31. Abrahams, "Sungusungu"; Heald, "Controlling Crime and Corruption from Below."

32. Brogden and Nijhar, *Community Policing*; Diphoorn and van Stapele, "What Is Community Policing"; Skilling, "Community Policing in Kenya"; Steinberg, "Crime Prevention Goes Abroad."

33. Sen and Pratten, "Global Vigilantes," 3.

34. Independent Policing Oversight Authority official, August 15, 2017.

35. Kibera community policing chairman, July 14, 2017.

36. Muiruri, "Policing a Willing Community"; Ruteere, "More than Political Tools," 11.

37. Government of Kenya, *Report of the National Task Force on Police Reforms*; Skilling, "Community Policing in Kenya."

38. Kioko, "Conflict Resolution and Crime Surveillance in Kenya."

39. Government of Kenya, *Fourth Draft Guidelines for Implementation of Community Policing*.

40. Government of Kenya, "Ulinzi Unaanza Na Mimi, Ulinzi Unaanza Na Wewe." The Swahili word *ulinzi* also translates to "surveillance" or "protection."

41. Diphoorn and van Stapele, "What Is Community Policing"; Mogire et al., "Policing Terrorism in Kenya."

42. Glück, "Security Urbanism and the Counterterror State in Kenya," 311.

43. UNHCR head of protection, Nairobi, March 3, 2017.

44. Kakuma, November 10, 2016.

45. Tazzioli, "Extractive Humanitarianism."

46. Griek, "Traditional Systems of Justice in Refugee Camps"; Jansen, *Kakuma Refugee Camp*.

47. Verdirame and Harrell-Bond, *Rights in Exile*, 141.

48. *Kitu kidogo* is colloquial Kiswahili for a bribe.

49. Senior police officer, Nairobi, January 14, 2017.

50. Senior CPPA, November 26, 2016.

51. Carter-White and Minca, "The Camp and the Question of Community."

52. Sagy, "Treating Peace as Knowledge."

53. Sagy, "Treating Peace as Knowledge," 372.

54. Interview, head of LWF peace building, Kakuma, 19 January 2017.

55. United Nations High Commissioner for Refugees, *Kakuma Refugee Camp Community: Constitution and Rules*, November 2011.

56. CPPT, Hagadera, Dadaab, April 12, 2017.

57. Director of LWF Djibouti-Kenya Program in Nairobi, April 3, 2017.

58. Crisp, "Lessons Learned from the Implementation of the Tanzania Security Package"; United Nations High Commissioner for Refugees, *Understanding Community-Based Protection*; Veroff, "Crimes, Conflicts and Courts."

59. United Nations High Commissioner for Refugees, *Reinforcing a Community Development Approach*.

60. Bulley, "Inside the Tent."

61. United Nations High Commissioner for Refugees, *Understanding Community-Based Protection*, 7.

62. Foucault, "The Subject and Power."

63. Conversation, Kakuma, August 23, 2016.

64. Foucault, *Discipline and Punish*, 181.

65. LWF senior supervisor, March 2, 2015.

66. CPPT, January 26, 2017.

67. Communication with the head of the LWF, October 7, 2015. The budget for community policing consists of contributions from the UNHCR (77 percent), the Church of Sweden (12 percent), and DanChurchAid (11 percent).

68. Kenyan CPPT supervisor, 3 November 2016.

69. Interviews in Nairobi, April 3, 2017, and Kakuma, August 3, 2017.

70. Intelligence officer, December 14, 2016; Spalek and Lambert, "Muslim Communities under Surveillance."

71. The notion of "real refugees" was constantly evoked by government officials and police officers when talking about camp security.

72. RAS officer, August 18, 2016.

73. CPPT, March 1, 2017

74. CPPT, May 16, 2017.

75. Spalek and Lambert, "Muslim Communities under Surveillance."

76. Opitz, "Government Unlimited."

77. Conversation, January 26, 2017.

78. Conversation, Kakuma, November 25, 2016.

79. Government official, Kakuma, February 24, 2017.

80. Interview, August 3, 2017.

81. Li, "Governmentality," 279.

82. Turner, "Angry Young Men in Camps," 13.

83. CPPT office, February 27, 2017.

84. Li, "Governmentality."

85. Hagmann and Péclard, "Negotiating Statehood," 549.

86. Halais, "They Call Him the Millionaire"; CPPT supervisor, August 1, 2016.

87. CPPT, March 20, 2015.

88. The bars' names have been changed.

89. Conversation, August 1, 2016.

90. Kelling and Wilson, "Broken Windows."

91. Meeting, January 20, 2017.

CHAPTER 5. EXTRACTION

My coauthors for the article "The Camp as Market Frontier: Refugees and the Spatial Imaginaries of Capitalist Prospecting in Kenya," *Geoforum* 145 (2023): 103843, generously allowed me to reuse some of our interview material for chapter 5.

1. UNHCR Kenya Budget and Expenditure Trend, accessed April 26, 2024, https://reporting.unhcr.org/operational/operations/kenya?_gl=1*xcsx35*_rup_ga*MTI4NjIzN zgoNC4xNjYwMDQ5NzU2*_rup_ga_EVDQTJ4LMY*MTcxNDEyMzEwNS4xMS4x LjE3MTQxMjUyMzIuMjguMC4w*_ga*MTgzMzA5MTI4MC4xNzExNTUwOTE5* _ga_WYV1L5CG21*MTcxNDEyMzEwNS4xOS4xLjE3MTQxMjUyMzIuMjguMC4w #toc-financials.

2. Bhandar, *Colonial Lives of Property*; Duschinski and Bhan, "Introduction"; Rodney, *How Europe Underdeveloped Africa*; Stirk, *The Politics of Military Occupation*.

3. Tsing, "Natural Resources and Capitalist Frontiers," 5100.

4. Tsing, *Friction*, 27.

5. Mezzadra and Neilson, *The Politics of Operations*.

6. Harvey, "Globalization and the 'Spatial Fix'"; Luxemburg, *The Accumulation of Capital*.

7. Mezzadra and Neilson, "On the Multiple Frontiers of Extraction," 194.

8. Mezzadra and Neilson, *The Politics of Operations*, 65.

9. Hardin, "Concessionary Politics," 115.

10. Henriet, *Colonial Impotence*.

11. Hopkins, *An Economic History of West Africa*; Marinelli, "Making Concessions in Tianjin"; Veeser, "A Forgotten Instrument of Global Capitalism?"

12. Barkan, "On the Systematic and Historical Analysis of Concessionary Zones"; Ferguson, *Global Shadows*; Sassen, *Expulsions*.

13. Brankamp et al., "The Camp as Market Frontier."

14. Chabeda-Barthe and Haller, "Resilience of Traditional Livelihood Approaches Despite Forest Grabbing"; Enns and Bersaglio, "Enclave Oil Development and the Rearticulation of Citizenship in Turkana, Kenya"; Hashimshony-Yaffe and Segal-Klein, "Renewable Energy and the Centralisation of Power."

15. Jansen, "Digging Aid."

16. Conversation with Kenyan police officer on leave, Nairobi, April 29, 2017. This notion is common among officers and other officials, documented—for example, on January 14, 2017, and January 27, 2017.

17. Balakian, "Money Is Your Government"; Nyaoro, "Policing with Prejudice."

18. Achtnich, "Accumulation by Immobilization."

19. United Nations Office of Internal Oversight Services, *Investigation into Allegations of Refugee Smuggling the Nairobi Branch Office of the Office of the United Nations High Commissioner for Refugees*.

20. Hope, "Police Corruption and the Security Challenge in Kenya"; Mwangi, "Political Corruption, Party Financing and Democracy in Kenya."

21. Interview, Nairobi, April 6, 2017.

22. Personal communication, May 2017.

23. Conversations in Kakuma, January 25, 2017; May 29, 2017; July 19, 2017; and July 20, 2017.

24. United Nations High Commissioner for Refugees, "UNHCR Refers Kenyan Staff to Police After Internal Investigation Finds Fraud at Kakuma Camp."

25. Newhouse, "More than Mere Survival," 2298.

26. Carruth and Freeman, "Aid or Exploitation?"; Farah, "Expat, Local, and Refugee."

27. Morris and Voon, "Which Side Are You On?" 3.

28. Clacherty and Clacherty, *Advocating for Refugee Incentive Workers*, 2.

29. KANERE, "Incentive Pay Raises and Terminations Targeting Incentive Staffs."

30. Coddington et al., "Destitution Economies," 1434; Pascucci, "The Local Labour Building the International Community," 745.

31. CPPT meeting, Kakuma, February 9, 2017.

32. Newhouse, "Creative Fictions."

33. Betts, *The Wealth of Refugees*; Betts et al., *Refugee Economies*; Easton-Calabria and Omata, "Panacea for the Refugee Crisis?"

34. Interview, June 15, 2021.

35. Bird and Schmid, "Humanitarianism and the 'Migration Fix'"; Harvey, "Globalization and the 'Spatial Fix.'"

36. Aradau and Tazzioli, "Biopolitics Multiple"; Brankamp et al., "The Camp as Market Frontier"; Martin and Tazzioli, "Value Extraction through Refugee Carcerality."

37. Martin, "Carceral Economies of Migration Control," 746.

38. Martin, "Carceral Economies of Migration Control," 747.

39. Coddington et al., "Destitution Economies."

40. Interview, June 4, 2021.

41. Brankamp et al., "The Camp as Market Frontier."

42. Interview, Kakuma, May 18, 2017.

43. Interview, July 20, 2021.

44. Interview, July 20, 2021.

45. Turner, "'#Refugees Can Be Entrepreneurs Too!'" 139.

46. Bhagat and Roderick, "Banking on Refugees"; Bhattacharyya, *Rethinking Racial Capitalism*; Rajaram, "Refugees as Surplus Population."

47. Kakuma Kalobeyei Challenge Fund website, accessed May 19, 2023, https://kkcfke.org.

48. UNHCR website, accessed May 3, 2024. https://www.unhcr.org/news/stories/feature-jolie-gives-refugee-girls-shot-school-kenya.

49. Conversation in Kakuma, December 2016.

50. Brankamp, "Camp Abolition"; Tazzioli, "Confining by Choking Refugees' Lifetime."

51. Marx, *Capital, Volume One*.

52. Brankamp and Ngutulu, "Poetry On the Run."

53. Jansen, "Between Vulnerability and Assertiveness"; Teferra, "Kakuma Refugee Camp"; Tegenbos and Büscher, "Moving Onward?"

54. Gatter, *Time and Power in Azraq Refugee Camp*, 22.

55. Qasmiyeh, *Writing the Camp*, 66.

56. Cacho, *Social Death*; Coutin, "Confined Within," 204; Khosravi, "Stolen Time"; Mbembe, *Necropolitics*; Patterson, *Slavery and Social Death*.

57. Qasmiyeh, *Writing the Camp*, 66.

58. Agamben, *Homo Sacer*.

59. Gilmore, "Abolition Geography and the Problem of Innocence," 227.

60. Gilmore, "Abolition Geography and the Problem of Innocence," 227.

61. Weima, "'Is It Commerce?'" 27.

62. Stoler, *Duress*, 77.

CONCLUSION

Epigraph: Fantaye Agaro, "Rise Kakuma!" KANERE website, December 31, 2022, accessed July 9, 2024, https://kanere.org/rise-kakuma/#more-2830.

1. In Kiswahili, *kushirika* means "to cooperate."

2. Government of Kenya, *Shirika Plan*.

3. "Dealing with Refugees: John Burugu on Shirika Plan (Part 1)," Kenya Broadcasting Corporation (KBC), *Prime Edition*, March 27, 2024, accessed May 7, 2024, https://www.youtube.com/watch?v=RsMcFXNLSA8.

4. "Mudavadi's Speech During the High-Level Dialogue on Shirika Plan for Refugees at Serena [Hotel]," Nairobi, video, posted June 20, 2023, accessed June 7, 2024, https://www.youtube.com/watch?v=n-_Ttom1fNw.

5. "Dealing with Refugees: John Burugu on Shirika Plan (Part 1)," Kenya Broadcasting Corporation (KBC), *Prime Edition*, March 27, 2024, accessed May 7, 2024, https://www.youtube.com/watch?v=RsMcFXNLSA8.

6. Interview, Kakuma, October 23, 2023.

7. United Nations High Commissioner for Refugees, *UNHCR Policy on Alternatives to Camps*.

8. Tuck and Yang, "Decolonization Is Not a Metaphor."

9. Conversation, WhatsApp, May 7, 2024.

10. Jansen, *Kakuma Refugee Camp*; Oka, "Unlikely Cities in the Desert."

11. Agier, "Between War and City," 336.

12. Davis, *City of Quartz*, 253; Kimari, "The Story of a Pump."

13. Rodney, *Decolonial Marxism*, 289.

14. Césaire, *Discourse on Colonialism*; Maldonado-Torres, "Césaire's Gift and the Decolonial Turn," 440; Ndlovu-Gatsheni, *Coloniality of Power in Postcolonial Africa*; Wynter, "Unsettling the Coloniality of Being/Power/Truth/Freedom."

15. Tamale, *Decolonization and Afro-Feminism*, 7.

16. Pallister-Wilkins, *Humanitarian Borders*, 199; Sabaratnam, *Decolonising Intervention*, 142.

17. Fanon, *Black Skin, White Masks*; Fanon, *The Wretched of the Earth*; Mbembe, *Out of the Dark Night*, 62.

18. Mbembe, *Out of the Dark Night*, 44.

19. Interview, Kakuma, July 19, 2022.

20. De Genova et al., "Autonomy of Asylum?"

21. Weima and Brankamp, "Camp Methodologies," 2.

22. Gilroy, *Between Camps*; Sharma, *Home Rule*.

23. Sharma, *Home Rule*, 6.

24. Moulin and Nyers, "We Live in a Country of UNHCR."

25. Getachew, *World-Making After Empire*.

Bibliography

Abdelaaty, Lamis E. *Discrimination and Delegation: Explaining State Responses to Refugees*. Oxford: Oxford University Press, 2021.

Abrahams, Ray. "Sungusungu: Village Vigilante Groups in Tanzania." *African Affairs* 86, no. 343 (1987): 179–96.

Abrams, Philip. "Notes on the Difficulty of Studying the State (1977)." *Journal of Historical Sociology* 1, no. 1 (1988): 58–89.

Achtnich, Marthe. "Accumulation by Immobilization: Migration, Mobility and Money in Libya." *Economy and Society* 51, no. 1 (2022): 95–115.

Active Learning Network for Accountability and Performance. *The State of the Humanitarian System*. Report, Overseas Development Institute, London, July 2012.

Aden, Halima. "A Place of Hope: From Refugee Camp to International Fashion Model." TEDxKakumaCamp, June 9, 2018. YouTube, 7 min., 39 sec. https://www.youtube.com/watch?v=roe-STL8JxI&t=53s.

Agamben, Giorgio. *Homo Sacer: Sovereign Power and Bare Life*. Stanford, CA: Stanford University Press, 1998.

Agamben, Giorgio. *State of Exception*. Chicago: University of Chicago Press, 2005.

Agier, Michel. "Between War and City: Towards an Urban Anthropology of Refugee Camps." *Ethnography* 3, no. 3 (2002): 317–41.

Agier, Michel. *Borderlands: Towards an Anthropology of the Cosmopolitan Condition*. London: Polity, 2016.

Agier, Michel. *Managing the Undesirables: Refugee Camps and Humanitarian Government*. Cambridge: Polity, 2011.

Agier, Michel, with Yasmine Bouagga, Maël Galisson,Cyrille Hanappe, et al. *The Jungle: Calais's Camps and Migrants*. Cambridge: Polity, 2019.

Albahari, Maurizio. *Crimes of Peace: Mediterranean Migrations at the World's Deadliest Border*. Philadelphia: University of Pennsylvania Press, 2015.

Al-Bulushi, Samar. "Race, Space, and 'Terror': Notes from East Africa." *Security Dialogue* 52, no. S (2021): 115–23.

Amir, Merav. "The Making of a Void Sovereignty: Political Implications of the Military Checkpoints in the West Bank." *Environment and Planning D: Society and Space* 31, no. 2 (2013): 227–44.

Amnesty International. *Police Reform in Kenya: "A Drop in the Ocean."* London: Amnesty International, 2013.

Amoko, A. "The 'Missionary Position' and the Postcolonial Polity, or, Sexual Difference in the Field of Kenyan Colonial Knowledge." *Callaloo* 24, no. 1 (2001): 310–24.

Anand, Dibyesh. "Colonization with Chinese Characteristics: Politics of (in)Security in Xinjiang and Tibet." *Central Asian Survey* 38, no. 1 (2019): 129–47.

Anderson, Ben, Kevin Grove, Lauren Rickards, and Matthew Kearnes. "Slow Emergencies: Temporality and the Racialized Biopolitics of Emergency Governance." *Progress in Human Geography* 44, no. 4 (2020): 621–39.

Anderson, David M. *Histories of the Hanged: Britain's Dirty War in Kenya and the End of Empire.* London: Weidenfeld and Nicholson, 2005.

Anderson, David M. "Punishment, Race and 'the Raw Native': Settler Society and Kenya's Flogging Scandals, 1895–1930." *Journal of Southern African Studies* 37, no. 3 (2011): 479–97.

Anderson, David M. "Remembering Wagalla: State Violence in Northern Kenya, 1962–1991." *Journal of Eastern African Studies* 8, no. 4 (2014): 658–76.

Anderson, David M. "Sexual Threat and Settler Society: 'Black Perils' in Kenya, c. 1907–30." *Journal of Imperial and Commonwealth History* 38, no. 1 (2010): 47–74.

Anderson, David M., and David Killingray. "Consent, Coercion and Colonial Control: Policing the Empire, 1830–1940." In *Policing the Empire: Government, Authority, and Control, 1830–1940*, edited by David M. Anderson and David Killingray, 1–17. Manchester, UK: Manchester University Press, 1991.

Anderson, David M., and Jacob McKnight. "Kenya at War: Al-Shabaab and Its Enemies in Eastern Africa." *African Affairs* 114, no. 454 (2015): 1–27.

Andersson, Ruben. *Illegality, Inc.: Clandestine Migration and the Business of Bordering Europe.* Berkeley: University of California Press, 2014.

Aradau, Claudia, and Martina Tazzioli. "Biopolitics Multiple: Migration, Extraction, Subtraction." *Millennium* 48, no. 2 (2020): 198–220.

Aretxaga, Begoña. "Maddening States." *Annual Review of Anthropology* 32 (2003): 393–410.

Asad, Talal. "Reflections on Violence, Law, and Humanitarianism." *Critical Inquiry* 41, no. 2 (2015): 390–427.

Atanasoski, Neda. *Humanitarian Violence: The U.S. Deployment of Diversity.* Minneapolis: University of Minnesota Press, 2013.

Audet, Francois. "Humanitarian Space." In *The Routledge Companion to Humanitarian Action*, edited by Roger MacGinty and Jenny H. Peterson, 141–52. London: Routledge, 2015

Bachmann, Jan. "Governmentality and Counterterrorism: Appropriating International Security Projects in Kenya." *Journal of Intervention and Statebuilding* 6, no. 1 (2012): 41–56.

Balakian, Sophia. "'Money Is Your Government': Refugees, Mobility, and Unstable Documents in Kenya's Operation Usalama Watch." *African Studies Review* 59, no. 2 (2016): 87–111.

Balaton-Chrimes, Samantha. "Statelessness, Identity Cards and Citizenship as Status in the Case of the Nubians of Kenya." *Citizenship Studies* 18, no. 1 (2014): 15–28.

Barkan, Joshua. "On the Systematic and Historical Analysis of Concessionary Zones." *Public Culture* 35, no. 3 (2023): 431–39.

Barnett, Michael. *Empire of Humanity: A History of Humanitarianism*. Ithaca, NY: Cornell University Press, 2011.

Barth, Boris, and Rolf Hobson, eds. *Civilizing Missions in the Twentieth Century*. Leiden: Brill, 2020.

Bartolomei, Linda, Eileen Pittaway, and Emma Elizabeth Pittaway. "Who Am I? Identity and Citizenship in Kakuma Refugee Camp in Northern Kenya." *Development* 46, no. 3 (2003): 87–93.

Bauman, Zygmunt. *Modernity and Ambivalence*. Ithaca, NY: Cornell University Press, 1991.

Beek, Jan. "Money, Morals and Law: The Legitimacy of Police Traffic Checks in Ghana." In *Police in Africa: The Street-Level View*, edited by Jan Beek, Mirco Göpfert, Olly Owen, and Johnny Steinberg, 231–48. London: Hurst, 2017.

Beek, Jan, Mirco Göpfert, Olly Owen, and Jonny Steinberg, eds. *Police in Africa: The Street-Level View*. London: Hurst, 2017.

Benton, Adia. "African Expatriates and Race in the Anthropology of Humanitarianism." *Critical African Studies* 8, no. 3 (2016): 266–77.

Benton, Adia. "Risky Business: Race, Nonequivalence and the Humanitarian Politics of Life." *Visual Anthropology* 29, no. 2 (2016): 187–203.

Berda, Yael. *Living Emergency: Israel's Permit Regime in the Occupied West Bank*. Stanford, CA: Stanford University Press, 2017.

Berman, Bruce. *Control and Crisis in Colonial Kenya: The Dialectic of Domination*. Oxford: James Currey, 1990.

Bernault, Florence. "The Politics of Enclosure in Colonial and Post-Colonial Africa." In *A History of Prison and Confinement in Africa*, edited by Florence Bernault, 1–53. Portsmouth, NH: Heinemann, 2003.

Besteman, Catherine. *Making Refuge: Somali Bantu Refugees and Lewiston, Maine*. Durham, NC: Duke University Press, 2016.

Besteman, Catherine. *Militarized Global Apartheid*. Durham, NC: Duke University Press, 2020.

Betts, Alexander. "International Cooperation Between North and South to Enhance Refugee Protection in Regions of Origin." Refugee Studies Center Working Paper Series, Oxford, 2005.

Betts, Alexander. *The Wealth of Refugees: How Displaced People Can Build Economies*. Oxford: Oxford University Press, 2021.

Betts, Alexander, and Louise Bloom. *Humanitarian Innovation: The State of the Art*. Geneva: United Nations Officer for the Coordination of Humanitarian Affairs, 2014.

Betts, Alexander, Louise Bloom, Josiah Kaplan, and Naohiko Omata. *Refugee Economies: Forced Displacement and Development*. Oxford: Oxford University Press, 2017.

Betts, Alexander, Gil Loescher, and James Milner. *UNHCR: The Politics and Practice of Refugee Protection*. Abingdon, UK: Routledge, 2012.

Betts, Alexander, Naohiko Omata, and Olivier Sterck. "The Kalobeyei Settlement: A Self-Reliance Model for Refugees?" *Journal of Refugee Studies* 33, no. 1 (2020): 189–223.

Bhabha, Homi K. "The Other Question." In *The Location of Culture*, 94–120. London: Routledge, 2004.

Bhagat, Ali, and Leanne Roderick. "Banking on Refugees: Racialized Expropriation in the Fintech Era." *Environment and Planning A: Economy and Space* 52, no. 8 (2020): 1498–515.

Bhalla, Nita. "Kenya Orders Closure of Dadaab Refugee Camp This Year, According to Leaked UN Document." Reuters, March 29, 2019. https://www.reuters.com/article/us -kenya-refugees-somalia-idUSKCN1RA1FN.

Bhalla, Nita. "Poets and Models Star at World's First Refugee Camp TEDx Event in Kenya." Reuters, June 10, 2018. https://www.reuters.com/article/us-kenya-refugees -tedx-idUSKCN1J50SE.

Bhandar, Brenna. *Colonial Lives of Property: Law, Land, and Racial Regimes of Ownership*. Durham, NC: Duke University Press, 2018.

Bhattacharyya, Gargi. *Rethinking Racial Capitalism: Questions of Reproduction and Survival*. London: Rowman and Littlefield, 2018.

Bialasiewicz, Luiza, David Campbell, Stuart Elden, Stephen Graham, Alex Jeffrey, and Alison J. Williams. "Performing Security: The Imaginative Geographies of Current US Strategy." *Political Geography* 26, no. 4 (2007): 405–22.

Bierschenk, Thomas, and Jean-Pierre Olivier de Sardan, eds. *States at Work: Dynamics of African Bureaucracies*. Leiden: Brill, 2014.

Bird, Gemma, and Davide Schmid. "Humanitarianism and the 'Migration Fix': On the Implication of NGOs in Racial Capitalism and the Management of Relative Surplus Populations." *Geopolitics* 28, no. 3 (2023): 1235–61

Blauner, Robert. "Internal Colonialism and Ghetto Revolt." *Social Problems* 16, no. 4 (1969): 393–408.

Bogonko, Sorobea Nyachieo. "Colonial Chiefs and African Development in Kenya with Special Reference to Secular Education." *Transafrican Journal of History* 14 (1985): 1–20.

Boochani, Behrouz. *No Friend but the Mountains*. London: Picador, 2018.

Branch, Adam. "Humanitarianism, Violence, and the Camp in Northern Uganda." *Civil Wars* 11, no. 4 (2009): 477–501.

Branch, Daniel. *Defeating Mau Mau, Creating Kenya: Counterinsurgency, Civil War and Decolonisation*. Cambridge: Cambridge University Press, 2009.

Brankamp, Hanno. "Camp Abolition: Ending Carceral Humanitarianism in Kenya (and Beyond)." *Antipode* 54, no. 1 (2022): 106–29.

Brankamp, Hanno. "Community Policing in Kakuma Camp, Kenya." *Forced Migration Review* 53 (2016): 51–52.

Brankamp, Hanno. "The Cynical Recasting of Refugees as Raconteurs Can't Mask the Grim Reality." *The Guardian*, June 18, 2018. Accessed January 20, 2019. https://www .theguardian.com/global-development/2018/jun/13/tedx-kenya-kakuma-refugee -camp-hanno-brankamp.

Brankamp, Hanno. "Feeling the Refugee Camp: Affectual Research, Bodies, and Suspicion." *Area* 54, no. 3 (2022): 383–91.

Brankamp, Hanno. "'Occupied Enclave': Policing and the Underbelly of Humanitarian Governance in Kakuma Refugee Camp, Kenya." *Political Geography* 71 (2019): 67–77.

Brankamp, Hanno. "Refugees in Uniform: Community Policing as a Technology of Government in Kakuma Refugee Camp, Kenya," *Journal of Eastern African Studies* 14, no. 2 (2020): 270–90.

Brankamp, Hanno, and Patricia Daley. "Laborers, Migrants, Refugees: Managing Belonging, Bodies, and Mobility in (Post)Colonial Kenya and Tanzania." *Migration and Society* 3, no. 1 (2020): 113–29.

Brankamp, Hanno, Sara de Jong, Sophie Mackinder, and Kelly Devenney. "The Camp as Market Frontier: Refugees and the Spatial Imaginaries of Capitalist Prospecting in Kenya." *Geoforum* 145 (2023): 103843.

Brankamp, Hanno, and Zoltán Glück. "Camps and Counterterrorism: Security and the Remaking of Refuge in Kenya." *Environment and Planning D: Society and Space* 40, no. 3 (2022): 528–48.

Brankamp, Hanno, and Kodi Arnu Ngutulu. "Poetry on the Run." *Migration and Society* 7, no. 1 (2024): 217–26.

Breton, André, Roger Caillois, René Char, René Crevel, et al. "Murderous Humanitarianism." Manifesto, translated by Samuel Beckett, 1932. https://criticallegalthinking .com/2010/11/24/murderous-humanitarianism.

Brogden, Mike, and Preeti Nijhar. *Community Policing: National and International Models and Approaches*. London: Routledge, 2005.

Brown, Wendy. *Undoing the Demos: Neoliberalism's Stealth Revolution*. Princeton, NJ: Princeton University Press, 2015.

Bulley, Dan. "Inside the Tent: Community and Government in Refugee Camps." *Security Dialogue* 45, no. 1 (2014): 63–80.

Buzan, Barry, Ole Weaver, and Jaap de Wilde. *Security: A New Framework for Analysis*. Boulder, CO: Lynne Rienner Publishers, 1998.

Byler, Darren. *Terror Capitalism: Uyghur Dispossession and Masculinity in a Chinese City*. Durham, NC: Duke University Press, 2022.

Cacho, Lisa Marie. *Social Death: Racialized Rightlessness and the Criminalization of the Unprotected*. New York: New York University Press, 2012.

Cacho, Lisa Marie, and Jodi Melamed. "'Don't Arrest Me, Arrest the Police': Policing as the Street Administration of Colonial Racial Capitalist Orders." In *Colonial Racial Capitalism*, edited by Susan Koshy, Lisa Marie Cacho, Jodi A. Byrd, and Brian J. Jefferson, 159–205. Durham, NC: Duke University Press, 2022.

Calhoun, Craig. "The Imperative to Reduce Suffering: Charity, Progress, and Emergencies in the Field of Humanitarian Action." In *Humanitarianism in Question: Politics, Power, Ethics*, edited by Michael Barnett and Thomas G. Weiss, 73–97. Ithaca, NY: Cornell University Press, 2008.

Calvert, Peter. "Internal Colonisation, Development and Environment." *Source: Third World Quarterly* 22, no. 1 (2001): 51–63.

Camminga, B. "Encamped Within a Camp: Transgender Refugees and Kakuma Refugee Camp (Kenya)." In *Invisibility in African Displacements: From Structural Marginalization to Strategies of Avoidance*, edited by Jesper Bjarnesen and Simon Turner, 36–52. London: Zed, 2020.

Campbell, Elizabeth H. "Urban Refugees in Nairobi: Problems of Protection, Mechanisms of Survival, and Possibilities for Integration." *Journal of Refugee Studies* 19, no. 3 (2006): 396–413.

Canadian Broadcasting Corporation. "Inside Dadaab: Growing Up in the World's Largest Refugee Camp." CBC Radio. May 12, 2015. Accessed February 6, 2025. https://www.cbc.ca/radio/thecurrent/the-current-for-may-12-2015-1.3070544/inside-dadaab-growing-up-in-the-world-s-largest-refugee-camp-1.3070667.

Carruth, Lauren, and Scott Freeman. "Aid or Exploitation? Food-for-Work, Cash-for-Work, and the Production of 'Beneficiary-Workers' in Ethiopia and Haiti." *World Development* 140 (2021): 105283.

Carter-White, Richard, and Claudio Minca. "The Camp and the Question of Community." *Political Geography* 81 (2020): 102222.

Césaire, Aimé. *Discourse on Colonialism*. New York: Monthly Review, 1972.

Chabeda-Barthe, Jemaiyo, and Tobias Haller. "Resilience of Traditional Livelihood Approaches Despite Forest Grabbing: Ogiek to the West of Mau Forest, Uasin Gishu County." *Land* 7, no. 4 (2018): 1–22.

Chakrabarty, Dipesh. *Provincializing Europe: Postcolonial Thought and Historical Difference*. Princeton, NJ: Princeton University Press, 2000.

Chalfin, Brenda. *Neoliberal Frontiers: An Ethnography of Sovereignty in West Africa*. Chicago: University of Chicago Press, 2010.

Chaulia, Sreeram Sundar. "The Politics of Refugee Hosting in Tanzania: From Open Door to Unsustainability, Insecurity and Receding Receptivity." *Journal of Refugee Studies* 16, no. 2 (2003): 147–66.

Chimni, B. S. "The Geopolitics of Refugee Studies: A View from the South." *Journal of Refugee Studies* 11, no. 4 (1998): 350–74.

Chouliaraki, Lilie. *The Ironic Spectator: Solidarity in the Age of Post-Humanitarianism*. Cambridge: Polity, 2013.

Christian, Jenna Marie, and Lorraine Dowler. "Slow and Fast Violence: A Feminist Critique of Binaries." *International Journal for Critical Geographies* 18, no. 5 (2019): 1066–75.

Clacherty, Glynis, and James Clacherty. *Advocating for Refugee Incentive Workers: A Qualitative Research Study in Three Refugee Contexts in Africa*. Kampala: Africa Refugee Network and Oxfam, 2022.

Clifford, James. "Anthropology and/as Travel." *Etnofoor* 9, no. 2 (1996): 5–15.

Coddington, Kate, Deirdre Conlon, and Lauren L. Martin. "Destitution Economies: Circuits of Value in Asylum, Refugee, and Migration Control." *Annals of the American Association of Geographers* 110, no. 5 (2020): 1425–44.

Collins, Robert O. "The Turkana Patrol of 1918 Reconsidered." *Ethnohistory* 53, no. 1 (2006): 95–119.

Comaroff, Jean, and John L. Comaroff. "Theory from the South: Or, How Euro-America Is Evolving Toward Africa." *Anthropological Forum* 22, no. 2 (2012): 113–31.

Connell, Raewyn. *Southern Theory: The Global Dynamics of Knowledge in Social Science*. London: Polity, 2007.

Cons, Jason, and Romola Sanyal. "Geographies at the Margins: Borders in South Asia—An Introduction." *Political Geography* 35 (2013): 5–13.

Coutin, Susan Bibler. "Confined Within: National Territories as Zones of Confinement." *Political Geography* 29, no. 4 (2010): 200–208.

Crawford, Emily, and Alison Pert. *International Humanitarian Law*. Cambridge: Cambridge University Press, 2015.

Crawford, Neil James Wilson. *The Urbanization of Forced Displacement: UNHCR, Urban Refugees, and the Dynamics of Policy Change*. Montreal: McGill-Queen's University Press, 2021.

Crisp, Jeff. "Lessons Learned from the Implementation of the Tanzania Security Package." Report. United Nations High Commissioner for Refugees, Geneva, 2001.

Crisp, Jeff. "A State of Insecurity: The Political Economy of Violence in Kenya's Refugee Camps." *African Affairs* 99, no. 397 (2000): 601–32.

Crowder, Michael. "Indirect Rule: French and British Style." *Africa* 34, no. 3 (1964): 197–205.

Cruikshank, Barbara. *The Will to Empower: Democratic Citizens and Other Subjects*. Ithaca, NY: Cornell University Press, 1999.

Crush, Jonathan. "Scripting the Compound: Power and Space in the South African Mining Industry." *Environment and Planning D: Society and Space* 12, no. 3 (1994): 301–24.

Da Costa, Rosa. *Maintaining the Civilian and Humanitarian Character of Asylum*. Legal and Protection Policy Research Series, United Nations High Commissioner for Refugees, Geneva, 2004.

Daley, Patricia. "Refugees and Underdevelopment in Africa: The Case of Barundi Refugees in Tanzania." PhD diss., University of Oxford, 1989.

Daley, Patricia. "Rescuing African Bodies: Celebrities, Consumerism and Neoliberal Humanitarianism." *Review of African Political Economy* 40, no. 137 (2013): 375–93.

Daley, Patricia. "Towards an Anti-Racist Humanitarianism in a Post-Liberal World." In *Amidst the Debris: Humanitarianism and the End of Liberal Order*, edited by Juliano Fiori, Fernando Espada, Andrea Rigon, Bertrand Taithe, and Rafia Zakaria, 351–67. London: Hurst, 2021.

D'Arcy, Michelle, and Agnes Cornell. "Devolution and Corruption in Kenya: Everyone's Turn to Eat?" *African Affairs* 115, no. 459 (2016): 246–73.

Das, Veena, and Deborah Poole. *Anthropology in the Margins of the State*. Oxford: Oxford University Press, 2004.

Davis, Mike. *City of Quartz: Excavating the Future in Los Angeles*. London: Verso, 1990.

Davis, Thom, and Arshad Isakjee. "Ruins of Empire: Refugees, Race and the Postcolonial Geographies of European Migrant Camps." *Geoforum* 102 (2019): 214–17.

De Coss-Corzo, Alejandro. "The Infrastructures of Internal Colonialism: State, Environment, and Race in Lerma, Mexico." *Antipode* 55, no. 3 (2023): 810–29.

De Genova, Nicholas. *The Borders of "Europe": Autonomy of Migration, Tactics of Bordering*. Durham, NC: Duke University Press, 2017.

De Genova, Nicholas. "Spectacles of Migrant 'Illegality': The Scene of Exclusion, the Obscene of Inclusion." *Ethnic and Racial Studies* 36, no. 7 (2013): 1180–98.

De Genova, Nicholas, Glenda Garelli, and Martina Tazzioli. "Autonomy of Asylum? The Autonomy of Migration Undoing the Refugee Crisis Script." *South Atlantic Quarterly* 117, no. 2 (2018): 239–65.

De León, Jason. *The Land of Open Graves: Living and Dying on the Migrant Trail*. Berkeley: University of California Press, 2015.

Diken, Bülent, and Carsten Bagge Laustsen. "The Camp." *Geografiska Annaler, Series B: Human Geography* 88, no. 4 (2006): 443–52.

Diphoorn, Tessa. "The 'Pure Apples': Moral Bordering within the Kenyan Police." *Environment and Planning D: Society and Space* 38, no. 3 (2020): 490–509.

Diphoorn, Tessa, and Naomi van Stapele. "What Is Community Policing? Divergent Agendas, Practices, and Experiences of Transforming the Police in Kenya." *Policing* 15, no. 1 (2021): 399–411.

Dirik, Dilar. *The Kurdish Women's Movement: History, Theory, Practice*. London: Pluto, 2022.

Dragsbaek Schmidt, Johannes, Leah Kimathi, and Michael Omondi Owiso, eds. *Refugees and Forced Migration in the Horn and Eastern Africa: Advances in African Economic, Social and Political Development*. Cham, Switzerland: Springer, 2019.

Duffield, Mark. "Challenging Environments: Danger, Resilience and the Aid Industry." *Security Dialogue* 43, no. 5 (2012): 475–92.

Duffield, Mark. "Getting Savages to Fight Barbarians: Development, Security and the Colonial Present." *Conflict, Security and Development* 5, no. 2 (2005): 141–59.

Duffield, Mark. "Governing the Borderlands: Decoding the Power of Aid." *Disasters* 25, no. 4 (2001): 308–20.

Duffield, Mark. "Risk-Management and the Fortified Aid Compound: Everyday Life in Post-Interventionary Society." *Journal of Intervention and Statebuilding* 4, no. 4 (2010): 453–74.

Duschinski, Haley, and Mona Bhan. "Introduction: Law Containing Violence: Critical Ethnographies of Occupation and Resistance." *Journal of Legal Pluralism and Unofficial Law* 49, no. 3 (2017): 253–67.

Duschinski, Haley, Mona Bhan, Ather Zia, and Cynthia Mahmood, eds. *Resisting Occupation in Kashmir*. Philadelphia: University of Pennsylvania Press, 2018.

Dyke, Tim. "Public Health Aspects of a Refugee Camp." *Journal of the Royal Society of Health* 111, no. 3 (1991): 101–4.

Easton-Calabria, Evan, and Maurice Herson. "In Praise of Dependencies: Dispersed Dependencies and Displacement." *Disasters* 44, no. 1 (2020): 44–62.

Easton-Calabria, Evan, and Naohiko Omata. "Panacea for the Refugee Crisis? Rethinking the Promotion of 'Self-Reliance' for Refugees." *Third World Quarterly* 39, no. 8 (2018): 1458–74.

Edkins, Jenny. "Sovereign Power, Zones of Indistinction, and the Camp." *Alternatives: Global, Local, Political* 25, no. 1 (2000): 3–25.

Efuk, Soforonio Oniama. "Operation Lifeline Sudan (1986–1996)." PhD diss., University of Leeds, 2001.

Ek, Richard. "Giorgio Agamben and the Spatialities of the Camp: An Introduction." *Geografiska Annaler, Series B: Human Geography* 88, no. 4 (2006): 363–86.

Elkins, Caroline. *Imperial Reckoning: The Untold Story of Britain's Gulag in Kenya*. New York: Henry Holt, 2005.

Enns, Charis, and Brock Bersaglio. "Enclave Oil Development and the Rearticulation of Citizenship in Turkana, Kenya: Exploring 'Crude Citizenship.'" *Geoforum* 67 (2015): 78–88.

Ensor, Marisa O. "Lost Boys, Invisible Girls: Children, Gendered Violence and War Time Displacement in South Sudan." In *Gender, Violence, Refugees*, edited by Susanne Buckley-Zistel and Ulrike Krause, 197–218. Oxford: Berghahn, 2017.

Estroff, Sue. "Identity, Disability and Schizophrenia: The Problem of Chronicity." In *Knowledge, Power and Practice: The Anthropology of Medicine and Everyday Life*, edited by Shirley Lindenbaum and Margaret Lock, 247–86. Berkeley: University of California Press, 1993.

European Council on Refugees and Exiles. *Guarding Refugee Protection Standards in Regions of Origin*. Brussels: ECRE, 2005.

Evans, Grant. "Internal Colonialism in the Central Highlands of Vietnam." *Sojourn* 7, no. 2 (2014): 274–304.

Falola, Toyin, and Olajumoke Yacob-Haliso. *African Refugees*. Bloomington: Indiana University Press, 2023.

Fanon, Frantz. *Black Skin, White Masks*. London: Pluto, 1986.

Fanon, Frantz. *The Wretched of the Earth*. New York: Grove, 2004.

Farah, Reem. "Expat, Local, and Refugee: 'Studying Up' the Global Division of Labor and Mobility in the Humanitarian Industry in Jordan." *Migration and Society* 3, no. 1 (2020): 130–44.

Fassin, Didier. *Humanitarian Reason: A Moral History of the Present*. Berkeley: University of California Press, 2011.

Fassin, Didier. "Inequality of Lives, Hierarchies of Humanity: Moral Commitments and Ethical Dilemmas of Humanitarianism." In *In the Name of Humanity: The Government of Threat and Care*, edited by Ilana Feldman and Miriam Ticktin, 238–55. Durham, NC: Duke University Press, 2010.

Fassin, Didier, and Mariella Pandolfi. "Introduction: Military and Humanitarian Government in the Age of Intervention." In *Contemporary States of Emergency: The Politics of Military and Humanitarian Interventions*, edited by Didier Fassin and Mariella Pandolfi, 9–25. New York: Zed, 2010.

Feldman, Ilana. "What Is a Camp? Legitimate Refugee Lives in Spaces of Long-Term Displacement." *Geoforum* 66 (2015): 244–52.

Feldman, Ilana, and Miriam Ticktin, eds. *In the Name of Humanity: The Government of Threat and Care*. Durham, NC: Duke University Press, 2010.

Ferguson, James. *Global Shadows: Africa in the Neoliberal World Order*. Durham, NC: Duke University Press, 2006.

Fiddian-Qasmiyeh, Elena. "Introduction: Recentering the South in Studies of Migration." *Migration and Society* 3, no. 1 (2020): 1–18.

Fleming, Melissa. "Let's Change the Way We Think About Refugee Camps." *Medium*, June 8, 2018. Accessed January 30, 2023. https://melissa-fleming.medium.com/lets-change-the-way-we-think-about-refugee-camps-5d93c0bc296a.

Forth, Aidan. *Barbed-Wire Imperialism: Britain's Empire of Camps, 1876–1903*. Berkeley: University of California Press, 2017.

Foucault, Michel. "The Birth of Biopolitics." In *Michel Foucault: Ethics, Subjectivity, and Truth*, edited by Paul Rabinow, 73–80. New York: New Press, 1997.

Foucault, Michel. *Discipline and Punish: The Birth of the Prison*. New York: Vintage, 1995.

Foucault, Michel. "Governmentality." In *The Foucault Effect: Studies in Governmentality*, edited by Graham Burchell, Colin Gordon, and Peter Miller, 87–104. Chicago: University of Chicago Press, 1991.

Foucault, Michel. *The History of Sexuality, Volume 1: The Will to Knowledge*. London: Penguin, 1998.

Foucault, Michel. *Security, Territory, Population: Lectures at the Collège de France 1977–1978*. London: Palgrave Macmillan, 2007.

Foucault, Michel. *Society Must Be Defended: Lectures at the Collège de France, 1975–76*. New York: Picador, 2003.

Foucault, Michel. "The Subject and Power." *Critical Inquiry* 8, no. 4 (1982): 777–95.

Fox, Gregory H. *Humanitarian Occupation*. Cambridge: Cambridge University Press, 2008.

Galaty, John. "Boundary-Making and Pastoral Conflict along the Kenyan-Ethiopian Borderlands." *African Studies Review* 59, no. 1 (2016): 97–122.

Galtung, Johan. "Violence, Peace, and Peace Research." *Source* 6, no. 3 (1969): 167–91.

Garelli, Glenda, and Martina Tazzioli. "Military-Humanitarianism." In *Handbook on Critical Geographies of Migration*, edited by Kathryne Mitchell, Reece Jones, and Jennifer Fluri, 182–92. Cheltenham, UK: Edward Elgar, 2019.

Gatrell, Peter. *The Making of the Modern Refugee*. Oxford: Oxford University Press, 2015.

Gatter, Melissa. *Time and Power in Azraq Refugee Camp: A Nine-to-Five Emergency*. Cairo: American University in Cairo Press, 2023.

Gazzotti, Lorena. *Immigration Nation: Aid, Control, and Border Politics in Morocco*. Cambridge: Cambridge University Press, 2021.

Getachew, Adom. *Worldmaking After Empire: The Rise and Fall of Self-Determination*, Princeton, NJ: Princeton University Press, 2019.

Ghai, Yash. "Devolution: Restructuring the Kenyan State." *Journal of Eastern African Studies* 2, no. 2 (2008): 211–26.

Ghoddousi, Pooya, and Sam Page. "Using Ethnography and Assemblage Theory in Political Geography." *Geography Compass* 14, no. 10 (2020): e12533.

Gilmore, Ruth Wilson. "Abolition Geography and the Problem of Innocence." In *Futures of Black Radicalism*, edited by Gaye Theresa Johnson and Alex Lubin, 225–40. New York: Verso, 2017.

Gilmore, Ruth Wilson. *Golden Gulag: Prisons, Surplus, Crisis, and Opposition in Globalizing California*. Berkeley: University of California Press, 2007.

Gilroy, Paul. *Between Camps: Nations, Cultures and the Allure of Race*. London: Routledge, 2004.

Glasman, Joël. *Humanitarianism and the Quantification of Human Needs: Minimal Humanity*. Abingdon, UK: Routledge, 2020.

Global System for Mobile Communications Association. *Mobile-Enabled Energy for Humanitarian Contexts: The Case for Pay-as-You-Go Solar Home Systems in Kakuma Refugee Camp*. Atlanta: GSMA, 2019. Accessed February 6, 2025. https://www.gsma.com/solutions-and-impact/connectivity-for-good/mobile-for-development/wp-content/uploads/2019/02/Mobile_Enabled_Energy_M4H.pdf.

Glück, Zoltán. "Security Urbanism and the Counterterror State in Kenya." *Anthropological Theory* 17, no. 3 (2017): 297–321.

Gonzalez Casanova, Pablo. "Internal Colonialism and National Development." *Studies in Comparative International Development* 1 (1965): 27–37.

Göpfert. Mirco. *Policing the Frontier: An Ethnography of Two Worlds in Niger*. Ithaca, NY: Cornell University Press, 2020.

Gordon, Neve. "From Colonization to Separation: Exploring the Structure of Israel's Occupation." *Third World Quarterly* 29, no. 1 (2008): 25–44.

Government of Kenya. *Fourth Draft Guidelines for Implementation of Community Policing—Nyumba Kumi (Usalama Wa Msingi)*. Nairobi: Government of Kenya, 2015.

Government of Kenya. *The Refugee Act 2006*. Nairobi: Government of Kenya/Parliament of Kenya, 2006.

Government of Kenya. *Report of the National Task Force on Police Reforms*. Nairobi: Government of Kenya, 2009.

Government of Kenya. *The Security Laws (Amendment) Act*. Nairobi: Government of Kenya/Parliament of Kenya, 2014.

Government of Kenya. *Shirika Plan: Socioeconomic Hubs for Integrated Refugee Inclusion in Kenya*. Nairobi: Government of Kenya, 2023.

Government of Kenya. "Ulinzi Unaanza Na Mimi, Ulinzi Unaanza Na Wewe." Video, 2014, Accessed February 6, 2025. https://www.youtube.com/watch?v=2X6xFNwjaSk.

Government of Kenya, Government of Somalia, and United Nations High Commissioner for Refugees. *Tripartite Agreement Between the Government of the Republic of Kenya, the Government of the Federal Republic of Somalia and the United Nations High Commissioner for Refugees Governing the Voluntary Repatriation of Somali Refugees Living in Kenya*. Nairobi: Government of Kenya, Government of Somalia, and UNHCR, 2013.

Graham, Stephen. *Cities Under Siege: The New Military Urbanism*. London: Verso, 2010.

Graham, Stephen, and Derek Gregory. "Security." In *The Dictionary of Human Geography*, edited by D. Gregory, R. Johnston, G. Pratt, and G. Watts, 672–73. Oxford: Wiley-Blackwell, 2009.

Grayson, Catherine-Lune. *Children of the Camp: The Lives of Somali Youth Raised in Kakuma Refugee Camp, Kenya*. New York: Berghahn, 2017.

Gregory, Derek. "Imaginative Geographies." *Progress in Human Geography* 19, no. 4 (1995): 447–85.

Griek, Ilse. "Traditional Systems of Justice in Refugee Camps: The Need for Alternatives." *Refugee Reports* 27, no. 2 (2006): 1–20.

Gupta, Akhil. *Red Tape: Bureaucracy, Structural Violence, and Poverty in India*. Durham, NC: Duke University Press, 2012.

Hagmann, Tobias, and Didier Péclard. "Negotiating Statehood: Dynamics of Power and Domination in Africa." *Development and Change* 41, no. 4 (2010): 539–62.

Halais, Flavie. "'They Call Him the Millionaire': The Refugee Who Turned His Camp into a Business Empire." *The Guardian*, May 10, 2017. Accessed March 10, 2018. https://www.theguardian.com/global-development-professionals-network/2017/may/10/millionaire-refugee-mesfin-getahun-kakuma-refugee-camp.

Hall, Peter A., and Michèle Lamont. "Why Social Relations Matter for Politics and Successful Societies." *Annual Review of Political Science* 16 (2013): 49–71.

Hall, Stuart. "The Spectacle of the 'Other.'" In *Representation: Cultural Representations and Signifying Practices*, edited by Stuart Hall, 223–79. London: Sage, 1997.

Hardin, Rebecca. "Concessionary Politics: Property, Patronage, and Political Rivalry in Central African Forest Management." *Current Anthropology* 32, no. 3 (2011): 113–25.

Harper, Ian, and Parvathi Raman. "Less than Human? Diaspora, Disease and the Question of Citizenship." *International Migration* 46, no. 5 (2008): 3–26.

Harrell-Bond, Barbara E. *Imposing Aid: Emergency Assistance to Refugees*. Oxford: Oxford University Press, 1986.

Harrell-Bond, Barbara, and Eftihia Voutira. "In Search of 'Invisible' Actors: Barriers to Access in Refugee Research." *Journal of Refugee Studies* 20, no. 2 (2007): 281–98.

Harvey, David. "Globalization and the 'Spatial Fix.'" *Geographische Revue* 2 (2001): 23–30.

Harvey, David. "The Right to the City." *New Left Review* 53 (2008): 23–40.

Hashimshony-Yaffe, Nurit, and Hilah Segal-Klein. "Renewable Energy and the Centralisation of Power: The Case Study of Lake Turkana Wind Power, Kenya." *Political Geography* 102 (2023): 102819.

Heald, Suzette. "Controlling Crime and Corruption from Below: Sungusungu in Kenya." *International Relations* 21, no. 2 (2007): 183–99.

Henriet, Benoît. *Colonial Impotence: Virtue and Violence in a Congolese Concession (1911–1940)*. Boston: De Gruyter, 2021.

Herbert, Steve. "For Ethnography." *Progress in Human Geography* 24, no. 4 (2000): 550–68.

Herbert, Steve. *Policing Space: Territoriality and the Los Angeles Police Department*. Minneapolis: University of Minnesota Press, 1996.

Hilhorst, Dorothea, and Bram J. Jansen. "Humanitarian Space as Arena: A Perspective on the Everyday Politics of Aid." *Development and Change* 41, no. 6 (2010): 1117–39.

Hill, Martin. *No Redress: Somalia's Forgotten Minorities*, London: Minority Rights Group International, 2010.

Hills, Alice. *Policing Africa: Internal Security and the Limits of Liberalisation*. Boulder, CO: Lynne Rienner, 2000.

Hoffmann, Sophia. "Humanitarian Security in Jordan's Azraq Camp." *Security Dialogue* 48, no. 2 (2017): 97–112.

Hogg, Richard. "Destitution and Development: The Turkana of North West Kenya." *Disasters* 6, no. 3 (1982): 164–68.

Hogg, Richard. "The New Pastoralism: Poverty and Dependency in Northern Kenya." *Africa* 56, no. 3 (1986): 319–33.

Hom, Stephanie Malia. *Empire's Mobius Strip: Historical Echoes in Italy's Crisis of Migration and Detention*. Ithaca, NY: Cornell University Press, 2019.

hooks, bell. *Feminist Theory: From Margin to Center*. London: Pluto, 2000.

Hope, Kempe Ronald. "Police Corruption and the Security Challenge in Kenya." *African Security* 11, no. 1 (2018): 84–108.

Hopkins, A. G. *An Economic History of West Africa*. London: Routledge, 2019.

Horn, Rebecca. "Exploring the Impact of Displacement and Encampment on Domestic Violence in Kakuma Refugee Camp." *Journal of Refugee Studies* 23, no. 3 (2010): 356–76.

Horst, Cindy. *Transnational Nomads: How Somalis Cope with Refugee Life in the Dadaab Camps of Kenya*. New York: Berghahn, 2006.

Howell, Alison, and Melanie Richter-Montpetit. "Racism in Foucauldian Security Studies: Biopolitics, Liberal War, and the Whitewashing of Colonial and Racial Violence." *International Political Sociology* 13, no. 1 (2018): 2–19.

Human Rights Watch. *Human Rights Watch World Report 1993—Kenya*. New York: HRW, 1993. Accessed May 6, 2018. http://www.refworld.org/docid/467fca5d1e.html.

Hyndman, Jennifer. *Managing Displacement: Refugees and the Politics of Humanitarianism*. Minneapolis: University of Minnesota Press, 2000.

Hyndman, Jennifer. "Refugee Camps as Conflict Zones: The Politics of Gender." In *Sites of Violence: Gender and Conflict Zones*, edited by Wenona Giles and Jennifer Hyndman, 193–212. Berkeley: University of California Press, 2004.

Hyndman, Jennifer. "To Help or Not to Help? Humanitarian Spaces, Power, and Government." In *Handbook on the Geographies of Power*, edited by Mat Coleman and John Agnew, 380–92. Cheltenham: Edward Elgar Publishing, 2018.

Hyndman, Jennifer, and Wenona Giles. *Refugees in Extended Exile: Living on the Edge*. London: Routledge, 2016.

Hyndman, Jennifer, and Alison Mountz. "Refuge or Refusal: Geographies of Exclusion." In *Violent Geographies: Fear, Terror, and Political Violence*, edited by Derek Gregory and Pred Allan, 77–92. New York: Routledge, 2007.

Hyndman, Jennifer, and Bo Viktor Nylund. "UNHCR and the Status of Prima Facie Refugees in Kenya." *International Journal of Refugee Law* 10, nos. 1–2 (1998): 21–48.

Iazzolino, Gianluca. "Power Geometries of Encampment: The Reproduction of Domination and Marginality Among Somali Refugees in Kakuma." *Geoforum* 110 (2020): 25–34.

Ikanda, Fred Nyongesa. "Animating 'Refugeeness' Through Vulnerabilities: Worthiness of Long-Term Exile in Resettlement Claims Among Somali Refugees in Kenya." *Africa* 88, no. 3 (2018): 579–96.

Ilcan, Suzan, and Kim Rygiel. "'Resiliency Humanitarianism': Responsibilizing Refugees Through Humanitarian Emergency Governance in the Camp." *International Political Sociology* 9, no. 4 (2015): 333–51.

Independent Policing Oversight Authority. *Monitoring Report on Operation Sanitization Eastleigh Publicly Known as "Usalama Watch."* Nairobi: IPOA, 2014.

International Committee of the Red Cross. *The Geneva Conventions of 12 August 1949*. Geneva: ICRC, 2012.

International Finance Corporation. "Kakuma: A Refugee Camp with Its Own Informal Economy." Video, posted May 3, 2018. Accessed January 12, 2023. https://www.youtube.com/watch?v=oXLpweEIA1E.

International Finance Corporation. *Kakuma as a Marketplace: A Consumer and Market Study of a Refugee Camp and Town in Northwest Kenya.* New York: IFC, 2018.

International Rescue Committee. "Moria Refugee Camp During the Coronavirus Pandemic," May 28, 2020. Accessed November 28, 2022. https://www.rescue.org/uk /article/moria-refugee-camp-during-coronavirus-pandemic.

International Rescue Committee and Twaweza. *Kenya: Citizens' Perceptions on Refugees.* Nairobi: IRC, Sauti za Wananchi, 2018. Accessed February 6, 2025. https://www .rescue.org/sites/default/files/document/2857/irckenya.pdf.

Isakjee, Arshad, Thom Davies, Jelena Obradović-Wochnik, and Karolìna Augustovà. "Liberal Violence and the Racial Borders of the European Union." *Antipode* 52, no. 6 (2020): 1751–73.

Jackson, Michael. "The Shock of the New: Migrant Imaginaries and Critical Transitions." *Ethnos* 73, no. 1 (2008): 57–72.

Jaji, Rose. "Social Technology and Refugee Encampment in Kenya." *Journal of Refugee Studies* 25, no. 2 (2012): 221–38.

Jamal, Arafat. "Minimum Standards and Essential Needs in a Protracted Refugee Situation: A Review of the UNHCR Programme in Kakuma, Kenya." United Nations High Commissioner for Refugees, Geneva, 2000.

Janmyr, Maja. "Revisiting the Civilian and Humanitarian Character of Refugee Camps." In *Refuge from Inhumanity? War Refugees and International Humanitarian Law*, edited by David Cantor and Jean-François Durieux, 225–46. Leiden: Brill, 2014.

Janmyr, Maja, and Are J. Knudsen. "Introduction: Hybrid Spaces." *Humanity* 7, no. 3 (2018): 391–95.

Jansen, Bram. "The Accidental City: Violence, Economy and Humanitarianism in Kakuma Refugee Camp, Kenya." PhD diss., Wageningen University, Wageningen, Netherlands, 2011.

Jansen, Bram. "Between Vulnerability and Assertiveness: Negotiating Resettlement in Kakuma Refugee Camp, Kenya." *African Affairs* 107, no. 429 (2008): 569–87.

Jansen, Bram. "'Digging Aid': The Camp as an Option in East and the Horn of Africa." *Journal of Refugee Studies* 29, no. 2 (2016): 149–65.

Jansen, Bram. *Kakuma Refugee Camp: Humanitarian Urbanism in Kenya's Accidental City.* London: Zed, 2018.

Jansen, Bram. "The Refugee Camp as Warscape: Violent Cosmologies, 'Rebelization,' and Humanitarian Governance in Kakuma, Kenya." *Humanity* 7, no. 3 (2016): 429–41.

Jansen, Bram J., and Milou de Bruijne. "Humanitarian Spill-Over: The Expansion of Hybrid Humanitarian Governance from Camps to Refugee Hosting Societies in East Africa." *Journal of Eastern African Studies* 14, no. 4 (2020): 669–88.

Jenkins, Sarah. "Ethnicity, Violence, and the Immigrant-Guest Metaphor in Kenya." *African Affairs* 111, no. 445 (2012): 576–96.

Jok, Jok Madut. "Diversity, Unity, and Nation Building in South Sudan." Special report, US Institute of Peace, Washington, DC, 2011.

Jolliffe, Pia. "Night-Time and Refugees: Evidence from the Thai-Myanmar Border." *Journal of Refugee Studies* 29, no. 1 (2016): 1–18.

Jones, Reece. *Violent Borders: Refugees and the Right to Move.* London: Verso, 2017.

Jumbert, Maria G., and Elisa Pascucci. *Citizen Humanitarianism at European Borders.* Abingdon, UK: Routledge, 2021.

Junaid, Mohamad. "Death and Life Under Occupation: Space, Violence and Memory in Kashmir." In *Everyday Occupations: Experiencing Militarism in South Asia and the Middle East,* edited by Kamala Visweswaran, 158–90. Philadelphia: University of Pennsylvania Press, 2013.

Justin, Peter Hakim, and Mathijs Van Leeuwen. "The Politics of Conflict in Yei River County, South Sudan." *Modern African Studies* 54, no. 3 (2016): 419–42.

Kagwanja, Peter, and Monica Juma. "Somali Refugees: Protracted Exile and Shifting Security Frontiers." In *Protracted Refugee Situations,* edited by Gil Loescher, James Milner, Edward Newman, and Gary Troeller, 214–47. New York: United Nations University Press, 2008.

Kallio, Kirsi P., Jouni Häkli, and Elisa Pascucci. "Refugeeness as Political Subjectivity: Experiencing the Humanitarian Border." *Environment and Planning C: Politics and Space* 37, no. 7 (2019): 1258–76.

KANERE. "Incentive Pay Raises and Terminations Targeting Incentive Staffs." *Kakuma News Reflector,* August 21, 2011. Accessed December 20, 2022. https://kanere.org /incentive-pay-raises-and-terminations-targeting-incentive-staffs/#:~:text=In%20 Kakuma%2C%20camp%20refugees%20hold,education%20or%20their%20 position%20titles.

KANERE. "Violence in Kakuma Kills 20." *Kakuma News Reflector,* December 25, 2014. Accessed February 6, 2025. https://kanere.org/violence-in-kakuma-kills-20.

Kariuki, Josiah Mwangi. *"Mau Mau" Detainee.* Oxford: Oxford University Press, 1963.

Kelling, George L., and James Q. Wilson. "Broken Windows: The Police and Neighbour-hood Safety." *Atlantic Monthly,* March 1982.

Kenya Defense Forces. *Operation Linda Nchi: Kenya's Military Experience in Somalia.* Nairobi: Kenya Literature Bureau, 2014.

Kenya National Bureau of Statistics. *The 2009 Kenya Population and Housing Census.* Nairobi: KNBS, 2009.

Kenya National Bureau of Statistics. *The 2019 Kenya Population and Housing Census.* Nairobi: KNBS, 2019.

Kenya National Commission on Human Rights. *Return of the Gulag: Report of KNCHR Investigations on Operation Usalama Watch.* Nairobi: KNCHR, 2014.

Khalili, Laleh. *Time in the Shadows: Confinement in Counterinsurgencies.* Stanford, CA: Stanford University Press, 2012.

Khosravi, Shahram. *"Illegal" Traveller: An Auto-Ethnography of Borders.* Basingstoke, UK: Palgrave Macmillan, 2010.

Khosravi, Shahram. "Stolen Time." *Radical Philosophy* 203 (2018): 38–41. Accessed February 26, 2021. https://www.radicalphilosophy.com/article/stolen-time.

Kibreab, Gaim. "The Myth of Dependency Among Camp Refugees in Somalia 1979–1989." *Journal of Refugee Studies* 6, no. 4 (1994): 321–49.

Kibreab, Gaim. "Pulling the Wool over the Eyes of the Strangers: Refugee Deceit and Trickery in Institutionalized Settings." *Journal of Refugee Studies* 17, no. 1 (2004): 1–26.

Kibreab, Gaim. *Refugees and Development in Africa: The Case of Eritrea.* Trenton, NJ: Red Sea, 1987.

Kimari, Wangui. "The Story of a Pump: Life, Death and Afterlives Within an Urban Planning of 'Divide and Rule.'" *Urban Geography* 42, no. 2 (2021): 141–60.

Kioko, Eric M. "Conflict Resolution and Crime Surveillance in Kenya: Local Peace Committees and Nyumba Kumi." *Africa Spectrum* 52, no. 1 (2017): 3–32.

Kiura, Annet Wanjira. "Constrained Agency on Contraceptive Use Among Somali Refugee Women in the Kakuma Refugee Camp in Kenya." *Gender, Technology and Development* 18, no. 1 (2014): 147–61.

Kleinfeld, Margo. "Misreading the Post-Tsunami Political Landscape in Sri Lanka: The Myth of Humanitarian Space." *Space and Polity* 11, no. 2 (2007): 169–84.

Kotef, Hagar. *Movement and the Ordering of Freedom: On Liberal Governances of Mobility*. Durham, NC: Duke University Press, 2015.

Kothari, Uma. "Spatial Practices and Imaginaries: Experiences of Colonial Officers and Development Professionals." *Singapore Journal of Tropical Geography* 27, no. 3 (2006): 235–53.

Krause, Ulrike. *Difficult Life in a Refugee Camp: Gender, Violence, and Coping in Uganda*. Cambridge: Cambridge University Press, 2021.

Krause, Ulrike. "Researching Forced Migration: Critical Reflections on Research Ethics during Fieldwork." Refugee Studies Center Working Paper Series, Oxford, 2017.

Lamphear, John. "Aspects of Turkana Leadership During the Era of Primary Resistance." *Journal of African History* 17, no. 2 (1976): 225–43.

Landau, Loren. "A Chronotope of Containment Development: Europe's Migrant Crisis and Africa's Reterritorialisation." *Antipode* 51, no. 1 (2019): 169–86.

Landau, Loren. *The Humanitarian Hangover: Displacement, Aid and Transformation in Western Tanzania*. Johannesburg: Wits University Press, 2007.

Lawrence, Benjamin N., Emily L. Osborn, and Richard L. Roberts, eds. *Intermediaries, Interpreters, and Clerks: African Employees in the Making of Colonial Africa*. Madison: University of Wisconsin Press, 2006.

Lawton, Rebecca. "Midnight at the Oasis." *Aeon*, November 6, 2015. Accessed June 2023. https://aeon.co/essays/palm-trees-amid-the-sand-the-origins-of-the-oasis-fantasy.

LeBrón, Marisol. *Policing Life and Death: Race, Violence, and Resistance in Puerto Rico*. Berkeley: University of California Press, 2019.

Lefebvre, Henri. *Writings on Cities*. Oxford: Blackwell, 1996.

Legassick, Martin, and Harold Wolpe. "The Bantustans and Capital Accumulation in South Africa." *Review of African Political Economy* 3, no. 7 (1976): 87–107.

Lemberg-Pedersen, Martin. "Manufacturing Displacement: Externalization and Postcoloniality in European Migration Control." *Global Affairs* 5, no. 3 (2019): 247–71.

Lemberg-Pedersen, Martin, Sharla M. Fett, Lucy Mayblin, Nina Sahraoui, and Eva Magdalena Stambøl, eds. *Postcoloniality and Forced Migration: Mobility, Control, Agency*. Bristol, UK: Bristol University Press, 2022.

Lenin, Vladimir I. *Lenin Collected Works, Volume 3: The Development of Capitalism in Russia*. Moscow: Progress, 1977.

Lester, Alan, and Fae Dussart. *Colonization and the Origins of Humanitarian Governance: Protecting Aborigines Across the Nineteenth-Century British Empire*. Cambridge: Cambridge University Press, 2014.

Lewis, Rachel A., and Nancy A. Naples. "Introduction: Queer Migration, Asylum, and Displacement." *Sexualities* 17, no. 8 (2014): 911–18.

Li, Tania Murray. "Governmentality." *Anthropologica* 49, no. 2 (2007): 275–81.

Lind, Jeremy. "Devolution, Shifting Centre-Periphery Relationships and Conflict in Northern Kenya." *Political Geography* 63 (2017): 135–47.

Lind, Jeremy, Patrick Mutahi, and Marjoke Oosterom. "'Killing a Mosquito with a Hammer': Al-Shabaab Violence and State Security Responses in Kenya." *Peacebuilding* 5, no. 2 (2017): 118–35.

Lingelbach, Jochen. *On the Edges of Whiteness: Polish Refugees in British Colonial Africa During and After the Second World War*. Oxford: Berghahn, 2020.

Lischer, Sarah Kenyon. *Dangerous Sanctuaries: Refugee Camps, Civil War, and the Dilemmas of Humanitarian Aid*. Ithaca, NY: Cornell University Press, 2006.

Lochery, Emma. "Rendering Difference Visible: The Kenyan State and Its Somali Citizens." *African Affairs* 111, no. 445 (2012): 615–39.

Loescher, Gil, and James Milner. "Protracted Refugee Situations and State and Regional Insecurity." *Conflict, Security and Development* 4, no. 1 (2004): 3–20.

Loizides, Neophytos. "Contested Migration and Settler Politics in Cyprus." *Political Geography* 30, no. 7 (2011): 391–401.

Lonsdale, John. "Moral Ethnicity and Political Tribalism." In *Inventions and Boundaries: Historical and Anthropological Approaches to Ethnicity and Nationalism*, edited by P. Kaarsholm and J. Hultin, 131–50. Roskilde: Roskilde Universitet, 1996.

Lonsdale, John. "Soil, Work, Civilisation, and Citizenship in Kenya." *Journal of Eastern African Studies* 2, no. 2 (2008): 305–14.

Lopez, Patricia J., Lisa Bhungalia, and Léonie S. Newhouse. "Geographies of Humanitarian Violence." *Environment and Planning A: Economy and Space* 47, no. 11 (2015): 2232–39.

Low, D. A., and John Lonsdale. "East Africa: Towards the New Order 1945–1963." In *Eclipse of Empire*, edited by D. A. Low, 164–214. Cambridge: Cambridge University Press, 2010.

Lowe, Lisa. *The Intimacies of Four Continents*. Durham, NC: Duke University Press, 2015.

Loyd, Jenna, Matt Mitchelson, and Andrew Burridge. *Beyond Walls and Cages: Prisons, Borders, and Global Crisis*. Athens: University of Georgia Press, 2012.

Lugard, Frederick D. *The Dual Mandate in British Tropical Africa*. Edinburgh: William Blackwood and Sons, 1922.

Lutz, Catherine. "Making War at Home in the United States: Militarization and the Current Crisis." *American Anthropologist* 104, no. 3 (2002): 723–35.

Luxemburg, Rosa. *The Accumulation of Capital*. London: Routledge, 2003.

Lynch, Gabrielle. "Kenya's New Indigenes: Negotiating Local Identities in a Global Context." *Nations and Nationalism* 17, no. 1 (2011): 148–67.

MacArthur, Julie. *Cartography and the Political Imagination: Mapping Community in Colonial Kenya*. Columbus: Ohio University Press, 2016.

Maciel, Mervyn. "Memoirs of a Frontier Man: The Goan Contribution to the Kenyan Administration." *Kenya Past and Present* (2006): 24–27.

Maina, Andrew. "Development of Refugee Law in Kenya." *Blog*, 2016. Accessed January 26, 2017. https://worldpolicy.org/2016/03/29/development-of-refugee-law-in-kenya.

Maina, Andrew. "Securitization of Kenya's Asylum Space: Origin and Legal Analysis of the Encampment Policy." In *Refugees and Forced Migration in the Horn and Eastern Africa: Trends, Challenges and Opportunities*, 81–91. Cham, Switzerland: Springer, 2019.

Maingi, Joy, and Kenneth Omeje. "Policing Refugees in Fragile States: The Case of Kenya." In *Policing in Africa*, 73–93. New York: Palgrave Macmillan, 2012.

Mainwaring, Cetta. *At Europe's Edge: Migration and Crisis in the Mediterranean*. Oxford: Oxford University Press, 2019.

Makdisi, Saree. *Palestine Inside Out: An Everyday Occupation*. New York: W. W. Norton, 2008.

Maldonado-Torres, Nelson. "Césaire's Gift and the Decolonial Turn." In *Critical Ethnic Studies: A Reader*, edited by Nada Elia, David M. Hernández, and Jodi Kim et al., 435–62. Durham, NC: Duke University Press, 2016.

Maldonado-Torres, Nelson. "On the Coloniality of Being: Contributions to the Development of a Concept." *Cultural Studies* 21, nos. 2–3 (2007): 240–70.

Malkki, Liisa H. *The Need to Help: The Domestic Arts of International Humanitarianism*. Durham, NC: Duke University Press, 2015.

Malkki, Liisa H. *Purity and Exile: Violence, Memory, and National Cosmology Among Hutu Refugees in Tanzania*. Chicago: University of Chicago Press, 1995.

Malkki, Liisa H. "Refugees and Exile: From 'Refugee Studies' to the National Order of Things." *Annual Review of Anthropology* 24, no. 1 (1995): 493–523.

Malkki, Liisa H. "Speechless Emissaries: Refugees, Humanitarianism, and Dehistoricization." *Cultural Anthropology* 11, no. 3 (1996): 377–404.

Mamdani, Mahmood. *Citizen and Subject: Contemporary Africa and the Legacy of Late Colonialism*. London: James Currey, 1996.

Mamdani, Mahmood. *Neither Settler nor Native: The Making and Unmaking of Permanent Minorities*. Cambridge, MA: Harvard University Press, 2020.

Mangala, Jack. *Africa and the New World Era: From Humanitarianism to a Strategic View*. New York: Palgrave Macmillan, 2010.

Marinelli, Maurizio. "Making Concessions in Tianjin: Heterotopia and Italian Colonialism in Mainland China." *Urban History* 36, no. 3 (2009): 399–425.

Martin, Diana. "From Spaces of Exception to 'Campscapes': Palestinian Refugee Camps and Informal Settlements in Beirut." *Political Geography* 44 (2015): 9–18.

Martin, Lauren L. "Carceral Economies of Migration Control." *Progress in Human Geography* 45, no. 4 (2021): 740–57.

Martin, Lauren L., and Martina Tazzioli. "Value Extraction Through Refugee Carcerality: Data, Labour and Financialised Accommodation." *Environment and Planning D: Society and Space* 41, no. 2 (2023): 191–209.

Marx, Karl. *Capital, Volume One: A Critique of Political Economy*. London: Penguin, 1976.

Masco, Joseph. *The Theater of Operations: National Security Affect from the Cold War to the War on Terror*. Durham, NC: Duke University Press, 2014.

Massey, Doreen. *For Space*. London: Sage, 2005.

Mayblin, Lucy. *Asylum After Empire: Colonial Legacies in the Politics of Asylum Seeking*. London: Rowman and Littlefield, 2017.

Mayblin, Lucy, Mustafa Wake, and Mohsen Kazemi. "Necropolitics and the Slow Violence of the Everyday: Asylum Seeker Welfare in the Postcolonial Present." *Sociology* 54, no. 1 (2020): 107–23.

Mbembe, Achille. "Bodies as Borders." *From the European South* 4 (2019): 5–18.

Mbembe, Achille. *Critique of Black Reason*. Durham, NC: Duke University Press, 2017.

Mbembe, Achille. "Necropolitics." *Public Culture* 15, no. 1 (2003): 11–40.

Mbembe, Achille. *Necropolitics*. Durham, NC: Duke University Press, 2019.

Mbembe, Achille. *On the Postcolony*. Berkeley: University of California Press, 2001.

Mbembe, Achille. *Out of the Dark Night: Essays on Decolonization*. New York: Columbia University Press, 2021.

McCabe, J. Terrence. *Cattle Bring Us to Our Enemies: Turkana Ecology, Politics, and Raiding in a Disequilibrium System*. Ann Arbor: University of Michigan Press, 2004.

McCabe, J. Terrence. "The Failure to Encapsulate: Resistance to the Penetration of Capitalism by the Turkana of Kenya." In *Pastoralists at the Periphery: Herders in a Capitalist World*, edited by Harold Koster and Claudia Chang, 309–27. Tucson: University of Arizona Press, 1994.

McConnachie, Kirsten. *Governing Refugees: Justice, Order and Legal Pluralism*. London: Routledge, 2014.

McCormack, Killian, and Emily Gilbert. "The Geopolitics of Militarism and Humanitarianism." *Progress in Human Geography* 46, no. 1 (2022): 179–97.

McKittrick, Katherine. "Plantation Futures." *Small Axe* 17, no. 3 (2013): 1–15.

Megoran, Nick. "For Ethnography in Political Geography: Experiencing and Re-Imagining Ferghana Valley Boundary Closures." *Political Geography* 25, no. 6 (2006): 622–40.

Meiu, George Paul. "Who Are the New Natives? Ethnicity and Emerging Idioms of Belonging in Africa." In *A Companion to the Anthropology of Africa*, edited by Roy Richard Grinker, Stephen C. Lubkemann, Christopher B. Steiner, and Euclides Gonçalves, 147–72. Oxford: Wiley, 2019.

Memmi, Albert. *The Colonizer and the Colonized*. London: Earthscan, 1974.

Mezzadra, Sandro, and Brett Neilson. "On the Multiple Frontiers of Extraction: Excavating Contemporary Capitalism." *Cultural Studies* 31, no. 2–3 (2017): 185–204.

Mezzadra, Sandro, and Brett Neilson. *The Politics of Operations: Excavating Contemporary Capitalism*. Durham, NC: Duke University Press, 2019.

Miller, Sarah Deardorff. *UNHCR as a Surrogate State: Protracted Refugee Situations*. London: Routledge, 2018.

Mills, Charles M. *The Racial Contract*. Ithaca, NY: Cornell University Press, 1997.

Milner, James. *Refugees, the State and the Politics of Asylum in Africa*. New York: Palgrave Macmillan, 2009.

Milner, James, Mustafa Alio, and Rez Gardi. "Meaningful Refugee Participation: An Emerging Norm in the Global Refugee Regime." *Refugee Survey Quarterly* 41, no. 4 (2022): 565–93.

Milton, Daniel, Megan Spencer, and Michael Findley. "Radicalism of the Hopeless: Refugee Flows and Transnational Terrorism." *International Interactions* 39, no. 5 (2013): 621–45.

Minca, Claudio. "Geographies of the Camp." *Political Geography* 45 (2015): 74–83.

Minca, Claudio. "Giorgio Agamben and the New Biopolitical Nomos." *Geografiska Annaler, Series B: Human Geography* 88, no. 4 (2006): 387–403.

Mitchell, Timothy. "Society, Economy and the State Effect." In *Anthropology of the State*, edited by Aradhana Sharma and Akhil Gupta, 169–86. Oxford: Blackwell, 2006.

Mkutu, Kennedy, and Gerald Wandera. "Policing the Periphery: Opportunities and Challenges for Kenya Police Reserves." Working Paper no. 15, Small Arms Survey, Geneva, 2013.

Mogire, Edward. "Refugee Realities: Refugee Rights Versus State Security in Kenya and Tanzania." *Transformation* 26, no. 1 (2009): 15–29.

Mogire, Edward, and Kennedy Mkutu. "Counter-Terrorism in Kenya." *Journal of Contemporary African Studies* 29, no. 4 (2011): 473–91.

Mogire, Edward, Kennedy Mkutu, and Doreen Alusa. "Policing Terrorism in Kenya: The Security-Committee Interface." In *Security Governance in East Africa: Picture of Policing from the Ground*, edited by Kennedy Mkutu, 79–104. London: Lexington, 2018.

Moran, Dominique, Nick Gill, and Deirdre Colon. *Carceral Spaces: Mobility and Agency in Imprisonment and Migrant Detention*. London: Ashgate, 2013.

Morris, Helen, and Frances Voon. "Which Side Are You On? Discussion Paper on UN-HCR's Policy and Practice of Incentive Payments to Refugees." United Nations High Commissioner for Refugees, Geneva, 2014.

Moulin, Carolina, and Peter Nyers. "'We Live in a Country of UNHCR'—Refugee Protests and Global Political Society." *International Political Sociology* 1, no. 4 (2007): 356–72.

Mountz, Alison. *The Death of Asylum: Hidden Geographies of the Enforcement Archipelago*. Minneapolis: University of Minnesota Press, 2020.

Mountz, Alison. *Seeking Asylum: Human Smuggling and Bureaucracy at the Border*. Minneapolis: University of Minnesota Press, 2010.

Moyd, Michelle R. *Violent Intermediaries: African Soldiers, Conquest, and Everyday Colonialism in German East Africa*. Athens: Ohio University Press, 2014.

Mudimbe, Valentin-Yves. *The Invention of Africa: Gnosis, Philosophy, and the Order of Knowledge*. London: James Currey, 1988.

Muggah, Robert, ed. *No Refuge: The Crisis of Refugee Militarization in Africa*. London: Zed, 2013.

Muiruri, Stephen. "Policing a Willing Community." *Daily Nation*, May 1, 2005. Accessed February 8, 2018. https://www.nation.co.ke/lifestyle/1190-57354-dmr26dz/index.html.

Muraya, Joseph. "Mobility of Cops in Kakuma, Dadaab Camps Enhanced." *Capital News*, March 28, 2017. Accessed February 6, 2025. https://www.capitalfm.co.ke/news /2017/03/mobility-cops-kakuma-dadaab-camps-enhanced/

Mutambo, Aggrey. "In Wake of Garissa Attack, Kenya Frustrated by Dadaab Issue." *Daily Nation*, April 14, 2015. Accessed January 10, 2018. https://www.nation.co.ke/news /Dadaab-Refugee-Camp-Terrorism-Somalia-Repatriation/1056-2686320-crh6p0 /index.html.

Mwangi, Annabel Namik. "Refugees and the State in Kenya: The Politics of Identity, Rights and Displacement." PhD diss., University of Oxford, 2005.

Mwangi, Oscar Gakuo. "Political Corruption, Party Financing and Democracy in Kenya." *Journal of Modern African Studies* 46, no. 2 (2008): 267–85.

Mwangi, Oscar Gakuo. "The 'Somalinisation' of Terrorism and Counterterrorism in Kenya: The Case of Refoulement." *Critical Studies on Terrorism*, 12, no. 2 (2019): 298–316.

Myers, J. C. *Indirect Rule in South Africa: Tradition, Modernity, and the Costuming of Political Power*. Rochester, NY: University of Rochester Press, 2009.

Nawyn, Stephanie J. "New Directions for Research on Migration in the Global South." *International Journal of Sociology* 46, no. 3 (2016): 163–68.

Ndlovu-Gatsheni, Sabelo J. *Coloniality of Power in Postcolonial Africa: Myths of Decolonization*. Dakar: Council for the Development of Social Science Research in Africa, 2013.

Ndzovu, Hassan J. *Muslims in Kenyan Politics: Political Involvement, Marginalization, and Minority Status*. Evanston, IL: Northwestern University Press, 2014.

Neocleous, Mark. *A Critical Theory of Police Power*. London: Verso, 2000.

Neocleous, Mark. *Critique of Security*. Edinburgh: Edinburgh University Press, 2008.

Netz, Reviel. *Barbed Wire: An Ecology of Modernity*. Middletown, CT: Wesleyan University Press, 2010.

Neu, Michael. *Just Liberal Violence: Sweatshops, Torture, War*. London: Rowman and Littlefield, 2017.

Nevins, Joseph. "Policing Mobility: Maintaining Global Apartheid from South Africa to the United States." In *Beyond Walls and Cages: Prisons, Borders, and Global Crisis*, edited by Jenna M. Loyd, Matt Mitchelson, and Andrew Burridge, 19–26. Athens: University of Georgia Press, 2012.

Newhouse, Léonie S. "Creative Fictions: Incentive Work and Humanitarian Labour in South Sudan." *Transactions of the Institute of British Geographers* 50, no. 1 (2024): e12682.

Newhouse, Léonie S. "More than Mere Survival: Violence, Humanitarian Governance, and Practical Material Politics in a Kenyan Refugee Camp." *Environment and Planning A: Economy and Space* 47, no. 11 (2015): 2292–307.

Newton, Huey. "A Functional Definition of Politics." In *The Huey P. Newton Reader*, edited by David Hilliard and Donald Weise, 147–49. New York: Seven Stories, 2002.

Ngo, Bic, and Sarah Hansen. "Constructing Identities in UN Refugee Camps: The Politics of Language, Culture and Humanitarian Assistance." *Critical Inquiry in Language Studies* 10, no. 2 (2013): 97–120.

Ngũgĩ wa Thiong'o. *Decolonising the Mind: The Politics of Language in African Literature*. Nairobi: Heinemann Educational, 1986.

Ngutulu, Kodi Arnu. "Paradise in Hell." *Unheard Journalism Project*, 2021. Accessed February 6, 2025. https://journal.unheardproject.com/paradise-in-hell.

Nguyen, Vinh. "Refugeetude: When Does a Refugee Stop Being a Refugee?" *Social Text* 37, no. 2 (2019): 109–31.

Nixon, Rob. *Slow Violence and the Environmentalism of the Poor*. Cambridge, MA: Harvard University Press, 2011.

Noji, Eric K. "Public Health in the Aftermath of Disasters." *BMJ* 330, no. 7504 (2005): 1379–81.

Nunan, Timothy. *Humanitarian Invasion: Global Development in Cold War Afghanistan*. Cambridge: Cambridge University Press, 2016.

Nyabola, Nanjala. "Decolonise da Police: How Brutality Was Written into the DNA of Kenya's Police Service." *African Arguments*, July 19, 2016. Accessed February 6, 2025. https://africanarguments.org/2016/07/decolonise-da-police-how-brutality-was -written-into-the-dna-of-kenyas-police-service.

Nyaoro, Dulo. "Policing with Prejudice: How Policing Exacerbates Poverty Among Urban Refugees." *International Journal of Human Rights* 14, no. 1 (2010): 126–45.

Nyaoro, Dulo. "Refugee Hosting and Conflict Resolution: Opportunities for Diplomatic Interventions and Buffeting Regional Hegemons." In *Refugees and Forced Migration in the Horn and Eastern Africa*, edited by Johannes Dragsbaek Schmidt, Leah Kimathi, and Michael Omondi Owiso, 17–32. Cham, Switzerland: Springer, 2019.

Nyers, Peter. *Rethinking Refugees: Beyond States of Emergency.* New York: Routledge, 2006.

Oesch, Lucas. "The Refugee Camp as a Space of Multiple Ambiguities and Subjectivities." *Political Geography* 60 (2017): 110–20.

Oka, Rahul Chandrashekhar. "Unlikely Cities in the Desert: The Informal Economy as Causal Agent for Permanent 'Urban' Sustainability in Kakuma Refugee Camp, Kenya." *Urban Anthropology* 40, nos. 3–4 (2011): 223–62.

Okech, Awino. "Asymmetrical Conflict and Human Security: Reflections from Kenya." *Strategic Review for Southern Africa* 37, no. 1 (2015): 53–74.

Olivius, Elisabeth. "Constructing Humanitarian Selves and Refugee Others." *International Feminist Journal of Politics* 18, no. 2 (2015): 270–90.

Ombati, Cyrus. "Refugees Ordered to Relocate to Kakuma, Dadaab Camps as Urban Registration Centres Shut." *The Standard*, March 25, 2014. Accessed February 6, 2025. https://refugeeresearch.net/ms/km/2014/03/25/refugees-ordered-to-relocate-to -kakuma-dadaab-camps-as-urban-registration-centres-shut.

Ophir, Adi, Michal Givoni, and Sari Hanafi, eds. *The Power of Inclusive Exclusion: Anatomy of Israeli Rule in the Occupied Palestinian Territories.* New York: Zone, 2009.

Opitz, Sven. "Government Unlimited: The Security Dispositif of Illiberal Governmentality." In *Governmentality: Current Issues and Future Challenges*, edited by Ulrich Bröckling, Susanne Krasmann, and Thomas Lemke, 75–93. London: Routledge, 2010.

Osse, Anneke. "Police Reform in Kenya: A Process of 'Meddling Through.'" *Policing and Society* 26, no. 8 (2016): 907–24.

Overton, J. D. "Social Control and Social Engineering: African Reserves in Kenya 1895–1920." *Environment and Planning D: Society and Space* 8, no. 2 (1990): 163–74.

Painter, Joe. "Prosaic Geographies of Stateness." *Political Geography* 25, no. 7 (2006): 752–74.

Pallister-Wilkins, Polly. *Humanitarian Borders: Unequal Mobility and Saving Lives.* London: Verso, 2022.

Pallister-Wilkins, Polly. "HuManitarianism: Race and the Overrepresentation of 'Man.'" *Transactions of the Institute of British Geographers* 47, no. 3 (2022): 695–708.

Papada, Evie, Anna Papoutsi, Joe Painter, and Antonis Vradis. "Pop-Up Governance: Transforming the Management of Migrant Populations Through Humanitarian and Security Practices in Lesbos, Greece, 2015–2017." *Environment and Planning D: Society and Space* 38, no. 6 (2020): 1028–45.

Parkinson, J. "Notes on the Northern Frontier Province, Kenya." *Geographical Journal* 94, no. 2 (1939): 162–66.

Pascucci, Elisa. "The Local Labour Building the International Community: Precarious Work Within Humanitarian Spaces." *Environment and Planning A: Economy and Space* 51, no. 3 (2019): 743–60.

Pasquetti, Silvia, and Romola Sanyal, eds. *Displacement: Global Conversations on Refuge*. Manchester, UK: Manchester University Press, 2020.

Patterson, Orlando. *Slavery and Social Death: A Comparative Study*. Cambridge, MA: Harvard University Press, 1982.

Pesek, Michael. "The Boma and the Peripatetic Ruler: Mapping Colonial Rule in German East Africa, 1889–1903." *Western Folklore* 66, nos. 3–4 (2007): 233–57.

Peteet, Julie. "Camps and Enclaves: Palestine in the Time of Closure." *Journal of Refugee Studies* 29, no. 2 (2015): 208–28.

Peteet, Julie. *Space and Mobility in Palestine*. Bloomington: Indiana University Press, 2017.

Pezzani, Lorenzo, and Charles Heller. "A Disobedient Gaze: Strategic Interventions in the Knowledge(s) of Maritime Borders." *Postcolonial Studies* 16, no. 3 (2013): 289–98.

Pfingst, Annie, and Wangui Kimari. "Carcerality and the Legacies of Settler Colonial Punishment in Nairobi." *Punishment and Society* 23, no. 5 (2021): 697–722.

Picozza, Fiorenza. *The Coloniality of Asylum: Mobility, Autonomy and Solidarity in the Wake of Europe's Refugee Crisis*. London: Rowman and Littlefield, 2021.

Pierre, Jemima. *The Predicament of Blackness: Postcolonial Ghana and the Politics of Race*. Chicago: University of Chicago Press, 2013.

Pincock, Kate, Alexander Betts, and Evan Easton-Calabria. "The Rhetoric and Reality of Localisation: Refugee-Led Organisations in Humanitarian Governance." *Journal of Development Studies* 57, no. 5 (2021): 719–34.

Pittaway, Eileen, Linda Bartolomei, and Richard Hugman. "'Stop Stealing Our Stories': The Ethics of Research with Vulnerable Groups." *Journal of Human Rights Practice* 2, no. 2 (2010): 229–51.

Priddy, Grace, Zoe Doman, Emily Berry, and Saleh Ahmed. "Gender-Based Violence in a Complex Humanitarian Context: Unpacking the Human Sufferings Among Stateless Rohingya Women." *Ethnicities* 22, no. 2 (2022): 215–32.

Pupavac, Vanessa. "Pathologizing Populations and Colonizing Minds: International Psychosocial Programs in Kosovo." *Alternatives* 27, no. 4 (2002): 489–511.

Purdeková, Andrea. *Making Ubumwe: Power, State and Camps in Rwanda's Unity-Building Project*. New York: Berghahn, 2015.

Qasmiyeh, Yousif M. *Writing the Camp*. Talgarreg, UK: Broken Sleep, 2021.

Quijano, Aníbal. "Coloniality of Power and Eurocentrism in Latin America." *International Sociology* 15, no. 2 (2000): 215–32.

Rajaram, Prem Kumar. "Refugees as Surplus Population: Race, Migration and Capitalist Value Regimes." *New Political Economy* 23, no. 5 (2018): 627–39.

Ramadan, Adam. "Spatialising the Refugee Camp." *Transactions of the Institute of British Geographers* 38, no. 1 (2012): 65–77.

Reid-Henry, Simon M. "Humanitarianism as Liberal Diagnostic: Humanitarian Reason and the Political Rationalities of the Liberal Will-to-Care." *Transactions of the Institute of British Geographers* 39, no. 3 (2014): 418–31.

Reid-Henry, Simon M. "On the Politics of Our Humanitarian Present." *Environment and Planning D: Society and Space* 31, no. 4 (2013): 753–60.

Rijke, Alexandra, and Claudio Minca. "Checkpoint 300: Precarious Checkpoint Geographies and Rights/Rites of Passage in the Occupied Palestinian Territories." *Political Geography* 65 (2018): 35–45.

Rodgers, Graeme. "'Hanging Out' with Forced Migrants: Methodological and Ethical Challenges." *Forced Migration Review*, no. 21 (2004): 48–49.

Rodney, Walter. *Decolonial Marxism: Essays from the Pan-African Revolution.* London: Verso, 2022.

Rodney, Walter. *How Europe Underdeveloped Africa.* Dar es Salaam: East African Educational Publishers, 1972.

Rodríguez, Encarnación Gutiérrez. "The Coloniality of Migration and the 'Refugee Crisis': On the Asylum-Migration Nexus, the Transatlantic White European Settler Colonialism-Migration and Racial Capitalism." *Refuge* 34, no. 1 (2018): 16–28.

Rodriguez, S. M., Liat Ben-Moshe, and H. Rakes. "Carceral Protectionism and the Perpetually (In)Vulnerable." *Criminology and Criminal Justice* 20, no. 5 (2020): 537–50.

Rose, Nikolas. "The Death of the Social? Re-Figuring the Territory of Government." *Economy and Society* 25, no. 3 (1996): 327–56.

Rostis, Adam. *Organizing Disaster: The Construction of Humanitarianism.* Bingley, UK: Emerald, 2016.

Rudoren, Jodi. "Calm Boss Overseeing a Syrian Refugee Camp's Chaos." *New York Times*, May 24, 2013. Accessed February 6, 2025. https://www.nytimes.com/2013/05/25/world/middleeast/kilian-kleinschmidt-calm-boss-at-center-of-a-syrian-refugee-camps-chaos.html.

Russell, Simon. "Challenging the Established Order: The Need to 'Localise' Protection." *Forced Migration Review* 53 (2016): 8–11.

Ruteere, Mutuma. "More than Political Tools: The Police and Post-Election Violence in Kenya." *African Security Review* 20, no. 4 (2011): 11–20.

Rutinwa, Bonaventure. "The End of Asylum? The Changing Nature of Refugee Policies in Africa." New Issues in Refugee Research, Working Paper no. 5, United Nations High Commissioner for Refugees, Geneva, 1999.

Rwimo, Aminah. "Telling Our Own Stories: Finding Hope Through Film." TEDx KakumaCamp, June 9, 2018. YouTube, 10 min., 35 sec. https://www.youtube.com/watch?v=ouy23z9BS3I&t=10s.

Rygiel, Kim. "Politicizing Camps: Forging Transgressive Citizenships In and Through Transit." *Citizenship Studies* 16, nos. 5–6 (2012): 807–25.

Sabaratnam, Meera. *Decolonising Intervention: International Statebuilding in Mozambique.* London: Rowman and Littlefield, 2017.

Sagy, Tehila. "Treating Peace as Knowledge: UNHCR's Peace Education as a Controlling Process." *Journal of Refugee Studies* 21, no. 3 (2008): 360–79.

Said, Edward. *Orientalism.* New York: Vintage, 1994.

Sander, Gilman. *Difference and Pathology: Stereotypes of Sexuality, Race and Madness.* Ithaca, NY: Cornell University Press, 1985.

Sandvik, Kristin Bergtora. "Now Is the Time to Deliver: Looking for Humanitarian Innovation's Theory of Change." *Journal of International Humanitarian Action* 2, no. 8 (2017): 1–11.

Sanghi, Apurva, Harun Onder, and Varalakshmi Vemuru. *"Yes" in My Backyard? The Economics of Refugees and Their Social Dynamics in Kakuma, Kenya.* Washington, DC: World Bank Group, 2016. Accessed February 6, 2025. http://documents.worldbank .org/curated/en/308011482417763778.

Santos, Boaventura de Sousa. *Epistemologies of the South: Justice Against Epistemicide.* London: Routledge, 2015.

Sassen, Saskia. *Expulsions: Brutality and Complexity in the Global Economy.* Cambridge, MA: Harvard University Press, 2014.

Scharrer, Tabea. "'Ambiguous Citizens': Kenyan Somalis and the Question of Belonging," *Journal of Eastern African Studies* 12, no. 3 (2018): 494–513.

Schechter, James Alan. "Governing 'Lost Boys': Sudanese Refugees in a UNHCR Camp." PhD diss., University of Colorado, 2004.

Scheper-Hughes, Nancy, and Philippe Bourgois. "Introduction: Making Sense of Violence." In *Violence in War and Peace: An Anthology*, edited by Nancy Scheper-Hughes and Philippe Bourgois, 1–27. Oxford: Wiley-Blackwell, 2004.

Schlee, Günther. "Territorializing Ethnicity: The Imposition of a Model of Statehood on Pastoralists in Northern Kenya and Southern Ethiopia." *Ethnic and Racial Studies* 36, no. 5 (2013): 857–74.

Schor, Naomi. "This Essentialism Which Is Not One: Coming to Grips with Irigaray." *Differences* 1, no. 3 (1989): 38–58.

Schouten, Peer. *Roadblock Politics: The Origins of Violence in Central Africa.* Cambridge: Cambridge University Press, 2022.

Scott-Smith, Tom. "Humanitarian Neophilia: The 'Innovation Turn' and Its Implications." *Third World Quarterly* 37, no. 12 (2016): 2229–51.

Scott-Smith, Tom, and Mark E. Breeze, eds. *Structures of Protection? Rethinking Refugee Shelter.* Oxford: Berghahn, 2020.

Seigel, Micol. *Violence Work: State Power and the Limits of Police.* Durham, NC: Duke University Press, 2018.

Sen, Atreyee, and David Pratten. "Global Vigilantes: Perspectives on Justice and Violence." In *Global Vigilantes*, edited by Atreyee Sen and David Pratten, 1–21. London: Hurst, 2007.

Sequeira, James H. "The Ethiopian Refugees in Kenya." *Journal of the Royal African Society* 38, no. 152 (1939): 329–33.

Shadle, Brett L. "Reluctant Humanitarians: British Policy Toward Refugees in Kenya During the Italo-Ethiopian War, 1935–1940." *Journal of Imperial and Commonwealth History* 47, no. 1 (2019): 167–86.

Shanguhyia, Martin S. "Insecure Borderlands, Marginalization, and Local Perceptions of the State in Turkana, Kenya, Circa 1920–2014." *Journal of Eastern African Studies* 15, no. 1 (2021): 85–107.

Sharma, Nandita. *Home Rule: National Sovereignty and the Separation of Natives and Migrants.* Durham, NC: Duke University Press, 2020.

Shelley, Toby. *Endgame in the Western Sahara: What Future for Africa's Last Colony?* London: Zed, 2004.

Sigona, Nando. "Campzenship: Reimagining the Camp as a Social and Political Space." *Citizenship Studies* 19, no. 1 (2015): 1–15.

Skilling, Louise "Community Policing in Kenya: The Application of Democratic Policing Principles." *Police Journal* 89, no. 1 (2016): 3–17.

Skinner, Rob, and Alan Lester. "Humanitarianism and Empire: New Research Agendas." *Journal of Imperial and Commonwealth History* 40, no. 5 (2012): 729–47.

Slaughter, Amy, and Jeff Crisp. "A Surrogate State? The Role of UNHCR in Protracted Refugee Situations." New Issues in Refugee Research, Working Paper no. 168, United Nations High Commissioner for Refugees, Geneva, 2009.

Slim, Hugo. "Violence and Humanitarianism: Moral Paradox and the Protection of Civilians." *Security Dialogue* 32, no. 3 (2001): 325–39.

Smirl, Lisa. *Spaces of Aid: How Cars, Compounds and Hotels Shape Humanitarianism.* London: Zed, 2015.

Soguk, Nevzat. *States and Strangers: Refugees and Displacements of Statecraft.* Minneapolis: University of Minnesota Press, 1999.

Spalek, Basia, and Bob Lambert. "Muslim Communities Under Surveillance." *Center for Crime and Justice Studies* 68, no. 1 (2007): 12–13.

Spijkerboer, Thomas. *Fleeing Homophobia: Sexual Orientation, Gender Identity, and Asylum.* Abingdon, UK: Routledge, 2013.

Squire, Vicki, ed. *The Contested Politics of Mobility: Borderzones and Irregularity.* London: Routledge, 2013.

Steinberg, Jonny. "Crime Prevention Goes Abroad: Policy Transfer and Policing in Post-Apartheid South Africa." *Theoretical Criminology* 15, no. 4 (2011): 349–64.

Steinberg, Jonny. *Thin Blue: The Unwritten Rules of Policing South Africa.* Johannesburg: Jonathan Ball, 2008.

Stenson, Kevin. "Community Policing as a Governmental Technology." *Economy and Society* 22, no. 3 (1993): 373–89.

Stirk, Peter M. *The Politics of Military Occupation.* Edinburgh: Edinburgh University Press, 2009.

Stoler, Ann Laura. *Carnal Knowledge and Imperial Power: Race and the Intimate in Colonial Rule.* Berkeley: University of California Press, 2002.

Stoler, Ann Laura. *Duress: Imperial Durabilities in Our Times.* Durham, NC: Duke University Press, 2016.

Stoler, Ann Laura. *Race and the Education of Desire.* Durham, NC: Durham University Press, 1995.

Straziuso, Jason, and Tom Odula. "One of Westgate Mall Attackers Lived in Kenyan Refugee Camp." *Washington Times*, November 11, 2013. Accessed 12 April 2018. https://www.washingtontimes.com/news/2013/nov/11/one-westgate-mall-attackers -lived-kenyan-refugee-c.

Sud, Nikita, and Diego Sánchez-Ancochea. "Southern Discomfort: Interrogating the Category of the Global South." *Development and Change* 53, no. 6 (2022): 1123–50.

Tamale, Sylvia. *Decolonization and Afro-Feminism*. Ottawa: Daraja, 2020.

Tascón, Sonia. "Refugees and the Coloniality of Power: Border-Crossers of Postcolonial Whiteness." In *Whitening Race: Essays in Cultural Criticism*, edited by Aileen Moreto-Robinson, 239–53. Canberra: Aboriginal Studies Press, 2004.

Taylor, Charles. "Modern Social Imaginaries." *Public Culture* 14, no. 1 (2002): 91–124.

Taylor, Rosemary C. R. "The Politics of Securing Borders and the Identities of Disease." *Sociology of Health and Illness* 35, no. 2 (2013): 241–54.

Tazzioli, Martina. "Confining by Choking Refugees' Lifetime." *Geopolitics* 29, no. 4 (2024): 1121–42.

Tazzioli, Martina. "Extractive Humanitarianism: Participatory Confinement and Unpaid Labor in Refugees Governmentality." *Communication, Culture and Critique* 15, no. 2 (2022): 176–92.

Tazzioli, Martina. *The Making of Migration: The Biopolitics of Mobility at Europe's Borders*. London: Sage, 2020.

Teferra, Gerawork. "Kakuma Refugee Camp: Pseudopermanence in Permanent Transience." *Africa Today* 69, no. 1–1 (2022): 162–89.

Tegenbos, Jolien, and Karen Büscher. "Moving Onward? Secondary Movers on the Fringes of Refugee Mobility in Kakuma Refugee Camp, Kenya." *Transfers* 7, no. 2 (2017): 41–60.

Tennant, Vicky, Bernie Doyle, and Raouf Mazou. "Safeguarding Humanitarian Space: A Review of Key Challenges for UNHCR." United Nations High Commissioner for Refugees, Geneva, 2010.

Tesfahuney, Mekonnen. "Mobility, Racism and Geopolitics." *Political Geography* 17, no. 5 (1998): 499–515.

Thomas, Peter James Matthew, Sarah Rosenberg-Jansen, and Aimee Jenks. "Moving Beyond Informal Action: Sustainable Energy and the Humanitarian Response System." *Journal of International Humanitarian Action* 6, no. 1 (2021): 1–20.

Throup, David. "Crime, Politics and the Police in Colonial Kenya, 1939–63." In *Policing and Decolonisation: Nationalism, Politics and the Police, 1917–65*, edited by David M. Anderson and David Killingray, 127–57. Manchester, UK: Manchester University Press, 1992.

Thürer, Daniel. "Dunant's Pyramid: Thoughts on the 'Humanitarian Space.'" *International Review of the Red Cross* 89, no. 865 (2007): 47–61.

Tignor, Robert L. "Colonial Chiefs in Chiefless Societies." *Journal of Modern African Studies* 9, no. 3 (1971): 339–59.

Toomey, Nisha. "Aid and Development at the Thailand-Myanmar Border: Mapping Humanitarianism as a Settler Colonial Construct." PhD diss., University of Toronto, 2023.

Tsing, Anna Lowenhaupt. *Friction: An Ethnography of Global Connection*. Princeton, NJ: Princeton University Press, 2005.

Tsing, Anna Lowenhaupt. "From the Margins." *Current Anthropology* 9, no. 3 (1994): 279–97.

Tsing, Anna Lowenhaupt. "Natural Resources and Capitalist Frontiers." *Economic and Political Weekly* 38, no. 48 (2003): 5100–5106.

Tuck, Eve, and K. Wayne Yang. "Decolonization Is Not a Metaphor." *Decolonization: Indigeneity, Education and Society* 1, no. 1 (2012): 1–40.

Ture, Kwame, and Charles V. Hamilton. *Black Power: Politics of Liberation in America.* New York: Random House, 1967.

Turner, Lewis. "'#Refugees Can Be Entrepreneurs Too!' Humanitarianism, Race, and the Marketing of Syrian Refugees." *Review of International Studies* 46, no. 1 (2020): 137–55.

Turner, Simon. "Angry Young Men in Camps: Gender, Age and Class Relations Among Burundian Refugees in Tanzania." New Issues in Refugee Research, Working Paper no. 5, United Nations High Commissioner for Refugees, Geneva, 1999.

Turner, Simon. "The Barriers of Innocence." PhD diss., Roskilde University, Roskilde, Denmark, 2001.

Turner, Simon. *Politics of Innocence: Hutu Identity, Conflict and Camp Life.* Oxford: Berghahn, 2010.

Turner, Simon. "Under the Gaze of the 'Big Nations': Refugees, Rumours and the International Community in Tanzania." *African Affairs* 103, no. 411 (2004): 227–47.

Turner, Simon. "What Is a Refugee Camp? Explorations of the Limits and Effects of the Camp." *Journal of Refugee Studies* 29, no. 2 (2016): 139–48.

United Nations High Commissioner for Refugees. *Conclusion No. 48 (XXXVIII): Military or Armed Attacks on Refugee Camps and Settlements.* Geneva: UNHCR, 1987.

United Nations High Commissioner for Refugees. *Global Report 2018.* Geneva: UNHCR, 2018.

United Nations High Commissioner for Refugees. *Global Trends in Forced Displacement in 2021.* Geneva: UNHCR, 2022.

United Nations High Commissioner for Refugees. *Guidance Note on Maintaining the Civilian and Humanitarian Character of Asylum.* Geneva: UNHCR, 2018.

United Nations High Commissioner for Refugees. *Kakuma Refugee Camp Community: Constitution and Rules.* Kakuma: UNHCR, 2011.

United Nations High Commissioner for Refugees. *Kalobeyei Integrated Socio-Economic Development Plan in Turkana West.* Geneva: UNHCR, 2018.

United Nations High Commissioner for Refugees. *Kenya Comprehensive Refugee Programme 2016: Programming for Solutions.* Nairobi: UNHCR, 2016.

United Nations High Commissioner for Refugees. *Kenya: Enhanced Security Partnership Project (SPP) 2011–2012.* Nairobi: UNHCR, 2012.

United Nations High Commissioner for Refugees. *Operational Protection in Camps and Settlements: A Reference Guide of Good Practices in the Protection of Refugees and Other Persons of Concern.* Geneva: UNHCR, 2006.

United Nations High Commissioner for Refugees. *Reinforcing a Community Development Approach.* Geneva: UNHCR, 2001.

United Nations High Commissioner for Refugees. *Understanding Community-Based Protection.* Geneva: UNHCR, 2013.

United Nations High Commissioner for Refugees. *UNHCR Comprehensive Policy on Urban Refugees.* Geneva: UNHCR, 1997.

United Nations High Commissioner for Refugees. *UNHCR Kenya Planning Summary 2017.* Nairobi: UNHCR, 2017.

United Nations High Commissioner for Refugees. *UNHCR Policy on Alternatives to Camps*. Geneva: UNHCR, 2014.

United Nations High Commissioner for Refugees. *UNHCR Policy on Refugee Protection and Solutions in Urban Areas*. Geneva: UNHCR, 2009.

United Nations High Commissioner for Refugees. "UNHCR Refers Kenyan Staff to Police After Internal Investigation Finds Fraud at Kakuma Camp." Accessed November 14, 2017. http://www.unhcr.org/news/press/2017/5/592dcf644/unhcr-refers -kenya-staff-police-internal-investigation-finds-fraud-kakuma.html.

United Nations High Commissioner for Refugees. *Visitor's Guide: Kakuma Camp and Kalobeyei Settlement*. Kakuma: Sub-Office of the UNHCR, 2019.

United Nations Human Settlements Programme. *Kakuma and Kalobeyei Spatial Profile*. Nairobi: UN-Habitat, 2021.

United Nations Office of Internal Oversight Services. *Investigation into Allegations of Refugee Smuggling at the Nairobi Branch Office of the Office of the United Nations High Commissioner for Refugees*. New York: United Nations Office of Internal Oversight Services, 2001.

Van Maanen, John. "Epilogue: On Watching the Watchers." In *Policing: A View from the Street*, edited by Peter K. Manning and John van Maanen, 309–49. Santa Monica, CA: Goodyear, 1978.

Vaughan, Megan. "Madness and Colonialism, Colonialism as Madness: Re-Reading Fanon. Colonial Discourse and the Psychopathology of Colonialism." *Paideuma* 39 (1993): 45–55.

Vaughan-Williams, Nick. *Europe's Border Crisis: Biopolitical Security and Beyond*. Oxford: Oxford University Press, 2015.

Veeser, Cyrus. "A Forgotten Instrument of Global Capitalism? International Concessions, 1870–1930." *International History Review* 35, no. 5 (2013): 1136–55.

Veney, Cassandra R. *Forced Migration in Eastern Africa: Democratization, Structural Adjustment, and Refugees*. London: Palgrave Macmillan, 2007.

Verdirame, Guglielmo. "Human Rights and Refugees: The Case of Kenya." *Journal of Refugee Studies* 12, no. 1 (1999): 54–77.

Verdirame, Guglielmo, and Barbara Harrell-Bond. *Rights in Exile: Janus-Faced Humanitarianism*. New York: Berghahn, 2005.

Veroff, Julie. "Crimes, Conflicts and Courts: The Administration of Justice in a Zambian Refugee Settlement." New Issues in Refugee Research, Working Paper no. 192, United Nations High Commissioner for Refugees, Geneva, 2010.

Vigh, Henrik. "Crisis and Chronicity: Anthropological Perspectives on Continuous Conflict and Decline." *Ethnos* 73, no. 1 (2008): 5–24.

Visweswaran, Kamala. "Introduction: Geographies of Everyday Occupation." In *Everyday Occupations: Experiencing Militarism in South Asia and the Middle East*, edited by Kamala Visweswaran, 1–28. Philadelphia: University of Pennsylvania Press, 2013.

Vitale, Alex S. *The End of Policing*, London: Verso, 2018.

Vradis, Antonis, Evie Papada, Joe Painter, and Anna Papoutsi. *New Borders: Hotspots and the European Migration Regime*. London: Pluto, 2018.

Wacquant, Loïc, Tom Slater, and Virgilio Borges Pereira. "Territorial Stigmatization in Action." *Environment and Planning A: Economy and Space* 46 (2014): 1270–80.

Walcott, Rinaldo. "The Problem of the Human: Black Ontologies and 'the Coloniality of Our Being.'" In *Postcoloniality-Decoloniality-Black Critique: Joints and Fissures*, 93–108. Frankfurt: Campus, 2014.

Walia, Harsha. *Border and Rule: Global Migration, Capitalism, and the Rise of Racist Nationalism*. New York: Haymarket, 2021.

Walkey, Claire Elizabeth. "Building a Bureaucracy: The Transfer of Responsibility for Refugee Affairs from United Nations Refugee Agency to Government of Kenya." PhD diss., University of Oxford, 2019.

Waller, Richard. "Towards a Contextualisation of Policing in Colonial Kenya." *Journal of Eastern African Studies* 4, no. 3 (2010): 525–41.

Walters, William. "Foucault and Frontiers: Notes on the Birth of the Humanitarian Border." In *Governmentality: Current Issues and Future Challenges*, edited by Ulrich Bröckling, Susanne Krasmann, and Thomas Lemke, 138–64. New York: Routledge, 2011.

Wambui, Mary. "Kenya to Close Kakuma, Dadaab Refugee Camps by June 2022." *Daily Nation*, April 29, 2021. Accessed September 20, 2023. https://nation.africa/kenya/news/kenya-to-close-kakuma-dadaab-refugee-camps-by-june-2022-3381886.

Wario Arero, Hassan. "Coming to Kenya: Imagining and Perceiving a Nation Among the Borana of Kenya." *Journal of Eastern African Studies* 1, no. 2 (2007): 292–304.

Watkins, Josh. "Spatial Imaginaries Research in Geography: Synergies, Tensions, and New Directions." *Geography Compass* 9, no. 9 (2015): 508–22.

Weheliye, Alexander G. *Habeas Viscus: Racializing Assemblages, Biopolitics, and Black Feminist Theories of the Human*. Durham, NC: Duke University Press, 2014.

Weima, Yolanda. "'Is It Commerce?' Dehumanization in the Framing of Refugees as Resources." *Refuge* 37, no. 2 (2021): 20–29.

Weima, Yolanda, and Hanno Brankamp. "Camp Methodologies: The 'How' of Studying Camps." *Area* 54, no. 3 (2022): 338–46.

Weima, Yolanda, and Claudio Minca. "Closing Camps." *Progress in Human Geography* 46, no. 2 (2021): 261–81.

Weiss, Thomas G., and Michael Barnett, eds. *Humanitarianism in Question: Politics, Power, Ethics*. Ithaca, NY: Cornell University Press, 2008.

Weiss, Thomas G, and Kurt M. Campbell. "Military Humanitarianism." *Survival* 33, no. 5 (2008): 451–65.

Weitzberg, Keren. *We Do Not Have Borders: Greater Somalia and the Predicaments of Belonging in Kenya*. Athens: Ohio University Press, 2017.

Weizman, Eyal. *Hollow Land: Israeli's Architecture of Occupation*. London: Verso, 2012.

Weizman, Eyal. *The Least of All Possible Evils: Humanitarian Violence from Arendt to Gaza*. London: Verso, 2011.

Whittaker, Hannah. *Insurgency and Counterinsurgency: A Social History of the Shifta Conflict, c. 1963–1968*. London: Brill, 2015.

Whittaker, Hannah. "Legacies of Empire: State Violence and Collective Punishment in Kenya's North Eastern Province, c. 1963–Present." *Journal of Imperial and Commonwealth History* 43, no. 4 (2015): 641–57.

Williams, Jill M. "From Humanitarian Exceptionalism to Contingent Care: Care and Enforcement at the Humanitarian Border." *Political Geography* 47 (2015): 11–20.

Wirth, Anna. "Reflections from the Encampment Decision in the High Court of Kenya." *Forced Migration Review*, no. 48 (2014): 81–82.

Wolpe, Harold. *The Theory of Internal Colonization: The South African Case*. Collected Seminar Papers, no. 18, Institute of Commonwealth Studies, London, 1975, 105–20.

Woroniecka-Krzyzanowska, Dorota. "The Right to the Camp: Spatial Politics of Protracted Encampment in the West Bank." *Political Geography* 61 (2017): 160–69.

Wynter, Sylvia. "1492: A New World View." In *Race, Discourse, and the Origin of the Americas: A New World View*, edited by Vera Lawrence Hyatt and Rex Nettleford, 5–57. Washington, DC: Smithsonian Institution Press, 1995.

Wynter, Sylvia. "Unsettling the Coloniality of Being/Power/Truth/Freedom." *CR: New Centennial Review* 3, no. 3 (2003): 257–336.

Yamashita, Hikaru. *Humanitarian Space and International Politics: The Creation of Safe Areas*. London: Routledge, 2004.

Yannakakis, Yanna. *The Art of Being In-Between: Native Intermediaries, Indian Identity, and Local Rule in Colonial Oaxaca*. Durham, NC: Duke University Press, 2008.

Yarnell, Mark, and Alice Thomas. *Between a Rock and a Hard Place: Somali Refugees in Kenya*. Washington, DC: Refugees International, 2014.

Zaiotti, Ruben. *Externalizing Migration Management: Europe, North America and the Spread of "Remote Control" Practices*. London: Routledge, 2016.

Zolberg, Aristide, Astri Suhrke, and Sergio Aguayo. *Escape from Violence: Conflict and the Refugee Crisis in the Developing World*. New York: Oxford University Press, 1989.

Index

Abdelaaty, Lamis E., 55–56
abolitionism, 195. *See also* Gilmore, Ruth Wilson
abolitionist future, 35
Acholi (ethnic group), 44, 130, 150
accumulation: by immobilization, 168; capital, 7, 74, 178, 181–82; logics of, 165; micro-, 87, 165, 167, 178; operations of, 163; opportunities for, 176; process of raw, 163. *See also* capitalism
Addis Ababa: 47; University, 22
Aden, Halima, 39, 66–67. *See also* TEDxKakumaCamp
Administration Police, 81, 209n40; history of, 79; in Kakuma camp, 88, 90, 96; National Police Service and, 80. *See also* police; policing
Africans: as sources of productivity, 19; "detribalized," 107; indirect rule and, 133–36; political autonomy among, 134; racialization as Black and "native," 57, 106–7; self-government and, 26; sexual panic and imaginings around, 117
Agamben, Giorgio, 18–19. *See also* bare life; state of exception
Agier, Michel, 17–19, 48
aid: archipelago, 50, 98; budgets, 29, 187; carceral, 30; civilizing effects of, 122; compounds, 31, 32, 179; craft, 2, 68, 83; decolonizing, 187–91; dependence, 16; development and, 13–14; economy,174; extraction and, 163; foreign, 22, 23, 25, 27,

30; geographies, 48, 50; global circuits of, 97; history of, 12–16; infrastructures, 6; intervention, 83, 99, 122; landscapes of, 17; logics of, 9; machinery, 142, 161; militarization and, 31; mutual, 131; oasis of, 68, 160; programs, 2–3, 8, 10, 16–17, 21–22, 23, 117, 159; space of, 27, 48–54; system, 12, 171, 177. *See also* camp; humanitarianism
aid actors, 4, 16, 22, 34, 47, 54, 81, 83, 111, 146. *See also* UNHCR
aid agencies/organizations, 2–4, 10, 17, 27, 28, 30, 41, 46, 50, 52, 63, 64, 79, 81, 85, 93, 102–3, 113, 132, 133, 139–40, 144, 146, 154–55, 161, 165, 170–71, 173, 176, 184, 185, 186. *See also* UNHCR
aid industry, 34, 38, 48, 81, 97, 161, 167, 172. *See also* NGO; UNHCR
aid operations, 38, 97, 142, 170, 188
aid workers, 5, 18, 29, 30, 32, 35, 38, 41, 50, 59, 63, 102–3, 112, 113–14, 117–18, 121, 124, 127, 144, 150, 161, 165, 169–70, 173. *See also* incentive work; labor
Ain al-Hilweh camp, 188
Al-Jazeera, 66
Al-Shabaab: attack on Westgate Shopping Mall and, 60; Dadaab camps and, 59; Garissa University College and, 60; in Kakuma camp, 149, 155; "refugee warriors" and, 64. *See also* terror; terrorism
Aluel, Mary, 178–80. *See also* TEDxKakumaCamp

anticolonialism, 13, 73, 194; agitators, 72; Frantz Fanon's writings, 190; insurgents, 19; "world-making," 195. *See also* Fanon, Frantz; decolonization

Anti-Terrorism Police Unit (ATPU), 84, 149. *See also* police; policing; terrorism

Anyanya II, 65, 207n128

askaris: 134, 136, 142–46

asylum, 9, 11, 114, 162; country of, 6, 22, 105, 124; claims, 116; in the global South, 8–9; politics of, 56, 58, 99; procedures, 23; rights, 61; urban, 188; seekers, 173, 193, 195; space, 15, 55, 60, 99; status, 27. *See also* refugee

Bamba Chakula, 84, 176. *See also* food; Kakuma

Bantustans, 76, 134

bare life, 18–19, 29, 33. *See also* Agamben, Giorgio

Bauman, Zygmunt, 110

belonging: autochthonous, 21; cultural, 105; diasporic, 140; ethno/racial, 107, 126, 163, 194; hierarchies of, 6, 25; Kenya's economy of belonging, 57, 77; legal categorization of, 86; moral, 123; national, 7, 56, 107, 115, 124; "native," 78; nonbelonging, 48; not quite, 42; precarious, 41, 113.
See also identities; ethnicity

Besteman, Catherine, xi, 99, 204n34

Bidi Bidi camp, 188. *See also* Uganda

biopolitical technology, 18, 82

biopolitics, 18, 19, 25, 82; intimate, 115; racialized subjects and, 19. *See also* Foucault, Michel

bios, 180. *See also* Agamben, Giorgio; *zoe*

Black: Africans, 107; majority rule, 7; collectivity, 106; colonized people, 13; containment, 20; policing Blackness/Black life, 17–21; Panther leader, 28; new political elites, 26; racialization as, 57. *See also* ethnicity; nativeness; race

boda boda, 2, 95, 185

Boinett, Joseph Kipchirchir, 69

boma, 71

border: areas, 9; between camp and Turkana countryside, 86; bordered nation-state, 196; carceral border technology, 193; control, 4, 7, 16; crossings, 76; disputes, 107; enforce-

ment, 186; fighting against, 190; guards, 3, 6; humanitarian, 15, 61; insecurity, 59; mobile, 87; regime, 11; region, 83; spaces, 78, 123; Tanzanian, 42; technology, 29; territories, 7; Thailand-Myanmar, 50; town, 42, 81, 130; violence, 3, 11

borderland, 8, 27, 81, 163, 177

borderwork, 4

Brauman, Rony, 49

Breton, André, 13

bribes, 2, 87, 88, 94, 98, 155; mining for, 166–70. *See also* extraction; police

bunna, 21, 139, 192

bureaucracy, 34, 70, 85, 89–94, 135.
See also state

Burugu, John, 185. *See also* RAS

Bundeskriminalamt (BKA), 33. *See also* police; policing

camp: abolition, 187–91, 193–96; administrators, 34, 85, 109; as a spatial artifact of colonization, 21, 33; as a border technology, 27; as a form of Black containment, 20; carcerality of, 95; closure, 54–55, 60–61, 62, 114; colony and, 28, 181–82; concessions and, 164–65; continent of, 17–21; cosmopolitan, 34, 42–48; expansion, 58, 159; geopolitics, 4; global aid and, 3–4, 6–7; governmentality, 144; history of, 12; infrastructure in, 49–53; manager, 58, 84, 91, 102, 113, 156, 159, 211n87; microgeographies of, 95; moral disorder in, 108–11; nation building and, 122–25; occupying the, 80–86; "pipeline" in Kenya, 73–74; research in, 31–33; time and, 179; violence within, 62–66, 70–71; within the camp, 155. *See also* humanitarianism; carcerality

camp life, 4, 30, 42, 48, 92, 102, 103, 112, 117, 126, 127, 151

capitalism: and its "outsides," 163; free market, 131, 175; frontiers of, 165; global, 164; 131; neoliberal, 195; racial, 29, 190. *See also* economy; marketization

capitalist: accumulation, 7, 178; circuits, 35; crisis, 3; economy, 13; ladder of productivity, 176; markets, 173, 175; plunder, 13; subjects, 165, 175; ways of thinking, 174; ways of valorizing human life, 181

carceral archipelago, 73

carceral care, 83, 131, 195

carcerality, 21, 40, 90, 95

carceral microgeographies, 94–95

carceral power, 6, 189, 195

carceral protectionism, 68, 86, 187, 196

carceral technology, 99, 193

carceral violence, 70, 95, 195

care, 110, 186, 187; and control, 20, 71; and commerce, 163; and maintenance, 53, 173, 185; carceral, 83, 131, 190; health, 23, 185; promises of protection and, 162

chang'aa: 112, 143, 151; hotspot of, 52

checkpoints, 76, 86, 127, 190. *See also* police; roadblocks

children, 29, 42, 116, 118, 149, 150, 172, 185, 192, 193. *See also* youth

citizens: ethnoracially subjugated, 26; citizen-led aid activities, 9; citizen-led community policing, 136–38; minority/minoritized, 6, 24, 57, 78; national, 29; not quite, 75; of former colonies, 8; of the camp, 191, 193; of the colonial state, 110; precarious/precaritized, 35, 91, 194, 195; quasi-, 22; question-mark, 7; second-class, 75; Somali minority, 57; white, 4. *See also* noncitizens

citizenship: claims to, 113; democratic, 133; excluded from, 76, 135; formal, 124; fragile, 108; graduated, 28; hierarchies of, 7; ideas of, 7; national, 27, 76; screenings of Kenyan Somalis, 77, unworthy of, 109; wages of, 188. *See also* belonging; ethnicity; nationalism

civilization: "custodians of the values of," 121; fiction of a superior morality and, 116; frontiers of, 181; hierarchies of, 106; madness and uncivilization, 119–22; racial civilizationalism, 134; spreading, 110; "Western," 120. *See also* colonization; racialization

civilizing mission, 13, 14, 16, 70, 106, 133. *See also* colonization

civil war: Ethiopia's, 44; in Sudan, 46, 207n128; in South Sudan, 46, 166, 123, 203n27, 203n37; in Somalia, 56, 191, 204n34

city, 12, 38, 20, 59, 60, 166, 167, 178, 191, 204n31; "accidental," 43; "carceral," 189; "city-camp," 189; "in the desert," 39; makeshift, 41–42; "naked," 189; "occupied," 189; "right to the," 47

colonial, 7, 8, 9, 12, 18, 20, 22, 52, 55, 56, 57, 77, 99, 127, 137, 165, 176, 179, 187, 208n9, 214n1; administration/administrators, 73, 86, 133; anti, 19; anthropology, 135; Britain's territories in Africa, 91; brutality, 25; camp as micro-territory, 186; cities, 110; classifications, 78; concession, 162; concession economy, 53; condition, 26; conquest, 12, 71; control, 6; difference, 13, 25, 126; discourses, 116, 120; domination, 74; enterprises, 13; expansionism, 13; formations, 181; geography/geographies, 25, 34, 79, 88; governmentality, 193; hierarchies, 126, 190; histories, 12; imaginaries/imaginations, 81, 162; imaginings of southern life-worlds, 10; logics of land enclosure, 189; machinery, 189; margins, 4; mobilities, 77; modernity, 18, 19, 110; modes of unfreedom, 97; narratives of protectionism, 11; occupation, 25, 34, 41, 70, 83, 98, 102, 162, 170, 182, 192; officials/officers, 20, 27, 71, 73, 107; oppression/repression, 7; order, 24–25, 29, 77, 105, 136, 194; paradigms of dispossession, 28; pass laws, 90; phantasms, 103; police, 24, 79; power, 14, 63, 72, 73, 136; projects, 25, 27, 74, 125, 186; racial orders, 24; regime, 24, 115, 208n13; relations, 6, 25, 26, 28, 30, 195; rule, 7, 33, 35, 71, 75, 80, 83–84, 95, 106–7, 132–33, 189, 193–94; sovereignty, 134; space, 13, 106; state, 21, 24, 26, 79, 134–35, 142; stereotypes, 121; subjugation, 191; technologies, 132, 134; techniques of differentiated mobility, 125; territoriality, 194; third colonial occupation, 26–30; tropes, 3, 102

colonialism, 134, 161, 163; as a fiduciary duty, 134; beyond coercion, 27; British, 57; "of compassion," 22; metaphorizing, 22. *See also* colonization

coloniality, 9, 23, 190, 195; geographies of, 4

colonization, 5, 13, 15, 19, 23, 71, 73, 78, 80, 83, 134, 172, 187–88; camp as system of, 33; cultural text of, 125; collaborative, 161; double bind of, 136; European, 9, 133, 164; for Mbembe and Fanon, 98; frontier, 34, 164; geographies of, 28, 198n24; humanitarian, 5, 7, 21, 25, 31, 35, 88, 98, 103, 109, 112, 118, 122, 132, 156, 161, 165, 170, 181, 186, 188, 193, 195; internal/home, 74–75, 99, 186; landscapes of aid and, 17; logics of, 8; of everyday life, 41; of Kenya's northern hinterland, 27; processes of, 6; spaces of, 12, 50; spatial artifact of, 21. *See also* colonialism community, 2, 35, 38, 64, 84, 91, 96, 115, 118, 124, 145, 179, 204n31, 207n128; as a technology of indirect rule, 132–36; -based violence work, 136; camp, 140; host, 160; imagined, 123, 137, 147; international, 54, 114, 174; leaders, 82; level political mobilization, 184; moral, 109; protection, 143–44; rule in Kakuma, 138–41, 149; deep, 132, 150–55; suspect, 137, 147, 151

community police/policing, 5, 29, 30, 35, 67, 129–32, 136–37, 141–42, 143, 146, 149, 151–52, 154–57, 172, 211n91. *See also* Nyumba Kumi; police

Community Peace and Protection Teams (CPPT), xi, 30, 35, 129–30, 138–39, 141, 155, 215n2; as humanitarian askaris, 142–46; as incentive workers, 172; as state proxies, 146–50; deep community and, 150–55; history of, 139–42

Comprehensive Peace Agreement (CPA), 46

Comprehensive Refugee Response Framework (CRRF), 133

concession: as territorial enclaves, 164; as an adaptable frontier geography, 165; as a model of fragmented economic ordering, 164; economy, 53; extractive frontiers and, 162–65; Kakuma as a, 181; camp and, 165. *See also* capitalism; colonialism; extraction

concessionary geographies, 164, 172. *See also* camp; extraction

confinement, 40, 73; "participatory," 139

Congolese refugee, 47, 86, 89, 97, 110, 148, 153–54, 167, 171; *boda boda* drivers, 95; Lamassia (football team), 94

containment, 3, 11, 15, 28, 48, 86, 89, 95, 98, 111, 126, 173, 180, 182; Black, 20; carceral, 8; edifice of, 188; planetary, 173; policies of, 127; politics of, 195; spaces of, 4. *See also* camp; encampment

counterinsurgency, 7, 75, 193. *See also* Kenya Land and Freedom Army; Mau Mau; Shifta War

counterterrorism, 34, 60, 63, 76, 99, 130, 147, 155, 173. *See also* Al-Shabaab; terror; terrorism

crime, 3, 23, 28, 41, 52, 63–64, 78, 89, 92–93, 95, 104, 109, 112, 114, 116, 130–31, 136, 139, 156, 168; rates, 93, 140; prevention, 142. *See also* policing; security

Crisp, Jeff, x, 64. *See also* UNHCR

cultural beliefs, 29, 103

cultural belonging, 105, 109

cultural diversity, 109, 117

cultural supremacy, 124

cultural text, 34, 102, 125–27

curfews, 1, 3, 28, 34, 89, 92–94, 189, 211n85

Dadaab camp, 31, 38, 44–46, 58–59, 62–63, 84, 147, 165, 184, 188; closure of, 55, 60–61; community policing in, 141; relocatees from, 46

Dandora, 189. *See also* city; Nairobi

Danish Refugee Council (DRC), 55. *See also* NGO

Dar es Salaam, 58

Davis, Mike, 189

decolonization, 10, 14, 21, 188, 190, 195. *See also* Fanon, Frantz; Rodney, Walter

decolonizing, 187–89

deep community, 132, 150–55. *See also* CPPT; ethnicity; identities

dehumanization, 7, 18, 97, 125, 195. *See also* race; racialization

de las Casas, Bartolomé, 12–13

Deng, Valentino Achak, 43

Department of Refugee Affairs (DRA), 58, 84, 146. *See also* DRS; RAS

Department of Refugee Services (DRS), 174, 190. *See also* DRA; RAS

deportations, 15, 57, 154. *See also* enforcement; police

de Sepúlveda, Juan Ginés, 13

desert, 39, 46, 49, 49, 71, 72, 74, 160, 178, 180. *See also* Turkana

detention, 3, 15, 60, 77, 95, 168; camps/centers, 17, 19, 73, 180

deviance, 104, 115, 117, 122

Didinga, 130

Dinka (ethnic group), 43–44, 47, 52, 87–88, 94, 114, 115, 130, 139, 203n27, 204n37

Directorate of Criminal Investigation (DCI), 33, 169

disobedient futurity, 191–93

disorder, 18, 19, 24, 25, 51, 102, 104, 108, 122, 125, 156; moral, 108–11, 120, 124, 127

dispossession, 13, 23, 27, 28, 75, 124, 162–63, 170, 189. *See also* capitalism

Dollo Ado camps, 176, 188

domination, 23, 23, 28, 74, 75, 94, 97, 105, 135, 138, 156, 180, 181–82, 188, 189; ethnoracial, 6, 13, 34

donors, 10, 29, 34, 55, 61, 63, 85, 112, 114, 116, 146, 156, 165, 171, 173, 174, 176, 180, 184, 187, 188, 190

Dunant, Henri, 12

durable solutions, 179, 187, 192. See also refugee; resettlement

Eastleigh, xi, 59, 60, 206n102. See also Nairobi

economy: aid/humanitarian, 172, 174; camp, 166; capitalist, 13; colonial, 53; "destitution," 174; global, 177; Kakuma's, 39; Kenyan, 26, 57, 184, 185; of difference, 164; of violence, 15, 28; of scarcity, 170; pastoralist, 107; political, 161

Eldoret, 87, 185

elections, 131, 137, 141. See also government; state

emergency, 2, 10, 15, 18, 43, 81–82, 85, 92, 97, 104, 161, 163, 180, 186; policing, 27, 71, 81; Kenya Emergency, 27, 73, 136, 208n9; Shifta Emergency, 57, 74, 76

Emergency Trust Fund (EUTF) for Africa, 10

empire, 14, 19, 25, 27, 74, 99; "biopolitical," 25; end of, 8, 28; legacy of, 107, 194; liberal, 4, 187; metaphorical, 23; space and, 18; subjects of, 13

empowerment, 67, 131, 156, 184–85, 186, 188, 192

encampment, 5, 6, 19, 22, 29, 35, 39, 42, 53, 68, 104, 131, 138, 151, 176, 195; accumulation and, 168; alternatives to, 187; archipelago of, 188; care-and-maintenance approach to, 173; citizenship and, 192; colonial, 73–74; concessionary, 181–82; effects of, 23, 54; extraction and, 162; geographies of, 20; humanitarian, 25, 34; logics of, 133, 181; nation building and, 122; policy in Kenya, 58–62, 184–85; process of, 111; refugee, 9, 90, 98, 142, 180–81, 194, 196; rules of, 178; structures of, 175; tactics of, 21; texture of, 127; violence of, 32. See also camp; containment

enclaves, 25, 49, 50, 76, 89, 98, 164, 167

enforcement: armed, 81–82; border, 186; community, 141, 152; heavy-handed, 104; law, 98; migration, 15; of rules, 93; of order, 98; powers, 54, 131; self, 141. See also deportations; police

Enlightenment, 9, 12, 110, 120

Equatoria: community, 44, 96, 108, 129; security office 138, 142; states, 143, 203n27

Equity Bank, 173

ethics, 30–33. See also methods

Ethiopia, 8, 21, 42, 74; civil war, 44; great famine, 10; Italy's invasion of, 20, 55; market, 44–45, 46, 48, 154, 155; police state, 22; refugee camps in, 176

Ethiopian People's Revolutionary Democratic Front (EPRDF), 44

ethnicity, 2, 21, 57, 76, 86, 106, 189; ethnic/ethnoracial identities, 27, 43, 44, 47, 52, 55, 63, 75, 77, 102, 105, 107, 123, 125, 131, 139, 141, 163, 177, 186, 194. See also identities; race

ethnography, 30. See also methods

expansionism, 5, 13. See also empire; nation building

extraction, 8, 13, 25, 34, 35, 162–63; camp as form of, 159–62, 164, 171, 175, 182; "frontiers of," 163; labor, 7, 75, 99; through bribes, 165–170; of wealth, 3. See also capitalism

Fanon, Frantz, 24, 98; on decolonization, 190. See also decolonization

Fassin, Didier, 12

Female Genital Mutilation (FGM), 122

Fleming, Melissa, 37–38, 66–67. See also TEDxKakumaCamp

food: distribution, 23, 31, 82, 112, 130, 142, 150, 178; rations, 5, 16, 52, 84, 146, 160, 178. See also Bamba Chakula

Foucault, Michel, on biopolitics, 18; on security, 143; on surveillance, 89; on the barbarian, 121; power of writing, 92. See also biopolitics; governmentality

freedom, ix, 2, 4, 14, 22, 25, 41, 56, 62, 68, 142, 147, 184, 189, 191, 193, 195; of Black and African life, 18; of movement, 185; places of, 190; promises of, 7; seeking, 190; spatiotemporal, 92. See also abolitionism frontier: colonization, 34, 71, 164; extractive, 162–64; internal, 7, 74; maritime, 15; nation building, 122, 125; of civilization, 181; of Kenya's north, 24, 72, 76, 78–80; of late capitalism, 165; of the free market, 174; prison, 73; town, 20, 42, 46; underdeveloped, 26. *See also* border

Gaddafi, Muammar, 44. *See also* Libya
Garang, John, 65, 142, 207n128.
    See also South Sudanese refugees
Garissa, 57, 58, 61, 108, 113; attacks, 147; county, 31, 71, 92; University College, 31, 60
Gaza Strip, 40
gender: -based violence, 3, 16, 115, 116; discrimination, 82; equality, 22, 117, 121, 131. *See also* homosexuality; women
General Service Unit (GSU), 79, 83, 94, 210n50. *See also* police; policing
Geneva, 22, 96, 98, 161. *See also* humanitarianism; UNHCR
Geneva Conventions, 14
genocide, 10, 13
Gilmore, Ruth Wilson, 5, 180. *See also* abolitionism
Gilroy, Paul, 125
global apartheid, 6, 99, 194, 196. *See also* border
Global Compact on Refugees, 132. *See also* UNHCR
global North, 6, 7, 25, 29, 55, 61, 99, 113, 168, 169, 174, 177, 180, 186, 194; borders/fringes of, 15–16
global South, 3, 4, 5, 8, 40, 74, 99, 180, 186, 188, 189; definition, 198n24; refugee aid programs in, 16–17
government: British colonial, 26; bureaucracies, 21; of Kenya, 53–54, 57, 59, 62, 109, 130, 156, 173, 185; of Turkana county, 53–54, 67; of Somalia, 60; of Sudan, 65; policies, 61; self, 27. *See also* state
governmentality, 145, 149; camp, 131–32, 144; colonial, 193; humanitarian, 154; pioneering, 162. *See also* Foucault, Michel
Grandi, Filippo, 177. *See also* UNHCR

Hall, Stuart, 118
Harrell-Bond, Barbara, x, 22, 32
Harvey, David, 47

health, 5, 29, 59, 80, 127, 174, 178, 179, 180; care, 23, 185; infrastructures, 53; humanitarians and, 115; mental, 74; public, 3, 116, 121; services, 3
HIV/AIDS, 115. *See also* health
Hobbes, Thomas, 120–21
homosexuality, 104, 118. *See also* gender; identities; minorities
Hong Kong: neighborhood of, 52, 90, 95, 114. *See also* Dinka (ethnic group); Kakuma
humanitarian: action, 9, 11; borders, 15, 61; character of camps, 62–63, 64–66, 84; colonization, 5, 7, 21–26, 27, 31, 35, 88, 98, 103, 109, 112, 118, 122, 132, 156, 161, 165, 170, 181, 186, 188, 193; crisis, 10, 104; encampment, 25, 34; geographies, 9, 11; infrastructure, 9; innovation, 52–53; interventions, 6, 10, 180; landscapes, 8; power, 9, 23, 132, 142; "present," 14; principles, 13, 53, 127, 145; protection, 3, 21, 27, 28, 49, 132, 142, 150; reason, 12, 50, 181; solutions, 104; space, 7, 49, 51, 53–54, 62, 65, 167; violence, 15, 16, 11–17; workers, 3, 5, 35, 160. *See also* aid
humanitarianism: "actually existing," 172; Africa as cradle of, 10; carceral, 195; colonization and, 83; decolonizing, 190; moral mission of, 34, 54; origins of, 9; political economy of, 161; refugee, 5, 178, 181; resiliency, 133; self-help, 39; violent, 11–17; white supremacist, 190
humanity, 37, 106, 110, 111, 176, 181, 186, 189; common, 12, 127; hierarchies of, 12; infra-, 122; pathologized category of, 122
humanness, 106
human rights, 3, 7, 16, 22, 63, 78, 83, 118, 121, 125, 131, 139, 145, 147, 149, 187
Hyndman, Jennifer, 16

identities, 112, 115, 125; cultural, 140; ethnic/ethnoracial, 43, 52, 99, 123; hierarchy of, 106; native, 107; self, 3. *See also* ethnicity; race
IKEA Foundation, 52, 176
immorality, 115, 116, 118
incentive work, 170–71; workers, 171–72. *See also* labor
independence, 6, 7, 10, 15, 25, 27, 72, 77–78, 80, 91, 105, 126, 136, 140, 163, 184, 189, 203n26. *See also* uhuru

Independent Policing Oversight Authority (IPOA), xi, 78–79, 137. *See also* police; policing

indirect rule, 8, 29, 34, 106, 107, 137, 155–56, 157; colonial technologies of, 132; genealogy of, 132–36; humanitarian iteration of, 35; reinvention of, 154. *See also* colonialism

integrated settlement, 53–54, 184, 189. *See also* camp; Kalobeyei

integration, 6, 38, 54, 68, 75, 109, 179; economic, 55, 62; national, 26

Intergovernmental Authority on Development (IGAD), 62

International Committee of the Red Cross (ICRC), 12

International Finance Corporation (IFC), 39–40, 176

Isiolo, 20, 71, 108

Jansen, Bram, x, 53, 65, 112

Jolie, Angelina, 177

Juba: 47, 142, 166–67; Arabic, 143

Jubilee Party, 55. *See also* Kenyatta, Uhuru

justice, 22, 23, 47, 60, 139, 141, 152, 190; administration of/administering, 135, 139, 151; decarceral, 35; formal, 78, 85; mobility, 195; "rough," 70; system, 132, 151; traditional/customary, 82, 132, 151

Kakamega, 119

Kakuma: administrative structures, 51–52; airstrip, 101; area, 51; as a "big university," 47; as a brand, 39, 68; as "city in the desert," 39; as a cosmopolitan camp, 42–48; as a place at the margins, 8–9; as "paradise in hell," 42; as surrogate homeland, 124; community rule in, 138–41; domestic frontline of the "War on Terror," 59; ethnocultural diversity, 109; geostrategic location, 123; history of, 39–41, 50–54; infiltration, 62; labor exploitation in, 170–72; Mission Hospital, 42; policing in, 81–86; research methods in, 30–33; TEDxKakumaCamp, 38–39, 66–68, 173; town, 46, 50, 169; violence in, 62–66. *See also* Kalobeyei

Kakuma Kalobeyei Challenge Fund (KKCF), 176

Kakuma News Reflector (KANERE), 95, 171

Kalobeyei, 53–54, 176, 184, 186. *See also* Kakuma

Kalobeyei Integrated Socio-Economic Development Plan (KISEDP), 184

Kampala, 47

Kapenguria Six, 72, 208n9. *See also* Kenyatta, Jomo

Kariuki, Josiah M., 73. *See also* detention; Mau Mau

Kashmir, 28, 75

Kenya: as country of asylum, 6, 22, 105, 124; downcountry, 40, 79, 87, 145, 160, 172, 186, 190; government of, 53–54, 57, 59, 62, 109, 130, 156, 173, 185; minorities, 7, 24, 44, 75, 76, 80, 91, 96, 105, 118, 137, 194; society, 57, 97, 103, 107, 118, 125, 192, 195; state, 3, 23, 27, 34, 53, 65, 67, 80, 85, 92, 93, 102, 104, 122, 126, 131, 146–47, 149–50, 154, 155, 186

Kenya Defence Forces (KDF), 123

Kenya Emergency, 27, 73, 136. *See also* Kenya Land and Freedom Army; Mau Mau

Kenya Land and Freedom Army, 73, 136, 208n13. *See also* Mau Mau

Kenya Police, 73, 79–80, 81, 82, 84, 96, 136, 139, 209n36, 209n40. *See also* police; policing

Kenya Police Reserves (KPR), 79, 136, 140, 209n36. *See also* police; policing

Kenyatta, Uhuru, 55, 60, 62, 69; and Nyumba Kumi, 137, 147

Kenyatta, Jomo, 72–74, 208n9; and Harambee, 184. *See also* independence; Kapenguria Six

Khartoum, 42, 47, 65, 204n37

khat, xi, 47, 144, 204n41. *See also* miraa

Kibaki, Mwai, 58, 137

Kibicho, Karanja, 54

Kibra, 189. *See also* city; Nairobi

Kiir, Salva, 46, 152, 204n37. *See also* South Sudanese refugees

Kim Il Sung, 44

King's African Rifles (KAR), 71

kipande (pl. *vipande*), 57, 77, 90–91. *See also* colonialism

Kitale, 87

kitu kidogo, 140, 170, 216n48. *See also* bribes

Kituo cha Sheria, 60

Kleinschmidt, Kilian, 42. *See also* Za'atari camp
Kurdistan, 28; regions of Turkey, 75
kutafuta maisha (life-seeking), 177
Kutupalong, 187

labor, 24, 144, 161, 165, 171, 177–78, 181, 182; camps, 17; captive, 171; division of, 47, 68; domestic, 55; exploitation, 7; forced, 12, 73; hard, 74; incentive, 172; involuntary, 89; land and, 23, 71, 181; of aid, 126; refugee, 29, 165, 175; relations, 170; reserves, 184; rights, 164, 171–72; schemes, 73; solidarity, 131; supplies of, 135; unpaid, 162. *See also* aid workers; incentive work
lagga, 40, 46, 148, 156. *See also* Tarach River
Lamu Port-South Sudan-Ethiopia-Transport (LAPSSET), 165
Lefebvre, Henri, 47
Lego Foundation, 52
Lenin, Vladimir, 74
liberal democracy, 4, 16, 25, 75, 80, 83, 131, 132
liberal order, 7, 14, 25, 27, 68
liberal violence, 14, 189, 195
liberation, 42, 63, 65, 74, 76, 130, 152, 190, 195–96. *See also* decolonization
Libya, 6, 19, 44
life: affirming, 19, 188; "bare," 18, 19, 29, 33; biographical, 180; biological, 180; Black, 17, 21; camp, 4, 30, 42, 48, 92, 102, 103, 112, 117, 126, 127, 151; chances, 5, 16, 161, 178; everyday, 16, 30, 41, 47, 94, 105; saving, 48, 52, 110; seekers/seeking, 3, 4, 15; time, 29, 165, 177–78, 180, 182
Locke, John, 120
Lodwar, 31, 49, 72–73, 82, 86
Lokichoggio, 31, 42, 81, 83. *See also* borderland; Turkana
Lokitaung, 72–73. *See also* Kapenguria Six
Lopit (ethnic group), 130. *See also* South Sudanese refugees
Lost Boys, 42–43, 82. *See also* South Sudanese refugees
Lotuko (ethnic group), 122, 130. *See also* South Sudanese refugees
Lugard, Lord Frederick, 134. *See also* indirect rule
Lukole camp, 109. *See also* Turner, Simon

Lutheran World Federation (LWF), 23, 31, 55, 65, 112, 129, 130, 139, 140–42, 144–46, 152, 156, 169, 172, 215n2, 216n67. *See also* aid agencies/organizations; NGO
Luxemburg, Rosa, 163

Machar, Riek, 46, 152, 204n37
Mae La camp, 188
Mai-Mai, 65, 207n128
Maina, Andrew, 57
Malkki, Liisa, 18, 109
Mamdani, Mahmood, 135
Mandera, 58, 71, 92
margins: as sites of knowledge, 8–8, 99; colonial, 4, 73; domestic/internal, 28, 74–75, 76, 98; global, 5, 8, 11, 33, 180, 196; rural, 5, 140
market, 30, 38, 39, 44, 50, 53, 74, 130, 131, 150, 154, 164–65, 171, 173–77, 181; -based approaches to aid, 29, 181, 185; Ethiopian, 44–46, 48, 154, 155; free, 131, 175, 186; Somali, 45, 191
marketization, 29, 173, 176, 181. *See also* capitalism
Marsabit, 44, 58, 71
Martin, Lauren, 174
Massey, Doreen, 105
Mastercard, 52, 176
Mathare, 189
Mau Mau, 136, 193, 208n13. *See also* Kenya Land and Freedom Army
Mazou, Raouf, 52, 173, 181. *See also* marketization; UNHCR
Mbatha, Nomzamo, 39
Mbembe, Achille, 13, 25, 98. *See also* necropolitics
Médecins sans Frontières (MSF), 49, 59
Mediterranean, 6, 15
Memmi, Albert, 121
Mengistu Haile Mariam, 44
methods, 30–33. *See also* ethics
Mezzadra, Sandro, 163
migration control, 3, 15, 16, 99. *See also* border; global apartheid
Milimani High Court, 55, 60, 149
militarization, 3, 15, 31, 34, 41, 64–65, 66, 84, 163, 189
Mill, John Stuart, 120
Mills, Charles, 105–6

Ministry of the Interior and National Administration, 54
minorities, 7, 24, 44, 75, 76, 80, 91, 96, 105, 118, 137, 194. *See also* identities
miraa, xi, 47, 144, 204n4. *See also* khat
mobility: apartheid, 8, 29, 194; control, 4, 29, 34, 99, 181; differentiated/differential, 7, 50, 125; justice, 195; policing of, 7, 189, 194, 196. *See also* migration control; movement
Mogadishu, 47, 177; Little Mogadishu, 60
Moi, Daniel arap, 57–58, 137
Mombasa, 44–45, 58, 87, 116, 191; police swoops in, 58; Port of, 158
moral disorder, 104, 108, 120, 124, 127
morality, 104, 109, 115–16, 118, 127
Mória camp, 40
Mountz, Alison, 8, 16
movement: clandestine, 190–91; free, 25, 185, 188; fugitive, 188; pass, 59, 86, 87, 89, 91–92, 102, 118, 188, 190; restrictions, 77, 81, 91. *See also* mobility
Mudavadi, Musalia, 184–86
Museveni, Yoweri, 44
Muslim communities, 147; Kenyans, 76; leaders, 149

Nadapal, 31, 42. *See also* Lokichoggio
Nairobi: xi, 29, 31, 33, 38, 59–60, 66–67, 70–71, 78, 81, 83, 114, 140, 149, 161; Declaration, 62; humanitarian staff from, 172; its periphery, 80; national government in, 53–54, 79; police swoops in, 58; slums and, 189; witness protection program in, 170. *See also* city
Nanok, Josphat, 39, 67. *See also* Turkana
narratives, 11, 30, 34, 127. *See also* moral disorder; TEDxKakumaCamp
national belonging, 7, 115, 124
nation building, 7, 19, 27, 115, 122, 125, 185–86, 187, 193. *See also* sovereignty; state
National Intelligence Service (NIS), 84
nationalism, 26, 56, 75, 76, 125, 193, 194, 195
national security, 58, 61, 63, 147, 156
national sovereignty, 4, 26, 74
native administration, 133–34, 136; aliens, 57; authorities, 135; reserves, 79, 90, 107, 110, 134. *See also* colonialism; indirect rule
nativeness, 7, 106, 110
necropolitics, 19, 95. *See also* Mbembe, Achille

Newton, Huey, 28
Ngutulu, Kodi Arnu, 41–42
Nguyen, Vinh, 48
Nkaissery, Ole, 55
noncitizens, 7, 24, 25, 26, 28, 35, 75, 78, 137, 148, 168, 186, 194. *See also* citizen
nongovernmental organization (NGO), 30, 58, 132. *See also* aid agencies/organizations
Northern Frontier District, 57, 76
Norwegian Refugee Council (NRC), 23. *See also* aid agencies/organizations; NGO
Nuer (ethnic group), 44, 46, 47, 92, 95, 96, 115, 130, 138, 139, 151, 152, 154, 172, 203n27, 204n37; council of elders, 153. *See also* South Sudanese refugees
Nyarugusu camp, 188. *See also* Tanzania
Nyumba Kumi, 130, 137, 147. *See also* community police/policing

occupation, 28, 68, 83, 85, 89, 90, 96, 98–99, 153, 157, 170; architecture of, 86, 94, 99; colonial, 25–27, 34, 41, 70, 74–78, 83, 98, 102, 104, 162, 182, 192; domestic, 25; foreign, 24; lifting the, 195; militarized, 4, 27, 28, 34, 59, 71, 81, 85, 186, 187, 196; of territories, 96, 106, 133; second colonial, 26; third colonial, 26–30, 83, 163; topography of, 89. *See also* colonization; militarization
occupied territories, 76, 96, 106
Octopizzo, 39
Officer Commanding Station (OCS), 1–2, 69–70, 84–85, 91–92; as "local sovereign," 93. *See also* police
Oka, Rahul, 66
Ole Lenku, Joseph, 60. *See also* camp; Kakuma
operational areas, 78, 80, 85, 145. *See also* police; policing
Operation Lifeline Sudan (OLS), 81, 159, 165
Operation Usalama Watch, 60. *See also* Eastleigh
Oxfam, 55, 79. *See also* aid agencies/organizations; NGO

pacification, 5, 75, 83, 97, 134, 141, 163
Palestine, 28; authorities, 76; camps in, 85; stolen land, 75
paramilitaries, 28, 30, 78, 79, 102, 140, 186. *See also* police

peace building, 16, 22–23, 131, 141, 149. *See also* CPPT; LWF

police: colonialism and, 24–25; commander/chief, 71, 84, 93, 94, 97, 112, 120, 146, 169, 170, 187; brutality, 151; extortion 2; OCS, 1, 2, 69–70, 84, 85, 91–92, 211n87; post, 89, 95, 119; station, 2, 24, 30, 34, 69–70, 86, 92, 96, 116, 169, 187. *See also* crime; OCS; security

policing: Blackness/Black life, 17, 19, 21; community, 29, 30, 35, 67, 129–32, 136–37, 141–42, 143, 146, 149, 151–52, 154–57, 172, 211n91; emergency, 27, 71, 81; militarized, 7, 11, 25; of mobility, 7, 189, 196. *See also* crime; security

politics: asylum, 58; concessionary, 182, ethnoracial, 107; global, 8, 99; moral, 12; multiparty, 137; of containment, 195; of security, 57; territorial state, 97; urban, 47

postcolonial state, 19, 20, 25, 29, 79, 83, 194; Kenyan, 57, 74, 76, 77, 103, 193, 195. *See also* independence; Kenya

postcolony, 26, 10, 195. *See also* nation building; *uhuru*

power: carceral, 6, 190, 195; hierarchies, 103, 11, 140; of writing, 92; penal, 5; police, 5; sovereign, 18, 25; state, 5, 18, 19, 22, 25, 33, 79, 85, 126, 140. *See also* Foucault, Michel

protection: humanitarian, 3, 21, 27, 28, 49, 132, 142, 150; refugee, 3, 27, 61, 84, 85, 150, 186

protectionism, 11, 68, 86, 134, 142, 187, 196. *See also* encampment; humanitarianism

Qasmiyeh, Yousif M., 179–80

Quijano, Aníbal, 106

race, 21, 76, 106, 124, 189, 190. *See also* ethnicity; identities

racialization 19, 57, 106–7

racism, 190

Rajaf police post, 88–90. *See also* police; Kakuma

rebels, 64, 65, 97

Reech, Chol, 86

refugee: Act, 23, 58, 59; aid, 4, 5, 7–8, 11, 15, 16, 17, 97; arrival of, 6, 26; encampment, 9, 90, 98, 142, 180, 181, 187, 196; history in Kenya, 54–62; humanitarianism, 5, 178, 181; law, 25, 63; LGBTQI+, 98; protection,

3, 27, 61, 84, 85, 150, 186; registration, 31, 59, 206n93; resettlement, 9, 44, 46, 112–13, 114, 168, 169, 179, 180, 193; status determination (RSD), 58, 59; "warriors," 64. *See also* asylum

Refugee Affairs Secretariat (RAS), 61, 84, 101, 146, 160. *See also* DRA, DRS

Refugee Consortium of Kenya, 55. *See also* aid agencies/organizations; NGO

refusal, 29, 99, 131, 155, 156. *See also* resistance

religious extremism, 3, 148

religious practices, 29, 142

repatriation, 46, 60, 62, 150, 166, 179, 184

reservations, 91, 134, 190. *See also* reserves

reserves, 24, 79, 90, 107, 110, 134, 163, 184. *See also* reservations

resettlement, 9, 44, 46, 112–13, 114, 168, 169, 179, 180, 193. *See also* durable solutions; refugee

resistance, 19, 30, 71, 72, 156. *See also* refusal

Rift Valley, 26, 71

rights: asylum, 61; collective, 106, 107; democratic, 14, 15, 24; equal, 75; human, 3, 7, 16, 22, 63, 78, 83, 121, 125, 131, 139, 145, 147, 149, 156, 186, 187; labor, 164, 171, 172; land, 76, 164; of citizenship, 133; of minorities, 6, 118; property, 7; refugee, 11, 58, 60, 114; reproductive, 116, 121; universal, 61; women's, 117

roadblocks, 30, 34, 86–87, 89, 98. *See also* checkpoints

Rodney, Walter, 189. *See also* decolonization

rule: colonial, 7, 71, 75, 80, 83, 84, 95, 106, 107, 134, 189, 193, 194; nationalized, 27; of law, 16, 103, 125; postcolonial, 7, 132; system of, 24

Ruto, William, 60–61

Rwimo, Aminah, 38, 42. *See also* TEDxKakumaCamp

Rygiel, Kim, 133

Safaricom, 52, 173, 176

Scheper-Hughes, Nancy, 16

security: as discourse, 56; committees, 137; community, 147, 155; forces, 27, 29, 60, 93, 147, 155; governance, 139, 154; guards, 52; interests, 54, 55; Laws Amendment Act, 60; national, 58, 61, 63, 147, 156; office, 94, 112, 129, 142, 145, 153–54; personnel, 81,

111; state, 19, 24, 93; "War on Terror" and, 58–59. *See also* crime; policing

Security Partnership Project (SPP), 83. *See also* Kakuma; UNHCR

Sharma, Nandita, 26. *See also* nationalism; nation building

Shifta War, 57, 74, 76, 193

Shirika Plan, 184–85, 187–88, 195. *See also* UNHCR

Smirl, Lisa, 50

social death, 179

sociality, 3, 92, 131, 143, 174, 182

Somalia, 10, 31, 44, 46, 56, 59, 60, 83, 150, 177, 179, 191, 204n31, 204n34, 208n9

Somali Bantu, 46, 91, 204n34; Bajuni, 44, 45, 191, 204n3; Barawa, 44–46, 204n31; Kenyans, 57, 74, 76–77, 91, 96, 113; minorities, 44; Somali market, 45, 191. *See also* ethnicity; identities; minorities

South Africa, 20, 39, 134; apartheid, 74, 76; white Boers in, 162

sovereignty, 4, 18, 19, 54, 78, 132, 134, 163, 186; colonial, 134; national, 4, 26, 74; of the state; postcolonial, 6, 56; territorial, 22. *See also* state; nationalism

spatial technology, 19, 23, 181, 187

state: actors, 3, 35, 41, 47, 83, 161, 188; agencies, 103, 132; control, 29, 81, 97, 105, 131, 154; Kenyan, 3, 23, 27, 34, 53, 65, 67, 80, 85, 92, 93, 102, 104, 122, 126, 131, 146–47, 149–50, 154–55, 186; machinery, 27; power, 5, 18, 19, 22, 25, 33, 79, 85, 126, 140; proxies, 146–50; violence, 14, 15, 21, 23–24, 35, 61, 68, 187, 195

statecraft, 2, 68, 83

statehood, 5, 97, 125

state of exception, 18. *See also* Agamben, Giorgio; bare life

Stoler, Ann Laura, 13, 21, 28, 181–82

South Sudanese refugees, 43, 44, 46, 52, 70, 82, 86, 87, 92, 94, 95, 96, 114, 120, 122, 129, 194. *See also* Dinka; Equatoria; Lost Boys; Nuer

Sudan People's Liberation Army/Movement (SPLA/M), 65. *See also* Anyanya II; Garang John

Support for Host Community and Refugee Empowerment (SHARE), 184. *See also* Shirika Plan

surrogate homeland, 124, 194

surrogate state, 22, 53. *See also* UNHCR

surveillance, 3, 15, 82, 85–86, 89, 90, 130, 137, 147, 216n40

Tamale, Sylvia, 189. *See also* decolonization

Tanzania: 42, 58, 109, 117; refugees in, 18, 126. *See also* Lukole camp; Nyarugusu camp

Tarach River, 39, 43, 148. See also *lagga*

technology, 6, 14, 18, 19, 35, 53, 188, 189, 194; anti-African, 20; biometric, 112; biopolitical, 82; border, 29, 193; carceral, 99, 193; colonial, 132; governmental, 131–32, 133–35, 151; of the camp, 6, 20; political, 125, 127, 157; spatial, 181, 187. *See also* Foucault, Michel

TEDxKakumaCamp, 34, 38–41, 63, 66–68, 173, 177

Tennet (ethnic group), 130

terror, 31; hotbed of, 41; War on, 31, 58–59, 67, 76, 84, 109. *See also* Al-Shabaab; terrorism; terrorist

terrorism, 38, 59–60, 62–63, 76–78, 104, 105, 108, 130, 148–49, 154–55. *See also* Al-Shabaab; terror; terrorist

terrorist, 3, 19, 56, 58–59, 62, 104–5, 109, 120, 137, 147, 155, 193. *See also* Al-Shabaab; terror; terrorism

Thika, 57

Thuku, Harry, 208n9

Toomey, Nisha, 50

Tsing, Anna, 163. *See also* margins

Tuck, Eve, 22, 188. *See also* colonization

Tunisia, 6

Turkana: as frontier, 78–79; county, 39, 53, 54, 66, 67; land, 53; landscape/countryside, 49–50, 71, 81, 107, 125, 163; pastoralists, 79; Patrol, 71–72; people/population, 43, 51, 71, 108, 115, 172

Turner, Simon, 109, 117, 126. *See also* Lukole camp

Uganda: 8, 44; internally displaced people in, 81; northern, 71

uhuru, 6–7, 26. *See also* independence; Kenya

United Nations High Commissioner for Refugees (UNHCR): as surrogate state, 22, 54; camp closure and, 55; civilian character of refugee camps and, 62–66; "country of," 195; global role, 9–11; historical role in

United Nations (*continued*)
  Africa, 15–16; humanitarian space in
  Kakuma and, 49–54; "in white hands," 8;
  Kakuma office, 1; officials/officers, 32, 82,
  170; partner organizations and, 3, 30,
  65, 82, 142, 146; publicity and branding,
  17, 38–40, 173–77; relation with Kenyan
  state, 23–24, 28–29; Security Partnership
  Project (SPP), 83–84; Tripartite Agreement
  with, 60
United Nations Environmental Program
  (UNEP), 6
United Nations Human Settlements Program
  (UN-Habitat), 6
United States, 21, 40, 74, 114, 134, 160, 162;
  embassy bombings, 58; resettlement to, 44,
  46, 177. *See also* resettlement

Valetta Summit on Migration, 10. *See also*
  global apartheid
violence: border, 3, 11; gender-based, 3,
  16, 115, 116; humanitarian, 11–17; liberal,
  14, 189, 195; of encampment, 32; "of kitu
  kidogo," 170; organized, 12, 24, 25, 66,
  96, 98; police, 5; "spirit of," 63; state, 21,
  23–24, 35, 61, 68, 187, 195; workers,
  24, 33, 35, 79, 98. *See also* enforcement;
  police
vulnerability, 5, 17, 113

Wajir, 57–58, 71, 92
Walda camp, 44

wananchi, 7, 105, 125, 130, 193, 194. *See also*
  citizen; noncitizens
Weizman, Eyal, 14, 76. *See also*
  occupation
Western Sahara, 28, 75
Westgate Shopping Mall, 60. *See also* Al-
  Shabaab; terrorism
West Papua, 28
white supremacy, 13, 105, 106
women: dispute between, 89, 143; fetishized,
  118; outcasts, 150; women's rights, 117.
  See also gender
workers: aid, 5, 18, 29, 30, 32, 35, 38, 41, 50, 59,
  63, 102, 103, 112, 113–14, 117–18, 121, 124,
  127, 150, 161, 165, 169–70, 173; humanitarian, 3, 5, 35, 160; incentive, 171–72
World Bank, 39–40, 52, 175–176. *See also* IFC;
  marketization
World Food Program (WFP), 23, 50, 112,
  166, 176
World Vision, 55

Xinjiang, 28, 75

Yang, K. Wayne, 22, 188. *See also* decolonization; Tuck, Eve
youth, 22, 82, 95, 114, 124, 144, 194. *See also*
  children

Za'atari camp, 43, 188. *See also* Kleinschmidt,
  Kilian
zoe, 180. *See also* Agamben, Giorgio; *bios*

www.ingramcontent.com/pod-product-compliance
Lightning Source LLC
Chambersburg PA
CBHW020843270326
41928CB00006B/529

* 9 7 8 1 4 7 8 0 3 3 1 3 4 *